Y0-BCM-927

LATINA HISTORIES — AND — CULTURES

FEMINIST READINGS AND RECOVERIES OF ARCHIVAL KNOWLEDGE

EDITED AND WITH AN INTRODUCTION BY MONTSE FEU AND YOLANDA PADILLA

Recovering the US Hispanic Literary Heritage

Arte Público Press
Houston, Texas

Latina Histories and Cultures is published in part with funds from the Department of World Languages and Cultures at Sam Houston State University. We are grateful for its support.

Recovering the past, creating the future

Arte Público Press
University of Houston
4902 Gulf Fwy, Bldg 19, Rm 100
Houston, Texas 77204-2004

Cover design by Mora Des¡gns Groups

Library of Congress Control Number: 2023933250

23 24 25   3 2 1

Contents

Part I. Feminist Readings of Latina Authors

Part II. Forum on Chicana Memory

Acknowledgements

This volume is possible because of Nicolás Kanellos' vision in founding the US Hispanic Literary Heritage Project and his tireless work in sustaining it and taking it in new directions. We thank him, Gabriela Baeza Ventura, and Carolina Villarroel for their support throughout the development of this project. Antonia Castañeda and Clara Lomas have been at the forefront of Latina recovery work and are models both in terms of the groundbreaking nature of their scholarship and their generosity as colleagues and mentors. María Cotera organized the forum on "Chicana Memory Work," which we are very pleased to feature here. We extend particular gratitude to our contributors for their patience and support.

—Montse Feu and Yolanda Padilla

Introduction
The Practice of Latina Feminist Recovery

MONTSE FEU
Sam Houston State University

YOLANDA PADILLA
University of Washington, Bothell

This volume presents new scholarship on Latina histories and cultures from the mid-nineteenth century to 1980, demonstrating the historical scope, interdisciplinary rigor, and critical energy around archives that constitute hallmarks of Latina feminist recovery work. The essays consider Latina pasts' complex and heterogeneous contexts that include, for instance, national, class, social and ideological structures, subject formations, public and private spheres, and gender and sex expectations. The authors analyze a range of source materials, including personal and institutional archives, literature, print culture, oral history and other forms of "memory work." They take a transnational approach to case studies situated in several locations throughout the Americas, such as the United States, Mexico, Cuba, and Puerto Rico. Taken together, the essays remind us of a principle that is still too often forgotten: that sex and gender should be centered as crucial variables in the study of the long history of Latina/o/x literature and culture.

This collection was conceived and developed under the auspices of the Recovering the US Hispanic Literary Heritage Project, a program founded in 1992 that works with scholars, librarians, and archivists to "constitute and make accessible an archive of cultural productions by Hispanic or Latino peoples who have existed since the sixteenth century in the areas that eventually became part of the United States" (Kanellos 371).[1] Prominent Latina feminist scholars have been members of the international advisory board from its inception, including founding members Edna Acosta-Belén, Antonia Castañeda, Erlinda Gonzales-Berry, María Herrera-Sobek, Clara Lomas, Nélida Pérez, and Virginia Sánchez Korrol. Their guidance and that of feminist scholars who joined subsequently has ensured that the Recovery Project, as it is known colloquially, has understood a significant part of its mission to be the recovery of women's writings and to recognize the importance of sex and gender as key categories of analysis.

In what follows, we map out the practice of Latina feminist recovery by reviewing principles of Latina feminisms especially relevant for such work and considering issues regarding archives and language. We then circle back to these points, providing an overview of the continuing importance of recovery work framed through a discussion of assertions that we are in a "post-recovery" era. We circle back to these points in the ensuing discussion, in which we provide an overview of the continuing importance of recovery work framed through an engagement with calls by some scholars that we move "beyond" recovery, or assertions that we are in a "post-recovery" era. The overview we provide is not meant to be comprehensive; rather, our aim is to touch on some of the key debates as well as theoretical and methodological developments that have informed Latina feminist recovery work over the past thirty years. We conclude by suggesting that more attention to queer studies frameworks and speculative approaches to recovery work will challenge and move the field forward. While we make our points about Latina recovery work generally, we organize our discussion through an emphasis on the Recovery Project's vision, achievements, and possible future directions.

Mapping Terms and Concepts

One of the defining attributes of Latina and women of color feminisms more generally is the intersectional methodology at their core, one characterized by the analysis of gender at the intersection of axes of identity such as race, class, sexuality, and nationality, among numerous others. Intersectionality counters the idea of an essential or stable category of "woman" predicated on the universalist claim that all women share a set of common experiences. As Sonita Sarker memorably explains, intersectionality demands that we ask "which women, where, and how," and, even more, "the axes themselves (gender, race, etc . . .) are understood in their historicity, in that they are mutually and contingently defined, not discrete and fixed" (10). Transnational approaches are also central to historically-oriented Latina feminist scholarship and complement intersectionality in that they "compel us to contend with this mobility and fluidity of terms" (Sarker 10).[2]

The concept of the transnational has multiple valences. In our usage, it refers both to a conceptual framework that allows scholars to track "the movement of goods, individuals, and ideas happening in a context in which gender, class, and race operate simultaneously" (Briggs, et al. 632), and to "transnational persons," a term Paula Moya and Ramón Saldívar use to mean individuals "whose lives form an experiential region within which singularly delineated notions of political, social, and cultural identity do not suffice" (2).[3] This latter meaning captures how Latina subjects who have been long settled and anchored in particular locales (often for generations) can nonetheless continue to be influenced and shaped by Latin American phenomena. With respect to transnational feminism specifically, Nicole Guidotti-Hernández offers a useful characterization when she describes it as a paradigm that focuses on "the intersections of sexuality, sexual violence, gender, and race as processes of making subjects in multiple national contexts simultaneously," enabling a consideration of overlapping colonialisms and diasporas, especially as influenced by gender and sexuality (*Unspeakable Violence*, 28).

In addition, transnational approaches are necessary for locating and analyzing the archives most pertinent to the recovery of Latina literary and cultural histories. Our usage of "archive" follows the "slippage" in the uses of the term that have arisen in recent years, and that have moved beyond the original reference to repositories of rare documents to now include reference to "a record of web postings, historical memory, libraries, and even a set of readings with a theme, among others" (Lazo, "Migrant," 40). Transnational approaches to archives challenge American studies scholars to move beyond the fixed archive of an Anglo-American nation. Rodrigo Lazo reminds us that in many ways the archive and the nation are mutually constituting: historically they have "come together to grant each other authority and credibility" ("Migrant," 36). Nation-based archives and methodologies "either forget certain people or frame mobile subjects in relation to a national lens, sometimes cutting out experiences in various countries" (Lazo, "Historical Latinidades," 10). In arguing that we need new "routes that allow for a way to move in and out of the nation," Lazo develops the concept of "migrant archives," which names archives that "reside in obscurity and are always on the edge of annihilation," containing texts "of the past that have not been written into the official spaces of archivization, even though they weave in and out of the buildings that house documents" ("Migrant," 37-38).[4] The concept includes but is not limited to the identification of texts that are illegible in nation-based frameworks. It also elaborates a transnational mode of reading that applies to documents that are "known" but that have been studied in ways that dismiss or are unable to make sense of "migrant" or linguistically and culturally diverse elements.

Among such elements one must include language, and in a US context this means that archives in languages other than English are perceived as foreign or "migrant." While numerous languages are relevant for the study of Latina histories and cultures, scholars engaging in Latina/o/x recovery work—especially pre-twentieth century—have emphasized the importance of working with Spanish-language materials. Lazo argues that texts written in languages other than English can "lead scholars to alternative ways of remembering the past, new ways of naming multiple nations and communities, and even the invention of new ontologies" (38). Working with Spanish-language materials brings to light an entire world—a Hispanophone world—constituted by extensive print cultures, artists and intellectuals, readerships, and the transnational circuits of exchange that sustained them. And this was not a hermetically-sealed world, but one that crisscrossed multiple and multilingual histories throughout the hemisphere, "connecting, dividing, and redrawing the Americas across literary, linguistic, national, and racial borders" (Alemán, *Latino Nineteenth Century*," vii).

The essays in this collection use Latina feminist frameworks in their recovery and analysis of migrant archives. Consequently, they recover or analyze Latina lives and writings in ways that elucidate social structures, ideologies, and relations of power. These frameworks align with the transnational orientation that runs throughout the volume to collectively "provincialize the United States," to adapt Dipesh Chakrabarty's well-known phrase. Transnational approaches challenge the idea of the United States as a monocultural, Anglo-Saxon "pinnacle of occidental culture," recasting it instead as a "transnational, multilingual, and multi-cultural society of mixed 'racial' heritage" and showing the Western Hemisphere to be a "historical and cultural system in itself" (Kanellos 372). In addition, a transnational analysis can shed light on women's agency in refusing the patriarchal construct of women as reproducers of national citizens and transmitters of national culture, a symbolic order dominant in various national contexts.

Latina Recovery Work, Then and Now

We find ourselves in an era of scholarship that increasingly calls for a move "beyond recovery" or that even muses about this being a "post-recovery" era. There are also separate but related questions raised about whether there is still value in studying women's literary history.[5] Given our commitments to this work, it is no surprise that we are in sympathy with Frances Smith Foster's assertion that "considering this a "Post-Recovery Era" is as ignorant as proclaiming this a post-racial period" (245). Despite this, and notwithstanding the fact that most of these calls come from outside the fields of Latina/o/x and ethnic studies, we believe that a brief engagement with the concerns raised provides a valuable starting point for discussing the work being done collectively by the essays featured here, especially as they relate to the principles outlined above.

Doubts about the value of feminist recovery work question whether it is an inert exercise in locating neglected literary and historical female figures and their archives simply for the sake of recovery. Another is that it is a separatist endeavor, as it attempts to construct "women's histories" in isolation. In fact, recovery work has much more expansive objectives. Bringing attention to unknown

xii   Montse Feu and Yolanda Padilla

or understudied women is simply the first crucial step, one that occurs in tandem with an interpretive framework. Scholars strive to show how this information enhances or disrupts what we think we know about a historical period or process and how it helps challenge or advance a given field.[6] Along these lines, the essays in this volume that bring to light overlooked Latinas and their cultural expressions engage precisely in the work of contextualization, analysis, and theorization. To take one example, Anita Huizar-Hernández's essay on the largely unknown *Álbum* created by a Mexicana exile of the Cristero War provides a framework for analyzing diasporic Cristero literature, one that foregrounds the intersections of gender, religion, and race in Mexican-American subject formation and complicates our understanding of early twentieth-century Latina/o literature.

As to the separatist nature of scholarship that uses women's writings, archives, histories, or cultures as its organizing category of analysis, Devoney Looser points out in the context of feminist literary criticism that precious little of this work investigates women entirely apart from men. In fact, "in most cases it would be impossible to leave out the male publishers, reviewers, mentors, and family members in a woman writer's circle" (223). She further notes that considering women together is useful—provided it is not done in an essentializing manner—because they were often perceived in ways that "demonstrate significant patterns, and these patterns appear to be based at least in part on sex (and sex and race, sex and class, sex and age, sex and nation, sex and sexuality, etc.)" (224). Ayendy Bonifacio's essay illustrates this point as he traces the circulation of the Cuban poet Gertrudis Gómez Avellaneda's public image in periodicals throughout the Americas, showing that her gender and literary talent were rarely separated in reviews of her publications, and this despite her level of fame and influence. He further demonstrates that the production of women's writing involves multiple agents, as male newspaper editors positioned and re-positioned her poetry and image to promote competing political interests. As this last point indicates, far from being isolationist, scholarship on women's histories and cultures opens avenues for interrogating the larger social field. We have long understood the power of individual women's stories as testimony of patriarchy's effects. Several of the essays in this volume provide a transnational sample of such testimonies, elucidating patriarchy's divergent and overlapping manifestations in distinct cultural, national, and historical contexts.

Jessica Berman argues that feminist recovery projects continue to be essential for their role in "erasing center-periphery distinctions." As she explains,

> the very impulse to question the dominance of an unmarked yet valorized, central position owes much to longtime feminist theoretical efforts to dethrone the perspective of the universal (Western, white, straight, able) male . . . one cannot debunk the universal, metropolitan West, without also explicitly debunking the universal (white, straight, able) male that undergirds the universal, metropolitan West. (9)

In making this argument, Berman rightly expresses concern that this work needs to be done in a manner that does not simply replace the "universal" white male with an essentialist view of the "universal" white woman (10). This is a concern that has been raised for decades by women of color, including Latina feminists who have contributed to the development of the intersectional methods that challenge essentialist tendencies.[7] In her now-classic essay "Women of Color and the Rewriting of Western History" (1992), Antonia Castañeda identified the problem with white feminist historians who were engaged in the work of decentering men from the historiography of the West, but who simply "substituted the experience of white males with that of white women and thus reproduced the same relationships of power and authority that male historians used when writing the canon of history" (517). Such work failed to ground its accounts of racial contact and cultural conflicts within their "historical, political, or ideological context," assuming instead that "concepts, categories, terminology, methodology, and language are universally applicable" (517).

Feminist recovery work has come a long way since then, not least because intersectionality is now considered fundamental to feminist theory. However, many of Castañeda's points still apply. She expressed the need for the use of multilingual sources, for example, highlighting the work of Chicana historian Deena González and her use of Spanish-language sources in her study of "Spanish-Mexican Women" in nineteenth-century Santa Fe. These resources enable González to "weave her analysis with the women's own language, imagery, and consciousness, which reveal the subjectivities, complexities, tensions, strategies, conflicts, and contradictions of their lives, as well as their sense of honor, propriety, justice, and right" (528).[8] The use of multilingual sources is still lacking in American studies, as scholars continue to point out.[9] And while intersectional frameworks have become more widespread, the increased prevalence of transnational and comparative approaches requires even more rigor in their implementation. Such work must ensure that it is grounded in cultural and historical specificity, that it attends to relationships of power, and, accordingly, that it guards against a collapsing of difference in the too quick search for convergence (Cotera 8-10).[10]

Being alert to difference includes differentiations internal to communities as well, and this is an issue that has been addressed consistently by scholars working to recover Latina histories and cultures. Emma Pérez's theorization of "third space" historiographical methods enables an attention to the Latina voices silenced by masculinist histories through an examination of "where in discourse the gaps, the interstitial moments of history, reappear to be seen or heard as that third space" (Decolonial, xvi). Pérez mobilizes the concept of the third space to examine nationalist discourses, showing how Mexicanas and Chicanas aligned themselves with the men of their communities at the same time that they "intervened interstitially with their own rhetoric about their place and meaning" as women in nationalist causes (Decolonial, 59). Suzanne Bost provides an apt characterization of the third space as a method that "critically recovers the repressed within the repressed: the queer and female voices that were marginalized by Mexican and Chicano histories" (624).[11] She adds that from a Chicana feminist perspective, "the past is not an ideal to return to but a contested terrain of competing truth claims" (624). In her essay, Monica Perales suggests ways to read in the "interstices" to recover evidence of women's agency in her analysis of food-related content in Spanish-language newspapers.

Attention to internal difference also applies to differences among Latinas. A concern raised about feminist recovery projects is that they are prone to projecting feminist ideals onto women from the past, and either ignore evidence to the contrary or jettison politically "problematic" women from consideration (Looser 222-3; Marsden 658-60). Understandably, feminist and ethnic studies scholars might project imperatives of resistance to the figures they recover, especially when such work was in its early stages. This is an issue that Recovery Program Scholars have engaged from the beginning in the pages of the Program's earliest publications (Gonzales-Berry and Tatum 14; Herrera-Sobek and Sánchez Korrol 4-5). Indeed, the nineteenth-century Californian author María Amparo Ruiz de Burton has been the subject of intensive critical attention since the recovery and publication of her two novels in the 1990s, *The Squatter and the Don* and *Who Would Have Thought It?* While she was initially and compellingly presented as a figure whose work aligned with Chicana/o counterhegemonic imperatives, that interpretation, while valid to a significant extent, was immediately complicated by scholars who juxtaposed her counter hegemonic voice with racist views that stake out what Jesse Alemán describes as a "hydra-hegemonic position" against indigenous peoples and African Americans ("Diachronics" 2016, 33). Kenya Dworkin y Méndez and Agnes Lugo-Ortiz attribute the "productive critical restlessness" that Ruiz de Burton's work has incited to the "discomfort and puzzlement produced by the dynamics of identification and disidentification it simultaneously allows" (12). Ruiz de Burton's importance continues unabated, as indicated by the generative essays on her work contributed by Evelyn Soto and Esmeralda Arrizón-Palomera.

Building on the work of Emma Pérez, Gloria Anzaldúa and Chela Sandoval, among others, María Cotera, Maylei Blackwell and Dionne Espinoza propose the concept of *movidas* as a decolonial historiographical method, which they theorize as "collective and individual maneuvers, undertaken in a context of social mobilization, that seek to work within, around, and between the positionings, ideologies, and practices of publicly visible social relations" (2). They apply the concept to the Chicano Movement, arguing that while Chicanas were key participants in the movement's "big" events, centering Chicana *movidas* "illuminates a multimodal engagement with movement politics that included everyday labor and support as well as strategic and sometimes subversive interventions within movement spaces" (2).

Moreover, as they demonstrate in their edited collection *Chicana Movidas*, the mapping of such *movidas* is in itself a historiographical intervention, a way of reading against the grain in order to examine "the array of political, social, analytic, and aesthetic strategies that Chicanas mobilized to imagine and enact social change" (3-4). "Memory work," one of the four types of *movidas* they identify, is well-represented in this volume, both in the "Forum on Chicana Memory Work" and in Vanessa Fonseca-Chávez's essay, which engages oral histories and personal archives to bring to light Chicana activism in Wyoming in the 1970s and 1980s, thus uncovering a specific regional *movida* and expanding our understanding of the moviniento's spatial reach.[12]

We conclude this overview by suggesting two areas that merit further attention in order to challenge and continue to expand the field. The potential in using queer studies frameworks in Latina recovery work has yet to be tapped extensively, although there have been discrete examples that show the importance of following such lines of research. For example, several of the essays in *Chicana Movidas* challenge the heteronormative limits of dominant movement historiographies, shedding light on feminist lesbians who were active in many of the movement's major efforts and who "shaped movement practices and culture" (Cotera, et al. 6). In his analysis of the 1876 Civil War narrative *The Woman in Battle*, which narrates the life of Loreta Janeta Velazquez, a Cuban-born, cross-dressing Confederate soldier, Jesse Alemán draws from queer studies scholarship in ways that demonstrate its importance for historicizing and troubling not only normative gender categories, but also markers of "race and national identity across the colonial terrain of the Americas" (113). Nicole Guidotti-Hernández's study of early-twentieth-century diasporic Mexican masculinities uses queer theory to "recapture intimacy and affect as forms of history meriting documentation and interpretation" (*Archiving*, 4), doing so in ways that are suggestive for future analysis of Latina recovery. In this volume, William Orchard opens new avenues of inquiry into the writings of the important author María Cristina Mena, and shows the importance of interrogating sex and sexuality in early Latina literature.

In her 2003 essay "Queering the Borderlands: The Challenge of Excavating the Invisible and Unheard," Emma Pérez expresses her frustration with history's text and archives. She speaks of her longing to find in the archives a "queer vaquera from the mid-nineteenth century whose adventures include finding Anglo squatters and seducing willing señoritas" (122). Unable to locate such records, she takes a creative approach to archival absence, writing a "*tejana* baby butch" into her novel *Forgetting the Alamo, Or, Blood Memory*. While she does not call it such, with this act she engages in a form of "speculative" recovery as a way of grappling with a lack of material evidence of queer Latinas who she is sure existed. Certainly, this paucity of evidence accounts at least in part for the relative lack of queer-studies informed work on Latina histories and cultures that we identify above. Scholars in African American studies have developed speculative methods for dealing with the impossibility of recovering the voices of the enslaved. Saidiya Hartman's influential concept of "critical fabulation," for example, names a double gesture "straining against the limits of the archive to write a cultural history of the captive, and, at the same time, enacting the impossibility of representing the lives of the captives precisely through the process of narration" (11). We wonder about the possibilities of employing methods such as informed speculation, critical fabulation, and other forms of evidence when dealing with historical fragments, archival traces or even absences. We do not expect these methodologies to supersede traditional archives, but perhaps they can contribute to the recovery not only of queer voices, but Afro and indigenous Latina voices as well.[13]

Archives and Counter-Archives

Latina archival recoveries are far from complete. There are still significant gaps because of patriarchy, among other forms of oppression. To generate Latina findings, perspectives, and knowledges, contributors have drawn information from bibliographic, artistic, and literary historiography; oral history and memory work; newspapers and genealogy databases; and physical, institutional, personal, community, and digital archives. With their research, contributors have helped reconstruct some Latina cultures and histories.

Using bibliographic, artistic, and literary historiography, Arrizón-Palomera, Orchard, and Soto have produced new readings of Latina classics. Arrizón-Palomera contextualizes *Who Would Have Thought It?* and Ruiz de Burton's correspondence *Conflicts of Interest* in the nineteenth-century Women's Movement. With the hemispheric legacy of Tapadas, Soto explores Lola's usage of a veil textile in *Who Would Have Thought It?* Bonifacio and Castañeda have combed periodical databases to find Avellaneda's and Capetillo's local and global press coverage. Their interdisciplinary approach has led to findings that expand our understanding of these well-known authors.

Fonseca-Chávez also employs oral histories and newspaper databases and oral histories to document Chicano activism in Wyoming. Nogar has centered her search on the Spanish-language press to show Adelina "Nina" Otero-Warren's concern for race-based violence in the Spanish-language media. Contributors also have advanced research on the political production of Latina's genealogies and government databases. Through FBI records, Landeros unfolds the influence of Communism on the political development of Chicana radical movements in California, focusing on the figure of Francisca Flores. Similarly, Hernández has used the newspaper databases generated by the Recovering the US Hispanic Literary Heritage and other digital and physical archives to track anarchist groups in México and the United States. In doing so, Hernández has established González Parra's anarcho-feminism. Similarly, Varela-Lago combs through letters to the editor to reconstruct De la Grana's political voice.

Contributors have unearthed and contextualized new authors, documents, and manuscripts by investigating databases and institutional and community archives meticulously. Huizar-Hernández explores María de La Torre's *Álbum* in the De La Torre family papers at the Special Collections at the University of Arizona Libraries. Losch examines another digital treasure with a similar diasporic approach: the only known copy of Aurora Mena's *The Pearl Key*, now available in the digital Latin American and Caribbean Collection of the University of Florida. Exploring a variety of records, contributors have shown the political power of Latinas' experiences and disclosed possibly self-imposed silences for fear of social ostracism.

Recovery scholars must acknowledge painful discoveries and silences when locating less-known Latina histories and cultures.

Oral history and memory work examine records of isolation and resistance in this volume's US Basque and Chicana chapters. To do so, contributors have applied "methodological interventions that center feminist oral history to dialogic approaches that foreground the give-and-take of knowledge production. The memory work elaborated in these projects insists on the deeply personal nature of historical meaning-making" (Cotera, this volume).

Using an ethnographic methodology, San Sebastian explores women in his family's papers, genealogy databases, and the literary historiography of US Basques. He uncovers the isolated lives of Basque-American women and the hard labor they endured in migration pockets in the United States. Genealogy studies can help us explore how women workers interacted. His findings show how isolation often limited Basque women's integration in the social fabric. Therefore, their US legacy is hard to unearth. Since US Basque women share historical, language, and migration experiences with other Latinas in the United States, further archival research departing from San Sebastian's might recover points of contact. Also, from a labor perspective, Perales has intentionally searched the Recovery databases. She has determined Mexicanas' agency through the early-twentieth-century gendered narratives of labor addressed to working-class Mexicanas in two prominent Texas periodicals.

Essays

The essays collected in Part I, "Feminist Readings of Latina Authors," examine privileged narratives with new lenses and apply archival practices that trace disregarded data in less obvious or traditional repositories. Evelyn Soto's "Translating the *Tapada*'s Veil in *Who Would Have Thought It?*" offers a reading of María Amparo Ruiz de Burton's 1872 novel that focuses on the protagonist Lola's shawl as a hemispheric translation of the *tapada*'s veil. These veils were face coverings used by nineteenth-century Spanish-creole women to expertly wrap and cover their faces leaving only one eye visible. Such anonymity enabled these women to have an insurgent presence, both hidden and public simultaneously. Soto reads the trace of this tapada style in Lola's shawl, arguing that the accessory transmits ideas of racial taint and feminine sedition that trouble dominant interpretations of the novel's resolution into conventional domestic and racial concepts associated with elite Anglo-American society. Soto's reading, then, is a textual analysis that is attuned to the possibilities of style and performance as alternative types of women's archives. It marks an attention to the subversive knowledge embedded in fashion, as preserved in the literary text.

If Soto presents a transnational reading that teases out the protagonist's potential as an insurgent figure that destabilizes US-based domestic and racial concepts, Esmeralda Arrizón-Palomera demonstrates the importance of keeping track of the novel's national contexts. In "Citizenship, Suffrage, and the (Un)making of the Mexican-American Woman Citizen in María Amparo Ruiz de Burton's *Who Would Have Thought It?*" Arrizón-Palomera situates the novel within the nineteenth-century US women's movement, a connection others have acknowledged but not pursued. She argues that by minimizing the importance of Ruiz de Burton's engagements with the movement, scholars inadvertently "reinforce the notion that Mexican-American women are foreign to the United States" and also "produce a myopic view of the development of Chicana feminist thought." Combining readings of Ruiz de Burton's letters with an analysis of her novel, Arrizón-Palomera makes a case for the role of literature in the formation and development of social movements and reframes our understanding of Chicana feminism and its relationship to white feminism.

In "Aurora Mena and *The Pearl Key*: Unlocking the Meaning of a Mambisa's Story," Paul Losch introduces a little-known memoir by the Cuban feminist educator and writer Aurora Mena, who lived in Florida in the 1890s. Titled *The Pearl Key, or Midnight and Dawn in Cuba* (1896), only one copy of the book is extant, which the University of Florida has digitized and made available online. Bringing together biographical information about Mena with literary analysis and reviews that appeared in various Florida newspapers, Losch shows that the memoir was part of a public relations effort to convince US readers to support the Cuban struggle for independence from Spain, which for Mena was closely related to her desire for greater opportunities for herself and other Cuban women. He further contextualizes the memoir's importance by reading it in conjunction with Evangelina Cosio y Cisneros' contemporaneously published and more renowned memoir, *The Story of Evangelina Cisneros*.

As William Orchard notes in his essay "Maria Cristina Mena and the Masturbating Boy," critics have productively studied Mena's writings through the categories of race and gender, but much less attention has been devoted to sexuality. Focusing on one of Mena's most well-known short stories, "The Education of Popo" (1914), Orchard intervenes in this gap by drawing from queer studies scholarship that connects masturbation to discourses of self-governance and self-sovereignty to argue that the story's eponymous protagonist is represented as a masturbating boy. This representation's significance lies in what it reveals about how Popo is attempting to formulate a sovereign identity in the face of cultural, political, and economic forces that threaten to overwhelm him and, by extension, the Mexican nation. Through this reading, Orchard not only makes an argument about Mena's use of sexuality as an aesthetic and political strategy, but more broadly positions his analysis of Mena's work as a queer extension of influential literary scholarship that has focused on gender and the heterosexual romance.

The Chicana Forum authors in this volume are pathbreakers in archival methods. These Chicanas have been committed to listening and exchanging knowledge with their communities and have meticulously created and preserved community centers that cared for their legacies. They have done this work because the state and knowledge-producing institutions have often disregarded or silenced their archives. With poetry—a personal and, thus, consequential genre to contest master and imperial narratives—Chicanas recall their legacy. Now, the Recovery Project has pushed the Chicano Movement date mark of the 1960s to the 1980s to retrieve Chicanas' *movidas* and other contributions further. Their personal and professional memories have political meanings that fill historiographic gaps for future and, we hope, empowered Latinas and Chicanas.

While essays throughout the collection draw from newspapers for their analyses, those gathered in Part II, "Gender, Politics, and Power in the Spanish-Language Press," consider newspapers in terms of "textual environments," indicating that they emphasize flows of texts and meanings across and within texts as they tease out how newspapers reinforced or challenged gendered relations of power

(Couldry 80). Ayendy Bonifacio's "Gertrudis Gómez de Avellaneda and Puerto Rico's Colonial Press" examines the public image of the celebrated Cuban poet and novelist in light of such textual flows. He argues that Puerto Rican newspapers controlled by the Spanish government understood her to be a threat to colonial dominance and to gender norms because of her popularity and the power of her work's anti-colonial overtones. Through an analysis of these newspapers' reprint processes and manipulative editorial practices, he shows how they attempted to recreate Avellaneda's public image by recontextualizing her poetry as "a patriotic performance of Spanish colonial control." His study elucidates how women writers could be simultaneously "included and excluded from participating in the public sphere and contributing to the discourse of nation-building," one that "subjected them to patriarchal colonial power."

While the early-twentieth-century Nuevomexicana Nina Otero-Warren did not have the same hemispheric level of fame as Avellaneda, she was highly celebrated on a regional level, both as a writer and a political candidate. As Anna Nogar argues in "Adelina 'Nina' Otero-Warren: A Nuevomexicana in Suffrage, Politics, and Letters in the Early Twentieth Century," historians have shown a renewed interest in Otero-Warren due to her role as a suffrage advocate, yet their focus on institutional records and Anglophone periodicals provides a limited view of her importance. Attending to how she was represented in the Hispanophone press and in popular culture, Nogar elucidates how Nuevomexicanos perceived Otero-Warren, showing that they identified with the land dispossession and race-based violence suffered by her family as a form of collective trauma. Nogar concludes by re-reading Otero-Warren's 1936 memoir *Old Spain in Our Southwest* in light of her career of advocacy for Nuevomexicanos in the public sector, "examining how the text corrected erroneous ideas about New Mexico and its people prevalent in the government institutions and Anglophone worlds in which Otero-Warren often moved."

Monica Perales' *"Entre la plancha y la página*: Early Twentieth-Century Mexicana Food Work and the Spanish-Language Press in Two Cities" reads elements of two Texan, Spanish-language newspapers to gain broader insights into the class and gender expectations that working-class Mexicanas confronted. Arguing that debates about women's food work serve as generative sites to explore gendered power relations, Perales analyzes household advice articles, recipes, advertisements, and employment notices and the multi-voiced meanings of women's food-related labor that emerge. As she shows, while editors and writers "promoted a middle-class ideal of domesticity, respectability, and the preservation of Mexican identity," food-related content reflected a more complex, multicultural reality that Mexicanas had to navigate, as they negotiated acculturation and cultural retention. Moreover, Perales suggests valuable ways of reading food content "against the grain" to tease out signs of Mexicana agency in providing for their families' emotional, nutritional, and economic needs. Ultimately, Perales demonstrates how women's everyday domestic concerns can reveal much about the challenges at the center of their political and social lives.

Even though radical Latinas have been historically marginalized and shunned by the state, patriarchy, and academia, contributors to Part III, "Radical Latinas' Politics," show Latinas finding tools to advance their rights in anarchism and other non-institutionalized, grassroots organizations. In turn, Latinas advanced radical movements by publishing in their periodicals and communicating nationally and transnationally. In "Luisa Capetillo, Free Love, and the *Falda-Pantalón*," Christopher Castañeda adds important insights to our understanding of the famed Puerto Rican anarcho-feminist by analyzing her life and writings from 1911 to 1913, a period that has received relatively little attention in Capetillo studies and during which she lived in the United States. Among the most famous episodes in Capetillo's life was her 1915 arrest in Havana for wearing pants while walking down a street, a provocative act that was part of her strategy to promote the gender equality that was her life's mission. While the Havana incident is understood to be a formative moment in her activism, Castañeda unearths US press coverage of a similar scandal in which Capetillo publicly wore pants in New York City three years earlier. Juxtaposing this public act with the writings on free love that she published contemporaneously in anarchist periodicals in the United States, he demonstrates that this was a significant period for the development of her anarcho-feminist ideas, which were based on her views regarding gender equality, love, and sex.

Historiographies of early-twentieth-century anarchism in the Gulf of Mexico region have centered on male workers and thinkers. Sonia Hernández's "Loud, Hidden Voices of the Revolution: Reynalda González Parra, Organized Labor, and *Feminismo Transfronterizo*" builds on and critiques this work by considering González Parra's largely unknown writings that appeared in the anarchist press between 1910-1920. There she developed a *feminismo transfronterizo* based on "revolutionary motherhood," which she conceptualized in anarchist terms as a process that required women to educate and emancipate themselves so that they could produce "free children" and thus contribute to the "reconstruction of a new society." In contrast to dominant politicized framings of motherhood in this period, González Parra's was staunchly anti-clerical and served the interests of the women themselves, promoting self-governance in a collective trans-border world void of any class distinction.

In "Josefina de la Grana's Letters to the Editor: A Window into her Activism in Tampa, Florida," Ana Varela-Lago analyzes letters published by de la Grana between 1927 and 1946 in Tampa's two leading newspapers. Born in Tamaulipas, Mexico, to a Cuban father and an Anglo-American mother, de la Grana was a feminist who was involved in labor causes, ran for mayor of Tampa as a Socialist in 1931, and was a vocal supporter of the international struggle against fascism, most specifically through her support of the Spanish Republic during the Spanish Civil War, an issue that was of great importance to Tampa's "Latin community." Varela-Lago stresses the importance of "letters to the editor" in providing access to individual and group perspectives marginalized in historical accounts. By recovering and contextualizing de la Grana's letters, Varela-Lago sheds light on an influential individual meriting further study and, more broadly, on "Latin women's activism" in the 1930s to defend the rights of women, immigrants, and workers.

Pablo Landeros' "AKA Frances: Francisca Flores and the Radical Roots of Chicana Feminism in California" explores an unexamined period in the renowned Chicana writer and organizer's political development. While Flores is acclaimed for establishing organizations such as the Comisión Femenil (1970) and for mentoring young women who faced sexism in the Chicano Movement, Landeros provides insights into Flores' activism before the Movement through close attention to the previously unstudied FBI surveillance files regarding her affiliation with the Communist Party USA in the 1940s and 1950s. The CPUSA's narrow focus on class struggle became increasingly problematic for Flores, who was always attuned to issues of race and gender due to her longstanding involvement in Mexican-American grassroots struggles. Landeros argues that these tensions pushed her to develop an ideological framework that understood race, class, and gender oppression to be interlinked, and which became the basis for the intersectional Chicana feminist praxis she became known for in the 1960s and 1970s. Landeros' essay thus expands our knowledge of an important figure for Chicana feminism and of the history of the Mexican-American Left.

To disestablish which past is silenced and which one is remembered (Michel-Rolph Trouillot 2015), contributors to Part IV, "Reclaiming Community, Reclaiming Knowledge," have retrieved various sources and perspectives to explore a history that is both traumatic and complex, beginning with Anita Huizar-Hernández's analysis of diasporic literature of the Cristero War. The Cristero War (1926-1929), a Catholic uprising against the Mexican government's secularization efforts, prompted many Cristeros—as the Catholic rebels were known—to flee across the border for safety and consequently become part of the Mexican diaspora in the United States. Cristeros on both sides of the border produced large amounts of writing engaging the War's meanings, from private documents to publications in Spanish-language newspapers and small presses, yet these writings have received little scholarly attention. In *"Mujeres y mártires*: Cristero Diaspora Literature,"* Huizar-Hernández argues that diasporic Cristero writings nuance our understanding of early twentieth-century Latino/a literature. To illustrate this point, she analyzes a little-known document by a Cristero exile, María de la Torre's tribute to a former suitor in her *Álbum sobre la vida y muerte de Fidel Muro*, which combines poetry, prose, images, and objects to commemorate Muro's martyrdom on behalf of the Cristero cause. Huizar-Hernández reads the *Álbum* through a transnational feminist lens, showing that Cristero diaspora literature highlights the destabilization of gender roles in the wake of the War and the role religion played in consolidating early twentieth-century US and

Mexican national identities, thus dramatizing the intertwined politics of modernization, assimilation, and racialization and their impact on Latino/a communities.

Koldo San Sebastian's contribution uncovers the research done on Basque women in the United States by generously sharing the migration history of his family. Like other migrants, his account gives insights into the social forces behind identity categories. His maternal grandmother was born in Cuba, where her Basque parents had migrated. His paternal grandmother was born in Idaho. His ethnographic piece on US Basque women shows how traditional and language expectations kept them in niches and mingled little outside their communities, contrary to their male counterparts, at least in the first generation. Patriarchy kept Basque women apart from Latinas, although both groups suffered the Spanish state and empire.

Through an analysis of little-known personal archives and oral histories, Vanessa Fonseca-Chávez recovers Chicana activism in Wyoming in the 1970s and 1980s in "'We Were Always Chicanos,' or, 'We Did it Our Way': Situated Citizenship in the Equality State." While Wyoming prides itself on being the first state or territory to grant women the right to vote, in fact it has a long history of failing to extend equality to Chicana/o and other marginalized populations. Centering the stories and community organizing efforts of Chicana residents in the city of Riverton, Fonseca-Chávez shows that they were keenly aware of their positionality as lesser citizens who had the legal right to vote but whose communities were regularly denied services as essential as water and sewage. Using theoretical frameworks such as "situated citizenship" and "memory *movidas*," Fonseca-Chávez maps collectivity-based understandings of citizenship and activism developed by Chicana community leaders to counter the "Equality State's" founding and exclusionary mythos based in "rugged individualism" and a "bootstraps mentality." In so doing, she adds Wyoming to our spatial understanding of Chicano Movement politics and shows how Chicana feminist activists challenge fundamental US notions of citizenship and equality.

Works Cited

Alarcón, Norma. "The Theoretical Subjects of *This Bridge Called My Back* and Anglo-American Feminism." *Making Face, Making Soul: Haciendo Caras*, edited by Gloria Anzaldúa, Aunt Lute P, 1990, pp. 356-369.

Alemán, Jesse. "Crossing the Maxon-Dixon Line in Drag: The Narrative of Loreta Janeta Velazquez, Cuban Woman and Confederate Soldier." *Look Away: The U.S. South in New World Studies*, edited by Jon Smith and Deborah Cohn, Duke UP, 2004, pp. 110-29.

___. "The Diachronics of Difference: *Chicano Narrative* Then, Now, and Before Chicanidad." *Bridges, Borders and Breaks: History, Narrative, and Nation in Twenty-First-Century Chicana/o Literary Criticism*, edited by William Orchard and Yolanda Padilla, U of Pittsburgh P, 2016, pp. 1-24.

___. "Preface." *The Latino Nineteenth Century*, edited by Rodrigo Lazo and Jesse Alemán, New York UP, 2016, pp. vii-ix.

Aranda, José F. "Recovering the US Hispanic Literary Heritage." *The Routledge Companion to Latino/a Literature*, edited by Suzanne Bost and Frances R. Aparicio. Routledge, 2013, pp. 476-484.

Berman, Jessica. "Practicing Transnational Feminist Recovery Today." *Feminist Modernist Studies*, vol. 1, no. 1-2, 2018, pp. 9-21.

Blackwell, Maylei. *¡Chicana Power!: Contested Histories of Feminism in the Chicano Movement*. U of Texas P, 2011.

Bost, Suzanne. "Messy Archives and Materials that Matter: Making Knowledge with the Gloria Evangelina Anzaldúa Papers." *PMLA*, vol. 130, no. 3, 2015, pp. 615-30.

Briggs, Laura, Gladys McCormick, and J.T. Way. "Transnationalism: A Category of Analysis." *American Quarterly*, vol. 60, no. 3, 2008, pp. 625-648.

Castañeda, Antonia I. "Women of Color and the Rewriting of Western History: The Discourse, Politics, and Decolonization of History." *Pacific Historical Review*, vol. 61, no. 4, 1992, pp. 501-33.

___. *Three Decades of Engendering History: Selected Works of Antonia I. Castañeda*, edited by Linda Heidenriech, U of North Texas P, 2014.

Chakrabarty, Dipesh. *Provincializing Europe: Postcolonial Thought and Historical Difference*. Princeton UP, 2000.

Coates, Lauren and Steffi Dippold. "Beyond Recovery." *Early American Literature*, vol. 55, no. 2, 2020, pp. 297-320.

Cotera, María Eugenia. *Native Speakers: Ella Deloria, Zora Neale Hurston, Jovita González, and the Poetics of Culture*. U of Texas P, 2008.

Cotera, María Eugenia, Maylei Blackwell, and Dionne Espinoza. "Introduction: Movement, Movimientos, and Movidas." *Chicana Movidas: New Narratives of Activism and Feminism in the Movement Era*, edited by Dionne Espinoza, María Eugenia Cotera and Maylei Blackwell, U of Texas P, 2018, pp. 1-30.

Couldry, Nick. *Inside Culture: Re-imagining the Method of Cultural Studies*. Sage, 2000.

Dworkin y Méndez, Kenya and Agnes Lugo-Ortiz. "Introduction." *Recovering the US Hispanic Literary Heritage*, vol. 5. Arte Público P, 2006, pp. 1-19.

Foster, Frances Smith. "Forgotten Manuscripts: How Do You Solve a Problem Like Theresa?" *African American Review*, vol. 40, no. 4, 2006, pp. 631-45.

___. "Intimate Matters in This Place: The Underground Railroad of Literature." *Legacy: A Journal of American Women Writers*, vol. 36, no. 2, 2019, pp. 245-8.

Gonzales-Berry, Erlinda and Chuck Tatum. "Introduction." *Recovering the US Hispanic Literary Heritage*, vol. 2. Arte Público P, 1996, pp. 13-19.

González, Deena J. *Refusing the Favor: The Spanish Mexican Women of Santa Fe, 1820-1880*. Oxford UP, 1999.

Gruesz, Kirsten Silva and Rodrigo Lazo. "Introduction: The Spanish Americas." *Early American Literature*, vol. 53, no. 3, 2018, pp. 641-664.

Guidoitti-Hernández, Nicole M. *Unspeakable Violence: Remapping U.S. and Mexican National Imaginaries*. Duke UP, 2011.

___. *Archiving Mexican Masculinities in Diaspora*. Duke UP, 2021.

Harris, Sharon M. "'Across the Gulf': Working in the 'Post-Recovery' Era." *Legacy*, vol. 26, no. 2, 2009, pp. 284-98.

Hartman, Saidiya. "Venus in Two Acts." *Small Axe*, vol. 26, 2008, pp. 1-14.

Herrera-Sobek, María and Virginia Sánchez Korrol. "Introduction." *Recovering the US Hispanic Literary Heritage*, vol. 3. Arte Público P, 1998, pp. 1-14.

Kanellos, Nicolás. "Recovering the U.S. Hispanic Literary Heritage." *PMLA*, vol. 127, no. 2, 2012, pp. 371-4.

Lazo, Rodrigo. "Migrant Archives: New Routes in and out of American Studies." *States of Emergency: The Object of American Studies,* edited by Susan Gillman and Russ Castronovo, U of North Carolina P, 2009, pp. 36-54.

___. "Historical Latinidades and Archival Encounters." *The Latino Nineteenth Century*, edited by Rodrigo Lazo and Jesse Alemán, New York UP, 2016, pp. 1-17.

Looser, Devoney. "Why I'm Still Writing Women's Literary History." *Minnesota Review*, vol. 71-72, 2009, pp. 220-227.

Marsden, Jean I. "Beyond Recovery: Feminism and the Future of Eighteenth-Century Literary Studies." *Feminist Studies*, vol. 28, no. 3, 2002, pp. 657-62.

Moya, Paula and Ramón Saldívar. "Fictions of the Trans-American Imaginary." *Modern Fiction Studies,* vol. 49, no. 1, 2003, pp. 1-18.

Orchard, William and Yolanda Padilla. "Chicana/o Narratives, Then and Now." *Bridges, Borders and Breaks: History, Narrative, and Nation in Twenty-First-Century Chicana/o Literary Criticism*, edited by William Orchard and Yolanda Padilla, U of Pittsburgh P, 2016, pp. 1-24.

Pérez, Emma. *The Decolonial Imaginary: Writing Chicanas into History*. Indiana UP, 1999.

___. "Queering the Borderlands: The Challenges of Excavating the Invisible and Unheard." *Frontiers: A Journal of Women's Studies*, vol. 24, no. 2-3, 2003, pp. 122-131.

___. *Forgetting the Alamo, Or, Blood Memory: A Novel*. U of Texas P, 2009.

Poovey, Mary. "Recovering Ellen Pickering." *The Yale Journal of Criticism*, vol. 13, no. 2, 2000, pp. 437-52.

Sarker, Sonita. "On Remaining Minor in Modernisms: The Future of Women's Literature." *Literature Compass*, vol. 10, no. 1; 2013, pp. 8-14.

Trouillot, Michel-Rolph. *Silencing the Past: Power and the Production of History*. Beacon P, Boston, Massachusetts, 2015.

PART I
FEMINIST READINGS OF LATINA AUTHORS

Citizenship, Suffrage, and the (Un)making of the Mexican-American Woman Citizen in María Amparo Ruiz de Burton's *Who Would Have Thought It?*

ESMERALDA ARRIZÓN-PALOMERA
University of Illinois, Chicago

María Amparo Ruiz de Burton's *Who Would Have Thought It?* (1872) is the first novel written in English by a Mexican-American woman and the first to engage the US women's movement. In this novel, Ruiz de Burton offers her impressions of an evolving movement in the years leading up to the Civil War and interrogates Mexican-American women's relationship to it. The novel's engagement with the women's movement, however, has received little critical attention. The criticism on Ruiz de Burton's work that approximates this subject is focused on gender and its significance within the larger Mexican-American struggle against US colonialism. This criticism, moreover, subordinates gender to issues of class, viewing gender "only in terms of romance and marriage," understanding it as a means to create or preserve racial and class privilege (J. Ruiz 118).

Literary scholars who center gender in analyses of Ruiz de Burton's work generally acknowledge her interest in women's rights, her awareness of the women's movement, and her familiarity with nineteenth-century feminist discourses, but they do not locate her work within those discourses or in conversation with the

3

women's movement. Instead, critics dismiss her engagement with the movement as "satirical," characterize it as peripheral to the larger Mexican-American struggle against US colonialism, or interpret it as anticipatory of Chicana feminism (Sánchez, "Introduction" xvi).[1] These interpretations of Ruiz de Burton's work locate her at the edges of the women's movement, which not only reinforces the notion that Mexican-American women are foreign to the United States, but also produces a myopic view of the development of Chicana feminist thought that excludes its connections to the nineteenth-century women's movement.

The tendency among literary scholars to locate Ruiz de Burton's work outside the women's movement may be explained by an oppositional impulse to locate Ruiz de Burton within a Chicana feminist genealogy where Chicana feminism is not only outside the women's movement, but also in opposition to the women's movement's investment in white supremacy.[2] However, as scholars who note the "conflicts of interest" in Ruiz de Burton's work suggest, white supremacy "both enabled and circumscribed" Ruiz de Burton's "field of action" and often "implicated" and made her "complicit" in this system (Sánchez and Pita, "Introduction" ix-x). In his analysis of what he calls the "contradictory responses" to Ruiz de Burton's work, for example, José F. Aranda gestures towards the entanglement between Chicana feminist politics and white feminism and calls for a reformulation of Chicana/o Studies to create space for privileged Mexican-Americans like Ruiz de Burton who, he notes, "are far from being always marginalized" and "have had a historic role in the cultural and literary production of the United States since 1848" (554). Writing specifically about Ruiz de Burton's positionality within Chicana/o Studies, Aranda notes,

> In the figure of María Amparo Ruiz de Burton, we have a complex person and a writer who easily exploded stereotypes in her day and continues to do so today. And yet—and here is the idea that needs to be entertained—she is not a Dolores Huerta of the United Farm Workers Union or a Gloria Anzaldúa of the borderlands in nineteenth-century clothes. (555)

Aranda's misrepresentation of Chicana feminists as static political subjects aside, his point invites a discussion about the relationship between Chicana feminism and white feminism beyond the conversations that took place among Chicana feminists in the 1960s and 1970s.

Suppose literary scholars correctly identify Ruiz de Burton as "a foremother of Chicana literature" and Chicana feminist thought (De La Luz, "See How" 187). How does a (re)reading of Ruiz de Burton's work that centers her engagement with an evolving women's movement reframe our understanding of the Chicana feminist movement, the nineteenth-century women's movement, and the relationship between Chicana feminism and white feminism? The answer to this question is complex and located in Ruiz de Burton's (re)construction of the women's movement in *Who Would Have Thought It?* When we turn to Ruiz de Burton's first novel and read it in conversation with nineteenth-century feminist discourses, what emerges is not simply a different genealogy of Chicana feminism, but a reconstruction of nineteenth-century feminisms. The reconstruction of nineteenth-century feminisms *Who Would Have Thought it?* offers, I argue, not only highlights the role of literature in the formation and development of social movements, it also challenges the "myth of Seneca Falls"—the origin myth that shaped "the development of nineteenth-century feminism" into a white, middle-class movement—by calling attention to the experiences of Mexican-American women that were excluded in the construction of this myth and their role in the development in nineteenth-century feminisms (Tetrault 1).

The Women's Movement, a (Re)construction

Who Would Have Thought it? is informed by Ruiz de Burton's experience as a Californiana in the northeast. The eleven years she spent there "intensified her sense of displacement" as a Mexican American and as a woman, but it also provided her with an education in the political forces and events reshaping the United States (*Conflicts* 180). In letters written to the Californio general and statesman Mariano Guadalupe Vallejo during her early years in the northeast, Ruiz de Burton remarks on the radical changes that have recently taken place in her life. She observes that her time in the northeast has given her much to think about, "particularly if one starts making comparisons," and determines that the best thing she can do to make sense of what she sees is "write a book" (*Conflicts* 244).[3] The comparisons in Ruiz de Burton's letters are concerned with include the southwest and northeast landscapes, the people with whom she interacts, the status of "married women," and the political situation in Mexico and the United States (277). Her 1872 novel reflects these concerns, particularly the political forces and events reshaping the United States and their effect on women who, as she notes in her 1869 correspondence with San Diego attorney and politician, Ephraim W. Morse, "can't vote yet" (296).

Ruiz de Burton's novel tells the story of María Dolores (Lola) Medina. Lola's story begins in 1846 when Doña Theresa, pregnant with Lola, is kidnapped from her home in "the northern part of Sonora" and held captive for ten years during which Doña Theresa amasses a great fortune (*Who* 193). Lola's story pivots in 1857 when her mother dies and Lola is rescued from captivity by Dr. James Norval, a Democrat from New England who promises to take care of Lola and find her family. Dr. Norval takes Lola and her inheritance with him to New England where Lola's transformation, from a ten-year old girl who is believed to be both an orphan and racially inferior into a young woman with skin that is "whiter than white," unfolds alongside an evolving women's movement and against the backdrop of the Civil War (Sánchez and Pita "Introduction" [*Who*] xvi). Ruiz de Burton's narrative choice positions Lola's struggles in New England and, by extension, the struggles of Mexican-American women in the United States as the other Civil War taking place in the country. *Who Would Have Thought it?*, in other words, brings the significance of the US-Mexico War and its aftermath into the Civil War by locating Lola at the center of the major political events in the United States in the mid-nineteenth century. In so doing, the novel enacts a redeployment of white women reformers' strategic use of the Civil War "to [white] women's advantage" in service of Mexican-American women (Etcheson 610).[4]

Lola's 1857 arrival in New England coincides with the only year, in ten years, that passed without a National Women's Rights Convention in the United States.[5] Lola's arrival in New England at this precise moment inserts Mexican-American women into a gap in the women's movement and recasts the movement from the perspective of the Mexican-American woman. Read as an engagement with nineteenth-century feminist discourses, *Who Would Have Thought it?* functions as an early attempt to narrate and examine an evolving and often contradictory movement. The novel appeared at pivotal moments in the women's movement's development and was published nine years before the first of six volumes of the *History of Women's Suffrage,* which sought to construct a cohesive history of the movement, were released.[6] The novel was completed in 1869, when the feminist movement was fractured into two national women's rights organizations due to disagreements about the Fifteenth Amendment, and it was published in 1872, the year in which Virginia Minor sued for women's suffrage in Missouri and lost.[7] The most significant part of Ruiz de Burton's examination of the women's movement, however, lies not in these interesting coincidences, but in its narration of Lola's relationship to abolitionists and emerging feminists in the novel and how these relationships shaped both Lola's transformation into a white political subject and her relationship to the United States and the women's movement.

Ruiz de Burton's analysis of the women's movement and Mexican-American women's relationship to it in *Who Would Have Thought it?* subverts the racialized citizen/alien dichotomy developed by white women reformers in the early nineteenth century to secure suffrage for white women only. Ruiz de Burton's subversion of this dichotomy acknowledges Mexican-American women's eligibility for legal citizenship in the United States. However, it also demonstrates the (im)possibility of their full incorporation into the nation-state and the women's movement due to Mexican-American women's sex and the racialization of their national origin. The subversion of this dichotomy begins in the novel's first chapter where Ruiz de Burton reverses the Anglo-American gaze Mexican and Mexican-American women encountered in the nineteenth century.

She parodies "travel, journalistic, and biographical accounts" (Castañeda 215) written by Anglo-American men that began to circulate
in the 1840s, as well as the "trashy novels" (*Who* 9) about Mexican
women inspired by Anglo-American men's accounts. In so doing,
she offers an account of New England as a place that is "politically,
sexually, and racially lacking in ethics" and therefore beneath the
Mexican-American woman who exemplifies the ideals of white
womanhood far better than the supposed abolitionist and emerging
feminists of New England (De La Luz, "Introduction" xiii).

In narratives written by "merchants, sailors, and adventurers"
(Castañeda 215) the writer encounters the Other, someone
characterized as foreign and described by a racialized, classed, and
gendered interpretative framework. However, in the opening scenes
of *Who Would Have Thought It?*, the Other, the foreigner, encounters
Anglo Americans. Channeling her contemporary, Victoria
Woodhull, Ruiz de Burton uses white characters' racialized, classed,
and gendered interpretative frameworks to expose their prejudice
and hypocrisy.[8] In "The Arrival," Ruiz de Burton introduces Mrs.
Cackle, Jemima Norval, her two daughters, Ruth and Mattie Norval,
and Lavinia Sprig, Jemima Norval's unmarried sister. The narrator
introduces the Norval and Sprig women through the perspective of
Mrs. Cackle who stands outside the Norval home observing and
judging the Sprig and Norval women, their "flat" faces and "high
nose[s]," as the women notice and ignore Mrs. Cackle (5).

Ruiz de Burton expands her characterization of the women as
participants of an evolving women's movement by describing their
actions towards Lola and the Mexican-American women she
represents. Lola and Dr. Norval are met by the Norval and Sprig
women who notice two wagons: one of them, a "government
wagon," carrying boxes full of what they assume are "rocks and
pebbles;" the other with Lola (6). When they see Lola, it is her gender
they notice first. They see a "female in a red shawl" clinging to Dr.
Norval (7). They then note the color of her skin after which they lose
sight of Lola's humanity and refer to her as a "specimen," an
"animal," who they suggest is another one of Dr. Norval's
acquisitions (8). The immediate shift in the women's perception of

Lola, from "female" to "specimen," is a commentary on New Englanders' racism and possibly a reflection of contemporaneous debates regarding the status of black people sparked by the Supreme Court's 1857 ruling on the Dred Scott case. However, it is also a pointed critique of the women's movement's inability or unwillingness to reconcile gender and race in its pursuit of women's suffrage.

The Norval and Sprig women's response to Lola illustrates a problem abolitionist and women's rights advocate Sojourner Truth first notes in her widely recognized "Ain't I a Woman" speech, delivered at the second National Women's Rights Convention in Akron, Ohio.[9] The women's reception of Lola signals towards white women reformers' refusal to address race in their campaigns for women's full legal, political, and economic incorporation into the United States. This scene, however, can also be interpreted as a commentary on the absent presence of Mexican-American women in the development of the women's movement. This commentary is made by noting that just as the women miss the real value of the "rocks and pebbles" the "government wagon" carries, they also miss Lola's real worth and potential contributions to the United States and the women's movement. This point is made clear by Dr. Norval when he shares with Mrs. Norval Lola's true identity and assures her that "instead of being *a burden*" Lola "will be a great acquisition" (18).

Lola's wealth makes her a "great" acquisition for the women's movement and the United States. Lola, like the Mexican people she represents in the novel, had claims to property in the United States and, like all Mexicans who chose to remain in the United States after the US-Mexico War, had to assert her whiteness by denying or distancing herself from Blackness and Indigeneity in order to exercise those rights.[10] Her wealth, in other words, signaled her admissibility to the United States, which in 1857 reserved legal citizenship for foreign or US-born white men and women only, and the women's movement, which at the time of Lola's arrival to New England was primarily a white, middle-class movement that struggled with its relationship to "other reform movements" (DuBois 201). Lola's admissibility to the United States and the women's movement is made clear when the women are prompted to observe Lola closely. Lola's whiteness is first recognized by Reverend Hackwell who observes Lola's European features and notes that she "is rather pretty, only very black" (8). The Norval and Sprig women then gather around Lola and Reverend Hackwell and proceed to inspect Lola's body in what strongly resembles a slave auction scene. With this scene, Ruiz de Burton suggests that Lola's rescue is no rescue but rather her entry into a different type of captivity.

At this point in the novel, Ruiz de Burton's characters' descriptions of Lola vacillate between three forms of captivity: black slavery, Indian slavery—what historian Andrés Reséndez terms "the other slavery," and the subordination of white women to white men, what white women reformers often described as enslavement. Ruiz de Burton's gesture towards these three forms of captivity illustrate for the reader the (im)possibility of Lola's incorporation into the United States and the women's movement. Ruiz de Burton makes this point clear by momentarily, with each character's speculation about Lola's origin, positioning Lola as a representative of women of color—black women, Native American women, and Mexican-American women—who were generally excluded from the nineteenth-century women's movement before returning to, and settling on, Lola's whiteness.[11]

Ruiz de Burton makes the reader take a closer look at Lola and notice, along with Mattie, the youngest of the Norval girls, that the skin of Lola's palms is "as white" as hers (9). Through Mattie's observation, Ruiz de Burton notes white women reformers' varying views and attitudes towards women of color, and signals the potential inclusion of white Mexican-American women in this movement. Mattie, who harbors racist ideologies and acts on them, is portrayed as kinder to Lola and more willing or able to recognize her humanity than her sister Ruth who riffs off Mrs. Norval's disparaging comments about Lola and Dr. Norval. The women, guided by Mattie, observe Lola closely and determine that she has "magnificent eyes," "red and prettily-cut lips," and palms "a prettier white" than themselves (8-9). At this point, Lola's racial ambiguity lunges the Norval and Sprig women into speculation about her origins. Lavinia, the only one who addresses Lola directly, echoes Mattie's observation and speculates that Lola might not be black while Ruth, resounding her mother's conclusions about Lola's race, suggests that she might be the daughter of "Indians or negroes, or both" (9). Dr. Norval settles the debate, he notes that they are all "mistaken" and stops Mrs. Norval from dismissing Lola to the kitchen with the white immigrant domestic workers she employs (9). With Mrs. Norval's attempt to dismiss Lola, Ruiz de Burton rejects Lola's possible welcome and reaffirms her inadmissibility to the nation-state and the women's movement. This scene, in short, illustrates the racism and nativism of Anglo-American women and portrays their refusal to recognize women of color as their equal as a result of, Ruiz de Burton's narrative suggests, the patriarchal order in which they exist and is evident in white men's dismissal of white women as we see Dr. Norval do to the women in his family.

Mrs. Norval's attempt to dismiss Lola underscores the influence of Anglo-American women's racist and nativist observations about women of color in the treatment of Mexican-American women like Lola in the United States. Mrs. Norval's attitude towards Lola strongly resembles the attitudes Anglo-American women like Susan Shelly Magoffin held towards Mexican women. Magoffin's diary, written between 1846 and 1847, offers a series of stereotypes about Mexican women that include the "greaser girl" (51), the "Spanish beauty" (102), and representations of Mexican women as "shrewd" (120) and solicitous. Magoffin's descriptions of herself as "venturesome" (28) and as "an American citizen" (63) often precede her description of Mexican women. As Magoffin's narrative demonstrates, Anglo-American women's representations of Mexican women as Other and as foreign were critical to their construction of themselves as women and as citizens. Pejorative images of Mexican women operated within what historian Antonia I. Castañeda describes as a "political economy" (213) of stereotypes which, she argues, "served the political and economic interests of an expanding United States" (220) and, I would add, those of Anglo-American women who demanded the "immediate admission to all the rights and privileges which belong to them as citizens of the United States" (Stanton et al., 75).

Anglo-American women's construction of themselves as citizens often entailed a deployment of what Beth Fisher describes as "competing discourses of womanhood" (6). These competing discourses provided women with "meaningful vocabulary, and rich symbols" (Romero 19) to participate in nation-building through their creation of "notions of the foreign against which the nation can be imagined as a home" (Kaplan 582). The stereotypical descriptions of Mexican women in Magoffin's diary functioned in this way and helped determine if or how women of color would be incorporated into the nation-state and the women's movement.[12]

By the 1860s, as Lola's New England reception illustrates, Anglo Americans believed that only "minor differences" separated Mexicans, African Americans, and Native Americans, and these differences often converged in the figure of the foreigner (De León 21). Anglo-American women's transformation of Mexican-American women into foreigners to advance their own legal, political, and economic interests was not lost on Ruiz de Burton. Ruiz de Burton, as evident in her depiction of Mrs. Norval's attempt to dismiss Lola, and Mrs. Norval's subsequent efforts to prevent Lola's true identity from becoming public, demonstrates that she understood the nature and function of these images and moved to confront them and those who produced them, by subverting the racialized alien/citizen dichotomy animated by pejorative images of Mexican women.

Ruiz de Burton's subversion of the alien/citizen dichotomy is first articulated by Dr. Norval who, during Lola's first encounter with the Sprig and Norval women, comments on Lola's "lovely and affectionate" disposition as he witnesses the Norval and Sprig women's behavior (9). The significance of Ruiz de Burton's subversion of the alien/citizen dichotomy in this scene, however, goes beyond exposing Anglo-American women's racism and nativism. This subversion can also be read as a commentary on the political movements of which they are a part and the political system these movements aimed to reform. The stakes of Ruiz de Burton's rhetorical strategy are put into words by Dr. Norval who, commenting on his wife's treatment of Lola, turns to Reverend Hackwell and asks him to note the inconsistencies between his wife's abolitionist beliefs and her dismissal of Lola due to the color of her skin. Dr. Norval asks,

> I beg you to remember, Mr. Hackwell, . . . and to draw from that fact a moral for a sermon, that my wife is a lady of the strictest Garrisonian school, a devout follower of Wendell Phillips's teachings, and a most enthusiastic admirer of Mr. Sumner. Compare the facts with the reception she gives this poor little orphan because her skin is dark; whilst I, a good-for-nothing Democrat, who don't believe in Sambo, but believe in Christian charity and human mercy, feel pity for the little thing. (10)

With this brief exchange between Dr. Norval and Reverend Hackwell, Ruiz de Burton indicts the hypocrisy of Democrats and Republicans alike. This exchange, moreover, echoes the criticism against reformers like Elizabeth Cady Stanton and Susan B. Anthony who claimed to subscribe to Garrisonian abolitionism while also ignoring women of color in their pursuit for women's rights and actively working against black male suffrage.[13] With this aside between Dr. Norval and Reverend Hackwell, in other words, Ruiz de Burton highlights the incongruences between Mrs. Norval's and Dr. Norval's beliefs and actions, and notes that despite the calls for equal rights issued by both the women's movement and the abolition movement in the late 1860s, both movements were plagued by white supremacy. Ruiz de Burton's use of Dr. Norval in the subversion of the alien/citizen dichotomy is a moment in the novel where we see the "conflicts of interest" and "contradictory responses" in her work noted by critics like Rosaura Sánchez, Beatrice Pita, and José F. Aranda. On the one hand, she uses Dr. Norval and the patriarchal order he represents to assert Lola's, and by extension, Mexican-American women's superiority. On the other hand, she's affirming a patriarchal order that exists and operates regardless of race, ethnicity, or nation. However, this contradiction is so obvious that her use of Dr. Norval to subvert the alien/citizen dichotomy, combined with

Dr. Norval's shortcomings which include abandoning his family for years, his racism, sexism, and paternalism, could make the reader wonder if Ruiz de Burton's use of Dr. Norval, particularly in the exchange between him and Reverend Hackwell, isn't a nod to the grievances Anglo-American women enumerated in the Declaration of Sentiments and that Ruiz de Burton herself echoed in correspondence to Mariano Guadalupe Vallejo to whom she laments that the legal, political, and economic "progress of the continent" will not benefit her "race" or her "sex" (*Conflicts* 280).[14]

(Un)making the Mexican-American Woman Citizen

Within the first three chapters of the novel, Ruiz de Burton presents her views on an evolving women's movement in the United States in the years leading up to the Civil War. She notes its limits and contradictions. She identifies racism, classism, heterosexism, and nativism as the factors stalling its development into the intersectional movement it had the potential to be. Her critiques, however, don't dismiss the women's movement on account of the *isms* that organize it. Rather, her critiques of the women's movement entertain the possibility of the white Mexican-American women's participation in it. Ruiz de Burton's inclination towards the women's movement is evident in her representation of Mattie Norval and Lavinia Sprig as redeemable Anglo-American women who are more willing than the others to recognize Lola's whiteness, and whom she develops, throughout the next fifty-eight chapters, into women with a political consciousness who cease to believe the things they hear or read "in printed political speeches" (100) about the church or the nation-state. These women can see that "the veritable source" of their troubles is "[*their*] *lawgivers*" (200).

Ruiz de Burton's inclination towards the women's movement, and its possibilities for the white Mexican-American woman citizen, is evident in Lola's proximity to the events that develop Mattie's and Lavinia's political consciousness. There is, for example, one pivotal scene in Lavinia's politicization where Lola makes an appearance that illustrates Ruiz de Burton's ambivalence towards the women's movement. This scene takes place soon after the Civil War begins and involves the moment in which Lavinia, at the height of "patriotic enthusiasm," sacrifices all but one of her canary birds to spare them the neglect they'd experience during the time she was planning to spend in Washington, DC, caring for wounded soldiers (79). Lola enters the scene after Lavinia has killed all except a canary named Jule, after Julian Norval, Lola's love interest. This scene signals the importance of the Civil War in the development of the women's movement which as Stanton, Anthony, and Gage note in their second volume of the history of women's suffrage, "threw new light on the status of woman in a republic" (1289). This scene, moreover, comments on the exclusion of Mexican-American women in the development of the women's movement. Whereas Lavinia is called upon to care for the wounded soldiers like Julian Norval, Lola, who wants to care for wounded soldiers, is only permitted to participate in the war effort symbolically by saving Jule from Lavinia's patriotism.

Lola's exclusion from this important event in the development of the women's movement can be explained in three ways. First, the subversion of the racialized alien/citizen dichotomy that organizes the novel may explain Ruiz de Burton's decision to sideline Lola. To carry out this rhetorical strategy and portray Lola as superior to the Norval and Sprig women, Ruiz de Burton has to exclude Lola from the patriotic fervor that makes Lavinia lose her composure. Lavinia's "patriotic enthusiasm" signals a mental and emotional instability, and to locate Lola in the patriotism Lavinia experiences would place her on equal footing with Lavinia and work against the organizing framework Ruiz de Burton uses to construct the white Mexican-American woman citizen (79). Second, the choice to locate Lola outside this important turning point in the development of the women's movement aligns with the critique of the nation-state the novel posits. Ruiz de Burton voices her critique of the US nation-state through Lavinia and Julian who learn that "American citizens as individuals . . . had lost the importance, the sacredness of old" (215). When Lavinia goes to Washington to "demand a right," she learns about the government's willingness to sacrifice soldiers who have been captured by the enemy (100).

Similarly, after enlisting in the army and being wounded in the line of duty, Julian discovers that he's been dismissed "by order of the President" without the opportunity to defend himself (207). On the other hand, Ruiz de Burton's critique of the Mexican nation-state is voiced through the narrator's commentary on Lola's mother's story. Reflecting on Doña Theresa's story, the narrator concludes, "Misery is, undoubtedly, 'the lot of mortals,' *but* there is no doubt that certain kinds of evils are impossible in some countries. If Mexico were well governed, if her frontiers were well protected, the fate of Doña Theresa would have been next to an impossibility" (200). Whereas in Ruiz de Burton's analysis of the US nation-state her critique is against the government's willful disregard for its citizens, in her analysis of the Mexican nation-state, her criticism is directed against the government's inability to protect its citizens. Finally, Ruiz de Burton's choice to locate Lola outside this important turning point in the development of the women's movement, falls within the narrative arc of Lola's transformation. When the Civil War begins, Lola is not yet eligible for citizenship.[15] Although the black ink on her skin had begun to fade, her skin was still "stained" (94). At this point in the novel, Lola has "spots" that make New Englanders question her claim to citizenship and speculate that Lola is Indian and that she must belong to "a tribe of Mexican Indians called 'Pintos,' who are spotted" (72).

Lola's transformation, the legitimization of her claim to citizenship and inheritance, faced challenges Mexicanos who remained in the United States after 1848 encountered. For Lola, these included the loss of Doña Theresa's "manuscript" (20), Dr. Norval's revision of Doña Theresa's "narrative" (20) into a last will and testament, the false "newspaper accounts" (116) of Dr. Norval's death, and finally, the attempts by "Solicitors and Attorneys-at-law" (218) to take advantage of Lola's situation. All of these, particularly the latter, prompted Lola's refusal of the second-class status the United States and the women's movement offered her. In the last of a series of intrigues, Reverend Hackwell tricks Lola, whose skin is now "whiter" (233) than that of the Norval and Sprig women, into claiming to be his wife in order to obtain information about her father by assuring her that "*only married* ladies" (220) can go into the "places" (220) she needed to go to receive that information. Lola is reunited with her family shortly after this incident and leaves New England with the help of Mattie and Lavinia. They lend themselves to a plot composed by Julian Norval to secure Lola's return to Mexico and prevent Reverend Hackwell's intrigues from harming Lola, particularly through the publication of the details of Doña Theresa's capture. Lola's departure, her refusal of the second-class status Dr. Norval offered her as his guardian, that Reverend Hackwell offered her as his wife, and that the women's movement presented to her under the tutelage of Mrs. Norval, is the logical conclusion of her story, not because Mexico is her home, or to prevent her subordination to the second-class status "*married* ladies" and single women occupied in the United States, but to maintain her claim to whiteness, her inheritance, and her eligibility to citizenship (220). Lola's return to Mexico, in other words, suggests that the only way for Lola to remain in control of her mother's "narrative" (20) is to exit the United States and remain outside the women's movement where her mother's history would call into question both Lola's whiteness and her incorporation into the women's movement.

Lola's departure, in short, maintains the possibility of an alliance between the Anglo-American woman, represented by Mattie and Lavinia, and the white Mexican-American woman citizen, represented by Lola. By the end of the novel Mattie, Lavinia, and Lola are identified as white and have come to understand that the "veritable source" of their troubles is their "*lawgivers*," a group that at this point is comprised of men (200). Having established the whiteness of the Mexican-American woman citizen, Ruiz de Burton continues to explore the possibility of this alliance by exploring the unjust laws and lawgivers shaping the lives of Californios in her 1885 novel, *The Squatter the Don*. This novel, published one year before the third volume of the *History of Women's Suffrage*, reconciles the white Mexican-American woman citizen, represented by Doña Josefa Alamar and her daughters, Elvira Alamar and Mercedes Alamar, and the Anglo-American woman citizen, represented by Mary Darrell and her daughter Alice Darrell, through

Mary Darrell's acknowledgement of Anglo-American women's wrongdoing, and under the mutual agreement that though "every true-hearted [American] woman" has "treated the conquered Spaniards most cruelly," it is "[their] lawgivers" who "have been most unjust to them" (*Squatter* 235-6).

Read as an engagement with nineteenth-century feminist discourses, *Who Would Have Thought It?* clarifies the need for further study of the relationship between the women's movement and the Chicana feminist movement. Ruiz de Burton's narration and interrogation of the nineteenth-century women's movement suggests that Mexican-American women were not disengaged from the movement. The novel, moreover, presents us with an alternative Chicana feminist genealogy that suggests Chicana feminism has not always been completely outside of or in opposition to the women's movement's investment in white supremacy. In so doing, *Who Would Have Thought It?* invites us to reject the "myth of Seneca Falls" and examine the entanglement between the development of Chicana feminist politics and white feminism to more fully understand the emergence and development of Chicana feminist thought (Tetrault 1).

Works Cited

Aranda, José F. "Contradictory Impulses: María Amparo Ruiz De Burton, Resistance Theory, and the Politics of Chicano/a Studies." *American Literature*, vol. 70, no. 3, 1998, pp. 551-79.

Castañeda, Antonia I. "The Political Economy of Nineteenth Century Stereotypes of Californians." In *Between Borders: Essays on Mexicana/Chicana History*. Edited by Adelaida R. Del Castillo, Floricanto, 1990.

Clinton, Catherine. *The Other Civil War: American Women in the Nineteenth Century.* Revised Edition, Hill and Wang, 1999.

Cotera, Martha. *The Chicana Feminist.* Information Systems Development, 1977.

_____. "Feminism: The Chicana and Anglo Versions (A Historical Analysis)." *Twice a Minority: Mexican American Women.* Edited by Margarita B. Melville, Mosby, 1980.

De La Luz Montes, Amelia María. "'See How I am Received': Nationalism, Race, and Gender in *Who Would Have Thought It?*" *María Amparo Ruiz De Burton: Critical and Pedagogical Perspectives.* Edited by Amelia M. L Montes, and Anne E. Goldman, U of Nebraska UP, 2004.

____. "Es Necessario Mirar Bien: Nineteenth-Century Letter Making and Novel Writing in the Life of María Amparo Ruiz de Burton." *Recovering the U.S. Hispanic Literary Heritage, Volume 3.* Edited by María Herrera-Sobek and Virginia Sánchez-Korrol. Arte Público, 1998.

____. "Introduction." *Who Would Have Thought It?* Edited by Amelia María de La Luz Montes, Penguin, 2009.

De León, Arnoldo A. *They Called Them Greasers: Anglo Attitudes Toward Mexicans in Texas, 1821-1900.* Texas UP, 1983.

DuBois, Ellen Carol. *Feminism and Suffrage: The Emergence of an Independent Women's Movement in America, 1848-1869.* Cornell UP, 1980.

Emmerich, Lisa E. "Civilization and Transculturation: The Matron Program and Cross-Cultural Contact." *American Indian Culture and Research Journal*, vol. 15, no. 4, 1991, pp. 33-48.

____. "Marguerite Laflesche Diddock: Office of Indian Affairs Field Matron." *Great Plains Quarterly*, vol. 13, 1993, pp. 162-171. Etcheson, Nicole. "'When Women Do Military Duty': The Civil War's Impact on Woman Suffrage." *Journal of American History*, vol. 107, no. 3, Dec. 2020, pp. 609-35.

Fisher, Beth. "The Captive Mexicana and the Desiring Bourgeois Woman: Domesticity and Expansionism in Ruiz De Burton's *Who Would Have Thought It?*" *Legacy*, vol. 16, no. 1, 1999, pp. 59-69.

García, Alma M., editor. *Chicana Feminist Thought: The Basic Historical Writings.* Routledge, 1997.

Griswold Del Castillo, Richard. *The Treaty of Guadalupe Hidalgo.* Oklahoma UP, 1990.

Haney López, Ian. *White by Law: The Construction of Race.* New York UP, 2006.

Hernandez-Jason, Beth. "Squatting in Uncle Tom's Cabin: Inter-textual References and Literary Tactics in Nineteenth-Century

U.S. Women Writers." In *Recovering the U.S. Hispanic Literary Heritage, Volume 8*. Edited by Gabriela Baeza Ventura and Clara Lomas, Arte Público, 2010.

Kaplan, Amy. "Manifest Destiny." *American Literature*, vol. 70, no. 3, 1998, pp. 581-606.

Magoffin, Susan Shelby. *Down the Santa Fe Trail and Into Mexico: The Diary of Susan Shelby Magoffin, 1846-1847*. Yale UP, 1962.

Menchaca, Martha *Naturalizing Mexican Immigrants, A Texas History*. Texas UP, 2011.

Moraga, Cherríe, and Gloria Anzaldúa, editors. *This Bridge Called My Back: Writings by Radical Women of Color*. Fourth edition, State U of New York P, 2015.

Reséndez, Andrés. *The Other Slavery: The Uncovered Story of Indian Enslavement in America*. Houghton, 2016.

Rivera, John-Michael. *The Emergence of Mexican America: Recovering Stories of Mexican Peoplehood in U.S. Culture*. New York UP, 2006.

Roesch Wagner, Sally. *Sisters in Spirit: Haudenosaunee (Iroquois) Influence on Early American Feminists*. Native Voices, 2001.

Romero, Lora. *Home Fronts: Domesticity and Its Critics in the Antebellum United States*. Duke UP, 1997.

Ruiz, Julie. "Captive Identities: The Gendered Conquest of Mexico in *Who Would Have Thought it?*" In *María Amparo Ruiz De Burton: Critical and Pedagogical Perspectives*. Edited by Amelia M. L. Montes and Anne E. Goldman U of Nebraska P, 2004.

Ruiz de Burton, María Amparo. *Who Would Have Thought It?* Edited by Amelia María de la Luz Montes, Penguin, 2009.

_____. *The Squatter and the Don*. Edited by Rosaura Sánchez and Beatrice Pita Arte Público, 1997.

_____. *Conflicts of Interest: The Letters of María Amparo Ruiz de Burton*. Edited by Rosaura Sánchez and Beatrice Pitta. Arte Público, 2001.

Sánchez, Rosaura, and Beatrice Pita. "Introduction." *Conflicts of Interest: The Letters of María Amparo Ruiz de Burton*. Edited by Sánchez and Beatrice Pita. Arte Público, 2001.

_____. "Introduction." *Who Would Have Thought It?* Arte Público, 1995.

Shaplen, Robert. "The Beecher-Tilton Affair." *New Yorker Magazine.* 12 Jun 1954, www.newyorker.com/magazine/1954/06/12/the-beecher-tilton-case-ii.

Soares, Kristie. "From Canary Birds to Suffrage: Lavinia's Feminist Role in *Who Would Have Thought It?*" *Letras Femeninas*, vol. 35, no. 3, 2009, pp. 211-229.

Stanton, Elizabeth C., et al. *The History of Women's Suffrage, Complete 6 Volumes (Illustrated): Everything You Need to Know about the Biggest Victory of Women's Rights and Equality in the United States—Written by the Greatest Social Activists, Abolitionists & Suffragists.* E-artnow. 2017.

Terborg-Penn, Rosalyn. *African-American Women in the Struggle for the Vote, 1850-1920.* Indiana UP, 1998.

Tetrault, Lisa. *The Myth of Seneca Falls: Memory and the Women's Suffrage Movement, 1848-1898.* North Carolina UP, 2014.

Truth, Sojourner. "Ain't I a Woman." *The Sojourner Truth Project.* https://www.thesojournertruthproject.com/. 30 April 2020.

Translating the Tapada's Veil in *Who Would Have Thought It?*

EVELYN SOTO

Sam Houston State University

Published in 1872, the novel *Who Would Have Thought It?* by María Amparo Ruiz de Burton formulates a capacious satire of US expansionism, Anglo-American hypocrisy, Civil War politics, and the degraded racial status of Mexican Americans in the aftermath of 1848. Linking together these strands of satire, the novel introduces Lola Medina—its orphaned Mexican protagonist—under the patriarchal guardianship of the New England geologist Dr. Norval. After a geological expedition in Gold Rush-era California, Dr. Norval returns to New England with Lola, who he extricates from Indian captivity following her mother's dying wish. Lola meets the rest of the supposedly upright and abolitionist Norval family as an early figure for Latina inscrutability: she is cloaked in a red shawl. At first, Lola's red shawl appears to be a salacious garment that alludes to a sexual scandal, gendered transgression, and mistaken identity. The shawl, however, drops off Lola when she is startled by the family dog to reveal "that what Mrs. Norval's eyes had magnified into a very tall woman was a little girl very black indeed" (8). Unveiled in a New England home, Lola's black skin shocks the Norval family and a neighborhood of judgmental onlookers.

The fall of Lola's shawl also discloses the problem of her uncertain racial status, which proliferates neighborhood gossip about her origin, status, and the fixity of her racial identity. According to Dr. Norval, Lola and her mother's skin had been dyed black by Native Americans to render them unrecognizable while in captivity. Secondly, Dr. Norval and a notary record her mother's last words attesting to Lola's "pure" Spanish descent, the address of her father, and her wishes for Lola's proper upbringing in the Catholic faith. This document functions as both a final will and personal history, but it is lost for years until it resurfaces toward the end. Finally, Lola's arrival in the Norval family home is accompanied by the unloading of heavy boxes filled with gold, precious gemstones, and other objects of old Spanish colonial wealth that Dr. Norval subsequently converts into modern assets through real estate and stock investments. Lola's lost genealogy, limitless wealth, and skin color pose competing proofs of her racial status that, in turn, vex Anglo-American social phobias and desires throughout the narrative.

In this essay, I argue that Lola's shawl is not merely a superficial accessory of sensational literature, but that it can be read productively through an underexamined Spanish-American creole cultural history of the tapadas' unique styles of face-covering or veiling (Fig. 1). This centuries-old fashion emerged from precolonial Moorish-Christian contact in peninsular Spain and it eventually traveled to the Americas, becoming most closely associated with the veiled women of Lima's plazas during the nineteenth century.[1] In early modern Spain and the nineteenth-century Americas alike, tapadas exercised their unaccompanied mobility and public presence by covering their faces with, most popularly, a jet-black mantle, although the material, color, and pattern of the textile varied according to period and place, as well as personal preference. However, as historians Laura R. Bass and Amanda Wunder concur, it was "the way that a woman handled her mantle that transformed her into a *tapada*," suggesting an intentional and performative aspect to this cultural practice (108). The most famous and reputationally seductive styling of the mantle was known as the *tapado de medio ojo*, where a woman would wrap the mantle around her head to reveal only one eye, and held in place by hand.

Without becoming a tapada, women could not leave the private sphere of the home without male accompaniment. Public life was available to a woman only by transforming her body into a different private enclosure through the fabric covering. Paradoxically, the anonymous reclusion of the face-covering afforded the tapada a revolutionary, public presence.

I begin by tracing challenges the tapada posed to patriarchal orderings of society throughout the cultural practice's transmission from early modern Spain to the nineteenth-century Americas, particularly Chile and Peru. I close read a 1586 appeal submitted by the Cortes de Castilla to King Philip II to outlaw the practice of tapadas alongside journal entries that record the public presence and practice of tapadas in an 1824 travel narrative by a British naval officer, Basil Hall. Across these two texts, I theorize distinct moral, social, and gendered forms of subversive agency that the tapadas' anonymous yet public presence made possible.

In what follows, I consider Lola's red shawl and the instability of her race as nineteenth-century hemispheric translations of the figural tapada's veil. Specifically, I examine the tapada as a vestigial figure in the novel that shapes hemispheric histories of race, nineteenth-century discourses of domesticity, and possible modes of early Latina subversion and critique in the United States. Current literary criticism of the novel focuses on Lola's gradual and ultimately triumphant restoration to white subjectivity as the indigenous "black" dye wears off to reveal white skin by the end of the novel. I focus instead on Lola's shawl in affinity with the tapada's veil, examining it as a wearable cultural textile and performative text. Defiant possibilities of the tapada's veil in Ruiz de Burton's novel, I ultimately argue, transmit ideas of racial taint and feminine sedition that significantly trouble interpretations of the novel's easy resolution into the conventional domestic and racial concepts associated with elite Anglo-American society.

Anonymity and Liberty through the Veil

The tapadas' veiled style exploits the unruly freedoms of anonymity. As historians of the garment Laura R. Bass and Amanda

Wunder observe that the veil in public space granted women to circumvent domestic confinement by willfully "enclosing" themselves within the veil. Put another way, tapadas embodied a mode of mobile domestic space. However, this confinement of domestic virtue within the veil also unleashed the social unruliness of anonymity. This section reads two texts that model distinct approaches to representing the anonymous tapadas and the forms of social upheaval they represent in their anonymous yet public presence. I include close readings of an official appeal submitted in 1586 to outlaw tapadas to interpret its social imaginary of gendered forms of power. I juxtapose close readings of the petition with selections from *Extracts from a Journal: Written on the Coasts of Chili, Peru, and Mexico in the Years 1820, 1821, 1822* (1824) by Basil Hall, a British naval officer. Instead of the legal constraints sought by the petition, Hall's travel narrative relies on sensationalist tropes of foreign exoticism to represent the tapadas for Anglophone audiences. Across my close readings of these early documents, I argue that the tapada's anonymity and performative presence in public space—such as the plazas of Spanish America—complicate the boundary between domestic and public life. Her skillful manipulation of the veil allows her to create unconventional forms of liberty that challenge racial and patriarchal orderings in the hemispheric Americas.

As one early modern petition from the Spanish Courts of Castile to the king in 1586 lamented, the veil allowed women to wield "la libertad y tiempo y lugar a su voluntad" (*Actas* 441). Although the precolonial conflicts of the Christian and Moorish past were in some sense woven into the threads of the tapada's veil, the presence of tapadas in public spaces like the city plazas of Seville and Lima posed a distinctly modern problem. In early modern Spain and colonial Spanish America alike, the tapada became associated with explosive urbanism fueled by the affluence and expansion of the colonies. Across colonial art, literature, and the law, the tapadas flaunted social legibility to proliferate mischievous tropes as "seductress, instrument of mayhem, figure of deception, [and] object of fetishistic worship" (Bass and Wunder 102). The scandal and seduction tapadas spurred in the public imagination resulted from unique performances of free will through the veil. Unseen and unrecognized beneath the veil, she could spy on others. Although the veil symbolically protected domestic virtue by concealing a woman's body, it could easily unravel feminine virtue by facilitating anonymous flirtation with others without risking consequence to her identity. A potentially elusive figure, a tapada could appear and vanish through the simple motion of drawing up or dropping the veil to thwart capture for any mischievous acts. The various forms of seduction, agency, and free will that women exercised under the veil often suggested to authorities a pervasive threat of moral and religious transgressions.

Veiled women were also imagined to pose concrete threats to social and political order. Returning to the 1586 petition submitted to the Spanish courts at greater length, the petitioning Cortes de Castilla complain that women's ability to travel in public under the veil had provoked "grandes ofensas De Dios y notable daño a la república, á causa de que en aquella forma, no conoce el padre á la hija, ni el marido á la mujer, ni el hermano á la hermana, y tienen la libertad y tiempo y lugar á su voluntad, y dan ocasión á que los hombres se atrevan á la hija ó mujer del más principal, como á las del más vil y bajo" (440-441). At first glance, the upheavals the petitioners identify concern not the veiled women's intention to deceive through her performance, but rather the mis-recognitions and passionate projections produced by the male gaze in public. When tapadas take the mantled form of anonymous publicity, she risks the potential breakdown and violation of appropriate kinship ties: the father cannot recognize his daughter, nor the husband his wife, nor the brother his sister. This confusion of family ties incited by the misperceptions of the male gaze not only implies marital scandal or even the danger of incest, but such disorder in domestic relationships extend to the undoing of class distinctions as well.

Male desires for tapadas become a gamble of hierarchical association whenever they fail to distinguish or willfully disregard differences in social strata. A man may approach the wife or daughter associated with those occupying the highest ranks of society as well as the wives or daughters linked to the lowest and most vile. The quoted passage struggles to relocate the problem of tapadas within the scope of patriarchal relations instead of the tapada's capacity to manipulate the social disorder she creates. For example, a man's inability to discern the correct rank of women under the veil is framed homosocially. The man who approaches the tapada enacts an unmerited or disgraceful association with another man who commands patriarchal authority, albeit of highest ranks or most "vile" orders. The petition constructs the tapada's disappearance from this scenario, where the social fabric of the "república" unravels through homosocial associations between misaligned classes. Strikingly, both examples of social disorder are linked by the petitioners' brief recognition of the tapada, who manipulates liberty, time, and place at will. The complaints issued in the petition therefore attempt to reign in the tapada's dangerous agency; the petitioner overwrites her agency and feminine modes of subversion by focusing instead on improper forms of masculine desire and affiliation. The tapada, then, obscures not only her individuality, but also undermines the ordering logics of familial relationships and social rank.

More than two centuries after the court's petition to the Spanish king, the British naval officer Basil Hall records multiple encounters with tapadas in Valparaiso, Chile and Lima, Peru in his *Journal Written on the Coasts of Chili* (1824). Unlike the court petition's suppression of women's exercise of free will through the veil, Hall's journals provide a glimpse into potential forms of unruly female agency enabled by the culturally specific textiles for anonymous publicity in the nineteenth-century Americas: the "saya" (petticoat) and "manto" (cloak) of the tapadas.[2] From Hall's foreign, British imperial gaze, the forms of anonymous disguise that the tapadas exercise "afforded much amusement, and, sometimes, not a little vexation" as they both captivate his attention and frustrate his discernment as a foreign, male subject (84). Hall attests, however, that the women's expertise in the disguise also eludes the discernment of the local men of Lima. He recollects:

I myself knew two young ladies, who completely deceived their brother and me, although we were aware of their fondness for such pranks and had even some suspicions of them at the very time. Their superior dexterity, however, was more than a match for his discernment, or my suspicions, and so completely did they deceive our eyes and mislead our thoughts, that we could scarcely believe our senses, when they, at length, chose to discover themselves. (84)

According to Hall, the success of the tapadas' disguise relies on more than the "covering" afforded by the manto. He notices performative expertise that he calls "their superior dexterity." This "dexterity" refers to the tapadas' skillful manipulation—not of the fabric itself, but of the men's perceptions, thoughts, and combined senses of both Hall and a local man from Lima, who Hall identifies to be the tapadas' brother. Implicitly, the experienced tapadas are capable of puppeteering the men's actions since they already exert influence, if not command, over their unwitting senses. Part of the captivating effect of the tapadas' performance also involves the moment they opt to disclose their identities. Hall acknowledges that the moment of their "reveal" is also a strategic maneuver of their performative control. He distrusts his senses only when the tapadas make the active choice "to discover themselves." In other words, the tapadas' will— their choice to reveal themselves—supplant the men's control over the scene and their capacities for discernment.

In Basil Hall's travel narrative, the naval officer describes his attempt to try on the veil in an entry dated December 30th, 1820, while visiting Valparaiso, Chile. This journal entry marks his first encounter with tapadas in the Americas. Hall departs to the bullring with a party of Chilean acquaintances and, afterward, the group of men attend the patriotic festivities of the Ramadas. One of the gentlemen "in" on the secret informs Hall that three of the ladies left in the mutual acquaintance's home were among the company, albeit disguised. The women aim to spy on "the master of the house, the husband of one of these Tapadas"; they reveal themselves and quickly disappear "after they detect him in treacherous flirtation" with another group of ladies they deem their "enemy" (24). A day later, Hall learns that the three ladies had returned that same evening, "differently disguised, and had amused themselves in watching the motions of such of us had been formerly admitted to their confidence, and who were still chuckling over the success of the first exploit" (24). Hall's first impression of the tapadas' disguise is one of sensational novelty: he perceives them "so completely metamorphosed, that, even when pointed out, they were with difficulty recognised." Furthermore, he experiences the secondhand knowledge of their plot as being made party "to the joke" and an indirect participant in "this escapo, or frolic" (24). Hall concludes the scene with an abbreviated mention of his failed mimicry of the tapadas: "I attempted, next evening to pass a similar jest upon [the three ladies,] but their practised eyes were not to be deceived, and they saw through it all at the first glance" (24). He omits all descriptive detail of the veiled disguise he presumably wears and any relevant context necessary for the reader to judge his attempt at a "similar jest." Indeed, this lack of contextual detail for Hall's cross-dress performance as a tapada renders the attempt itself comedic and transparent in its failure, just as the women "saw through it all at the first glance."

Ultimately, Hall admires the exotic feat of the tapadas' "metamorphosis" and is subject to what he calls their "superior dexterity," but he cannot correctly reenact the expert repertoire of their anonymous performances and reconnaissance under the veil. The tapada's transformations under the veil remain a specifically feminine and potentially queer mode of subversive agency that remain inaccessible to the foreign officer who acknowledges the power of their metamorphosis.

Textile Traces and Racial Taint

At a glance, the link between the tapada's mantle and Lola's red shawl; or by extension between Lima or Chile and California; or between colonial Spanish America and the legacy of 1848 in Ruiz de Burton's novel might seem geographically and contextually disjointed. My approach here does not pursue a robust equivalence between the two textiles. Instead, I aim to translate ideological affinities about colonial formations of race and gender that are interwoven across the cultural history of these two figural face-coverings. In this section, I turn to colonial discourses of racial taint that affix to tapadas in the Americas, and in turn, to Lola when the shawl falls to reveal her racial alterity—the artificial black dye of her skin—to both the reader and to the Norval family. I argue that Lola's marginalized racial status becomes a screen onto which Anglo-American characters project their desire for imperial expansion at odds with their control over the boundary between domestic ideals and foreign contaminants. Although Lola does not wear the shawl for long, the narrative veils her in other ways—through the black "dye" that reveals Anglo-American sociopolitical hypocrisies and finally through the novel's formal literary strategies of satire that mimic the anonymous publicity and mischief of the tapada. These hemispheric translations of the tapada's veil and cultural history inform an emergent Latina critique of the nineteenth-century United States.

Through its dispersal to the Americas especially, the typically dark mantle or veil of the tapadas heightened anxieties about unstable racial hierarchies in colonial society. According to Bass and Wunder, the jet-black mantle could be "worn by almost all women regardless of their station" (118). In Spanish-American society, colonial impositions created a form of demographic chaos that the racial ideology of the *sistema de castas* sought to contain, reorder, and rescript through logics of whitening, wherein the taint of "native" or "black" blood might one day be restored to whiteness (Fig. 2). The casta paintings of eighteenth-century Mexico are the most familiar and visually compelling representations of this ideology. In verse satires and theatrical productions, the tapadas featured in deception plots were racially tainted subjects who could pass as white. Bass and Wunder aver, furthermore, that the Baroque genre "of desengaño found fertile ground in Lima, where people of non-European descent outnumbered the Spanish population, and where literary satires of miscegenation were widespread" (136). The preponderance of the figural tapada in colonial-era theater and literature reminds us that, while she could spy on others in disguise, her veil became a screen onto which the public imagination projected its desires and fears. In the Americas, those desires and fears reckoned with the indeterminacy of racial and social status forged in the furnace of colonization. For example, legislation in Lima not only banned the mantle's full concealment of the face, but it also outlined more severe punishments for *negras* (black women), *mulatas* (women of black and Spanish ancestry), and *mestizas* (of mixed indigenous and Spanish ancestry) who could spend up to thirty days in prison while upper-class offenders of "pure" Spanish ancestry faced ten days (137).

In the first chapter of Ruiz de Burton's novel, titled "The Arrival," Mrs. Jemima Norval's scandalized reaction precedes Lola's formal introduction to the reader. When Dr. Norval arrives in a wagon loaded with large boxes, his wife, Jemima Norval, exclaims, "What upon earth is he bringing now?" (6). The Norval daughters initially perceive a heap of boxes in the carriage and assume that their father has returned with the geological samples of his profession, or, in an ironic answer to Jemima's question, he brings parcels of the earth itself. One of the Norval daughters replies in answer to the question, "More rocks and pebbles, of course," which another daughter anticipates will be added to his barn-loft collection of prehistoric, commercially useless "bones and petrified woods" (6). The family eventually learns that the boxes carry not just any "rocks and pebbles," but Lola's inheritance of rare earth minerals in the antiquated form of Spanish colonial treasure: gems, gold, and silver.

Through the redirection and clarification of Mrs. Norval's question, the shawl is linked to Lola. Mrs. Norval clarifies her initial question in a stammer, "I don't mean the boxes in the large wagon. I mean the—the—*that*—the red shawl" (6). Only then does the outline of Lola's character appear to other onlookers at the New England home: "And now the three other ladies noticed for the first time a figure wrapped in a bright plaid shawl, leaning on the doctor's breast, and around which he tenderly encircled his arm" (6). Between bewildered reactions among members of the Norval household, Mrs. Norval initially fixates on the shrouded figure's gender as her husband approaches the gates of the home. Ruiz de

Burton narrates this process of observation as follows: "The doctor again tenderly throwing his arm around the female in the shawl,— *for it was a female*: this fact Mrs. Norval had discovered plainly enough" (7, emphasis mine). In the first few paragraphs of the second chapter, the shawl drops off Lola to reveal her minor age and black skin. This racial disclosure reformulates Mrs. Norval's initial social distress from the hint of an extramarital affair, or at best a gendered rivalry, to a foreign disruption of her Puritanical reign over her household.

Although the shawl doesn't stay put on Lola for long, beyond it lies another screen: the stubborn indigenous "dye" that blackens her skin. Lola's racial illegibility obsesses the Anglo-American characters in the early chapters of the novel and the perceived status of her dyed skin becomes a recurrent question throughout. Lola's initial racial blackness might be attributed to binary frameworks for racial difference in Anglo America, unlike the Spanish colonial casta system that distinguished between various gradations of a bloodline's "stain" of descendance from peoples of the African diaspora or the possibility of purifying, and therefore assimilating, bloodlines from mixed indigenous and European Spanish ancestry. As we will see, her unstable racial belonging throughout the narrative is socially constructed through networks of gossip and second-hand testimony by Dr. Norval. However, since the New England gossip about Lola is an unreliable source of knowledge, the narrative disproves the possibility that Lola's father is the chief of the Gila River Indians. The novel omits a neat timeline of Lola's birth and her mother's captivity. Later on, Lola reveals that she knows her father's name— Don Luis Medina—only because she remembers "perfectly well that my mother *told me* that such was his name" (229, emphasis mine). The chief refers to Lola's mother as his wife, calling her "ña Hala" (translated in the novel as "my lady"), and calls her by the name "Euitelhap" (26). Lola's mother, who calls herself Doña Theresa Medina, informs Dr. Norval that she has been living in Indian captivity for the past ten years and promises him a glittering treasure of gems and gold in exchange for Lola's rescue "from those horrid savages," to bring her up as a Roman Catholic, and to locate her white, Spanish father (30). Lola's possible indigenous affiliation is never objectively annulled since the narrative disallows any putatively objective or verifying measure of race beyond the social domain of testimony and community consensus.

The telos of the novel's romantic plot hinges on Lola's racial whitening, which depends on social acknowledgments of her white racial status. Lola's initial perception as a "little girl very black indeed" and the taint of her "black dye" figures the Norval family's unreliable interpretation of racial difference and belonging—perhaps even their initial inability to discern her possible indigenous heritage. The New England protagonists of Ruiz de Burton's novel initially conceive of all racial differences in reference to blackness, although with time they ignorantly grasp for other terms and categories to reference Lola's racial belonging. The Anglo-American characters refer to Lola as a combination of antiblack racial slurs, an Aztec, "a true emanation of the black art," an Indian, and a member of the "Pinto" tribe when the black dye begins to wear off in spots during her adolescence, among other designations for racial difference. The last example is a particularly absurd misattribution of her possible indigenous affiliation, which collapses the Pinto Indian tribe with the dappled variation of a horse's coat that became popular among Native Americans.

From the screen of the shawl to the "stain" of nonwhite racial difference on Lola's skin, the observational politics figured by the tapada's veil appears to be turned inside out in the novel. Despite being the putative main character of the story, Lola scarcely speaks. She vanishes from domestic narrative space in the middle of the novel when Mrs. Norval keeps her away at a convent to discourage a potential yet inevitable romance plot between Lola and her son Julian. Furthermore, even when present in the narrative she is silent by comparison, others speak about her; Mrs. Norval micro-manages her location; Reverend Hackwell tricks her into a false marriage; and she is otherwise acted and strategized upon, even in her final rescue.

However, the contrast between Lola's passivity and the proactive mischief of the figural tapada conditions the very method of Ruiz de Burton's satirical analysis of Anglo-American society. The more Anglo-American characters gossip and therefore project their interpretations onto the screen of Lola's skin, the more their ideological convictions, self-interests, and corruptions become audible and overt confessions available for critical exposure through the narrator's satire. Put another way, the narrator manipulates the screen of Lola's uncertain racial status not only as a demonstration of the failed promise of the Treaty of Guadalupe-Hidalgo to enfranchise Mexican Americans, but to critique the hypocrisies of Anglo-American personalities and values.

But the critical bite of the novel's satire is diminished, many scholars note, by Ruiz de Burton's own investment in translating white racial politics for elite Mexicans, creating an uneasy alliance between the dispossession of the Californios with the Confederacy's losses in the Civil War. Current scholarly consensus interprets Lola's gradual whitening of the skin as Ruiz de Burton's bid for mutual recognition between elite Californios and enfranchised Anglo-Americans. For instance, Margaret Jacobs writes, "Clearly Ruiz de Burton, like many other Californios and Californianas, believed it more advantageous to throw in her lot with her conquerors and hope to be classified as White than to demote herself into the undifferentiated mass of 'non-White' Mexicans and Indians" (228). Literary scholar Jesse Alemán likewise situates the novel through a prevalent concern in Chicano scholarship, which grapples with "the problem of Mexican American whiteness." This strand of whiteness constructs itself in "response to Anglo American imperialism but [is] ultimately performed in contrast to nonwhite racial others." Over the course of the narrative, Lola progresses gradually through various stages of whitening evocative of the racial imaginaries prevalent in the Spanish colonial casta system. As Alemán summarizes, she passes through "black, Indian, brown, 'spotted' white, and finally 'pure' white" (100).

Toward the end of the novel, when she re-enters Mrs. Norval's domestic dominion, which is now located in a New York mansion purchased off the profit from Lola's invested inheritance. Initially, all the women in the mansion "eyed Lola, but said nothing to her" (233). Gradually, as the sisters observe themselves in the mirror for final adjustments before entering the grand reception, they begin to bring

Lola into the fold. Mattie Norval remarks, "Talk of Spanish women being dark! Can anything be whiter than Lola's neck and shoulders?" Ruth Norval interjects, correcting Mattie on the fact that "Lola is not Spanish; she is Mexican" (233). Finally, Emma Hackwell, who is Lola's rival for Julian's affection, pointedly notes, "I think Lola might teach us the secret of that Indian paint that kept her white skin under cover, making it whiter by bleaching it. I would bargain to wear spots for awhile" (233). In this scene, Lola's ascent to whiteness is constructed through observations and interpretations that posit her whitened racial status as an artificial spectacle instead of the nineteenth-century biological rationales that essentialized race as an objective or irrefutable category. Emma's comment is specifically cosmetic (the artificial result of make-up or skin treatment, "that Indian paint"). Lola's "purified" skin tone, therefore, remains an illegitimate and, ultimately, an unassimilable kind of white to Anglo-American society. Scholars such as Laura Gómez and María DeGuzmán theorize this process as "off-whiteness," a legal and social construction of early Latinx racial difference. Rather than neatly progressing toward a fully assimilated, Anglo-American whiteness, Lola's estranged whiteness lingers in the Norval family bloodline when she is forced to relocate to Mexico and marries Julian Norval.

Current scholarly conversations draw contradictory conclusions from Lola and Julian's marriage in Mexico as the plot's final location. On the one hand, Lola's expulsion from the United States can be read as a form of surrender to its expansionist designs (Szeghi 113). Literary scholar Tereza Szeghi elaborates this apparent defeat by her final expulsion outside the US border: "It seems there is no place for Lola in the United States where she will be accepted and treated as her [alleged Spanish] ancestry, in Ruiz de Burton's view, merits" (113). Other scholars, however, discern Lola's triumphant fulfillment of domestic ideals and gendered virtues that elevate her character over Anglo-American subjects who represent the degradations of expansionist avarice. As Beth Fischer points out in her article "Precarious Performances" (2004), Mrs. Norval exemplifies the corruption of traditional domestic values when she forsakes her puritanical domestic life in New England for public acts of ostentatious consumerism that she exercises through lavish expenditures of Lola's annexed wealth in New York City. Strikingly, Mrs. Norval attends public venues such as the theater to display her newfound wealth, which becomes one of the surest signs of her deviation from traditional domestic duties and a factor in her eventual moral downfall. In contrast to Mrs. Norval's moral ruin, scholar A. Laurie Lowrance argues that Lola and Julian's romantic reunion in Mexico significantly defies the fate usually ascribed to racialized women by the genre of the sentimental novel wherein "the racialized woman *does not* end up exiled or dead but instead becomes the truly 'white' character in the work who finally ends up within a superior domestic sphere in Mexico" (399, emphasis mine). The possibility of Lola's triumph over Mrs. Norval's moral downfall and the racial tropes of sentimental literature nonetheless confine Lola to a conventional appraisal of the domestic sphere that affords her no public agency. Given that Ruiz de Burton herself "was certainly—for her time and place—a woman with 'unladylike ambitions'" who partook in "spheres from which nineteenth-century women were, for the most part, excluded," can Lola's agency be truly redeemed within a superior domestic sphere in Mexico? (Sánchez and Pita, *Conflicts* xi)

Reading Lola's racial alterity and the novel's satirical critique in the context of the tapada's cultural history instead unravels the conventional separation between the public sphere and private domain. Consider that Lola's passivity in the novel—as a foreign yet domestic subject to be racially scrutinized by Anglo-Americans—coexists and conditions the novel's satirical mode of narration. In other words, Lola's characterization in the novel formally functions as a screen or veil for the narrative's incisive critique of expansionism, ideological hypocrisies, and Civil War-era corruption at both the individual and national scales. Recall, too, that the tapadas exercise forms of performative, public agency through the anonymity of the veil, which doubles as a form of mobile enclosure that radically dislocates the subjects and affairs of private domesticity into public realms like the plaza or street market. The anonymous publication and narration of *Who Would Have Thought It?* provides a final translation of the tapada's agency through the veil. The narrator's satirical commentary on members and associates of the Norval family who are scandalously embroiled in a mix of private and political corruptions resembles the discerning movement of the tapada, who traverses private and public domains. The novel's narrator, unlike Lola, obtains the critical distance necessary for satirical critique that is furnished by anonymous authorship and various literary modes at the narrative's disposal: allegory, picaresque, romance, and sentimentalism, among others.

The narration also breaks into an individuated, first-person voice to address itself and potentially the reader as a foreign "insider" with gossip to share on various social and political developments. For example, in a passage that contemplates past amorous connections between Lavinia (aunt to Julian Norval) and the morally degenerate New England priests, Hammerhard and Hackwell, who leave her jilted and childless, the narration answers its rhetorical question in untranslated Spanish: "Was [Lavinia] drawing mental comparisons between that grate and her virginal bosom? *¿Quién sabe?*" (31). At other points, the narration unpredictably breaks into asides to share a potentially relevant anecdote or subjective experience, as evinced toward the beginning of Chapter 31, "I have read somewhere the fable of a priest . . ." (131). It is as though the authorial voice of Ruiz de Burton reveals itself briefly—for mischievous and ironic commentary—through the veil of omniscient narration.

In *Who Would Have Thought It?* we ultimately observe Lola's red shawl undergo transformations: from textile (as melodramatic prop) to racialized difference (the dye of Lola's skin) to the satirical method of narration. The incisive social and political commentary of the novel's satirical mode mimics the tapada's free will through anonymity and her unruly intervention in public space. Reading Lola's red shawl as an adaptation of the cultural history and performances of the tapada's veil allows us to discern an early mode of Latina critique that vexes distinctions between domestic scandal and political corruption in Anglo America. Ultimately, the novel's ending in Mexico locates Lola beyond the boundaries of the United States to reaffirm the critical distance necessary for a satirical analysis of hemispheric perspective on Anglo-American culture and politics.

Fig. 1. Francisco Fierro. *Tapada de pie*. Watercolors, 16x23 cm, 1800, Pinacoteca Municipal Ignacio Merino, Lima, Peru.

Fig. 2: Anonymous. *Las castas*. Oil on canvas, 148×104 cm, eighteenth century Museo Nacional del Virreinato, Tepotzotlán, Mexico.

Works Cited

Actas de las Cortes de Castilla. Vol. 9. Madrid, 1885.

Alemán, Jesse. "Thank God, Lolita is Away from Those Horrid Savages: The Politics of Whiteness in *Who Would Have Thought It?*" in *María Amparo Ruiz De Burton: Critical and Pedagogical Perspectives.* U of Nebraska P, 2004, pp. 95-111.

Bass, Amanda and Amanda Wunder. "The Veiled Ladies of the Early Modern Spanish World: Seduction and Scandal in Seville, Madrid, and Lima." *Hispanic Review*, vol. 77, no. 1, 2009, pp. 97-144.

DeGuzmán, María. *Spain's Long Shadow: The Black Legend, Off-Whiteness, and Anglo-American Empire.* U of Minnesota P, 2005.

Fischer, Beth. "Precarious Performances: Ruiz de Burton's Theatrical Vision of the Gilded Age Female Consumer" in *María Amparo Ruiz De Burton: Critical and Pedagogical Perspectives.* U of Nebraska P, 2004, pp. 187-205.

Gómez, Laura. *Manifest Destinies: The Making of the Mexican American Race.* New York UP, 2007.

Hall, Basil. *Extracts from a Journal, Written on the Coasts of Chili, Peru, and Mexico: in the Years 1820, 1821, 1822.* Third edition. Edinburgh: Archibald Constable and Co., and Hurst, Robinson and Co., London, 1824.

León, Marco Antonio. "Entre lo público y privado: acercamientos a las *tapadas y cubiertas* en España, Hispanoamérica y Chile." *Boletín de la Academia Chilena de la Historia*, 1993, pp. 273-311.

Lowrance, A. Laurie. "Resistance to Containment in Sarah Winnemucca's *Life Among the Piutes* and María Amparo Ruiz de Burton's *Who Would Have Thought It?*" *Western American Literature*, vol 52, no. 4, 2018, pp. 379-401.

Jacobs, Margaret D. "Mixed-Bloods, Mestizas, and Pintos: Race, Gender, and Claims to Whiteness in Helen Hunt Jackson's *Ramona* and María Amparo Ruiz de Burton's *Who Would Have Thought It?*" *Western American Literature*, vol. 36, no. 3, 2001, pp. 212-232.

Katzew, Ilona. *Casta Painting: Images of Race in Eighteenth-Century Mexico.* Yale UP, 2004.

Ramirez, Pablo A. "Conquest's Child: Gold, Contracts, and American Imperialism in María Amparo Ruiz de Burton's *Who Would Have Thought It?*" *Arizona Quarterly: A Journal of American Literature, Culture, and Theory*, vol. 70 no. 4, 2014, pp. 143-165.

Ruiz de Burton, María Amparo. *Who Would Have Thought It?* Penguin Classics: New York, 2009. 1872.

Sánchez, Rosaura and Beatrice Pita. "Introduction" in *Who Would Have Thought It?* Arte Público, 1995, pp. vii-lvi.

_____. "Introduction" in *Conflicts of Interest: The Letters of María Amparo Ruiz de Burton.* Arte Público, 2001, pp. ix-xxii.

Szeghi, Tereza M. "The Vanishing Mexicana/o: (Dis)Locating the Native in Ruiz de Burton's *Who Would Have Thought It?* and *The Squatter and the Don.*" *Aztlán: A Journal of Chicano Studies*, vol. 36, no. 2, 2011, pp. 89-120.

Aurora Mena and *The Pearl Key:* Unlocking the Meaning of a Mambisa's Story

PAUL S. LOSCH
University of Florida

Aurora Mena, a Cuban teacher who lived in Florida in the 1890s, wrote *The Pearl Key, or Midnight and Dawn in Cuba* (1896), her only known published work. Only one copy of that book is reported to exist today, and it is in the Latin American and Caribbean Collection of the University of Florida (UF). The UF Libraries have digitized the book and made it available online.[1] This seems very appropriate since, in 1894, Mena was the first Spanish instructor hired by the Florida Agricultural College in Lake City, one of UF's predecessor institutions.[2]

Figure 1. Book cover image of *The Pearl Key* from UF Digital Collections https://ufdc.ufl.edu/AA000618410 001/1j

Mena was teaching Spanish to English-speakers and wanted to enlighten them about the Cuban struggle for independence. Her stated aim in writing the book was to provide US readers a firsthand account of the difficulties of life in Cuba under Spanish rule:

Inspired by the desire of giving to this country, whose whole people show so much sympathy for my suffering land, a more intimate knowledge of the truth concerning the misfortunes of the noble Cuban people, and the cruelty and injustice of a despotic and tyrannical government, I write this simple story of my life, as it touched these questions. I surely need not say that every incident and description in this narrative is strictly and literally the truth. (34)

The book is more than what Mena called a "simple story of my life." Her biography was used to win readers over to the Cuban cause, and it was published in English as part of a coordinated public relations campaign. This influenced how the manuscript was prepared, how it was published and how it was received. In this regard, it has many similarities with *The Story of Evangelina Cisneros,* which came out about a year later. Readers today should appreciate that Mena was writing during wartime and that her book was a contribution to the war effort.

The narrative follows the adventure genre that was popular at the time, perhaps to attract readers' attention. While parts of the story are fanciful, many passages offer insightful commentary on Cuban society, especially on the role of women. "A woman is not an authority for anything; even if she saw a murder committed and attempted to inform the authorities, she would not have the least attention paid to her complaints and no action would be taken" (109). Mena was a feminist, and clearly her interest in Cuban independence was closely related to her desire for greater opportunities for herself and for other Cuban women. She returned to Cuba after the war to pursue her goals as an educator and various political, philanthropic, and business ventures. By examining the scant record we have of Mena's life outside of what she tells in her "simple story," we can better appreciate her observations.[3]

The Book and Its Story

The publication of *The Pearl Key* in English was a collaborative effort of various people, all of whom shared the goal of enlisting support for the Cuban cause in the US. Mena was active in the Cuban exile community in Florida and was reported to have served as the secretary of the "Cuban Junta" in Jacksonville. This organization, led by tobacco merchant José Alejandro Huau, was engaged in collecting money for the war effort, arranging illegal arms shipments to Cuba, and pressuring the US government to lift the embargo on those shipments.[4] *The Pearl Key* seems to have been a part of the organization's fundraising and public relations efforts.[5] Huau's cigar shop and other local merchants subsidized the printing costs through advertising so that the proceeds from book sales could go towards the cause.

Mena's supporters were not only Cuban exiles. Eliza M. Souvielle, a prominent Jacksonville resident and a sympathizer with Cuban independence, served as Mena's editor, and in her preface, she states that *The Pearl Key* was meant to build support in the US for the Cubans, specifically for the lifting of the arms embargo:

> Cuba, the Pearl of the Antilles and key to the gulf, reveals the hidden meaning of the title of this book . . . whose woes should give strength to the most feeble pen and eloquence to the most timid tongue!
>
> May this book be the key to unlock many secrets, . . . may it open for the American people more fully the knowledge which another language makes it difficult to impart [. . .] may this 'PEARL KEY' also unlock the hearts in all this broad land [the US] which are yet untouched for this persecuted country [Cuba], and loose the bands of policy or statecraft which keep back from them the help which the small concession of recognition would give. (1-2)

An entry in a biographical dictionary from 1899 indicates that Souvielle may have seen *The Pearl Key* as her literary creation: "Her last work is a book upon Cuba, written originally in Spanish expressly for her purpose, and of which she is the editor and translator."[6] The book's title page identifies the translator as Pearl Mann, one of Mena's students in Lake City. Mena reportedly took sick leave from the college and stayed in the Mann family's Ocala home in late 1896, shortly before the book was published. The "Pearl" and "Dawn" ("Aurora" in Spanish) of the full title likely refer to the collaboration of the teacher and student in developing the story.

Mena and her team were working to produce a book that would help promote Cuban independence. Her collaborators obtained some advance publicity for the book, with notes in newspapers around the country, such as the following:

THE PEARL KEY, or Midnight and Dawn in Cuba, is the name of a book that is being written by Miss Aurora de Mena. The book will treat on the Cuban fight for liberty, and Miss de Mena will give stories in real life of the persecution of Cubans, bringing in the expressions of members of her own family. The proceeds from the sale of the book will go to the Cuban cause." *Riverside (Cal.) Enterprise* (November 19, 1896)

Miss Aurora de Mena, professor of Spanish in the state agricultural college at Lake City [. . .] is about to issue a book of great interest at the present time, owing to the attention that is being directed to Cuba. [. . .] It will contain a thrilling story of Miss de Mena's own experiences in Cuba up to the time of her escape from the island about a year ago. *Savannah Morning News* (December 12, 1896)[7]

Mena begins her book with episodes in her early childhood that inspired her patriotism. She describes her own coming of age and development of political consciousness, and she ends with a dramatic escape into exile, narrowly avoiding capture by Spanish soldiers led by her own brother, Theodore. This older brother personifies patriarchy and colonialism, and Mena clashes with him throughout the book. She describes, at length, the abuses and atrocities of Spanish authorities, and these descriptions are tinged with what Ivette García and Lisbeth Paravisini-Gebert have identified as a sense of Gothic horror present in many portrayals of life in colonial Cuba.

Towards the end of the book, she describes a fantastic journey into the rebel camps in the mountains. Among the characters Mena encounters in her travels are Matagás and his gang of patriotic outlaws, Yariguaz, the last of the Taínos, and General Enrique Varona, a figure who seems loosely based on the Cuban educator and writer of that same name.[8] A high point in the story is the banquet in the wilderness where Mena, the bandit, the Indian, and the philosopher-general come together in a kind of national pageant to sing popular songs and to share a meal of roast pork and plantains around the campfire. At this point, the narrator is thanking readers who would have abandoned her fanciful story if they were not also supporters of Cuban independence: "If you, my friends, have followed me so far, you are dear to me, for your sympathy must by this token, belong to the cause I love, and your heart mourn with me over the misfortunes of my country" (171).

The few recorded reactions of contemporary readers were mixed, and those who were pro-Spanish were highly dismissive. The *Florida Daily Citizen* (December 10, 1896) offered this somewhat dubious evaluation: "Those who have seen the manuscript say it reads more like a tale of days of the Inquisition than a story of real life in this Nineteenth Century." The *Tampa Tribune* commented, "It deals rather harshly with the Spaniards, and attacks the rule of that nation in the island with vitriolic pen. [. . .] Some of the statements in Miss De Mena's book [. . .] are, to say the least, remarkable. The Spaniards who saw it were very indignant" (October 19, 1899).

Indeed, one prominent member of the Spanish-American community in Tampa, Judge Joseph R. Torres, was outraged after reading the book. He arranged for Mena's expulsion from a social club, the Centro Español in Ybor City, and wrote to the *Tampa Tribune* to defend his actions (October 24, 1899):

> Mr. Editor, if you have not yet read Miss De Mena's book and desire to form an intelligent idea of whether or not the lady in question should be expelled from the Spanish Casino, I will gladly lend you a copy so that you can form your own conclusion. A person that writes such a book, a person that is capable of saying so many things against another should never of her own free will attempt to mingle with people that she so badly and basely defamed. What I did I would do again as a member of the organization.[9]

The Pearl Key and The Story of Evangelina Cisneros

Two Cuban writers of the nineteenth-century became known outside of Cuba for autobiographical writings published in English,

Juan Francisco Manzano and Evangelina Cosio y Cisneros. As Sylvia Molloy notes, Manzano's autobiography, published by British abolitionists in 1840, "was a text used by others, over which Manzano had little to no control. That the text was wielded to further a worthy cause, one dear to Manzano's own heart, does not lessen the importance of that manipulation." The nature of *The Pearl Key* as a Cuban woman's text shaped by English-speaking intermediaries becomes more apparent when we examine it together with another mambisa's first-person narrative of persecution and escape. *The Story of Evangelina Cisneros* became a bestseller in 1898, about a year after *The Pearl Key* was published. The book was a retelling, in Cisneros' words, of the story that had already been told in the pages of William Randolph Hearst's *New York Journal*.

Cisneros is appreciated today as an early example of a Cuban-American woman who shaped US public opinion through her dramatic account of daring and resistance. However, critics also recognize that her self-expression was very limited by the circumstances in which her book was published. For Teresa Prados Torreira, Cisneros was willingly used by others, for the sake of her cause, and became something of a pawn in what was billed as her own story. Belinda Linn Rincón finds that Cisneros' authorship is obfuscated, but still worthy of study: "Although Cisneros' text is highly mediated by Hearst's demands, language barriers, and perhaps her desire to meet US readers' expectations, it is important because it is one of the few published voices of a nineteenth-century Cuban woman in the United States" (88).

These and other evaluations of the Cisneros book seem useful for appreciating *The Pearl Key*. For Silvio Torres-Saillant, *The Story of Evangelina Cisneros*, as a text of the Cuban experience in the United States, "offers a wealth of interpretative possibilities that Latino studies scholars may wish to pursue" (442). Cisneros' book "remains insufficiently explored as a vibrant source of analytical provocation for scholars interested in mining its potential for dramatizing the problems of the location of US Cuban writing, the complex texture of US-Cuban relations and the unique character of Cuban-American identity *vis-`a-vis* the other subsections of the

Latino population" (436). Like Cisneros, Mena also wrote from this delicate position of wanting to present Cuban problems in a way that would interest an English-speaking public and having to rely on others to communicate that message in another language.

In terms of ambiguous location, Louis A. Perez [1994] describes the "circle of connections" between the US and Cuba during this time, when many leading Cubans were temporarily at home in one place or the other and had to adjust their writing to suit their local audience. Torres-Saillant recognizes that this duality affected many writers of the period: "Contributing to the unstable location of US Cuban texts is the inescapable frame of the peculiar history of American society's rapport with the island" (433). Mena never expresses anything but admiration for the US, and we are left to wonder if she would have dared to offend US sensibilities, given her need to win allies in her new home.[10]

Torres-Saillant's second observation is that Cisneros and other writers of this period had to deal with the thorny issue of how deeply the US should become entangled in Cuban affairs (434). For Karen Roggekamp and for Perez [2008], Cisneros presented an image of Cuba as a damsel in distress inviting an American hero to rescue her, a metaphor that was not welcomed by all Cubans. While Mena tends to describe Cubans as working hard for their own independence, at one point, she (or her editor) seems to support US military intervention. "May your sympathy be so awakened that your aid must soon be ours, and your swords leap from the scabbard to succor the downtrodden and oppressed who call upon you at your very doors. Shall they yet longer ask in vain?" (112-113).

Torres-Saillant's third observation about the Cisneros book is that it carefully presents Cubans as a special and acceptable class of foreigners in the US, different from other Latin American migrants. Sympathetic press coverage of Cisneros emphasized not only her patriotism and heroism, but also her whiteness and her social status. Mena seems to have created a similar kind of elite persona to gain acceptance in Boston society after the war, with stories about having renounced her aristocratic heritage to join the rebels.[11] In 1909, when Mena presented an album to retiring Harvard President Charles Eliot on behalf of the Cuban teachers' association, the local press recognized her for spreading the Harvard physical education program's "gospel of healthy bodies and clean living where such instruction is most needed."[12] In short, those aspects of Cisneros' work that make it valuable for study today are also present in Mena's, and having these two Cuban-American women's narratives that can be analyzed together will enrich the scholarship.

Mena's Feminist Ideals as Presented in The Pearl Key

The Pearl Key was produced through the collaboration of various individuals and so we may be left wondering the degree to which the opinions expressed are Mena's own. Fortunately, we can piece together a record of Mena's life, and we can appreciate that social commentary that we find inside seems to be very consistent with her words and actions in her actual life. Mena was a feminist for whom freeing Cuba from Spanish rule represented an opportunity to dismantle repressive economic and social structures of the island's colonial past. K. Lynn Stoner [2003] observes that *mambisas* were valued for propaganda purposes during the fight against Spain, but were expected to return to traditional gender-based roles after the war. Only a few organized feminists continued to press for changes in the new republic, and Mena was one of them as an active member of the National Suffragist Party. The specific reforms she identifies in her book were the aims of that larger movement, according to Raquel Vinat. These included a new school curriculum focused on human development, expanded economic opportunities for women, and the separation of Church and state.

Attention to Child Development

As Stoner [1991] notes, early-twentieth-century Cuban feminists focused heavily on children's issues. The early chapters of *The Pearl Key* give us a sense that Mena felt trapped indoors during her own childhood, and Mena compares her painful experience with that of US children:

It is a very important event for a young lady of that age to be allowed a few moments at the window, and constitutes a break in the monotony of a Cuban girl's life which makes a great impression. The houses in Cuba are not constructed as in America, with windows and doors of crystal, and where one lives as free as the bird in the forest, which builds its nest in the tree best suited to its fancy. There every house is constructed with the strength and security of a jail. (37-38)

Mena's later dedication to promoting physical education in Cuba seems to be based on this concern with fostering self-confidence in children, and especially in girls. Mena's professor at Harvard, Dudley Sargent, later recalled that, "[a]mong the many things that interested the Cubans in our people was the freedom of our women and the opportunities they enjoyed for growth and development, both mentally and physically" (854). Mena spent various summers at Harvard receiving training in new techniques, such as dances, ball games, and group gymnastics. In Cuba, she led public demonstrations of these activities and trained teachers in them, to great acclaim in the press.[13] Educational authorities expanded her responsibility for overseeing physical education from the provincial to the national level. In this role and as chair of a committee of the National Suffragist Party, she gained attention as a campaigner to create public playgrounds so that urban children could enjoy a "happy life and a complete and harmonious development."[14]

Economic Opportunity for Women

In the following passages from *The Pearl Key*, Mena expressed a concern that women lacked the legal standing and the education to achieve economic autonomy in Spanish Cuba:

A Cuban girl has no liberty whatever; if her father is dead, she is under the authority of her eldest brother, no matter if he be younger than herself. [. . .]. Think of this, you who have freedom of speech and action, who are listened to, respected and trusted. Is it not abominable and barbarous? Do you blame me that I am wild to give the same liberties to my poor, oppressed countrywomen? (109-110)

This may look strange to my American readers, but it is nevertheless true, that in Cuba no girl is allowed to earn her living. Such an attempt would be followed by social ostracism. Indeed, they are taught nothing by which they could help themselves and earn a livelihood, nor are there any places open to them. (230)

We see here that Mena addresses US readers, and the women among them, seeking to enlist their assistance.[15] After returning to Cuba from the United States, Mena became an example of financial independence. In addition to her position in the public schools, she also offered private lessons in calisthenics, and even patented her arthritis crème.[16] She was successful enough to engage in leisure travel to the US on her school vacations. After her official retirement in 1923, she was vocal in demanding that authorities honor retired teachers' pensions, and she supplemented her pension with a mining operation on a rural property she owned.[17] Still, Mena continued to work as an educator, directing the Instituto Popular Carlos Miguel Céspedes, a philanthropic trade school where young women could learn practical skills such as sewing, typing, and English (*Diario de la Marina*, 3 November 1929, 10). Thus, she took care of her own needs and helped other women become more economically independent through education.

Separation of Church and State

Various characters in *The Pearl Key* call attention to the close relationship between the Catholic Church and the Spanish regime in Cuba. One of the story's villains is a priest who abuses a young woman, and is then protected by civil authorities, who punish those who denounce the crime. In another example, a political prisoner refuses the chance to confess before his execution and complains, "I know that my humble fortune would never permit me to go to a country where a man is free to adopt the religion which most appeals to him, and where there is a government impartial and just" (87).

Mena's objections to the established Church were apparently connected to her own beliefs and her desire for women to play a greater role in religious affairs. Mena participated in the Congregational Church while living in the US, in part because of the relative freedom enjoyed by women in that denomination. This is indicated by a summary of an address she made at a church meeting in Massachusetts in 1900:

> The Christian religion in [Mena's] country, and particularly the Protestant form of it, was the great thing needed for the uplifting and development of Cuba. This was the first time she had ever addressed an audience like this, as women had no idea of freedom in her country. She looked forward to the greater freedom of women in Cuba under the new condition of things and hoped that all present would carry home the tidings of the new life.[18]

By making *The Pearl Key* available online, the University of Florida is recovering part of its own heritage, as well as a part of the US Hispanic Literary Heritage. Readers today should be aware that the work is much more than what Mena called the "simple story of my life." It is best appreciated with some understanding of the wartime context in which it was published and some knowledge of Mena's life in postwar Cuba. As in the case of *The Story of Evangelina Cisneros*, the publication of *The Pearl Key* was an opportunity for a Cuban woman to promote the independence movement in the United States, even if she had to share her narration of the story with editors and translators. Cisneros became a celebrity and achieved much greater success in bringing attention to the Cuban cause than Mena did. However, as a record of Cuban-American feminist writing of the time, *The Pearl Key* today offers valuable social commentary not found in Cisneros' work, and therefore deserves further attention today.

Works Cited

"About A Book: A Cuban Authoress Arrested on the Charge of Defaming the Character of the Wife of a Spaniard." *Tampa Weekly Tribune*, 19 Oct. 1899, p. 7, ufdc.ufl.edu/UF0009 3470/00160/7.

"Acuerdos de las Sufragistas." *Diario de la Marina*, 27 Jul. 1922, p. 2.

Del Corral, José Isaac. "Nuestra Contribución Bélica en Minerales. *Revista de Agricultura,* vol. 26, 1943, pp. 34-41.

"Cuban Patriot: Tragic Romance of Senorita de Mena, Who Arrives Here." *Boston Daily Advertiser*, 13 June 1900, p. 2.

Dabove, Juan Pablo. *Nightmares of the Lettered City: Banditry and literature in Latin America, 1816-1929*. U of Pittsburgh P, 2007.

"De Mena Case Dismissed." *Florida Times Union*, 22 Oct. 1899, p. 6.

"Dr. Sargent's Work." *Cambridge Tribune*, 18 Sept. 1909, p. 4, cambridge.dlconsulting.com/?a=d&d=Tribune19090918-01.

Florida Agricultural College Board of Trustees. *Minutes.* Series 157, University Archives, Smathers Library, University of Florida.

García, Ivonne M. *Gothic Geoculture. Nineteenth-Century Representations of Cuba in the Transamerican Imaginary*. Ohio State UP, 2019.

Godoy, Gustavo J. "Jose Alejandro Huau: A Cuban Patriot in Jacksonville Politics." *Florida Historical Quarterly* 54.2, 1975, pp. 196-206.

Jameson, Fredric. "Third-World Literature in the Era of Multinational Capitalism." *Social Text*, no. 15, 1986, pp. 65-88, www.jstor.org_stable_466493.

"Letter from Cuban Students." *Cambridge Tribune*. 28 Aug. 1909, p. 5, cambridge.dlconsulting.com/?a=d&d=Tribune19090828-01.2.49.

"A Life of Tragedy in the Cause of Freedom: Senorita Aurora de Mena, A Summer Student at Harvard." *Boston Globe,* 9 Sept. 1906, p. 41, www.newspapers.com/image/?clipping_id= 31293428.

Lizaso, Félix. *José Martí Recuento de Centenario*. Ucar García, vol. II, Havana 1953, p. 333.

Losch, Paul S. "The Fleeting Fame of Florida's Filibuster, 'Major' Frank Hann." *The Florida Historical Quarterly*, vol. 91, no. 4, 2013, pp. 491–525, www.jstor.org/stable/43487530.

Molloy, Sylvia. *At Face Value: Autobiographical Writing in Spanish America*. Cambridge UP, 2005.

O'Brien, John, and Horace H. Smith. *A Captain Unafraid: The Strange Adventures of Dynamite Johnny O'Brien*. New York: Harper & Row, 1912.

Paravisini-Gebert, Lizabeth. "Colonial and postcolonial Gothic: the Caribbean." Edited by Jerrold E. Hogle, *The Cambridge Companion to Gothic Fiction*. Cambridge UP, 2002, pp. 229-257.

Perez, Louis A., Jr. "The Circle of Connections: One Hundred Years of Cuba-U.S. Relations," *Michigan Quarterly*, XXIII, summer 1994, pp. 437-455.

___. *Cuba in the American Imagination: Metaphor and the Imperial Ethos*. U of North Carolina P, 2008.

Prados-Torreira, Teresa. *Mambisas: Rebel Women in Nineteenth-Century Cuba*. Gainesville, UP of Florida, 2005.

Proctor, Samuel. *The University of Florida, The Early Years, 1853-1906 Ph.D. Dissertation;* 1958. https://ufdc.ufl.edu/AA00038581.

Rea, George B. *Facts and Fakes About Cuba: A Review of the Various Stories Circulated in the United States Concerning the Present Insurrection*. G. Munro's Sons, 1897.

Rincón, Belinda Linn. "From Maiden to Mambisa: Evangelina Cisneros and the Spanish-Cuban-American War of 1898." *The Martial Imagination: Essays on the Cultural History of American Warfare*. Edited by Jimmy Bryan. Texas A&M P, 2013, pp. 88-106.

Roggenkamp, Karen. "The Evangelina Cisneros Romance, Medievalist Fiction, and the Journalism that Acts." *Journal of American Culture,* vol. 23, no. 2, 2000, pp. 25-37.

Sargent, Dudley Allen. "The Height and Weight of the Cuban Teachers." *Popular Science Monthly*, vol. 58, 1901, pp. 480-92.

Sebreli, Juan José. "Indigenismo, indianismo y el buen salvaje." *Cuadernos Hispanoamericanos* 487, 1991, pp. 45-68.

"La Señorita Mena en Harvard." *La Instrucción Primaria: Revista Quincenal*, vol. 8, 1909, p. 103.

Schwartz, Rosalie. *Lawless Liberators: Political Banditry and Cuban Independence*. Duke UP, 1989.

"Slander Case Today." *Tampa Tribune*, 20 Oct. 1899, p.1.

Sommer, Doris. *Foundational Fictions: The National Romances of Latin America*. U of California P, 1991.

"Spanish Instructress: Secretary of the Cuban Junta Will Teach Spanish in Tampa." *Tampa Weekly Tribune*, 29 Dec. 1898, p. 3, ufdc.ufl.edu/UF00093470/00058/3.

Stoner, K. Lynn. *From the House to the Streets: The Cuban Woman's Movement for Legal Reform, 1898-1940*. Duke UP, 1991.

Stoner, K. Lynn. "Militant Heroines and the Consecration of the Patriarchal State: The Glorification of Loyalty, Combat, and National Suicide in the Making of Cuban National Identity." *Cuban Studies*, 2003, pp. 71-96.

Torres, Joseph R. "A Card: Judge Torres Writes About a Recent Case in the Courts," *Tampa Tribune*, Oct. 24, 1899, p. 7.

Torres-Saillant, Silvio. "Recovering US Cuban Texts." *Latino Studies*, vol. 3, no. 3, 2005, pp. 433-42.

"Unsatisfactory Affair: Cuban-American Religious Meeting All One Sided: Twenty-five Parts Spanish to One English." *Cambridge (Mass.) Tribune*, 11 Aug. 1900, p. 1, cambridge.dlcons ulting.com/?a=d&d=Tribune19000811-01.2.9.

Vinat de la Mata, Raquel. *Las cubanas en la posguerra (1898-1902): acercamiento a la reconstrucción de una etapa olvidada*. EditoraPolítica, 2001.

"The Woes of an Authoress: A Little Book Causes Commotion in Spanish Circles." *Weekly Tampa Tribune*, 31 Aug. 1899, p.1, ufdc.ufl.edu/UF00093470/00153/1j.

María Cristina Mena and the Masturbating Boy

WILLIAM ORCHARD
Queens College CUNY

This essay's title alludes to Eve Kosofsky Sedgwick's "notorious" 1991 article, "Jane Austen and the Masturbating Girl," in which she gives due consideration to "the muse of masturbation."[1] Noting that scholars have, following Foucault, seen sexuality as entangled with historical conditions, epistemologies, and literary representations, Sedgwick argues that "masturbation itself . . . like homosexuality and heterosexuality, is being demonstrated to have a complex history" (820).[2] Although often coded as an aberrant or juvenile form of sexual expression, Sedgwick contends that masturbation offers "a reservoir of potentially utopian metaphors and energies for independence, and a rapture that may owe relatively little to political or interpersonal abjection" (821). In his cultural history of masturbation, Thomas Lacquer also sees masturbation as connected to discourses of self-control, self-governance, and self-sovereignty, claiming that, in the early eighteenth century, "[m]asturbation is the sexuality of modernity and of the bourgeoisie who created it" (18). In this essay, I offer a reading of Maria Cristina Mena's "The Education of Popo" (1914) that argues that the eponymous character is finally represented as a masturbating boy, and this representation is consequential for what it tells us about how Popo is attempting to formulate a sovereign identity in the face of cultural, political, and economic forces that threaten to overwhelm him. Moreover, if we understand Popo in these terms, we also can reflect further on Mena's aesthetic strategies, viewing her stories not as a coherent statement on Mexican national identity, but as work that experiments with the ideas of her historical moment and that attempts to imagine the possible futures these ideas entail.

Although Mena's work was initially dismissed as sentimental local-color literature, more recent scholars have reassessed her as a writer who produced complex representations of Mexico that were alert to evolving discourses about race in both the United States and Mexico.[3] These critics reflect on how Mena, who fled Mexico for New York in 1907 at the age of fourteen as the Mexican Revolution approached, was sensitive to how race and gender figured in Mexico's changing sense of national identity. Marissa K. López, for instance, notes how Mena's stories are attentive to Mexico's indigenous populations and to the "constraints of culturally defined womanhood" (101), but argues that Mena's fiction expresses "divided loyalties" that make "natives central to a definition of the Mexican nation while simultaneously distancing Mexico from its poor" (98). For López, Mena can see gender as "social, discursive, and abstract but stop[s] short of making this same argument about race" (108). Examining Mena's representation of beauty and cosmetic surgery, Kyla Schuller focuses on how gender and race are co-constitutive in Mena's work. In stories such as "The Gold Vanity Set" (1913), "The Vine Leaf" (1914), and "Marriage by Miracle" (1916), Schuller argues that Mena "repurpose[s] cosmetics use as a vehicle of Mexican cultural self-determination rather than an imitation of whiteness" (86).[4] While Schuller sees race and gender in the Mexican context working in tandem, rather than in competition, as López suggests, both scholars show the centrality of these two categories for understanding how Mena is engaging with the political and cultural upheavals of her historical moment.

Although Mena criticism's focus on gender sometimes broaches sexuality, sexuality has rarely been the central focus. This is somewhat surprising because some of her contemporaries saw her representations as fitting in with modernism's franker discussions of sexuality. Mena was friendly with a number of modernist writers like D. H. Lawrence, T.S. Eliot, and Aldous Huxley. Her tie to Lawrence was especially notable. Aside from a shared interest in Mexico, Mena came to Lawrence's aid when *Lady Chatterley's Lover* was banned in the United States by "offering to sell book volumes to booksellers in New York" (Doherty xiv). Reflecting on their fiction, Lawrence writes to Mena, "I think you and I instinctively turn to the same thing, the life implicit instead of the life explicit. And the life implicit is embodied and has touch: and the life explicit is only ideas and is bodiless" (xiv). Doherty notes that Mena "shared with Lawrence an openness about sexuality that is evident in the way in which she challenged both sexual mores and stereotypes in fiction" (xiv). Mena thus circulated in a literary public whose participants wrote and spoke openly about sexuality in its more corporeal forms.

When critics have tended to sexuality in her works, they most often focus on heterosexual romance. This is connected to Doris Sommer's arguments about how national romances of nineteenth-century Latin America form "foundational fictions" that symbolical-ly consolidate conflicting forces. As Sommer explains, "national ideals are all ostensibly grounded in 'natural' heterosexual love and marriages that provided a figure for apparently nonviolent consoli-dation during internecine conflicts" (6). Insofar as these unions are meant to engender a new nation, foundational fictions are future ori-ented. Jolie Sheffer sees the stories responding to the United States' racial regimes in romances "about the possibilities for a more mul-tiracial and egalitarian national identity" (91). Sheffer detects two kinds of romantic plots in Mena's fiction: an incestuous plot that reaffirms Mexico's colonial hierarchies and a miscegenation plot that gestures toward a post-revolutionary future.[5] This leads Sheffer to conclude that "the mestizo is the figure of futurity," which is con-sistent with Renee Hudson's arguments that Mena's work represents a kind of speculative fiction that captures the "former futures" of the period before the revolution. By "former futures," Hudson means that Mena's fiction is set in the recent past "to imagine better futures than those given to us by the Mexican Revolution" (71). Although she also draws upon Sommer's work, Hudson ultimately sees the stories' representations of failed romances as a critique of forging a coherent identity. By focusing on romance, these critics highlight how erotic plots look to the future.

This sort of future orientation is integral to the rethinking of race that is occurring in the midst of the Mexican Revolution. This rethinking of mestizaje promoted the mestizo—the mix of Spanish Creole and Indian—as embodying Mexican national identity, symbolically incorporating the Indian from the margins to the center of the nation. This view of race would find its most famous expression in José Vasconcelos' *La raza cósmica* (1925) but appears as well in earlier works like Manuel Gamio's *Forjando patria* (1916). Mena is thus writing at a moment when these ideas about race and nation were beginning to congeal into some of their most potent forms. Her fiction registers the fluctuations in understandings of mestizaje and its significance for the future of Mexico and the United States. The valorization of the mestizo has been rightly criticized for appropriating the historical and symbolic power of the Indian while erasing the Indians who exist in the present.[6] Although some might regard mestizaje as something internal to Mexico, Juliet Hooker reminds us that Vasconcelos' theorizing considered the role of the United States in Mexican identity: "Vasconcelos's ideas about mixture should therefore be read as part of an anti-colonial strand of Latin American thought for which the comparisons to the United States on race were a central feature of the response to US imperialism" (158). Hooker further coins the term "mestizo futurism" to describe the "ways in which utopian fantasies of mixture" allowed thinkers to imagine a "decolonized South that was yet-to-be" (4). Hooker helps us see how mestizaje relies on heterosexual romance to achieve its futures, and how these futures are conditioned by Mexico's relationship to the United States and are registered in discourses about race. As productive as attention to the romance plots of the stories has been, attending to other dimensions of sexuality helps us understand different aspects of Mena's fiction.

"The Education of Popo" is often read as a story concerned with the cultural invasion of the Mexican landscape by ugly Americans who mindlessly use the land and people for their own pleasure.[7] The story begins with the household of Governor Fernando Arriola making preparations to welcome and "[give] the most favorable impression of Mexican civilization" to the wife and daughter of Señor Montague Cherry of the US. Although Señor Cherry "was manipulating the extensions of certain important concessions in the State in which Don Fernando was governor," the story turns away from this capitalist venture and toward a light romantic plot involving Cherry's daughter, Alicia, and the governor's son, Popo (47).

Popo fulfills many US stereotypes of Mexicans. Although he is the only person in the house who knows English, his language is filled with several comical mistakes. We learn, for instance, that his study of English has equipped him to say, "prettily, although slowly, 'What o'clock is it?' and 'Please you this,' and 'Please you that,' and doubtless much more if he were put to it" (48). In addition to his juvenile command of the language, which prepares us for how he will misunderstand his encounters with the visiting Americans, Popo also possesses naïve notions of romance that are informed by a strict adherence to Catholicism. The two combine to transform his flirtations into metaphysical problems. Insofar as he represents Mexico, Popo embodies Anglo fantasies of a childlike, backward nation that is ruled by superstitious traditions and not conversant with modernity. Popo's failings are primarily legible to the reader through Alicia's interpretations. To his family, he is a young man of promise who will soon depart to the United States to attend a university. Indeed, that promise seems to be contained in his full name, Próspero, which both invokes prosperity and alludes to the main character of Shakespeare's *The Tempest* (which I return to below).

While Alicia often gives voice to some of the harsher ways in which US readers might imagine Mexico, the narrator—either through direct observation or through Popo's reactions—also provides an account of some of the ways a stereotypically uncouth American might be received abroad. Indeed, Mena is frequently lauded for the skill with which she discerns the dynamic scopic relations at play in encounters between Americans and Mexicans. Mena satirizes Mexican hospitality and the culinary tastes of the

American tourists when she mentions how the Arriola family "requisitioned from afar . . . American canned soups, fish, meats, sweets, hor d'oeuvres, and nondescripts; ready-to-serve cocktails, a great variety of pickles and much other cheer of American manufacture" (47), showing how, in their attempts to give "the most favorable impressions of Mexican civilization," the Arriolas have procured US goods to feed to US guests. The story is most biting about American tourists in its representation of a conversation between the two Cherry women early in the story. Alicia's mother sourly complains that no one speaks English. "Even the parrots here speak nothing but Spanish," she states, adding, "I am too old to learn to gesticulate, and I refuse to dislodge all my hairpins in the attempt" (52). Alicia, in reply, is much more enthusiastic about learning Spanish. Her mother sharply responds to this enthusiasm by saying: "If you continue studying the language . . . you will soon be speaking it like a native" (51). In the Cherry women, we witness two versions of the ugly American. On the one hand, there is the imperial expectation that the nation will conform to the linguistic and social conventions of the United States. On the other, there is the woman who is about to "go native."

Another aspect of this scene is revealed when Popo spies on the Cherry women and is dismayed because the two women do not speak in the manner of mother and daughter but rather appear to act in a manner "of an indifferent sisterliness, with a balance of authority in favor of the younger" (49). This scene contains an eroticism that anticipates Popo's later appearance as a masturbating boy: his peeping is as voyeuristic as it is inquisitive as he discerns the seeming perversion of disordered familial relations. This upending of the social order foreshadows the later revelation that Alicia Cherry is actually an American divorcee, a fact that comes to light when her ex-husband arrives to woo her and, in the process, abruptly ends Popo's first romance. When Popo notices the sisterly relationship between mother and daughter, the narrator remarks, "that revolutionary arrangement would have scandalized Popo had he not perceived from the first that Alicia Cherry was entitled to extraordinary consideration" (49). The use of the word "revolutionary" is noteworthy here. Although Popo is amenable to revolutionary alterations to established hierarchies, it is the Cherry women who are positioned as the revolutionaries, not Popo himself. The story thus posits the dangers the United States poses to Mexico, which in its zeal for social and political transformation may inadvertently fall prey to predatory Americans. In this reading of the romance, Popo's education is largely cultural: he comes to recognize the pain that cultural misunderstanding can cause, and the ways in which Mexico and Mexicans are poorly regarded by US citizens.

However, Popo's education is also sexual. In particular, this is conveyed in the final image that the story provides of Popo. Sullen and distraught over his failed relationship, Popo retreats to his beloved cañoncito. Earlier in the story, Popo's family takes Alicia and her mother to visit his grandmother's house to escape the clamor of preparations for a ball at his family's home. While there, he takes Alicia to the canyon in hopes of kissing her for the first time and declaring his love. To get there, the pair trounce through "a terraced Italian garden peopled with marble nymphs and fauns" and then travel down "an avenue of orange-blossoms" and across a field of lilies that their "feet crushed" before arriving at the canyon, in which there is a cave that lies behind a waterfall that Popo often stares at in contemplation. The narrator's description of the cañoncito can be read as a move from innocence to experience: he leaves the civilization of family, governed by his mother and grandmother, and proceeds into increasingly wild nature. If the crushing of lilies did not convey his sense of sacrificing innocence and entering maturity, Popo's description of the canyon as beyond the knowledge of *mamagrande* and as a location for self-reflection and meditation marks it as a private zone for maturation. By taking Alicia there, the private, reflective aspects blend with an erotic one, which becomes significant when Popo flees to this place after discovering Alicia with her ex-husband at the ball. Although Alicia does not reciprocate Popo's affection, she becomes familiar enough with him to know where Popo escaped. After going to the canyon to look for Popo, Alicia reports to Edward that she discovered him there: "He had eaten a few bananas, but as they are not recognized as food here, they only increased his humiliation" (60). I argue that this embarrassed, banana-devouring youth is a masturbating boy, and that this allows us to link the story to early twentieth-century debates about national sovereignty and eugenics.

Aside from the banana's phallic shape and the shame Popo evinces while consuming them, the banana's masturbatory connotations are connected to Popo's eating of them. Kyla Wazana Tompkins connects eating and sexuality, noting that "eating functions as a metalanguage for genital pleasure and sexual desire" (5), and further argues that "eating is central to the performative production of race" (7). If his consumption of this phallic fruit has sexual connotations, Alicia's remark that bananas "are not recognized as food here"—ostensibly referring to how banana trees were used to shade coffee plants and not to produce fruit for consumption—not only explains Popo's shame but marks his actions as transgressive and forbidden. It also marks him as "other" to the "civilization" that exists beyond the canyon. In addition to these figurings of his actions at the story's conclusion, we must remember that Popo's education from the onset is linked to his sexual maturity. When we first encounter him, fourteen-year-old Popo protests to his mother that he should graduate from short to long pantaloons because "since the last day of my saint I have shaved the face scrupulously on alternate mornings; but that no longer suffices, for my maturing beard now asks for the razor every day, laughing to scorn these legs which continue to lack the investment of dignity" (48).[8] After Popo promenades arm in arm with Alicia, he is overwhelmed with bodily sensations—"his finger throbbed" (54) while his ribs recall her warmth. The small sensations precipitate a more substantial confrontation: "Popo found himself looking into the seething volcano, which was his manhood. That discovery, conflicting as it did with the religious quality of his love, disturbed him mightily. Sublimely he invoked all his spiritual strength to subdue the volcano" (54). Throbbing digits, extending limbs, masculine eruptions, and carnal urges that need sublimation: this is the constellation in which the embarrassed banana eater is situated.

At the story's conclusion, several things follow from understanding Popo as a masturbating youth. First, we can insert him into a genealogy of masturbating Mexicans and Mexican Americans, one that we might chart from, say, the group masturbation scenes in José Villareal's novel *Pocho* (1959) to Alfonso Cuarón's film *Y tu mamá también* (2004). In her reading of Cuarón's film, María Josefina Saldaña-Portillo remarks that the poolside masturbatory fantasy of Tenoch and Julio—who, while laying down on parallel diving boards, ejaculate as they recall the image of Luisa, the Spanish wife of Tenoch's cousin, whom they call at this moment "la Española"—"stands for a desired independence from the foreign investment facilitated by NAFTA" (761). This reading of the film hinges upon understanding it as a national allegory and a psychoanalytic understanding of masturbation as propelled by fantasies of composure, mastery, and self-sovereignty. This aligns with Sedgwick and Lacquer's arguments that representations of masturbation respond to political events and express a desire for control in experiences of upheaval. In this connection, we can also see that Popo is not only a boy who is trying to demonstrate sexual competence in the face of overwhelming stimulation, but also one who, insofar as he is representative of the nation, is staking a similar independence from the influx of US capital in Mexico.

While these similarities bridge two works produced ninety years apart, it is important to note key differences. For Mena's early twentieth-century readers, a masturbating child would be a familiar figure from a growing body of literature concerned with regulating the sexual lives of children. George Mosse and Michel Foucault have taught us that, in nineteenth and early twentieth-century Europe and the United States, such a regulation of sexuality was imbricated with the ideological work of nation formation.[9] On this account, masturbation threatens the health of the child, who represents the future of the nation. Medical and educational institutions should therefore join with the family to police children so that they grow into healthy sexual maturity. Such biopolitical regulation of lives was associated with the science of eugenics, which was approaching its moment of greatest influence at the time of the story's publication. In 1912, the First International Congress of Eugenics was held in London, with follow-up meetings planned in New York City (Stepan 5).

The story is saturated with some of the language and concerns of eugenics. In particular, Alicia's report of her final meeting with Popo reflects this thinking. She tells her ex-husband, Edward Winterbottom, that she offered to kiss Popo, but Popo refused. For Winterbottom, Popo's restraint and his refusal to be seduced into a kiss by a woman of questionable sexual mores make the young man "worthy of being American" (62). Alicia, however, checks this response, declaring, "Why that was his Indian revenge, the little monkey" (62). Although her "little monkey" comment may simply be a term of endearment, when combined with the racialization of Popo as an Indian, the remark is congruent with the anthropometry of the period that attempted to draw equivalences between the skulls of simians and those of Irish immigrants and African Americans. "Little monkey" could also refer to his banana consumption, which, as noted above, contains racial overtones that distance Popo from some unnamed norm. Alicia also lauds herself for providing Popo, who is about to head to the United States, with an education in the "college widow breed" (62). When Alicia refers to social types as breeds and national types as races, the story consistently evokes how a biological understanding of race is a factor in social relations. Finally, Alicia, after being called a saint by Edward and "a name which ought not to be applied to any lady in any language" by Popo, exults in the story's final lines, "I suppose we are all mixtures of one kind or another" (62).

Alicia's remarks about her final moments with Popo help us understand the significance of Popo's name. Jolie Sheffer argues that the story plays on Shakespeare's *The Tempest*.[10] Próspero's name alludes to the magus in the Bard's late play, while his last name, Arriola, evokes Ariel, the spirit who serves Próspero after Próspero liberates Ariel from Sycorax's imprisonment. As Sheffer notes, "Ariel" is also the title of an influential book by José Enrique Rodó. In *Ariel* (1900), Rodó declares Latin America "to be Ariel, the spirit of beauty, culture, and morality" while the United States "fulfilled the role of Caliban due to its obsessions with vulgarity and materialism"

(Sheffer 102). For Sheffer, Popo is transformed into a Caliban while Alicia assumes Prospero's mastery: "While Alicia Cherry may see herself as a female Prospero, teaching her ignorant Mexican Caliban about the ways of the world, Mena suggests that she is, in fact, a crude, capitalist Caliban á la Rodó" (103). Sheffer concludes that Popo can only achieve the prosperity in his name when "he refuses to see himself as Caliban" (104). Although Sheffer's interpretation is compelling, Popo's transformation into Caliban seems like less an American illusion than a reckoning with the paradoxical state Mexican subjects find themselves in as they articulate a new national identity.

If masturbation is a figure through which Popo is able to assert sovereignty and guard himself against manipulation from the North, it is an assertion that requires him to be perceived as debased or degenerate. Mena's story suggests that, despite the claims of figures like Rodó, Mexicans will always be seen in these terms by the United States. This is apparent when Alicia racializes him as an "Indian" and "monkey." Popo's connection to Caliban is confirmed in Alicia's last observation about their final conversation: he called her "a name which ought not to be applied to any lady in any language" (62). Popo, like Caliban, learned to curse.[11] Caliban is thus not a figure that Popo refuses, but rather a position from which he represents national identity. In this way, Mena foreshadows Roberto Fernández Retamar's challenge to Rodó in his 1974 essay "Caliban: Notes Toward a Discussion of Culture in Our America." While Rodó, writing in the wake of the Spanish American War, understands the aesthetic and spiritual vitality of Latin Americans as akin to Ariel in *The Tempest*, Retamar, writing from the aftermath of the Cuban Revolution, views the enslaved Caliban as a more fitting figure for a Latin America oppressed by a neocolonial United States.[12]

If Próspero is rendered a Caliban when Americans invade his home, the name Popo also suggests another referent that relates to the place he retires for his banana consumption. In the story, Popo is a diminution of Próspero, but to many Mexicans, especially those from Mexico City like Mena's family, Popo would evoke a connection to

Popocatépetl and Iztaccíhuatl, the two mountains that surround the Valley of Mexico and that are often referred to colloquially as Popo and Izta. Popocatépetl is the Nahuatl word for "smoking mountain," which is fitting because the mountain is a volcano. Given that Popo's emerging manhood is earlier described as a "volcano," Mena's story further connects the two. Iztaccíhuatl, on the other hand, translates as "white woman" because the mountains are snowcapped. This translation seems especially important if we see Popo and Alicia's romance encoded in the Aztec myth: Alicia becomes the "white woman," a racialization that further distances Popo from whiteness. However, most Mexicans referred to the mountain as Mujer Dormida because it resembles a woman lying down in slumber. The mountains were named after an Aztec myth about Iztaccíhuatl, an Aztec princess, who falls in love with a warrior named Popocatépetl. When Popocatépetl goes off to battle, a rival for Iztaccíhuatl's affection tells her that Popocatépetl has died, which causes the princess to die of grief. When Popocatépetl returns victorious from battle and finds his love dead, he has a mountain built, where he lays her body down and sits beside her for eternity.

Mena's other stories reveal that she was familiar with Aztec myths. In her short story "The Birth of the God of War" (1914), published two months after "The Education of Popo," a grandmother recounts to the narrator the story of Huitzilopochtli, the Aztec god of war, whose mother was the goddess Coatlicue. In "The Education of Popo," the allusion to Popocatépetl associates Popo not with the prosperous future that transcends the nation but with Mexico's land and long history. Popo's connection to an Aztec past could be read, as Marissa K. Lopez argues of "The Birth of the God of War," as an instance of "Mena turning indigeneity into a historical relic," or the story might also be seen as an instance in which an elite class symbolically absorbs the indigenous past while ignoring the Indians alive in the present. Such an assessment of this connection between Popo and the past should also acknowledge the transformations occurring in the story's present. If we follow the logic of the masturbating boy, for whom sovereignty is achieved at the price of appearing degenerate or backward, Mena's story similarly attempts to transvalue categories of identity that Alicia and other Americans have devalued. In this instance, Popo's "Calibanization" racializes him and his family, and the story thus argues that, to American eyes, Mexicans will always be juvenile, racially other, and under-developed. However, through the association of Popo and Popo-catépetl, the story reveals how what seems juvenile, such as the nickname "Popo," can be something momentous, such as an Aztec warrior or national landmark.

Understanding that Popo signifies differently depending on who is regarding him also helps us understand Alicia's surprising claim that "I suppose we're all mixtures of one kind or another" (62). At the narrative's end, the white woman is "mixed," a figure whose sexual mores seemed to have been contaminated by the excesses of US capitalist modernity. In contrast, Popo remains "pure"—racially and spiritually—but through assuming a sexual position that moves him backward on a developmental scale, in many ways intimating the tricky ground on which Mexican sovereignty was achieved. This would seem to invert the usual way of thinking about racial purity and racial mixing in eugenicist thought in the historical moment Mena writes. In *The Hour of Eugenics*, historian Nancy Stepan argues European and US eugenicists saw racial hybridization as a source of degeneration, while in Latin America racial mixing was a path toward national regeneration (137). Alicia's flippant tone about mixture at the end of the story implies how there are limits to the forms of mestizaje that will regenerate Mexico, and that the nation needs to define and understand what those limits are. When Popo attempts to maintain sovereignty against these Northern forces in his cañoncito, he provides one lesson for beginning this project: by turning inward toward Mexico—its history, its land, and its indigenous peoples.

Significantly, the place that we find Popo in his moment of banana consumption is a "cañoncito," a geographical depression in the earth. In addition to being a place of privacy and repose from the public life of his family, the little canyon also evokes the mountain Popocatépetl: both are geographical bodies formed by dramatic accumulations of rock and sediment. If Popo's journey into the canyon suggests a move toward a private, interior space, it also suggests a movement into the landmass of Mexico, a way of attuning his spirit to the nation. The cañoncito is thus a setting for Popo's masturbatory fantasies, whether these are erotic or about self-governance. As psychoanalysts Jean LaPlanche and J. B. Pontalis remind us, "Fantasy is not the object of desire, but its setting" (17). Popo's fantasies take place in a setting that allows him to rehearse his responses to stimuli and new information he encounters in the world beyond his sanctuary. This sort of intellectual play sometimes gets labeled "mental masturbation," but marks an attempt to figure out the contours of new situations (Sedgwick 820).

This mirrors the short story form itself. Mary Louise Pratt argues that, among other things, the short story's fragmentary nature, against the novel's "wholeness," has made it an ideal vehicle "to introduce new regions or groups into an established national literature" (188). Like much local color or regionalist fiction from the early twentieth century, Mena's stories function in this way. This view of Mena's work is confirmed by *The Household Magazine*'s epigraph to her final published story, "Son of the Tropics" (1931), which reads, "a story of revolution by the foremost interpreter of Mexican life" (137). The short story's affinity for representing fragments over wholes, Pratt also notes, makes it well suited for representing different forms of social disorder or disintegration (180). Instead of seeing Mena's stories as a cohesive statement on the Mexican Revolution by a Mexican-American writer—as we would in later novels like Josefina Niggli's *Mexican Village* (1945), Luis Pérez's *El Coyote, The Rebel* (1947), and Américo Paredes' *The Shadow* (1950s)—we can see the stories as documentary, trying to capture the recent past and immediate present, while also attentive to the possible futures contained within them.[13] Mena exploits what Pratt sees as the short story's propensity for experimentation in order to use the story as a setting for thinking, much as Popo uses his cañoncito as a retreat for pleasure in the face of his catastrophic misunderstanding of his social situation. Seeing Popo as a mastur-bating boy entails recognizing his attempts to remain sovereign in the face of the "revolutionary" Cherry women's social upheavals.

Popo recognizes, in the end, the ways that the Americans threaten to coopt mestizaje and the need to guard against this by locating national identity and development in the resources of Mexico's land, nation, and people.

Works Cited

Doherty, Amy. "Introduction." *The Collected Stories of María Cristina Mena,* by María Cristina Mena, Arte Público P, 1997, pp. vii-l.

Foucault, Michel. *The History of Sexuality, Vol. 1*. Translated by Robert Hurley, Vintage, 1978.

Hooker, Juliet. *Theorizing Race in the Americas: Douglass, Sarmiento, Du Bois, and Vasconcelos*. Oxford UP, 2017.

Hudson, Renee. "Former Futures and Absent Histories in María Cristina Mena, Rosaura Sánchez, and Beatrice Pita." *CR: The New Centennial Review*, vol. 19, no. 2, 2019, pp. 69-92.

Kimball, Roger. *Tenured Radicals: How Politics Corrupted Higher Education*. Ivan Dee, 1990.

Lacquer, Thomas. *Solitary Sex: A Cultural History of Masturbation*. Princeton UP, 2003.

LaPlanche, Jean, and Jean Bertrand Pontalis. "Fantasy and the Origins of Sexuality." *International Journal of Psychoanalysis*, vol. 49, 1968, pp. 1-18.

López, Tiffany Ana. "'Tolerance for Contradictions': The Short Stories of María Cristina Mena." *Nineteenth-Century American Women Writers: A Critical Reader*, edited by Karen L. Kilcup, Blackwell Publishing, 1998, pp. 62-80.

López, Marissa K. *Chicano Nations: The Hemispheric Origins of Mexican American Literature*, NYU P, 2011.

Mena, María Cristina. *The Collected Stories of María Cristina Mena*, edited by Amy Doherty, Arte Público P, 1997.

Mosse, George L. *Nationalism and Sexuality: Respectability and Abnormal Sexuality in Modern Europe*, Fertig, 1985.

Ortíz, Ricardo L. "Revolution's Other Histories: The Sexual, Cultural, and Critical Legacies of Roberto Fernández Retamar's 'Caliban.'" *Social Text*, vol. 58, 1999, pp. 33-58.

Padilla, Yolanda. "The 'Other' Novel of the Mexican Revolution." *Borders, Bridges, and Breaks: History, Narrative, and Nation in Twenty-First-Century Chicana/o Literary Criticism*, edited by William Orchard and Yolanda Padilla, U of Pittsburgh P, 2016, pp. 63-79.

Paredes, Raymund. "The Evolution of Chicano Literature." *MELUS*, vol. 5, no. 2, 1978, pp. 70-110.

Pratt, Mary Louise. "The Short Story: The Long and the Short of It." *Poetics,* vol. 10, 1981, pp. 175-94.

Retamar, Roberto Fernández. "Caliban: Notes Toward a Discussion of Culture in Our America." *Massachusetts Review*, 15. 1/2, 1974, pp. 7-72.

Saldaña-Portillo, María Josefina. "In the Shadow of NAFTA: *Y Tu Mamá También* Revisits the National Allegory of Mexican Sovereignty." *American Quarterly,* vol. 57, no. 3, 2005, pp. 751-777.

_____. "Who's The Indian in Aztlán? Re-writing Mestizaje, Indianism, and Chicanismo from Lacandón." *The Latin American Subaltern Studies Reader*, edited by Ileana Rodríguez and María Milagros López. Duke UP, 2001, pp. 402-423.

Saldívar, José David. *The Dialectics of Our America: Genealogy, Cultural Critique, and Literary History*. Duke UP, 1991.

Sedgwick, Eve Kosofsky. "Jane Austen and the Masturbating Girl." *Critical Inquiry*, vol. 17, no. 4, 1991, pp. 818-837.

Schuller, Kyla. "Facial Uplift: Plastic Surgery, Cosmetics and the Retailing of Whiteness in the Work of María Cristina Mena." *Journal of Modern Literature*, vol. 32, no. 4, 2009, pp. 82–104.

Sheffer, Jolie. *The Romance of Race: Incest, Miscegenation, and Multiculturalism in the United States, 1880-1920*. Rutgers UP, 2013.

Sommer, Doris. *Foundational Fictions: The National Romances of Latin America*. U of California P, 1991.

Stepans, Nancy Ley. *The Hour of Eugenics: Race, Gender, and Nation in Latin America*. Cornell UP, 1991.

Tompkins, Kyla Wazana. *Racial Indigestion: Eating Bodies in the 19th Century*. NYU P, 2012.

PART II
FORUM ON CHICANA MEMORY

A Forum on Chicana Memory Work, Past, Present, and Future: Nuestras Autohistorias

History, Memory and Chicana Futures

MARÍA COTERA

The University of Texas at Austin

In recent years Chicana memory has emerged as a critical site for the historical interrogation of the past. From scholarly books like Maylei Blackwell's *Chicana Power! Contested Histories of Feminism in the Chicano Movement* (2011), to large-scale recovery projects like the Chicana por mi Raza Digital Memory Collective (initiated in 2009), to more recent collections like *Chicana Movidas* (2018), a new generation is actively recovering the "hidden insurgencies" (Blackwell 2011) of Chicanas in the Movement years (roughly 1965-1980). In the process, they have developed new frameworks of analysis and approaches to recovery that challenge long-held values of historical scholarship, particularly concerning objectivist norms that rely on distinctions between scholars and their "objects of inquiry." From methodological interventions that center feminist oral history to dialogic approaches that foreground the give-and-take of knowledge production, the memory work elaborated in these projects insists on the deeply personal nature of historical meaning-making.

Whereas dominant scholarly discourse values interpretation—the act of applying one's theoretical expertise to the "evidence" of history—memory work privileges the *process* of memory-keeping

(typically, the province of feminized labor) as a critical site of trans-
formative knowledge. I have written elsewhere about how students
who work with the Chicana por mi Raza Digital Memory Project are
impacted by their role as critical witnesses, and how the memory
work (reflective writing, short biographies, timelines and other
curations) they produce in and through their *encuentro* with the past
is a form of "theorizing from the flesh" that often leads to a "deeper
understanding of the connections between theory, experience, and
political action."[1] At the center of this *encuentro* is an intimate, even
familial, process of transgenerational memory exchange in which
questions of affect, relationality, and intersubjectivity take center
stage. In this sense, memory work can be understood as a praxis of
engaging with the past that has personal, ethical, political, and
historical dimensions.

Memory work can take many forms, from the maintenance of
family memory through altars, photo albums, and stories told across
the kitchen table, to more recognizable scholarly practices like oral
history, memoir, and personal writing, archival development, artistic
creation (murals and other homages to feminist icons of the past),
and fiction-writing (for example Jovita González's folklore and
historical fiction). Whatever form it takes, memory work is essential
not just as a way to offer a more comprehensive picture of the past,
but also as an avenue to discover new visions of resistance. Indeed,
at the center of memory work is the idea that the past contains
survival knowledges that can help us cope with the present and build
a future in which Chicanas are a central part of the story. As the
contributions to this Forum amply demonstrate, memory work is
healing work.

The collection of brief essays included in this Forum were first
presented as part of a Roundtable on Chicana Memory at the 2020
Recovery Conference, *Histories and Cultures of Latinas: Suffrage,
Activism and Women's Rights*. The Roundtable featured presen-
tations from contributors to *Chicana Movidas*, a volume that
includes incisive essays from women who were active participants
in the Chicana/o movement like Anna NietoGomez, Martha Cotera,
and Dr. Inés Hernández Ávila, all of whom presented papers as part

of the Roundtable. Historian Dr. Samantha Rodriguez, and poet Dr. Stalina Villareal—who co-wrote an essay for *Chicana Movidas* on Houston-area activist María Jimenez—also participated in the Roundtable, sharing their reflections on collaborating with María (Stalina's mother) to write her story. Presenters were asked to address the ways in which their particular approaches to memory work engaged the past not as a documentary imperative but as a process that is at once historical and deeply personal. As a prompt to consider the self-reflexive nature of this approach to understanding the past—and whether or not we can lay claim to a particular form of historical meaning-making that draws from a deep font of Chicana tradition—presenters were asked to consider Gloria Anzaldúa's formulation of *autohistoria-teoría*, a methodological and spiritual practice that excavates the past as a process of politicized self-reflection and *concientización*: Her first step is to take inventory. *Despojando, desgranando, quitando paja.* Just what did she inherit from her ancestors? This weight on her back—which is the baggage from the Indian mother, which is the baggage from the Spanish father, which is the baggage from the Anglo?

Pero es difícil differentiating between *lo heredado, lo adquirido, lo impuesto*. She puts history through a sieve, winnows out the lies, looks at the forces that we as a race, as women, have been a part of. *Luego bota lo que no vale, los desmientos, los desencuentros, el embrutecimiento. Aguarda el juicio, hondo y enraizado, de la gente antigua.* This step is a conscious rupture with all oppressive traditions of all cultures and religions. She communicates that rupture, documents the struggle. She reinterprets history and, using new symbols, she shapes new myths.[2]

How might the recuperation of Chicana memory transform not only the ways we think about the past but also how we imagine our work as public intellectuals? What are the interconnections and genealogical threads that unite these varied practices of memory, some of which are deeply personal? Can memory be an act of healing, even as it brings long buried experiences of marginalization and violence to the surface? What does the emergence of Chicana memory at this particular juncture suggest about the development of

Chicana studies as a field of inquiry? And what do these stories of the past teach us about the present, and even the future of Chicana feminism? Reflecting on how the essays they wrote for *Chicana Movidas* illuminated these questions, roundtable participants offered deeply personal accounts of their own engagements with memory as a praxis of historical meaning-making. This Forum gathers these methodological and personal reflections in hopes that we might continue the dialogue on how Chicana memory work fundamentally shifts both the practices and the aims of historical recovery.

Memory Work

ANNA NIETOGOMEZ

Publisher of One of the First Chicana Feminist Newspapers, Hijas de Cuauhtémoc, 1971

I am an archive resource for scholars of the Chicano and Chicana feminist movement.

I am also writing my memoirs.

It is difficult to write about something that happened almost fifty years ago, for I never kept diaries.

What happened? What was the cause? And what was the effect? Or, was it the other way around?

Remembering is similar to conducting an archeological dig of the mind and body.

The problem is, I am part of the ruin.

Some artifacts are on the surface of my memory banks and easily available. But often they are only shards, bits and pieces scattered here and there. As a consequence, they reveal only fragments. Pages of my story are also buried I have to hunt for them. In caverns scattered underneath the layers of memory. If I am not ready, the story or stories stay hidden. At times, memory work can be retraumatizing. Then I have to step away, until I am ready to revisit that memory site.

University and personal archives help me remember.

Once my personal archives were dead files because I rarely used them. Thanks to scholars like María Cotera, and Maylei Blackwell, and many of you in the audience, I have revived them, and now they almost speak to me. They are part of the paper trail to my story.

Archives help me create, and update timelines. Timelines help me picture in my mind what happened. I remember why these documents are essential to my story. I analyze and reinterpret the data. This process is often unconscious and takes time, and then I must go back and picture in my mind what I did and how I felt about what happened.

Scholars like yourselves help me with my dig, the telling, and retelling process. You call for an interview. I ask for questions. The questions are limited to what the scholar knows. Therefore, they limit my search. I prepare for your visit, I go to my files, to conduct the dig. It is a manual data search. Then I assemble, dis-assemble, and reorganize my files. The next phase is a collaborative process. Together, the scholar and I engage in collaborative telling and retelling. The telling is dependent on your insightful feedback and additional questions. The more you know, the more I can tell you. Consequently, together, we work as a team trying to understand more with each telling. It is through the telling and retelling that I can uncover more of the memory site link it together, analyze, interpret, and reinterpret what I remember.

This is comparable to a fermenting process, for, I often remember and understand much more six months after we have concluded our collaboration. However, I don't always have a collaborator. And the telling is then internal and consequently a slower process, or so it seems.

Memory work involves going on an intuitive journey without a map. I use my intuition to engage my unconscious mind to uncover my story. In doing research for my memoir, for example, I made a list of people to interview. However, I didn't always know why they were on my list. I just knew they were essential to my story. For instance, the first person on my list was Olga Talamante. In 1974, she was a Chicana activist working in Argentina. The Argentine government imprisoned and tortured her. The nation rallied to free Olga and brought her home. In 1976, Olga came home.

In May 1976 in *La Gente*, a UCLA Chicano Student newspaper, I remembered reading about her trials and tribulations in Barbara Carrasco's interview with Olga Talamante. Forty years later, Olga was gracious enough to grant an interview. On the drive from Los Angeles to San Francisco, my husband, Richard asked me, "When did you first meet Olga?" I said, "This will be my first time." Richard asked, "Then, why are you going to interview her. What does she have to do with your story?" I said, "I don't know. I just know she does." After the interview, on the journey home, Richard asked me. "Well, now! Do you know why Olga is important to your story?" I said, "Nope." I asked myself, "What does Olga Talamante mean to me?" I worked on the dig and dived down into the shafts of my unconscious. Finally, when we reached Santa Barbara, an intuitive guide awoke. It led me to that place we call clarity. Immediately before the memory tunnel closed again. I said, "Olga is vital because she helped me move on.

In 1976, I fought for tenure and lost. I battled with the underbelly of toxic paternalistic Chicano studies. Those who supported me, including my four-year-old boy, were bullied and terrorized. Once I was la Adelita in the movement. Then I became a pariah because I accused Chicano studies of gender discrimination. Rather than obey its request to resign and leave immediately, I chose to exercise my right to due process, and I appealed their decision to deny tenure. I felt abandoned and betrayed. The movement demanded its equal rights but did not feel obliged to grant it to its own.

I was alone. Only my mother, though she was against my activism, came to help me move on. I was devastated and felt sorry for myself. Then I remembered Olga. I compared her situation with mine. I imagined her physical pain and life of terror. I was going home to a safe place to recover and heal. Then I said to myself, "My situation is nothing compared to Olga's. If Olga can make it through, Then, so, can I!"

It was then that I understood why Olga was the first name on the list. Through her, I had moved on and left behind a toxic world. And it was through Olga that I would make my re-entry, though this time it would be on my terms.

Memory work also included understanding how family history shaped my feminist ideas. I grew up hearing stories about the women in my family. I recalled comparing the movement's version of the Chicano history of men and the patriarchal family. I suspected a false narrative because they were so vastly different from what I learned from my family's oral histories. Looking back, I wondered why the men and the women in my family made different choices and had different narratives. I conducted family interviews and studied history. The stories I heard as a child had a different meaning as an adult. I realized that the stories of my grandmothers were about violence against women, human trafficking, and slavery. Class, race, and gender discrimination. They were working mothers. Life decisions were based on a fusion. A fusion of religious superstitions, and laws from a colonial theocratic Mexico. The Mexican liberal laws of *La Reforma* and the 19th amendment to the United States constitution.

Similar to the 1964 civil rights legislation, these laws were specific about women they restricted or opened the choices and opportunities available to my great grandmothers and their daughters. The men had stories too.

Both my father and my maternal grandfather mindfully strived to break away from patriarchal values. When they were toddlers, their fathers died. And they became homeless and destitute. Their mothers were illiterate and unskilled. They had to depend on the kindness of others to survive. There were too many children. Some took in the children as indentured servants under the pretense of providing free room and board. Though their mothers worked, it was not enough to feed the family. Marriage was the only safety net available for a single working mother. When their mothers married, the stepfathers were ambivalent and resented providing free room and board for children fathered by another man. Father and grandfather resented that they and their mothers were treated as possessions of "El Don" the patriarchal master of the house. My father and grandfather promised themselves that their daughters would get at least a high school education.

With an education, their daughters could keep the family together without having to exchange their rights as human beings for the economic support of another man. I was taught that education was life insurance. It guaranteed that I would have more choices than my grandmothers. It guaranteed that my children and I would not become destitute and homeless. Education ensured that I would be able to earn enough to provide for my children and keep my family together.

The moral of each of my family's stories motivated me to become La Feminista.

For the moral was: A mother's place is in the labor market. If women do not get an education and fight for their rights, they cannot protect themselves nor their children.

This was their legacy to me.

This is a glimpse into my memory work.

Los cuentos que contamos e historias que conservamos (Stories We Tell and History We Preserve)

MARTHA P. COTERA
Founding member of the National Women's Political Caucus, Texas Women's Political Caucus, Partido Raza Unida and Mexican American Cultural Center in Austin

I was literally born and raised in an archive in Casas Grandes, Chihuahua, the ancient town of PAQUIME, of the Anazasi and Mogollon culture. As a young child, playing in the still buried montículos (mounds) with artifacts revealed by rainfall, and shamed into reburying them in respectful deference to our ancestors, I was admonished to learn my culture, history, and stories; to retell them, keeping our ancestors alive and in our lives. I was literally born in the throes and mounds of ARCHIVE FEVER.[3] And so, I live. I learned that the ancient ceramic tokens I admired were "Moctezumas," possibly receipts for tribute paid to the Aztec Empire, headquartered 2,000 miles away from our beloved peaceful *valles* and *sierras* of northern Mexico.

I absorbed tales of wars for liberation from the Aztec empire, from the European invaders, and later from would be autocrats. *Embelesada* (spellbound), I encountered the courageous Doña Josefa Ortiz de Dominguez, Leona Vicario, and grief-stricken la LLORONA in grandmother's conversations, forever seeking liberation. *Comadres, madres*, and aunts bemoaned the maligned Malinche/ Doña Marina, reimagined as the creator of the cosmic race, and channeling Sor Juana Inés, they complained, "*pues hombres necios que culpan a la pobre esclava violada*," (foolish men, slut shaming a raped slave), now elevated by Chicana feminists, including me, from *Chingada* to *Chingona*. Of course, *la rebelde* Sor Juana Inez de la Cruz (the Tenth Muse), became a favorite, the seventeenth-century feminist who adored learning, an international celebrity admired for her intellectual prowess; all these heroines populated my first work, *Diosa y Hembra* (1976), and my entire life, *no agraviando lo presente* (I live surrounded by excellent women).

With my own hands, my entire life, I excavated, shared, and preserved my indigenous feminist heritage, aspiring to become what my grandmother and mother exhorted me to be, a storyteller. The story I tell in *Chicana Movidas* is one of many, with a backstory, a beginning, a middle (strategies), and a moral "*Te lo dije*" ("I told you so") ending. Nevertheless, there is also a happy ending of our own making.

In 1976-1977 following the first International Women's Year conference in Mexico City (1975) the federal government proposed a series of International Women's Year state conferences to culminate in a national conference with the goal of planning a progressive agenda for women in decades to come. Chicana feminists throughout the nation coalesced with other women of color, radical women, and LGBTQ women to elaborate strategies for inclusion that could overcome the racism of the mainstream women's movement. In my essay in *Chicana Movidas*, I write about this conference, and name names involved in our successful "*movidas*" especially here in Texas, which brought in hundreds of women of color participants. By replicating successful strategies of inclusion in Chicano movement and mainstream feminist activism of the southwestern and midwestern states, Chicanas led women of color representatives who advanced a progressive national plan of action at the state levels, and then on to the 1977 National Conference for Women where it was approved, in Houston, Texas. The Women's Plan of Action included ratification of the Equal Rights amendment, LGBTQ rights, reproductive choice, and other progressive issues furiously opposed by many in the mainstream women's movement. This successful proposal for a progressive national plan for women was unfortunately derailed post conference by mainstream women's movement leaders typically supportive of the male-dominated neoliberal order which protects the status quo empowerment of white communities in the United States. *"Te lo dije"* ("I told you so"). This was the reason I had been a reluctant organizer for this conference in Texas, after having experienced obstruction of progressive policies by the mainstream women's movement for years.

Following the failure to launch the Woman's Plan of Action approved at the 1977 National Conference for Women, Chicana feminists nevertheless continued our community activism, which included archival preservation efforts through institutions like Chicana Research and Learning Center and projects like the Benson Latin American Collection's Mexican American Library Program, the Recovering the US Hispanic Literary Heritage Project of the University of Houston, and in the past decade, the Chicana Por Mi Raza Digital Memory Collective. Also, and most importantly, our efforts launched a generation of empowered Chicanas who are changing the political and academic landscape, many of them active in events recovered and retold in *Chicana Movidas*. Among them, of course, is Sylvia Garcia, United States Representative who was a member of the US House of Representatives impeachment manager team. Another outcome of 1977 has been the focused continuity of Latina feminists working 24/7 on progressive public policy and institution building primarily at the local level as a long-term strategy for statewide and national impact.

I believe every story has an agenda, and part of mine in retelling this narrative has been to offer content useful for revisiting third wave feminist critique of diversity issues in second wave feminism, by providing just one amply documented and meticulous example of coalition building between Chicana feminists, radicals, and the LGBTQ community. This is also a cautionary tale for storytellers to be deliberate and smart in their critiques; to search, document, listen, *antes de andar con cuentos* (before telling tales) of individual and collective history. As in Casas Grandes (Paquimé), Chihuahua, the mounds are all around, waiting for you to get your hands dirty.

El Amoridolor del Movimiento

INÉS HERNÁNDEZ-AVILA
University of California
Founding Member of the Native American and Indigenous Studies Association

> *The information in my body tells me that I am whole but scarred, many scars, many lives, many wounds not healed: healer, make me whole, healer that I am, take hold of my life and nurse the cuts that have reached inside so deep I will think of them when I die. I know I am not alone. At the same time, I witness(ed) the radiance of heightened consciousness—I learn(ed) and play(ed) a part in lifting up the hearts of our people (as we would say among my mom's people). Would I have preferred to turn a blind eye to the movimiento? There is no way I would trade that experience for anything. I went into it with my eyes wide open and my heart ready.[4]*

The Movimiento was imbued with love-and-pain, *amoridolor*, one word. We love(d) deeply, so we hurt deeply. We hurt so much because we love(d) so much. We felt injustice, we felt its historical intergenerational impact on our communities, on our families, so we fought for justice with passion and determination. We were, and are, fiercely loving and committed. We didn't always do things right. With every step we took as activists, we were unlearning domination, subjugation, forced assimilation, internal colonialism. We were unlearning the normalized allegiance to the heteropatriarchy. We were unlearning rampant misogyny and homophobia. We were unlearning the racism of Indian-hating that permeate(d/s) Mexican culture. At the same time, we were learning to be proud of other aspects of our mexicanidad. But in that process, we made mistakes, we took missteps. We could not always see how sometimes we had (unknowingly) internalized oppressive mindsets.

We were figuring out how to name precisely what was wrong, and in that naming, free ourselves to imagine and envision new ways of being. This new freedom, these acts of liberation, were exhilarating. For me, my heart filled to bursting every time we did something right, which is something I measured by the response in the community to our organizing, to our actions, to our *palabra*. When we tapped into the collective hopes and dreams, and the ongoing concerns, of our *comunidad*, and engaged them with our hearts, we could feel, I could feel, the joy, the collective *"¡Eso!"* to our growing/expanding *conciencias*, to our realization that we were not only possible, but that we were inevitable—who we were and what we were doing was *meant to be*. We were not victims; we were a broad-based community of protagonists. Those were the moments that gave us/me strength, that confirmed that we were on the right path.

Those of us who were artists, poets, singers, performers understood the power of the arts to transform. We contributed to a gran *florecimiento* of expressions that touched the hearts and spirits, the very being of our community—many of us in Austin going into schools, grades K-12, to work as volunteers with young ones, to inspire in them the power of creativity, resulting in annual citywide Floricanto Festivals featuring the art and literature of the youth in our communities. I am grateful that I moved fairly smoothly (though not without cost) between the different arms or fronts of the Movimiento—*academia*, Raza Unida Party organizing, *mujeres* organizing, solidarity work with other fronts of the socio-political movement, cultural work, the arts, work of the spirit, and solidarity work with Indigenous struggles in the US.

I am a "rememberer," a term from distinguished Stó:lōō writer, Lee Maracle, who writes: "The rememberer must choose what to witness, what to commit to ready and accurate recall, and who to discuss the event with. This process is at once historical, sociological, political, legal, and philosophical."[5] I have a keen memory, I have always been this way, and what I am realizing as I am writing this, is that I have woven memory over the years, which in so many ways, has served me well. If memory is history, and history encompasses all that we did, thought, felt, and longed for, then those actions, and the thinking, feeling, and longing are living, teaching moments that have shaped me in all of these subsequent years, along with the other life experiences I have had. I have never stopped being an organizer. I have never stopped the work of the heart, through my writings, through my teachings, in my life. My inclination is always to bring people together, *buscar justicia, siempre*. One of the major life lessons from the Movimiento? Autonomy. Self-determination. How does this happen unless each of us knows deeply, truly what autonomy means to us as conscious individuals who want to strengthen our communities?

Another major life lesson from the Movimiento? We must find the words, find the inspiration in our own people, in their words, their acts, their writings, their love. Those long decades ago, my intuition told me to look to our own for inspiration and guidance, so I was not so interested in mainstream feminism because I sensed our connections to *lo mexicano*, and my *hermana en la lucha*, María Jiménez, very early on, told me about Sor Juana Inés de la Cruz, and my *hermano en la lucha*, Emilio Zamora, told me about Sara Estela Ramírez. As I began to be more acutely attentive to our own, I saw that our people had never been passive, and that we had/have the tools and strategies necessary to engage in our struggle(s). I realized deep in my being that we were a manifestation of the legacy that had been left by our ancestors to guide us. Because of them, we have always known how to fight back, talk back, and bring back.

What is one of the critical challenges for us today as we re-gather memory to reshape the historiography of the Chicano movement and the women's movement? We must work against erasure. Erasure is deadly. What could be worse than for women activists' lives to be written out of the larger story, for their/our contributions to become invisibilized? For it to be that they/we never existed? We must continue to affirm, validate, and honor all the *mujeres* who gave of themselves, *con valor, pasión y conciencia*, in any and every way to the life-altering transformations we achieved.

¿Que si me acuerdo? Claro que sí. My body remembers. My spirit remembers. My *conciencia* remembers. My heart remembers. Memory is powerful. My personal story is part of our history, just as every single personal story is part of our history. History is not only the story of the ones named as leaders. History is what each of us lived singly and collectively during those Movimiento years, and each story matters. As N. Scott Momaday wrote, "If I were to remember other things, I should be someone else."[6] *Así es.*

María Jiménez: Fronteras and Memory Movidas
SAMANTHA M. RODRIGUEZ
Houston Community College

In 2006, immigrant rights activists flooded urban streets to resist H.R. 4437, a xenophobic bill designed to criminalize immigrants and anyone who assisted immigrants. María Jiménez, a political elder who was always seeking to empower the next generation, was a steady presence at these protests, and her keen analyses and potent energy left a deep impression upon me as a young student and community activist. I was not only captured by her *palabras*, but also ignited by her *movidas*. At the request of Jiménez, her daughter, Stalina Emmanuelle Villarreal, and I wrote an essay for *Chicana Movidas* that documented how her *movidas* destabilized race, gender, and class *fronteras* in Texas during the Chicana/o Movement.

A central feature of our memory *movida* was a collective and dialogic process of historical reconstruction. Stalina and I shared all drafts with Jiménez, demonstrating how the process of storytelling (oral histories) can be inclusive and empowering for both the writers and the subject. This process of memory-making has important implications for public scholarship. For public historians, the task is to not just extract information from the community for our research agendas. We have to take part in a larger collective process of creating "vernacular histories" that shift and deconstruct the dominant narrative where "Mexicans are all rapists, criminals, and migrants," and where Mexicans have long been considered to be foreigners even though they are generational residents of the borderlands. As historian Monica Muñoz Martínez notes, vernacular histories shape popular understandings of the past by making histories of racial violence available to the public, opening "new opportunities to recover marginalized histories."[7] María Jiménez's story contributes to this process because it recovers the history of how Tejanas maneuvered anti-Mexican sentiments and claimed liberation in the "Juan Crow South," particularly in multiracial urban communities like Houston, Texas. Indeed, as she reveals in her *testimonio,* Jimenez's childhood experiences with segregation in the context of Black and Brown Texas taught her important lessons that she would later draw upon in her work within the Chicano Movement in Houston. Recalling her first experiences with Juan Crow as a child, María Jiménez proclaimed, "I remember seeing for the first time on the buses there were African Americans in the back and white people in the front. I remember I had never seen an African American. I remember asking my father why that was, and he said, 'Well, they have to by law sit in the back.' I also remember that . . . on the way to Houston there were certain little towns like Schulenberg and others where *we* were not permitted to eat in certain restaurants."

Jiménez's *testimonio* also reflects her sense of being a *nueva* Tejana, part of a "new breed" of ethnic Mexican women in the protest era (1960s and 1970s) who built upon histories of Mexican female insurgents of the past (through a practice of intergenerational memory) to rail against socio-economic oppression and work towards collective male and female empowerment. Jiménez recalled, "In those years, I would eventually shed all pretenses of the cultural concept of womanhood. I fought along [with] feminists at the [University of Houston] to get the Women's Studies program and childcare for students started . . . I participated in events that fought for reproductive rights . . . I fought for a women's right to decide what to do with her own body and imposed motherhood." Jimenez's *testimonio* thus illuminates how concepts central to contemporary Chicana feminism, such as Gloria Anzaldúa's new mestiza consciousness, were articulated on the ground in the political *movidas* of *nuevas* Tejanas. As Anzaldúa asserts, the borderlands is not just as a physical boundary, but also a mental and cultural space that activates fluid consciousness, in which "energy comes from continual creative motion that keeps breaking down the unitary aspect of each new paradigm." *Mestiza* consciousness acts as an elastic modality for cultivating tolerance and freedom pathways that rupture "all oppressive traditions of all cultures." Jiménez's activism as a grassroots organizer for ethnic self-determination, cross-racial justice, and feminist liberation demonstrates how she, and other "*nuevas* Tejanas" of her era (particularly those who worked across communities of struggle), were the architects of an intersectional feminism based on intergenerational feminist gatherings where women of color influenced and learned from one another, as described by Maylei Blackwell, Marisela Chavez, Samantha Rodriguez, and others. As a university and community activist, Jiménez remembered, "I had a very distinct identity . . . . Because I was . . . Mexican and Chicana, I fought for that first. I mean, I had to fight for that because that was my community. But I'm also a woman, so I had to fight for that . . . . But also, the whole issue of income inequality would fit with poor whites and blacks." Jiménez's intersectional perspective, born from her early experiences of segregation and the gendered contradictions of the Chicano Movement were foundational to her community bridging efforts in the Houston Chicana/o Movement. As a La Raza Unida Party candidate, she canvassed historic African American neighborhoods, she stated: "I remember going with Omowali [Lithuli], and we said—when we were knocking on doors— "We are representing the Raza Unida Party." We had to immediately translate—it is the People's United Party . . . it was seeing the tremendous impact of social systems not just for Latinas/os, but for African Americans as well."

Presently, we continue to grapple with establishing an intersectional feminism that embraces anti-racism and class issues within movements for women's equality. Fifty years ago, and up until her untimely passing in December of 2020, Jiménez fought for the collective community; advocating for broad racial and gender liberation based on the freedom of all members of *la familia*. While the paternalism and racism that existed in the mainstream Women's Liberation Movement of the 1960s and 1970s persists today, Jiménez offers a potent example of how to navigate such exclusionary structures and foster new paradigms for resistance. Indeed, Jiménez's life and example have inspired my own movements toward collective freedom when addressing women's issues. I am a co-founder of *Más Que Tres*, a Chicana collective that addresses the core topics of feminism, health, empowerment, race, and justice. MQ3 has presented at the "We are Girl" Girls Empowerment Network Conference where we focused on instructing young girls of color to engage in self-care and heal as well as honor our hearts as women. We have also had elders speak on the women's roles in Mexica/Aztec society. Lastly, we have generated art, virtual talks, poetry, and writings centered on broad women's empowerment. In commem-orating suffrage and women's activism, we construct vernacular histories to remember ethnic, Mexican women's long trajectory in that movement and how women such as María Jiménez contributed their own values and pursuits of freedom. Indeed, her experiences in the Juan Crow South and her life-long struggle to build bridges between justice movements demonstrate how it is imperative for Tejanas to traverse multiple *fronteras* in their fight for liberation and justice.

My Mother's Palabras: The Chain Reaction of Intergenerational Memory

STALINA EMMANUELLE VILLARREAL

In elementary school, when my twin brother and I asked our mom, María Jiménez, why we were the only kids eating brown bread, she told us about a scientific experiment in which mice that ate white bread died, whereas the mice that ate wheat bread lived. We could never argue with her because she always had an answer. She raised us with the power of her *palabras*, the *palabras* that attracted so much attention in her activism. After my lifetime of noticing her speaking patterns, I was delighted to collaborate with Samantha Rodriguez to write about my mother's *testimonio* for

Chicana Movidas. We used transcripts of her *testimonio* that left me with a profound impact, influencing my own *palabras* as a daughter, poet, and artivist.

In our article, I focused on how my mom's *palabras* embedded anecdotes with arguments:

> [She] refined her skills at the time by transcending masculinist forms of speaking—the "bombasti" oratory style that is "culturally accepted." She confronted sexism, classism, and racism by learning how to weave concrete analysis and storytelling into a formidable rhetorical strategy. This cross-genre style is emblematic of [her] ability to surpass boundaries . . . Alongside poetic political commentary, [she] developed her argumentative style through the narrative traditions of her father's lineage. Her paternal relatives invoked rhetorical devices that combined imagery with situational irony . . . During [her] rhetorical formation, she bridged symbolism and context to scrutinize the fallacy of arguments.[8]

An example from my mom's *testimonio* that Samantha and I quoted shows some of these very strategies. As she recalled:

> From my mother, what I learned was how to deal with absolute power because she would figure out what to do to obtain our objectives which Papá said we could not do . . . I remember that she would organize us clandestinely: "*No le digan a [su] papá* [Don't tell your father], but we are going to do this." So, from her I learned to deal with that type of absolute power.[9]

In this passage, my mom narrates how my *abuelita* circumvented my abuelito's authority while contextualizing sexism and its power dynamics. My mom's references to "absolute power" are analytical. In particular, I had heard my *abuelita* say, "*No le digan a [su] papá*" repeatedly, but I had not contextualized her expression until I read my mother's *testimonio* while working on *Chicana Movidas*. Learning from my mom and *abuelita*, I once tried to help organize adjunct professors to unionize clandestinely, although eventually, to avoid being fired for aiding and abetting against the administration, as advised by the AFL-CIO, I had to break the silence as a Faculty Senate representative and tell my bosses. I had to learn when to voice a problem and when to delay the response, but I witnessed the power of intergenerational *testimonio*.

While writing the article in *Chicana Movidas*, I understood my mother from a more multifaceted perspective. For instance, I recall my mother telling me that, during the Chicano Movement, some of her male peers would accuse her of breaking up the family. She would respond by reminding them that the poet Sor Juana Inés de la Cruz and *soldaderas* were part of Mexican history. She would say: "I don't know about your history, but in my history, women were always leaders." Those are the words I remember her expressing. Nevertheless, until I read my mother's *testimonio*, I did not know that she learned about Sor Juana and *soldaderas* at an early age from reading my bisabuelito's books.[10] I was able to get a more complete picture of my mother from both my dialog with her and her documented *testimonio*.

My mom's maneuvers with words have shaped me as a poet. For my artivism, I wrote a poem about environmental justice, as I kept in mind what I have learned from my mother for my own *testimonio*. I begin my poem "Breath Distres" with a narrative element:

> . . . and I am
> transplanted as a child,
> four generations of immigrants
> *en Magnolia el mismo barrio*
> where my mother developed
> asthma, *es posible que la
> causa sea la contaminación.*[11]

Here I establish a setting and begin the conflict in the plot by speculating that environmental pollution is the cause of my mother's asthma. Remembering how my mom referenced the expertise of scientists in the mice experiment, remembering how my mom referenced Sor Juana and *soldaderas*, I next cite an expert in environmental justice Robert D. Bullard:

> [T]he current system has (1) institutionalized unequal enforcement, (2) traded human health for profit, (3) placed the burden of proof on the "victim" and not the polluting industry, (4) legitimated human exposure to harmful chemicals, pesticides, and harmful substances, (5) promoted "risk" technologies such as incinerators, (6) exploited the vulnerability of economically and politically disenfranchised communities, (7) subsidized ecological destruction, (8) created an industry around risk assessment, (9) delayed cleanup actions, and (10) failed to develop pollution prevention as the overarching and dominate strategy.[12]

This excerpt explicates the cause of environmental injustices. I then proceed to document the pollutants of my barrio:

> [W]here diesel fuel gets emitted
> and sold, where trains leak
> chemicals, where tugboats and boats
> on the ship channel pollute, where
> eighteen wheelers and commercial
> buses exhaust. With Houston's
> lack of zoning laws polluting
> industries neighbor houses.[13]

Much like my mother invokes imagery when she spoke of my grandmother organizing her children "clandestinely." I wanted my audience to visualize the environmental hazards of my barrio. Last, I list the effects of such hazards:

> *En el mismo barrio*
> where cancer is rampant.
> My *abuelita* had pancreatic cancer.
> I had skin cancer.
> *Es un orgullo que respiro.*

My *mamá* has primary peritoneal cancer—It's a cancer of the lining of the abdomen;
It has spread to her lung.
And sighs are not enough.[14]

I combine the narration of my matrilineal relationships with an explication of the roots of environmental injustices to reiterate, through cause and effect, an argument within my poem. This process was inspired by my mother's *testimonio*.

Ultimately, I develop my own *testimonio*, as the poem explores my own relationship to breath and my sense of community, but that commitment to my community and my *testimonio* have been molded by mom's activism and *testimonio*. It has been an intergenerational chain reaction, for my mother learned how to organize people by watching my *abuelita* organize her own children, and my poetry raises awareness of social issues I learned from my mom. My activism involves circles of poetry readers and listeners instead of the audience at large, so I cannot say that I am more successful than my mother who organized large masses of people. What I admit is that I am lucky to have had such a heartfelt yet intellectual mother, a believer in social justice.

PART III
GENDER, POLITICS, AND POWER IN THE SPANISH-LANGUAGE PRESS

Gertrudis Gómez de Avellaneda and Puerto Rico's Colonial Press

AYENDY BONIFACIO
University of Toledo

The transamerican poet Gertrudis Gómez de Avellaneda (1814-1873) was one of the most celebrated writers to emerge from the nineteenth-century Hispanophone world. Born in Puerto Príncipe (modern-day Camagüey), Cuba, she lived most of her life in Spain. Her father, Manuel Gómez de Avellaneda, was an aristocratic Spanish navy officer, and her mother, a wealthy creole of the landed gentry. Like many young women of the landed caste, Avellaneda received an unparalleled education. One of her tutors was the foremost Romantic poet of the Americas, José María Heredia (1803-1839), whose influence on Avellaneda's writing is evident in poems like "A Washington" and "A Vista del Niagara."

Like many women writers of the mid- to late-nineteenth-century, Avellaneda maneuvered a literary landscape governed by a separate-spheres ideology that deemed women unfit for public letters. Yet, no other Hispanophone woman poet of her time was reprinted more in newspapers. As a famous poet and a woman in the public sphere, Avellaneda's literary talents were often measured against her gender. In fact, her gender and talents were rarely separated from critiques, celebrations, and reviews of her publications. For instance, the Spanish poet José Zorrilla writes of Avellaneda, "she was a woman—

99

but undoubtedly only by an error of nature, which had absent-mindedly placed a manly soul in that vessel of womanly flesh."[1] Zorrilla is one of the many Spanish writers who fault nature, or God, for misgendering Avellaneda, i.e., for erroneously placing her in a woman's body. Critics like Zorrilla dispossessed Avellaneda of her body. Along with the gendered dispossession of her body, critics of her work regularly positioned and repositioned Avellaneda's body of work within opposing Spanish nationalist and Caribbean anticolonial discourses.

A poststructuralist, print-culture reading of Avellaneda's gendered body (embodiment and work) is helpful for better understanding Avellaneda's public image within the press' varying colonial and anticolonial discourses. The opposing discourses and power dynamics that contextualized Avellaneda's public image must be examined diachronically and synchronically to understand the semiotic relationship between text and public image. The newspaper is the ideal artifact for horizontal/vertical readings of Avellaneda because newspapers provide paratexts and extended print runs from which to examine what Jaques Derrida terms, the "systematic play of differences."[2] Derrida famously argued that discourse, whether textual, cultural, or institutional, is a battle of "philosophical opposi-tion [where] we are not dealing with the peaceful coexistence of a vis-a-vis, but rather with a violent hierarchy. One of the two terms governs the other (axiologically, logically, etc.), or has the upper hand. To deconstruct the opposition, first of all, is to overturn the hierarchy at a given moment."[3] Indeed, the logical and axiological contentions, inconsistencies, and contradictions that simultaneously included and excluded women writers from participating in the public sphere and contributing to the discourse of nation-building — a discourse that subjected them to the patriarchal colonial power — required constant overturning of various hierarchies. To make sense of Avellaneda's appearance in the colonial press, I use decon-struction as a type of decolonial option, or as Walter Mignolo states, a way of "confronting and delinking from coloniality, or the colonial matrix of power" (xxvii).

By using the term "colonial," I invoke Mignolo's definition of coloniality as the "darker side of modernity" that contributes to the legacy of the term colonialism: "Moderdernity[/coloniality] is a complex narrative whose point of origination was Europe" and in our specific case Spain. It is a narrative that "builds Western civilization by celebrating its achievements while hiding at the same time its darker side, 'coloniality'."[4] In the case of Avellaneda's publication in the colonial press, what's hidden in plain sight is the colonial printscape. This paratextual structure holds and pieces together her work and public image for readers. Coloniality and modernity go hand in hand, according to Mignolo. They cannot exist without each other in the western world because they depend on Eurocentric epistemes, i.e., the "western code."[5] Thus, in this chapter, "colonial" refers to western modernity as much as it does to the historical/cultural/social phenomenon of colonialism and its axiological and logical forms of oppression and domination.

This chapter examines how print practices shaped and reshaped Avellaneda's poetics and public image within and among colonial spaces. Vying colonial and anticolonial discourses meet in the pages of newspapers where Avellaneda's works were published. These discursive differences amount to printscapes that frame her work and public image for complex social groups. Some of the pieces in this chapter were culled from Spanish books and periodicals and reprinted in colonial contexts. Through the reprint process, certain manipulative editorial practices, including public censorship and political reportage, allowed newspapers to concomitantly create and recreate Avellaneda's public image for their audience.

My focus is the nineteenth-century Puerto Rican colonial press for two primary reasons: first, although Cuba and Puerto Rico were Spanish colonies throughout Avellaneda's lifetime (they were often called sister islands because of their converging interest for liberation from Spanish, a study of Avellaneda's work in the Puerto Rican colonial press has never been done. Avellaneda's popularity in Puerto Rico blurs the lines of Caribbean belonging in ways that can help us better understand the rhizomatic networks of colonial/anticolonial projects. And second, the colonial island of Puerto Rico reveals an aperture through which to study Avellaneda's trans-Caribbean and transcolonial poetics in the Hispanophone press. In other words, Puerto Rico functions as a vantage point, liminal space and colonial parallel, where Spanish nationalist discourses can be examined. Avellaneda's presence in the periodical press reveals a tryptic image of colonial, anticolonial, and decolonial desires that linked the Hispanophone Caribbean to Spain and the United States. This transnational triangulation of print culture, which circulated poems, discourses, and political interests to English and Spanish readerships, contributed to Avellaneda's multifaceted image in the public sphere.

As a celebrity poetess with nationally recognized affiliations in Cuba, Spain, Puerto Rico, and the United States, Avellaneda's poems and public image were bound up in the push and pull of colonial, anti-colonial, and decolonial discourses. Some newspapers claimed her as a Spanish loyalist and/or nationalist. In contrast, others framed her as a feminist abolitionist—aligning her with Cuban freedom fighters like the Afro-Cuban abolitionist and formerly enslaved poet Gabriel de la Concepción Valdés, known by the pseudonym Plácido, and the revolutionary architect of Cuban liberation, José Martí. As a woman in the nineteenth century with disputed connections to the imperial metropoles and colonial territories, Avellaneda never had complete ownership of her work or public image. Like many poets of the period, her poems were printed, reprinted, and disseminated throughout the Hispanophone world without her consent or compensation, and reportage about the author speculated about her political views according to the partisanship and agendas of the press that published them. It is important to trace this messy production of her work and public image to better understand Avellaneda not so much as a nationalist/loyalist poetess but as a woman who maneuvered a dissonant landscape of voices advocating for different futures. Did she see herself as an anti/decolonial poet advocating for Cuba Libre, a Spanish nationalist loyal to Queen Isabella and Spain, or both? Was she indifferent? The media played an understudied role in shaping these very questions. This chapter shows that the colonial and anticolonial press politicized and depoliticized Avellaneda for specific political ends. I examine how Avellaneda's public image and poems were filtered through the specific political agendas of the partisan newspapers that published her. This created a knotted image of the writer throughout the Hispanophone world that we are still disentangling today. Ultimately, this chapter is about the dispossession of Avellaneda's body, i.e., how her embodiment as a Cuban-born white colonial Spanish subject and citizen and her body of work as a kaleidoscopic projection of the vying discourses of the trans-Caribbean Hispanophone colonies were regularly repackaged in the press for specific colonial and/or anticolonial social groups. To understand this gendered landscape, we must understand Avellaneda's role in refuting it.

As a woman and celebrity, Avellaneda blended the social lines between the public and private spheres. At the same time, she merged political and national lines, which has historically presented a categorical conundrum for students of literature and culture attempting to pinpoint her to a school of thought and/or national literary tradition. Beth Miller reads Avellaneda from a historical and feminist perspective. She argues that Avellaneda's "literary production is feminist for its times in some of its themes, plots, characters, and statements."[6] As a creole woman of means and fame, Avellaneda's career did not come without its fair share of gendered challenges. She maneuvered a sexist, patriarchal colonial culture and acquired, as Miller argues, endurance.[7] Through a feminist historiographical approach, Catherine Davies takes on an important set of questions about Avellaneda's literary reputation: "Should she be credited to (or appropriated by) the cultures and literary traditions of the colony or the metropolis? Why not to both? Clearly, what is at issue here is not Avellaneda's work but her status as a cultural icon and repository of colonial or anticolonial sentiment."[8] Her status as a repository for competing (anti)colonial futures importantly reveals how nation-formation is inherently a patriarchal project in which gender norms function as epistemic forces in the colonial and imperial spaces Avellaneda maneuvered. Davies posits that "consideration of the polemics that arose on account of Avellaneda may show us how cultural nationalism produced women as a social category in colonial Cuba and how [Avellaneda] negotiated subsequent contradictions."[9] Miller and Davies teach us that the social values of the cult of domesticity and nation-formation that shaped Avellaneda's public life share a patriarchal episteme that formed women into social categories in the service of cultural nationalism.

Avellaneda in the US Periodical Press

In the US press, Avellaneda was considered a major poet of the Americas. In articles published from Pennsylvania to California, her poems were likened to her mentor, José María Heredia's work for its Romantic and Cuban characteristics. Many US editors reprinted poems and published lengthy columns about the poet introducing US readers to her work and celebrity. In their deep dive into Avellaneda's presence in the US press, María C. Albin, Megan Corbin, and Raúl Marrero-Fente read Avellaneda's reprint poems in the United States as political verses that unveil the nature of Spanish tyranny (in the case of her poem "A Washington") and the terrors of slavery (in the case of *Sab*.) Scholars have made clear that *Sab* was particularly important in shaping Avellaneda as an abolitionist in the eyes of the anticolonial press in Cuba, Puerto Rico, and the exile press in New York City.

Published in 1841, eleven years before Harriet Beecher Stowe's *Uncle Tom's Cabin*, *Sab* is considered the first anti-slavery work of fiction published in the Americas and Spain. Although it was banned in Cuba, many copies were smuggled into the Hispanophone Caribbean. The book was also reprinted in periodicals in New York and Europe, gaining Avellaneda notice for her abolitionist writings. Scholars of *Sab* read the novel as evidence of "an early and genuine concern for the emancipation of the slaves, and . . . one example of [Avellaneda's] lifelong commitment to the abolitionist cause."[10] In her comparative study of US and Cuban nineteenth-century poets, Anna Brickhouse examines the impact of *Sab*'s censorship in Cuba and New York. She argues that "late in Avellaneda's life, *Sab* had emerged again as anticolonial fodder," stoking the flames of revolution and abolitionism. Brickhouse continues,

> Obviously aware of the potential impact of her novel, Avellaneda herself claims in a foreword that she wrote the novel purely for "amusement" and never intended to publish it,

though many details in the novel, as well as the explanatory notes that accompany it, suggest that she intended all along to introduce Cuba and its folk customs to a foreign readership. Indeed, Avellaneda ambiguously disavows the ideas in *Sab* as "somewhat different" from those she holds at present; at the same time, however, she acknowledges having opted not to change them—but declines to specify "whether out of laziness or our unwillingness to alter something we wrote with real conviction."[11]

Avellaneda's cautious response to *Sab*'s political message is a symptom of what Davies calls the "contradictions of the political discourse (liberal individualism) as a gendered formation. . . . Men were free to make identity choices. Women, on the other hand, represented the unchanging, natural qualities of the nation, and therefore were denied progressive agency and citizenship."[12] In other words, a cautious response was the only publicly acceptable answer for a woman. Such an answer sides with ambiguity, abstraction, indifference, and "unchanging, natural qualities of the nation." Avellaneda's irresolution was often not simply taken out of context but resituated within the pages of the Puerto Rican colonial press.

Avellaneda in the Puerto Rican Colonial Press

Avellaneda print scholars have made clear that in the Cuban-New York press, she was claimed as one of their own, as a liberator and abolitionist writer, central to the Cuban fight for independence and abolitionism. However, this was not the case in Hispanophone colonial newspapers that painted Avellaneda in a light that was more palatable to their readers. The abolitionist and Cuba Libre overtones that Avellaneda's New York publications display are wiped-out in the reportage and reprint poems in the colonial Hispanophone press. In colonial Puerto Rico, these overtones were replaced by a patriotic performance of Spanish colonial control of which Avellaneda was a part.

In Puerto Rico, the Spanish government utilized two major newspapers as a means of communication and colonial control: *La*

Gaceta de Puerto-Rico and the *Boletín Mercantil de Puerto Rico*. Both papers used Avellaneda's image and poetics to represent the colonial interests of Spain in Puerto Rico. The four-page newspaper, *La Gaceta de Puerto-Rico,* was the earliest Spanish colonial newspaper published on the island. Its earliest issues date back to 1806, commemorating the arrival of the first printing presses on the island.[13] As the official newspaper of the Spanish crown, *La Gaceta* served the readerly needs of the Spanish land- and slave-owning elites. According to the Library of Congress, which made available one of the largest print runs of the paper, *La Gaceta* published local and international news, "speeches, arrival of vessels in San Juan, people arrested for illicit gambling, the lottery, and the escape and capture of fugitives."

La Gaceta obscured Avellaneda's private and public lives through reports and reprint poems that seemed to align her poetics and personal life with the colonial project. In a front page column titled "España" printed in the July 28, 1846 issue, for example, *La Gaceta* announces "el matrimonio . . . [del] Sr. Sabater actual jefe político de Madrid, y la conocida y aplaudida escritora Doña Gertrudis Gomez Avellaneda."[14] Avellaneda's marriage ceremony and French honeymoon appear alongside news about the exiled "obispo de Barbastro, who has returned "á España en virtud de un decreto de la Reina," the establishment of the Banco de Cadiz, and news of a society gathering "en el Real Palacio." The imbrication of Avellaneda's private and public lives as colonial fodder can also be seen in the poems *La Gaceta* published. On April 20, 1858, *La Gaceta* reprinted a poem titled "Serenata: A su Alteza Real, la Serma, Sra. Infanta Duquesa de Montpensier, La víspera de su Cumpleaños" (Serenade: To Her Royal Highness, Mrs. Infanta Duchess of Montpensier, On the eve of her Birthday). Avellaneda dedicates the poem to the eponymous Duchess of Montpensier, Luisa Fernanda, the youngest sister of Queen Isabella II. The poem was later collected in Avellaneda's *Obras Literarias* in 1869. In the poem, the speaker serenades the Duchess with sentimental and adorning compliments to the royal family:

Luisa su nombre bendecir vea;
Y honra no habiendo que no le cuadre,
La augusta hermana de Isabel sea
De bella prole dichosa madre.

This poem is a colonial serenata that pays homage not only to Luisa but also to Queen Isabella II, and their mother, Maria Christina of the Two Sicilies (1806-1878). The deferential speaker illustrates a continuation of the Spanish royal line, which inherently extends to Spain's colonies. The poem performs an exaggerated faultless devotion, an old-world custom of polite deference over 5,000 miles away from Spain that models "good" colonial subjectivity.

Along with the poem's addressees and colonial overtones, *La Gaceta* provides a paratextual note that depicts Avellaneda as a good colonial subject.

Esta poesía fue leída por la señora Avellaneda a los señores Duques de Montpensier con motivo del cumpleaños de S. A. D. Luisa Fernanda, y al siguiente día los Príncipes enviaron a la poetisa un rico regalo que consiste en un lindo estuche con una rica joya de brillantes perlas y rubíes de exquisito trabajo.[15]

This formal exchange of goods—a poem and reading for precious jewels—is a performance of good colonial subjectivity printed and promoted in the pages of *La Gaceta*. This patriotic performance displays two essential components of colonial subjectivity: 1) that the good colonial subject will be well compensated for honoring the royal family and 2) that the crown is enormously wealthy, no matter that the rubies and pearls were likely plundered from the very land on which Avellaneda was born. The pearls might as well be a metonym for Avellaneda herself, who was famously nicknamed "la Perla de Las Antillas" (the pearl of the Antilles).[16] In *La Gaceta*'s context, the pearl is more than a sobriquet. It is also a colonial consequence of plundering Caribbean islands, people, and aesthetics in the name of Spain. *La Gaceta*'s paratextual note offered readers access to this patriotic performance and, most importantly, to the poet's metonymic collapse and her plundered pearls, which begs the rhetorical question, was the poet a gift to Spain, or is Spain a gift to the poet? The vertical exchange of goods suggests the latter. The paratextual note applies value and ownership to Avellaneda's genius, implying that it too can be purchased or perhaps rewarded. At the same time, like Avellaneda, the colonial subject will benefit from the charity of the colonizer if the colonized works to sustain the imperial power. This is the logic that sustains colonization at a distance. *La Gaceta* is part of the imperial machinery of propaganda, and Avellaneda's poem was an ideal cultural artifact to strengthen the unequal cultural relationship between caribeños and españoles. However, not all of *La Gaceta*'s poems focused on the poet's relationships with Spanish royals. Some, like the following example, placed Avellaneda in conversation with poets that challenged colonial values like gender norms.

Avellaneda's celebrity presented newspapers an opportunity to edit, as it were, the poet's public image. On May 14, 1861, *La Gaceta* reprinted three of Avellaneda's poems: "A la Virgen," "A Washington," and "A Sabater." The poems' byline, "La Avellaneda Poetisa," appears in bold type, larger than the poem titles. At the end of the column, a paratextual note authored by the famous Spanish abolitionist and Romantic poet Carolina Coronado (1820-1911), complements the paper's emphasis on Avellaneda's celebrity.

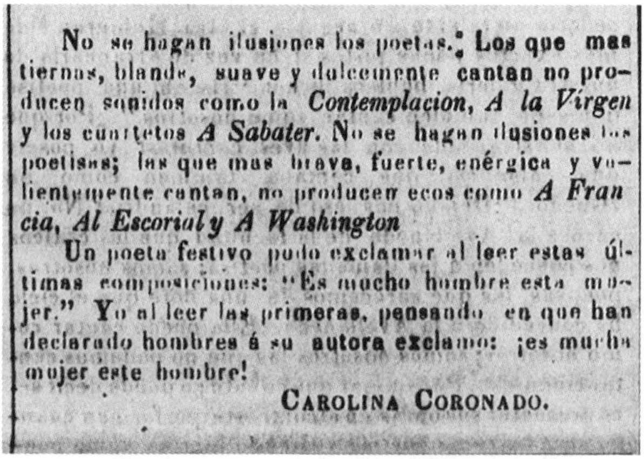

No se hagan ilusiones los poetas. Los que mas tiernos, blandos, suave y dulcemente cantan no producen sonidos como la *Contemplacion, A la Virgen* y los cuartetos *A Sabater*. No se hagan ilusiones los poetisas; las que mas brava, fuerte, enérgica y valientemente cantan, no producen ecos como *A Francia, Al Escorial y A Washington*

Un poeta festivo pudo exclamar al leer estas últimas composiciones: "Es mucho hombre esta mujer." Yo al leer las primeras, pensando en que han declarado hombres á su autora exclamo: ¡es mucha mujer este hombre!

CAROLINA CORONADO.

Figure 1. Library of Congress, *La Gaceta* de Puerto Rico, May 14, 1861.

Poets don't get your hopes up. Those who sing the most
tender, soft, and sweet sounds cannot produce those like
Contemplación, A la Vírgen and the quartets A Sabater.
Poetesses don't get your hopes up; the ones that sing the most
valiant and brave the loudest and the most energetically do
not produce echoes like A Francia, Al Escorial y A
Washington.

A celebrated poet was able to exclaim when reading these
last compositions: "This woman is a lot of man." Upon
reading this for the first time, [and] thinking about what men
have said of the author, I exclaim: there is a lot of woman in
this man! Carolina Coronado[17]

Speaking directly to Hispanophone poets, Coronado emphasizes
Avellaneda's singular greatness among poets. She asserts that
Avellaneda's poetics is unmatched within the world of Hispanophone
poetry. Borrowing from Bretón de los Herreros' famous phrase—
"¡Es mucho hombre esta mujer!"—Coronado resists the sex-gender
system that the patriarchy deploys to categorize women's literary
production. Gendered hierarchy inheres within the original claim:
"this woman is a lot of man" implicitly measuring women up to a
portion of masculinity. By comparison, Coronado upends this gender
dynamic with her new statement, "es mucha mujer este hombre!" In
Coronado's version, women are the ontological template, not men's
equal, but subtly above them; for it is a woman, Avellaneda, who
defines men's poetic tastes.

The above examples of Avellaneda's appearance in the colonial
La Gaceta show a complex colonial impression of Avellaneda's
poems and public image, which she had a limited part in painting.
Patriotic performativity, as evinced in *La Gaceta*, resists some
colonial values like gender norms as long as this form of colonial
resistance does not threaten the royal and colonial social order. The
contextualization of Avellaneda for colonial propagandistic ends is
also part of the print culture of the second largest Puerto Rican pro-
Spanish newspaper, *El Boletín mercantil de Puerto Rico.*

Published in San Juan between 1839 and 1918, *El Boletín Mercantil de Puerto Rico* was, along with *La Gaceta*, one of the most important newspapers for Spanish loyalists and merchants on the island. Starting as a bi-weekly and later changing to a daily, the *Boletín* was a Spanish organ that catered to the interest of Spain and Spaniards doing business on the island. In his foundational study of the Puerto Rican press, *El periodismo en Puerto Rico*, Antonio S. Pedreira emphasizes the *Boletin*'s saliency as "a newspaper of transcendental significance in the history of newspapers in Puerto Rico."[18] From a colonial perspective, the *Boletín*'s news columns, editorials, and literary offerings illustrated the everyday life of Spaniards and their descendants on the island. This newspaper serves as an important resource for analyzing how the colonial pro-Spanish press framed Avellaneda concomitant with the political currents and interests of the colony.

As a merchant paper, the *Boletín*'s readers would have been made up in large part by the mercantile class: business owners, exporters, planters. Many of the *Boletín*'s readers "grouped as conservatives in the Partido Conservador (1869), shortly after renamed Partido Incondicional Español (Unconditional Spanish Party)."[19] However, the work of periodical scholars reveals that partisan newspapers were often read by social groups outside of the intended political party. In part because of the relative scarcity and cost of reading materials, any literate person with access to the *Boletín* would have read the paper.[20] Like many merchant papers in the mid-century, the *Boletín* was not all business. It was a disseminator of culture, and its editors, as Kirsten Silva Gruesz would argue, acted as curators.[21] The *Boletín* regularly printed and reprinted poems, dramas, short stories, literary reviews, and announced book publications and their prices, providing a glimpse of the literature that circulated in the colony during the last four decades of Spanish domination in Puerto Rico.

The *Boletín* was part of the periodical machinery that turned Avellaneda into a Romantic barometer, or, as I call it, the "Avellanedaen barometer," for measuring the prowess and cultural expectations or lack thereof of other women literary figures. The *Boletín* often marketed her as a cosmopolitan poet, in equal footing with, and at times above, other women celebrity writers of her day. In 1871, the *Boletin* serialized essays from the five-volume O*bras Literarias de la Señora Doña Gertrudis Gomez de Avellaneda*. Published in Madrid between 1869 and 1871, *Obras* collected Avellaneda's fiction, autobiographical essays, and essays written about her. The *Boletín*'s selected reproductions describe Avellaneda as the ideal woman nationalist writer and publicly good colonial subject, that is, an apolitical and non-propagandistic poetess. On September 22, 1871, less than two years before her death, the *Boletín* reprinted selections from *Obras a*uthored by the Spanish writer and diplomat, Leopoldo Augusto de Cueto (1815-1901) and retitled them, "Noticias Literarias."[22] The article compares Avellaneda to the English novelist and poet Dinah Maria Mulock (also known as Dinah Maria Craik) (1826-1887). Cueto writes, "The only one of the writers of the sentimental analytic school that compares to Mrs. Gómez de Avellaneda is Miss Mulock, because, with her vigorous instinct, she recounts events with an unfettered and firm style, comments soberly, and does not abuse philosophical analysis."[23] The fabricated barometrical link between Avellaneda and Mulock suggests that Avellaneda's own poetics, politics, and style (which served as a model for other women writers to achieve a measure of literary success) were polite, submissive, and non-critical.

Cueto focuses almost exclusively on Avellaneda's Romantic poems and ignores her more political and widely read abolitionist, anticolonial, and feminist work (including *Sab* and "A Washington"). He does not evaluate literary talents, but rather attempts to reconcile domestic colonial values with women in the public sphere. Cueto goes on to argue that Avellaneda's and Mulock's sober and "not abusive" philosophical thinking result from their feminine natures: "This creation of popular fantasy, skillfully reproduced by Miss Mulock, came to our memory as a delicate analogy of feminine natures, when reading Mrs. Gómez de Avellaneda's 'The Angel Flower,' a deva flower very similar in shape to a bee."[24] The "feminine natures" and the natural world collapse in Cueto's analogy. Women, literary women at that, are like the deva flower and the bee which are part of

Romanticized nature. In addition to these "feminine natures," Cueto claims that Avellaneda's aesthetic sentiment distinguishes her from men: "Women understand and feel more delicately and intensely than men these fantastic illusions of the muse of the mountains, and Mrs. Gómez de Avellaneda has nothing to envy in this part the dreamy imagination of the northern races."[25] It is this myopic vision of Avellaneda as Romantic, sentimental, and non-political that writers like Cueto fixated on and that pro-Spanish newspapers reproduced.

To emphasize Avellaneda's aesthetics as non-political and pro-Spanish, Cueto uses the Avellanedaen barometer to compare the Cuban/Spanish poetess to celebrity writers who threatened the patriarchy. For example, later in the column, Cueto contrasts Avellaneda to George Sand (1804-1876) by way of a rebuke of the popular French novelist's protofeminist views.

> Esta nunca prescinde de sus insanos designios sistemáticos por lo general tan inciertos, que hasta Proudhon, que no es, por cierto, escrupuloso y asustadizo en materias de audacias y de innovaciones, condene con energía y hasta con desabrimiento su encarnizado afán de emancipación femenina sin restricción y sin medida, y todas las consecuencias inevitables de esta filosofía de *vacante revelada* según la expresión violenta de Proudhon, a saber: la igualdad absoluta de ambos sexos; la libertad en el amor, la proscripción del matrimonio; o en otros términos, envidia y odio al hombre, y espontáneo envilecimiento de la mujer.[26]

Cueto relies on the anarchist Pierre-Joseph Proudhon (1809-1865), known for his anti-feminist views, to substantiate critiques about Sand's antipatriarchal politics. Citing Proudhon, Cueto attempts to discredit Sand for "her fierce desire for feminine emancipation" which he equates with the "envy and hatred of men, and spontaneous debasement of women." Cueto continues by "add[ing] nothing to this tremendous judgment of the French critic," implicitly agreeing with Proudhon's position that feminist writers like Sand posed as threats to the social and gendered patriarchal order. The article continues, referring to Avellaneda as antagonistic to

Sand: "Ms. Gómez de Avellaneda is a novelist and not a propagator of risky and ambitious doctrines; she does not denaturalize the novel or the theater, which are literary genres destined for the refined and honest recreation of the people, and does not transform them into publications of upheaval and moral agitation."[27] Cueto subscribes to a patriarchal Romantic aesthetics where politics and "literary genres" are irreconcilable. Unlike her contemporary Sand, Cueto affirms that Avellaneda does not work against this Romantic aesthetics which is devoid of ambitious doctrines. In other words, it is because Avellaneda is a woman writer and not a propagator of feminist ideology that she does not "denaturalize" her writing, a logic that assumes that nature in essence is always already patriarchal.

Avellaneda is contextualized in the *Boletin*'s heteropatriarchal context of Romantic aesthetics to serve as a fabricated model for the comportment of women in the colonial public. Ultimately, Cueto offers a moral argument for examining Avellaneda's aesthetics: "The morality of the legends and novels of Mrs. Gómez de Avellaneda is frank, resolute, and healthy, which is offered by the sincere study of human nature, without hints of social doctrine and without fussiness of form."[28] For Cueto, this non-political study of human nature is the duty of women writers who wish to partake in nation building: "Women . . . cultivate themselves and help civilization and ease the weight of patriotism through literature and the arts."[29] Cueto's article exemplifies how Romanticism was often used as a tool of censorship in Avellaneda's poetics. He emphasizes the Romantic beauties and affective devices of Avellaneda's writing to depoliticize her work and undermine the political potential of Romanticism. Such efforts to depoliticize Avellaneda suggest her powerful influence in the public sphere and her potential threat to not just the colonial order but the patriarchy as well.

Men fabricating truisms about powerful and influential women to maintain power and influence over them, of course, did not start or end with Avellaneda. The fabrication of the apolitical muse of la patria in the form of the poetess was a common trope of the colonial and nationalist patriarchy throughout the Hispanophone Caribbean. Dixa Ramírez provides another example in her seminal study of the

Dominican Republic's foremost woman poet of the nineteenth-century, Salomé Ureña. Ramírez interrogates "the complex but clearly gendered scripts of patriotic performance in which [Ureña's] readers partook. Ureña's poems elicited a set of reactions and behaviors from her readers. The poems themselves did not *have* to elicit these behaviors, but . . . they did so due to the developing and firming of gendered assumptions in Dominican nationalist discourse."[30] Ureña's place within the Dominican nationalist discourse can be explained as an attempt to reconcile what Ramírez calls, "colonial neglect," (i.e., "Ureña's never-mentioned Blackness and her elite class status") with white Dominican elite's colonial desires of Europeanization and culturalization.[31]

Although Ureña was a non-white woman and Avellaneda was white, between them, at least through the lens of the white Europeanizing patriarchy, existed a colonial tethering to the "the muse of the nation," for which Avellaneda served as its template and ideal. This could not be made any clearer than in a celebration for Ureña in 1878, five years after Avellaneda's death. Ramírez details this occasion: "In the words of Justo, a society columnist, these important personalities, a crowd of approximately 80 women and 70 men, had gathered in order to 'render the tribute of estimation and justice to the Dominican Avellaneda' . . . to whom Ureña was compared repeatedly."[32] Here the Avellanedaen barometer crosses the color line to measure the national poetess of a racially diverse nation. As a non-white woman, Ureña's embodiment presented a racial inconsistency for what white Dominican intellectual elites subconsciously understood as nonwhite and civilized. The Avellanedaen barometer, along with the generational whitewashing of Ureña's national portraits throughout the twentieth century (as Ramírez discusses in *Colonial Phantoms*), was a way to reconcile this racial-national inconsistency. Like all such ethnographic comparisons, "the Dominican Avellaneda" presents a hierarchy of the ideal and non-ideal that is grounded in a racialized colonial and anticolonial dialectic. In other words, when Justo used the expression "the Dominican Avellaneda," Ureña became second to Avellaneda, and most significantly, the public image of

Avellaneda as a Cuban/Spanish poetess, ambiguously progressive and conservative, was mapped onto Ureña.

Parallel of Dispossession: Her Corpse and Corpus

Soon after Avellaneda's death on February 1, 1873, Avellaneda's obituaries began appearing across the Hispanophone and Anglophone press. Newspapers devoted a significant amount of their pages to the famed author expounding on her talents and celebrity. In two full columns, the April 9, 1873, issue of the *Boletín*, for example, confirmed with an exclamation that "It is true! The body that belonged to Gertrudis Gómez de Avellaneda rests in a niche in Madrid's San Martin Sacramental Cemetery."[33] The exclamation seems to answer a question or a debate about where Avellaneda's body was to be buried, that is, what nation and people will lay the final claim. The question of corporeal ownership is answered by burying her in Spain's capital city in the grounds of colonial power. There is an obvious parallel of dispossession between Avellaneda's literal and figurative body, i.e., her corpse and corpus. The phrase, for example, "el cuerpo de la que fue" functions as an appropriate metaphor if there ever was one for her body of work. Yet it also hearkens back to this chapter's key question: was Avellaneda ever in complete control of her body? Even in death she is quite figuratively exhumed from the colonial grounds as scholars attempt to contextualize her within a broader literary national tradition.

The *Boletín* obituary's insistence on aligning the poetess with apolitical and gendered aesthetics suggests that even in death, Avellaneda presented a threat to the colonial social order. The column asks, "Who was Avellaneda?" and answers its own question: "La Avellaneda, in life, possessed . . . the power of attraction: talent, beauty, wealth, social position; her sex put her outside the range of political opinion, which poisons everything . . ."[34] Avellaneda's very being, according to the colonial press, amounted to two characteristics: her power of social attraction and her sex. The former decorated her public image and social position; the latter, her womanhood, silenced her political opinions. Avellaneda's writing threatened to dismantle this fabricated colonial assumption.

Conclusion

Avellaneda's popularity meant that her work was published regardless of partisanship. Her influence across the Spanish-Speaking world was unmatched for any poet of her generation. She was read and revered in both the metropole and colonies. In the exile press of New York City, Avellaneda represented an anticolonial liberation movement. In these freedom-fighting newspapers, she symbolized Cuban independence, feminism, and abolitionism. However, the Hispanophone pro-Spanish newspapers, particularly in Puerto Rico, depicted Avellaneda as an apolitical and anti-propagandist Spanish national poet. As shown above, two of Puerto Rico's most popular Spanish organs shaped a specific vision of Avellaneda for their readers. Editors and publishers attempted to contain and manipulate her influence and cultural capital in these Hispanophone locations, framing her work and public image within agreeable discursive and rhetorical structures. Aware of the threat posed by a public figure with known ties to abolitionist and liberation efforts, the colonial press published Avellaneda within paratextual critiques that frame and reinforce the Spanish *status quo*.

This study teaches us that the reproduction of Avellaneda's writing often meant the dispossession of her corpus and corpse. Her diverse newspaper production reveals the intimate relationship between politics and culture in the Hispanophone Caribbean, how a place's literary production and what it reveals about that place's culture is a political act shaped and reshaped by artists and the editors and publishers that make their work available to readers. Avellaneda, thus, was never just simply a poet but a shaper of the always already political culture of the Hispanophone world.

Works Cited

Bonifacio, Ayendy. "'Se habla Español': Hispanophone-Merchant Advertisements in José Ferrer de Couto's *El Cronista* (1878)." *American Periodicals: A Journal of History & Criticism* vol. 30, no. 2, 2020, pp. 118-121.

Bravo-Villasante, Carmen. *Una vida romántica: la Avellaneda.* Instituto de Cooperación Iberoamericana, Ediciones Cultura Hispánica, Madrid, 1986.

Brickhouse, Anna, *Transamerican Literary Relations and the Nineteenth-Century Public Sphere. Cambridge Studies in American Literature and Culture.* Cambridge UP, 2009.

Davies, Catherine. "Founding-Fathers and Domestic Genealogies: Situating Gertrudis Gómez de Avellaneda." *Bulletin of Latin American Research* vol. 22, no. 4, 2003, pp. 423–44.

Derrida, Jacques. *Margins of* Philosophy. Translated by Alan Bass, U of Chicago P, 1982.

____. *Positions.* Translated by Alan Bass, U of Chicago P, 1972.

La Gaceta de Puerto Rico. Chronicling America Database, Library of Congress,

Mignolo, Walter. *The Darker Side of Western Modernity: Global Futures, Decolonial Options.* Duke UP, 2011.

Miller, Beth. "Gertrude the Great: Avellaneda, Nineteenth-Century Feminist." *Women in Hispanic Literature: Icons and Fallen Idols*, U of California P, 1982.

Pedreira S., Antonio. *El periodismo en Puerto Rico. Bosquejo histórico desde su iniciación hasta el 1936.* Monografías de la Universidad de Puerto Rico, tomo 1. serie A. Núm. 3.

Ramírez, Dixa. *Colonial Phantoms: Belonging and Refusal in the Dominican Americas, from the 19th Century to the Present.* New York UP, 2018.

Silva Gruesz, Kirsten. *Ambassadors of Culture: The TransAmerica Origins of Latino Writing.* Princeton UP, 2002.

Entre la plancha y la página: Early Twentieth-Century Mexicana Food Work and the Spanish-Language Press in Two Texas Cities

MONICA PERALES
University of Houston

In July 1936, *El Continental*, the Spanish-language daily newspaper in El Paso, Texas, ran an article with the provocative title, "The Matrimonial Career Isn't as Easy as it Used to Be." Written by the feminist Spanish journalist Teresa de Escoriaza, the article critiqued the complex gendered domestic labor that fell on the shoulders of Mexican women of the middle class.[1] Asserting a lack of preparation for marriage among the women of the modern generation, Escoriaza laid out the multitude of spoken and unspoken demands facing homemakers. "The modern wife, for as modern as she may be, learns very quickly that to run a household and make a husband happy requires baggage other than an electric stove, a can opener, and a cocktail shaker," she wrote. "Because the happiness of a marriage depends, one must not forget, as much on the woman's knowing how to prepare a stew as on the husband's ability to provide the essential ingredients" (Escoriaza 2). On its surface, the article presented household duties that were presumed to ensure marital harmony. More subtly, the article highlighted the complicated set of cultural pressures centered on domestic labor that women confronted daily, ideas that appeared regularly in the Buzón feminino section of

El Continental. Keeping one's husband "happy" likely involved adhering to rigid patriarchal divisions of labor and maintaining the family's cultural affinity to Mexico, including through one's cooking. It also meant negotiating constant messages about assimilation coming from public schools and popular culture, and becoming consumers of modern technology and household goods like electric stoves, can openers, and cocktail shakers. If the matrimonial career was not easy, Escoriaza warned, it was in part because women's household labor was laden with expectations and carried significant cultural meaning beyond what was cooking on the stove.

Escoriaza's commentary opens a window into the daily challenges Mexicanas faced as they navigated the demands on their food-centered labor inside and outside of the home. This essay examines the multi-faceted cultural meaning of Mexicana food work as presented on the pages of two large Spanish-language newspapers in Texas—*El Continental* (El Paso) and *La Prensa* (San Antonio). The term "food work" in this analysis encompasses both the physical and cultural labor of procuring and producing food inside the home for families—and outside of it for wages. As the opening vignette attests, women's lives were often consumed with the work of food preparation. It defined them as "good" Mexican women and homemakers, and for many, it afforded opportunities to support their families as wage earners. Household tips and recipes, product advertising, and employment ads reveal the pressures Mexicanas faced in early twentieth century Texas cities, as they tried to live up to middle class expectations of female domesticity and cultural integrity. This goal often conflicted with the lived reality of most of the working-class Mexicanos, who were developing new, increasingly US focused ties and cultural allegiances. As literary scholar Catalina Castillón argues, articles relaying recipes and domestic advice in Spanish-language newspapers illuminate the "interests, intentions, and expectations" of the women writers and readers, serving as spaces wherein women could "exchange concerns, counseling, and other ideas" that sometimes challenged rigid gender expectations (260). Building on her study, this article analyzes how domestic advice and advertising reveal changing class and cultural identities in El Paso and San Antonio, and how Mexicanas attempted to navigate the expectations of their labor, while asserting their own preferences through the recipes they perused, the foods and products they purchased, and the jobs they accepted (or rejected). Reading against the grain suggests Mexicanas' adaptability in the face of daily economic hardship, and how they were active agents in providing for their families' emotional, nutritional, and economic needs.

The View from El Continental and La Prensa

At the turn of the twentieth century, El Paso and San Antonio were vibrant southwestern urban centers, home to long-standing Mexican communities that pre-dated Anglo settlement in the nineteenth century.[2] Their populations grew exponentially with large waves of migration precipitated by the Mexican Revolution. With diverse economies rooted in industry, manufacturing, agriculture, food processing, and tourism, El Paso and San Antonio became attractive destinations for Mexican migrants of all classes. Wealthy exiles opposing revolutionary politics and displaced laborers seeking economic stability found refuge and navigated growing (and largely segregated) cities where social class and race determined access and opportunity. By 1920, San Antonio and El Paso had the largest Mexican populations in the United States, and El Paso was the only US city with a Mexican majority population (M. García, *Desert Immigrants* 36). They were dynamic communities in flux, a mix of longtime residents and recent arrivals, of laborers and a notable class of merchants and professionals. As varied as these communities were, they shared a common need for information — news about home, about where to find employment and goods, and stories that reinforced a sense of individual and collective identity in an ever-changing environment.

The Spanish language daily fulfilled this need. According to Nicolás Kanellos, these newspapers served a vital leadership role in Latinx communities, promoting a sense of cohesion and protection of rights, acting as "purveyors of education, culture and entertainment," and appealing to a wide array of political, cultural, and ideological interests. (Kanellos and Martell 7). *La Prensa* and *El Continental* originated in the tradition of the immigrant press and evolved into large metropolitan newspapers for a wide Spanish-speaking readership. Founded in 1913 by Mexican businessman Ignacio E. Lozano, *La Prensa* represented the conservative world-view of the Mexican exile elite. Directing its focus to the *México de afuera*, *La Prensa*'s content emphasized the preservation of the Spanish language, Mexican cultural integrity, and Catholicism with the hope of an eventual return to Mexico. Less is known about *El Continental*'s origins, but we know it grew from El Paso's dynamic Hispanic publishing environment. Beginning in 1926, *El Continental* was published daily (except Saturdays), its masthead declaring it the "independent afternoon newspaper for Mexicans." World-News Publications acquired it at some point, which gave it national distribution and reach. By the mid-1930s, *El Continental*'s publisher/ manager was a Jewish businessman named Morris J. Boretz (Howells and Dearman 240). While much research remains to be done on the history of *El Continental*, it seems that like *La Prensa*, the newspaper was well on its way to being a prominent metropolitan daily and community institution.[3]

Both newspapers' readership extended beyond the small, educated urban middle class, providing us a glimpse into the changing demographics and sensibilities in these cities. While *El Continental*'s circulation numbers are hard to determine, in the 1930s, *La Prensa's* daily circulation was more than 22,000 (Rivas-Rodriguez 76). Both had vast subscription networks throughout the United States, Mexico, and Latin America. Many more copies traveled across the country and internationally through formal and informal networks (Morales 63). Nationalist and class-centered sentiments undergirded much of the newspapers' content, yet publishers of *La Prensa* and *El Continental* increasingly included content aimed at a diverse audience that included working-class migrants and long-time residents developing identities connected to their lives in the United States (Treviño 468-70; Morales 60-8). *La Prensa* offered daily coverage of local stories providing readers important information about their immediate surroundings, even as it continued to reinforce Mexican culture and identification (Morales

66). It was not uncommon to find bilingual advertising and stories about the Fourth of July in the pages of the Spanish metro dailies, a sign of what historian Roberto Treviño calls the "persistent undercurrent of biculturalism" among Tejanos (460). Despite limited educational opportunities in Texas, working-class readers enthusiastically consumed *La Prensa* and *El Continental*. Escuelitas run by educated Mexicanos—some in collaboration with newspapers and the Consulates—promoted Spanish literacy and cultivated an appreciation of Mexican history and culture by sharing stories from *La Prensa* with their students (Morales 63).[4] Those who could not read could still access newspaper content. Literate workers read them aloud to their compatriots in railroad camps, a practice that was common in homes and barrios in both cities (Morales 63). In this way, newspapers crossed class-based boundaries and informally educated workers even as they promoted class distinctions in their content.

Household Tips and Recipes

Mexicana readers of *La Prensa* and *El Continental* encountered the tension between idealized Mexican middle-class domesticity and the demands of their daily lives in articles sharing household advice and recipes. Appearing mostly on pages dedicated to "women's interests," this content forced readers to balance the newspapers' nationalist imperatives with their families' changing tastes. According to historian Nancy Aguirre, middle-class Mexican women—including professional journalists—promoted a "Porfirista femininity" that reinforced the patriarchal family structure and asserted the power of women within the domestic realm to mold the meanings of *mexicanidad* in Mexico and in diaspora (150). Spanish-language cronistas further encouraged conformity to such norms by criticizing and ridiculing women's dress, behavior, and even food choices as examples of declining morality and increased assimilation into US culture.[5] *La Prensa*'s and *El Continental*'s women's pages sometimes fell in line with this view. *La Prensa*'s "Página para el hogar"—including the "La buena cocina" and "Para las amas de casa" columns—first appeared in 1918, and was edited by Beatriz

Blanco, a professional journalist and member of San Antonio's Mexican society (Aguirre 150-1). El Paso's *El Continental* had a regular "Sociales y página femenina" section, edited from at least the mid-1930s by Elena Gutierrez M., which featured the "Buzón femenino" and "Para el ama de casa" columns. These articles contained useful information, but the content was intended to influence the terms of Mexicanas' cooking and eating habits, their spending power, and their labor inside and outside the home from a middle-class perspective. What to eat, when and how to eat, and who prepared the food were important factors Mexicanas considered as they browsed the women's pages. In practice, Mexicanas probably also maneuvered prescriptive messages and claimed their kitchens, tables, and labor as sites of empowerment, creativity, and self-expression (Abarca 18-49; 78-108). A closer reading of this food-related content opens new possibilities for understanding complex racial, gender, and class hierarchies, how power relations between and within groups are defined, and how women crafted multilayered social identities in discrete spaces and regions.[6]

Pressures to conform to middle-class domestic ideals came from many directions. Articles on household tips and recipes also reflected the application of scientific methods to the domestic sphere promoted by Progressive Era reformers. Tips on proper cleaning affirmed the belief that good housekeeping was the marker of good women, wives, and mothers. Middle-class women reformers in the United States and Mexico campaigned to make "good mothers" of women of all classes, but especially those who were impoverished, non-white or immigrant, and Indigenous.[7] This scientific approach applied to advice on the maintenance of domestic space and kitchen tools, similar to that found in US women's magazines like *Ladies' Home Journal* (Scanlon 50). Household tips rarely credited authorship leaving us to wonder about the source of the household wisdom, but the advice was both practical and useful. The *El Continental* column "Para el ama de casa" instructed women on meticulously cleaning the home, removing grease stains from wallpaper, cleaning spots from drinking glasses, and eliminating food residue from casserole dishes (October 22, 1937; June 3, 1938;

June 6, 1937). Mexicanas could manage home budgets and prevent waste if they followed the tips for keeping eggs fresh, soaked overripe tomatoes to extend their life, and used cold water and baking soda to revive wilting vegetables ("Para el ama de casa," October 15, 1937; September 19, 1937; July 18, 1937). Consumed by middle-class and working-class Mexicanas, the messages operated on multiple levels. Editors reinforced the connection between good housekeeping and proper middle-class gender roles. Working-class readers may have learned tips they could use as wage-earning domestic workers. Readers of both classes surely discovered ways to make their household duties easier, but they also bore the added burden of negotiating class-centered demands on their labor embedded in the articles.

Although in its early years *La Prensa* embraced a Mexico-facing orientation, advice columns also presented more complex food advice and competing interests that Mexicanas had to navigate. In the spring of 1917, *La Prensa* published several articles by the USDA Office of Information that offered suggestions for tasty, nutritious, and easy family meals ("Buenas combinaciones de alimentos" 1). Emphasizing economically priced ingredients, cleanliness of cooking spaces, ease of preparation, and avoidance of waste, the USDA articles provided guidance to women in managing their homes. The articles must be read in the context of the creation of the Extension Service that offered courses on food preservation and conservation to rural families, the development of USDA nutritional guidelines, and World War I food rationing.[8] On the pages of *La Prensa*, these articles added to women's food work by introducing the expectations of a US governmental agency that sought to dictate what foods should be eaten and in what manner in support of the war effort. The USDA recommended women keep staples like pastas, breads, vegetables, and fruit on hand, and suggested economizing by using proteins like leftover meat, canned fish, and beans ("Buenas combinaciones de alimentos" 1). Another lengthy article detailed the nutritional and economical qualities of soups, and offered recipes for multiple varieties ("Como se prepapran las sopas alimenticias" 1). More than providing simple messages requiring culinary Americanization, the

USDA content offered an alternative way of eating from the perspective of a US (not Mexican) agency, even as the newspaper asserted continued identification with Mexico. We cannot know the factors behind the editorial decision to include the USDA's recommendations, or if Mexicanas followed the advice to alter their cooking habits. But by offering suggestions or specific prescriptions on the kinds of foods deemed "healthy" by government agencies and editors, these articles likely influenced what American and Mexican families should eat and reinforced women's central role in making daily food related decisions.

Recipes provide another glimpse into Mexicanas' complex daily food choices. Recipes in the women's sections of the newspapers rarely credited authorship, leaving few clues as to who created them. It is likely women writers played some role. Kimberly Wilmot Voss notes that food sections in large city newspapers defined and reflected a community's engagement with the food around them, and women were essential in developing food-related content that appealed to the "average home cooks in their community" (Voss 16). It is possible that staffers at *El Continental* and *La Prensa* were responsible for writing recipes or copying them from other publications. Maybe some came from community cookbooks, historically written collectively by women in religious and civic organizations to raise funds for charitable causes (Longone *par*. 19; Stoller-Conrad *par*. 4-6). Regardless of their sometimes-obscure origins, these recipes made their way to the page and spoke to the social and cultural meaning of food, that is, what certain foods meant to the people who ate them.

Many of the recipes in *La Prensa* and *El Continental* make no overt reference to ethnic or national cuisines, even in the earliest years of publication. This can be attributed to several factors. Food historian Jeffrey Pilcher explains that Mexico's attempts at defining what we recognize today as a national cuisine took a circuitous path in the nineteenth and twentieth centuries, moving from the haute European cuisine favored by the Porfirian elite, to the post-revolutionary subordination of corn in favor of wheat, to the acceptance of Indigenous foods as part of the national identity. In his study of Mexican foodways in El Paso, Juan Manuel Mendoza

Guerrero confirms that none of the newspapers in that city published recipes for Mexican foods, opting instead for Europeanized dishes intended to "civilize" the readers' palates (Mendoza Guerrero 242). For all of the emphasis on Mexican cultural identity and allegiance in other sections of the newspapers, recipes contained multiple messages. *La Prensa*'s 1915 recipe for "Pudding Graham"—a cake with apples and raisins—intriguingly had a name that appeared in English and also made reference to the addition of "baking powder" (in English and with quotation marks) (Fig. 1).

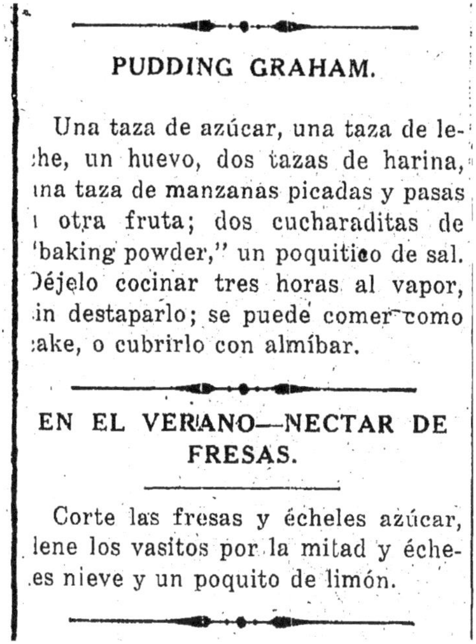

PUDDING GRAHAM.

Una taza de azúcar, una taza de le-
;he, un huevo, dos tazas de harina,
ına taza de manzanas picadas y pasas
ı otra fruta; dos cucharaditas de
'baking powder," un poquitıo de sal.
)éjelo cocinar tres horas al vapor,
ın destaparlo; se puede comer como
:ake, o cubrirlo con almíbar.

EN EL VERANO—NECTAR DE FRESAS.

Corte las fresas y écheles azúcar,
lene los vasitos por la mitad y éche-
.es nieve y un poquito de limón.

Fig. 1 Recipes, *La Prensa,* August 2, 1915.

These snippets of English catch the eye of a modern reader, and may have done the same for a Mexicana scanning the page in 1915. "Recetas para hacer panes con harina de maíz," published July 21, 1918, stressed frugality and home economy. Here, too, polvo de levadura is consistently translated into "baking powder" within the recipes, and one—semola de harina de maíz—is translated into "cornmeal grits" (8). The bilingual recipes suggest that as early as the 1910s, accommodation was taking place at the table. The corn flour recipes also reflected Texas' diverse history and Southern roots, fueling debates in Mexico and the United States about the nutritional and cultural superiority of wheat flour over corn (Pilcher 77-97; Engelhardt 51-82). Southern staples may also have given working-class Mexicanas the skills necessary to make these preferred items in the home of a potential employer.

Other recipes with pricier ingredients and fashionable preparations reflected the middle-class taste for haute cuisine as well as the legacy of the Porfirian-era cultural project in Mexico connecting European-style foods to modernization (Pilcher 77-97). "Recetas de cocina selecta" included several un-credited recipes for dishes with elegant names (7). Recipes for liver a la Cubana, rice *a la andaluza*, *bacalao a la vizcaína*, and leg of lamb Provençal referred to Latin American, Spanish, and French cuisines, evoking a refined dining experience. Perhaps writers assumed these cuisines were superior to the Mexican-American or "Tex-Mex" fare favored by the working classes. In a similar way, recipes from El Paso's *El Continental* in the 1930s that required ingredients like lobster or salmon carried cachet but would have been difficult to prepare on a worker's budget, especially during the Great Depression ("Para el ama de casa" August 4, 1938; Jul 24, 1938; September 25, 1938). Their presence on a middle-class table might have been a mark of distinction, and a woman's ability to prepare an elegant and expensive seafood meal with imported ingredients—in her own home or an employer's— could have been a way to distinguish her cooking skills.

Product Advertisements

Advertisements for consumer products entwined food work with consumer habits and also illuminated the pressures Mexicanas faced as they balanced competing messages about how to dress their homes and feed their families. With the growth of national, mass-produced brands and retailers, and the increased trend of buying-on-credit, the advertising industry exploded into a multimillion-dollar industry (Pope 2-3). Advertising does not just sell products, but also ideas about convenience and modernity.[9] In Porfirian Mexico, for instance, advertisements for foreign products represented a way for middle-class women to contribute to the making of a more modern nation through their spending (Sanders 2). Advertising in *El Continental* and *La Prensa* promoted Mexican businesses and products, but also featured Anglo-owned stores and American goods, inundating readers with messages that tugged at their loyalties and consumer desires. As historian Vicki Ruiz explains, advertising in Spanish-language newspapers was a critical site where Mexicanas negotiated acculturation and cultural retention through their purchasing power (Ruiz 51-71). Advertisements for foods, products, and services not only promised convenience for the busy homemaker, they reflected the social meaning embedded in those products that gave shoppers a way of asserting class and Mexican and American cultural identities. Sorting through those meanings added to Mexicanas' food work.

As early as the 1910s, advertisements for local Anglo-owned stores offered a wide selection of items for kitchens, encouraging women to embrace modern technologies and dress their kitchens with the latest appliances and gadgets. King's Furniture Company in San Antonio advertised $20 used stoves (accessible on modest budgets) and cabinet pieces that could be purchased on credit ("King Furniture Company"). The ad featured a woman in an apron standing before a furniture piece with space to hold all her essential kitchen tools (Fig. 2). King's ad fueled further consumer desires. The well-dressed kitchen pictured in the advertisement had cabinets filled with pots, pans, dishes, and other utensils. These could be purchased at Hull Brothers Company Household Department Store, or Newton, Weller & Wagner, Company, which carried an array of casserole sets, glassware and crystal, cutlery, and aluminum pots and pans (Hull Brothers; Newton, Weller & Wagner). Specialty items like nickel-plated vessels for cooking eggs or casseroles made of "the best quality of metal for cooking" may have appealed to the woman looking to have a truly fashionable kitchen (Newton Weller & Wagner). In addition to giving readers a glimpse into how "American" kitchens were furnished, the ads for Anglo-operated stores introduced shoppers to retail options beyond the world of Mexican-owned retailers.

Food advertising compelled Mexicanas to filter through many ethnic and national identities on their tables. Buying US-based

Fig. 2. "King Furniture Company, advertisement." *La Prensa,* September 15, 1915.

brands presented Mexicanas with options that allowed them to express more Americanized identities through their food selections, and recipes in the ads made it easy for women to incorporate new dishes into their repertoire. Some ads overtly presented American traditions and foods, forcing Mexicanas to confront ideas about food and ethnicity head-on. An ad for Hubig's baked goods exemplifies this complex cultural work (Fig. 3).

The ad, in English, offered "pumpkin pies for Thanksgiving Day—Old Mammy Lou's Creole recipe" (Hubig's). The remainder of the ad, in Spanish, extolled the virtues of the Louisiana-style pumpkin pie—"a delight for both the palate and the eye." Bilingual ads for American companies and products were not uncommon in *La Prensa*, but this ad stands out for its multiple layers of messaging. Of course, Hubig's main objective was to sell pies. But this ad also promoted acculturation among readers by encouraging them to partake of food associated with an American holiday. As food historian Andrew F. Smith explains, national Thanksgiving celebrations

Fig. 3 "Hubig's Pies, advertisement." *La Prensa,* November 21, 1924.

emerged in the nineteenth century and became a vehicle for Americanizing the large wave of immigrants arriving in US cities. By participating in Thanksgiving celebrations, immigrants "demonstrated their loyalty to their adopted country, and their belief in American abundance" (64). The ad also perpetuated racial tropes of African American women as "mammies," offering Mexican readers lessons in American racism. Read in conjunction with stories on nutrition by the USDA and other state agencies, the Hubig's ad suggests that being "American" had specific culinary characteristics, including partaking in national holidays and racist stereotypes. These ideas increasingly found their way onto the pages of newspapers that simultaneously asserted women's duty to maintain the Mexican cultural identity of her family. It was up to Mexicanas to filter through these messages and decide what made sense for their families.

To assume that this was the only perspective—transforming Mexican families into American ones one meal at a time—would be a mistake. Some ads did carry coded language that proposed a static "American" way of eating and being. Running this ad in *La Prensa* was not necessarily an endorsement of the ideas embedded in it. It did, however, make such ideas more accessible, offering readers a different way of partaking in new foods and expressing evolving tastes and identities. The newspapers also consistently ran advertising that promoted Mexican cultural integrity through food. Stores like Domingo Fernandez in San Antonio knew that there were some American ingredients that Mexicana customers wanted, like Karo Syrup for hotcakes and Mazola corn oil (Fig. 4).

But those customers might also want a *molino para nixtamal*, a *máquina para tortillas*, or a *molcajete de piedra* for making Mexican

Fig. 4. "Domingo Fernandez, advertisement." *La Prensa*, November 27, 1919.

foods as well ("Domingo Fernandez"). At Domingo Fernandez, Mexicanas could also find medicinal herbs, Mexican brands of chocolate, pastries, chiles, and other specialty items. The classified section advertised Mexican food items like specialty chocolates, sweet bread, chiles, caramels, cinnamon, tortillas, and sausages ("Ventas," September 26, 1920; February 5, 1921; December 30, 1928; June 25, 1928). These advertisements reflect stores' marketing strategies, but they also provide important clues as to what people wanted to buy and cook, and how tastes and identities were negotiated on the page and at the dinner table.

Employment Advertisements

Employment notices directly linked women and food work, highlighting the pressures they faced to provide for their families while managing the expectations of idealized middle-class domesticity. The labor that women performed outside their homes was often an extension of the domestic work they performed inside it. Contractors in both cities recruited women to work in industries including food processing, laundries, garment work, and manufacturing. Additionally, vocational schools, such as the Smelter Vocational School in El Paso, trained women in cooking, cleaning, and childcare and opened doors to domestic labor in the homes of plant supervisors and other wealthy El Pasoans (Perales, *Smeltertown* 144-5; 205-9). One of the most common recruiting tools was, in fact, the classified section in Spanish- and English-language newspapers. Historian Mario T. García found ads from companies in search of Mexicanas to work in the city's manufacturing and garment firms (García, "The Chicana" 328). San Antonio's *La Prensa* consistently ran a page dedicated to job listings that included regular solicitations for women to engage in some form of food work outside the home. Some asked for women to work as cooks in private homes. Other forms of food work available to Mexicanas included shelling pecans, making tamales, delivering sandwiches and sodas, and working at fruit stands. One unique opportunity in 1928 called for one hundred young women to sell pecan candies and nuts during the American Legion Convention ("Empleos" October 6, 1928).

Employment ads were written from a middle-class worldview. While the household tips, recipes, and product advertising may have afforded Mexicanas the possibility of accessing a measure of middle-class domesticity, job ads for domestic workers and cooks reinforced class boundaries. Historian Pablo Mitchell has argued that the language and content in the local press defined people's places in social and racial hierarchies (Mitchell 149-73). Potential employers drew upon stereotypes and preferred characteristics that asserted working-class Mexicanas' place as low-wage domestic laborers and occupants of a lower racial and social position. The language of age and marital status presented the domestic worker as one detached from her *own* food work to maintain a romanticized domestic space in someone else's kitchen. There was often a noted preference for a young, single *muchacha,* or *señora* or *mujer* of a certain age. The August 20, 1921, edition of *La Prensa*, contained several ads for housekeepers and family cooks that specified age — one for a "girl of 15 to 16 years of age who speaks English for housework," another for a "*señorita* of medium age to cook" ("Empleos" August 20, 1921). A *muchacha* might be presumed to be more trainable, more likely to speak English, and less likely to have children of her own. On the other hand, an older *señora* would possess experience and may not have small children needing her attention at home. In either case, a working Mexicana's ability to meet the expectations of wage work made it harder for her to live up to that domestic ideal in her own family.

Preferences regarding skills and personal characteristics further reflected changing cultural identities among working Mexicanas as well as class tensions. Ads requiring English language proficiency, the ability to cook "*a la americana,*" or for work in an "American" home ("Empleos" May 5, 1925; March 13, 1926; July 26, 1930; October 7, 1928) shared space with ads for cooks with knowledge of Mexican cuisine and the occasional work in a Mexican home ("Empleos" February 26, 1925; October 14, 1928). This combination hints at the ways working Mexicanas navigated multiple cultural worlds and negotiated their labor in American and Mexican contexts. Other desired qualities blurred the line between necessary skills and moral character that speak directly to racial and class tensions. Multiple references to women who were "clean," "neat," "decent," "honorable," "serious," "educated," and "stable" appear throughout the employment section ("Empleos" September 24, 1924; February 5, 1921; October 17, 1928; August 26, 1942; August 17, 1938; October 20, 1924; February 1, 1925; July 6, 1921). While it would stand to reason that someone hired to keep house and cook should be neat and reliable, when read in the context of Texas' racial and social structure in the early twentieth century and *La Prensa*'s middle-class politics as a whole, these terms carry a different meaning. Whether coming from an Anglo or Mexican employer, such words encoded racial and class-based presumptions about working-class Mexicanas who might fill those jobs and about the larger Mexican population. To seek out a "clean" or "decent" Mexican woman to work one's home suggested that the successful candidate was an exception to the rule, particularly when the stereotype of the so-called dirty Mexican was pervasive in many Southwestern cities. Such language also fed into stereotypes about Mexicanas' sexual behavior, evidenced in terms like "honorable" and "decent."[10]

While the classifieds say a lot about what employers expected of Mexicanas' food work and moral character, we can also read something about women's desires and the choices made when securing wage work to support themselves and their families. A close analysis of feminist Spanish-language newspapers might yield an entirely different perspective on women's food work and readers' responses to it; this is the focus of ongoing research. In *La Prensa* and *El Continental*, Mexicana voices are fragmented but perceptible. Advertisements for Mexican food items like tortillas, breads, and specialty ingredients shared column space with employment ads. Mexicanas might consider applying for a job requiring them to cook "a la americana," and also use their earnings to purchase the Mexican food items they or their families might prefer. Advertisements crafted the "ideal" worker to fit employers' needs and prejudices, but these jobs were filled (or rejected) by women who made choices based on their family's own needs. There is no way of knowing which ads were filled, by whom, and for how long, but their wording suggests what might have made one job more or less attractive to a potential candidate. Several indicated the job required cooking "for a small family" or for a couple with no children ("Empleos" January 11, 1925; May 28, 1942). Perhaps having fewer people to cook for was more appealing? Maybe cooking for a small Mexican family of three was more enticing than cooking for an Anglo family, whatever the size ("Empleos" August 14, 1921). The fact that several ads for housekeeping positions explicitly noted no cooking responsibilities (or cooking jobs that required no cleaning) might suggest that certain kinds of duties would have been more attractive to potential employees ("Empleos" June 5, 1916; November 2, 1924; January 6, 1926; March 21, 1926; January 30, 1927; December 31, 1943). Even within a limited range of choices, Mexicanas held a small measure of control over their labor and their hard-earned dollars.

Conclusion

Household advice, recipes, and product and employment advertising in *La Prensa* and *El Continental* offer insight into the history of Mexican women's complex and multi-layered food work in two rapidly changing borderlands cities. Both newspapers played a key role in defining and promoting cultural and class-based expectations related to women's food work that reflected and influenced broader societal views. Women of all classes negotiated the demands to conform to the idealized domestic space embraced by the Mexican middle class, while at the same time managing the pressures (or the allure) of American consumer culture, the educational system, and their own tastes. Articles with household and cooking tips and advertising did more than simply direct readers on what to eat, when, and in what manner, or where to give their dollars and labor. This rich and multilayered set of sources illuminates the rocky terrain of class and racial tensions at work in Southwestern cities that Mexicanas confronted daily. Household advice held out the idealized kitchen and table that preserved Mexican identity, but sometimes that table may have included USDA recommended soups or a Thanksgiving pie. Advertisements for consumer goods similarly presented women with ideas about what modern kitchens should contain and what should be cooked in them, even as Mexican housewives negotiated their own family budgets and shifting tastes, perhaps drawing them into Anglo-owned stores outside the boundaries of their segregated communities. The employment ads played on popular prejudices and prevailing attitudes to control and exploit Mexican women's food work, but Mexicanas likely made choices that aligned with their own needs and exerted a measure of control over their labor. Sorting through the cacophony of expectations and balancing the weight of gender and cultural demands, Mexicanas engaged in the hard food work that was essential to their family's survival.

Works Cited

Primary Sources

de Escoriaza, Teresa. "La Carrera Matrimonial ya no es tan Facil Como Antes." *El Continental* [El Paso, TX], 1 July 1936, p. 2. Readex: America's Historical Newspapers, Hispanic American Newspapers (1808-1980).

Departamento de Agricultura de los Estados Unidos, Oficina de Información. "Buenas combinaciones de alimentos en el hogar." *La Prensa* [San Antonio, TX], 29 Apr. 1917, p. 1. Readex: America's Historical Newspapers, Hispanic American Newspapers (1808-1980).

Departamento de Agricultura de los Estados Unidos, Oficina de Información. "Como se preparan las sopas alimenticias." *La Prensa* [San Antonio, TX], 12 May 1917, p. 1. Readex: America's Historical Newspapers, Hispanic American Newspapers (1808-1980).

"Domingo Fernandez, advertisement." *La Prensa* [San Antonio, TX] 27 Nov. 1919, p. 6. Readex: America's Historical Newspapers, Hispanic American Newspapers (1808-1980).

"Empleos." La Prensa [San Antonio, TX] 5 June 1916, p. 5. Readex: America's Historical Newspapers, Hispanic American Newspapers (1808-1980).

_____. *La Prensa* [San Antonio, TX] 5 Feb. 1921, p. 7. Readex: America's Historical Newspapers, Hispanic American Newspapers (1808-1980).

_____. *La Prensa* [San Antonio, TX] 6 July 1921, p. 7. Readex: America's Historical Newspapers, Hispanic American Newspapers (1808-1980).

_____. *La Prensa* [San Antonio, TX] 14 Aug. 1921, p. 8. Readex: America's Historical Newspapers, Hispanic American Newspapers (1808-1980).

———. *La Prensa* [San Antonio, TX] 20 Aug. 1921, p. 9. Readex: America's Historical Newspapers, Hispanic American Newspapers (1808-1980).

———. *La Prensa* [San Antonio, TX] 24 Sept. 1924, p. 8. Readex: America's Historical Newspapers, Hispanic American Newspapers (1808-1980).

———. *La Prensa* [San Antonio, TX] 20 Oct. 1924, p. 7. Readex: America's Historical Newspapers, Hispanic American Newspapers (1808-1980).

———. *La Prensa* [San Antonio, TX] 2 Nov. 1924, p. 7. Readex: America's Historical Newspapers, Hispanic American Newspapers (1808-1980).

———. *La Prensa* [San Antonio, TX] 11 Jan. 1925, p. 7. Readex: America's Historical Newspapers, Hispanic American Newspapers (1808-1980).

———. *La Prensa* [San Antonio, TX] 1 Feb. 1925, p. 6. Readex: America's Historical Newspapers, Hispanic American Newspapers (1808-1980).

———. *La Prensa* [San Antonio, TX] 26 Feb. 1925, p. 10. Readex: America's Historical Newspapers, Hispanic American Newspapers (1808-1980).

———. *La Prensa* [San Antonio, TX] 5 May 1925, p. 11. Readex: America's Historical Newspapers, Hispanic American Newspapers (1808-1980).

———. *La Prensa* [San Antonio, TX] 6 Jan. 1926, p. 9. Readex: America's Historical Newspapers, Hispanic American Newspapers (1808-1980).

———. *La Prensa* [San Antonio, TX] 13 Mar. 1926, p. 9. Readex: America's Historical Newspapers, Hispanic American Newspapers (1808-1980).

———. *La Prensa* [San Antonio, TX] 21 Mar. 1926, p. 7. Readex: America's Historical Newspapers, Hispanic American Newspapers (1808-1980).

———. *La Prensa* [San Antonio, TX] 30 Jan. 1927, p. 7. Readex: America's Historical Newspapers, Hispanic American Newspapers (1808-1980).

____. *La Prensa* [San Antonio, TX] 17 Aug. 1928, p. 9. Readex: America's Historical Newspapers, Hispanic American News-papers (1808-1980).

____. *La Prensa* [San Antonio, TX] 7 Oct. 1928, p.11. Readex: America's Historical Newspapers, Hispanic American News-papers (1808-1980).

____. *La Prensa* [San Antonio, TX] 14 Oct. 1928, p. 11. Readex: America's Historical Newspapers, Hispanic American News-papers (1808-1980).

____. *La Prensa* [San Antonio, TX] 17 Oct. 1928, p. 9. Readex: America's Historical Newspapers, Hispanic American News-papers (1808-1980).

____. La Prensa [San Antonio, TX] 6 Oct. 1929, p. 9. Readex: America's Historical Newspapers, Hispanic American News-papers (1808-1980).

____. *La Prensa* [San Antonio, TX] 26 July 1930, p. 9. Readex: America's Historical Newspapers, Hispanic American News-papers (1808-1980).

____. *La Prensa* [San Antonio, TX] 20 May 1934, p. 6. Readex: America's Historical Newspapers, Hispanic American News-papers (1808-1980).

____. *La Prensa* [San Antonio, TX] 17 Aug. 1938, p. 6. Readex: America's Historical Newspapers, Hispanic American News-papers (1808-1980).

____. *La Prensa* [San Antonio, TX] 28 May 1942, p. 6. Readex: America's Historical Newspapers, Hispanic American News-papers (1808-1980).

____. *La Prensa* [San Antonio, TX] 26 Aug. 1942, p. 6. Readex: America's Historical Newspapers, Hispanic American News-papers (1808-1980).

____. *La Prensa* [San Antonio, TX] 31 Dec. 1943, p. 7. Readex: America's Historical Newspapers, Hispanic American Newspapers (1808-1980).

Howells, John and Marion Dearman. *Tramp Printers: Adventures and Forgotten Paths Once Traced by Wandering Artisans of Newspapering and Typography*. Discovery P, 2003.

"Hubig's Pies, advertisement." *La Prensa* [San Antonio, TX] 21 Nov. 1924, p. 4. Readex: America's Historical Newspapers, Hispanic American Newspapers (1808-1980).

"Hull Brothers Co., advertisement." *La Prensa* [San Antonio, TX] 4 Nov. 1919, p. 8. Readex: America's Historical Newspapers, Hispanic American Newspapers (1808-1980).

"King Furniture Company, advertisement." *La Prensa* [San Antonio, TX] 15 Sept. 1915, p. 3. Readex: America's Historical Newspapers, Hispanic American Newspapers (1808-1980).

"Newton, Weller & Wagner Co., advertisement." *La Prensa* [San Antonio, TX] 25 Jan. 1920, p. 3. Readex: America's Historical Newspapers, Hispanic American Newspapers (1808-1980).

"Para el ama de casa." *El Continental* [El Paso, TX], 22 Nov. 1936, p. 7. Readex: America's Historical Newspapers, Hispanic American Newspapers (1808-1980).

____. *El Continental* [El Paso, TX], 6 June 1937, p. 7. Readex: America's Historical Newspapers, Hispanic American Newspapers (1808-1980).

____. *El Continental* [El Paso, TX], 19 Sept. 1937, p. 8. Readex: America's Historical Newspapers, Hispanic American Newspapers (1808-1980).

____. *El Continental* [El Paso, TX], 15 Oct. 1937, p. 6. Readex: America's Historical Newspapers, Hispanic American Newspapers (1808-1980).

____. *El Continental* [El Paso, TX], 22 Oct. 1937, p. 4. Readex: America's Historical Newspapers, Hispanic American Newspapers (1808-1980).

____. *El Continental* [El Paso, TX], 3 June 1938, p. 5. Readex: America's Historical Newspapers, Hispanic American Newspapers (1808-1980).

____. *El Continental* [El Paso, TX], 24 July 1938, p. 6. Readex: America's Historical Newspapers, Hispanic American Newspapers (1808-1980).

____. *El Continental* [El Paso, TX], 4 Aug. 1938, p. 3. Readex: America's Historical Newspapers, Hispanic American Newspapers (1808-1980).

____. *El Continental* [El Paso, TX], 25 Sept. 1938, p. 7. Readex: America's Historical Newspapers, Hispanic American Newspapers (1808-1980).

"Pudding Graham." *La Prensa* [San Antonio, TX], 2 Aug. 1916, p. 6. Readex: America's Historical Newspapers, Hispanic American Newspapers (1808-1980).

"Recetas de cocina selecta." *La Prensa* [San Antonio, TX], 28 Mar. 1931, p. 7. Readex: America's Historical Newspapers, Hispanic American Newspapers (1808-1980).

"Recetas para hacer panes con harina de maíz." *La Prensa* [San Antonio, TX], 21 July 1918, p. 8. Readex: America's Historical Newspapers, Hispanic American Newspapers (1808-1980).

"Ventas." *La Prensa* [San Antonio, TX] 26 Sept. 1920, p. 7. Readex: America's Historical Newspapers, Hispanic American Newspapers (1808-1980).

____. *La Prensa* [San Antonio, TX] 5 Feb. 1921, p. 7. Readex: America's Historical Newspapers, Hispanic American Newspapers (1808-1980).

____. *La Prensa* [San Antonio, TX] 25 June 1928, p. 7. Readex: America's Historical Newspapers, Hispanic American Newspapers (1808-1980).

____. *La Prensa* [San Antonio, TX] 30 Dec. 1928, p. 11. Readex: America's Historical Newspapers, Hispanic American Newspapers (1808-1980).

Secondary Sources

Abarca, Meredith. *Voices in the Kitchen: Views of Food and the World from Working-Class Mexican and Mexican American Women*, Texas A&M UP, 2006.

Abarca, Meredith, and Consuelo Carr Salas, *Latin@s' Presence in the Food Industry: Changing How We Think About Food,* U of Arkansas P, 2016.

Aguirre, Nancy. "Porfirista Femininity in Exile: Women's Contributions to San Antonio's La Prensa, 1913–1929." *Women of the*

Right: Comparisons and Interplay Across Borders, edited by
Kathleen M. Blee and Sandra McGee Deutsch, Penn State UP,
2012, 147-62.

Baeza Ventura, Gabriela. "La imagen de la mujer en la crónica del
'México de afuera.'" Ph.D. diss. University of Houston, 2001.

Barragán Goetz, Philis M. *Reading, Writing, and Revolution:
Escuelitas and the Emergence of a Mexican American Identity in
Texas,* U of Texas P, 2020.

Barrera, Magdalena. "Of Chicharrones" and Clam Chowder: Gender
and Consumption in Jorge Ulica's Crónicas Diabólicas." *Bilingual
Review/La Revista Bilingüe*, vol. 29. no. 1 January-April. 2008-
2009. 49-65, JSTOR, stable URL www.jstor.org/stable/257458 85.

Castillón, Catalina. "Domestic Advice and Culinary Articles in
Hispanic Newspapers from the Turn of the Twentieth Century:
Recovering Tradition or Subversion?"*Recovering the U.S.
Hispanic Literary Heritage,* vol. 9, edited by Donna Kabalen de
Bichara and Blanca López de Mariscal. Arte Público P, 2014, 243-
65.

Counihan, Carole. *A Tortilla is Like Life: Food and Culture in the
San Luis Valley of Colorado*, U of Texas P, 2009.

Engelhardt, Elizabeth. *A Mess of Greens: Southern Gender and
Southern Food,* U of Georgia P, 2011.

Ferguson, Kennan. "Intensifying Taste, Intensifying Identity:
Collectivity through Community Cookbooks." *Signs*, vol. 37, no.
3, 2012, pp. 695-717, *JSTOR*, www.jstor.org/stable/10.1086/66
2697.

Feu López, Maria Monserrat. "The U.S. Hispanic Flapper: Pelonas
and Flapperismo in U.S. Spanish-Language Newspapers, 1920-
1929." *Studies in American Humor*, vol.1, no. 2. Special Issues
American Humor Across Media in the 1920s and 1930s, 2015, pp.
192-217. JSTOR, www.jastor.org/stable/10.5325/studamerhu
mor.1.2.0192.

García, Mario T. "The Chicana in American History: The Mexican
Women of El Paso, 1880-1920: A Case Study," *Pacific Historical
Review*, vol. 49, no. 2, May 1980, pp. 315-337.

_____. *Desert Immigrants: The Mexicans of El Paso, 1880-1920*, Yale UP, 1981.

García, Richard T. *Rise of the Mexican American Middle Class: San Antonio 1929-1940*, Texas A&M UP, 1991.

Garza-Falcón, Leticia. *Gente Decente: A Borderlands Response to the Rhetoric of Dominance,* U of Texas P, 1998.

Inness, Sherrie A. *Secret Ingredients: Race, Gender, and Class at the Dinner Table,* Palgrave Macmillan, 2006.

Kanellos, Nicolás and Helvetia Martell. *Hispanic Periodicals in the United States, Origins to 1960: A Brief History and Comprehensive Bibliography*, Arte Público P, 2000.

Longone, Jan. "Feeding America: The Historic American Cookbook Project," Clements Library, University of Michigan, d.legacy.lib.msu.edu/fa/introduction. Accessed 28 July 2021.

Marchand, Roland. *Advertising the American Dream: Making Way for Modernity, 1920-1940*, U of California P, 1985.

Mendoza Guerrero, Juan Manuel. "Mexican Immigrants' Foodways in El Paso, Texas, 1880-1960s: Identity, Nationalism, and Community." Ph.D. Diss, University of Texas at El Paso, 2012.

Mitchell, Pablo. *Coyote Nation: Sexuality, Race, and Conquest in Modernizing New Mexico, 1880-1920.* U of Chicago P, 2005.

Morales, Daniel. "Tejas, Afuera de México: Newspapers, the Mexican Government, Mutualistas, and Migrants in San Antonio 1910-1940. Journal of American Ethnic History, vol. 40. no. 2 Winter 2021, pp. 52-91, JSTOR, www.jstor.org/stable/10.5406/jamerethnhist.40.2.0052.

Muncy, Robyn. *Creating a Female Dominion in American Reform, 1890-1935*. Oxford UP, 1991.

Perales, Monica. "'Who has a greater job than a mother?': Defining Motherhood on the U.S.-Mexico Border in the Early Twentieth Century." *On the Borders of Love and Power: Families and Kinship in the Intercultural American Southwest*, edited by in David Wallace Adams and Crista DeLuzio, U of California P, 2012, 146-163.

_____. *Smeltertown: Making and Remembering a Southwest Border Community.* U of North Carolina P, 2010.

Pilcher, Jeffrey M. *¡Que Vivan Los Tamales!: Food and the Making of Mexican Identity.* U of New Mexico P, 1998.

Pope, Daniel. "Making Sense of Advertisements." *History Matters: The U.S. Survey on the Web*, George Mason University. historymatters.gmu.edu. Accessed 28 July 2021.

Ramos, Raúl A. *Beyond the Alamo: Forging Mexican Ethnicity, 1821-1961.* U of North Carolina P, 2009.

Ruíz, Vicki L. *From Out of the Shadows: Mexican Women in Twentieth Century America.* Oxford UP, 1998.

Rivas-Rodriguez, Maggie. "Ignacio Lozano: The Mexican Exile Publisher Who Conquered San Antonio and Los Angeles." *American Journalism*, vol. 21, no. 1, Winter 2004, pp. 75-89. EBSCOhost, doi: 10.1080/08821127.2004.10677569.

Sánchez, George. "'Go after the women': Americanization and the Mexican Immigrant Woman, 1915-1929." *Unequal Sisters: A Multicultural Reader in U.S. Women's History*, second ed., edited by in Vicki L. Ruíz and Ellen Carol DuBois, Routledge, 1994, 284-97.

Sanders, Nichole. "Gender and Consumption in Porfirian Mexico: Images of Women in Advertising, *El Imparcial*, 1897-1910." *Frontiers: A Journal of Women Studies*, vol. 38. no. 1, 2017, pp. 1-30. JSTOR, www.jstor.org/stable/10.5250/fronjwomestud.38.1.0001.

Scanlon, Jennifer. *Inarticulate Longings: The Ladies' Home Journal, Gender, and the Promises of Consumer Culture*, Routledge, 1995.

Sharpless, Rebecca. *Cooking in other Women's Kitchens: Domestic Workers in the South, 1865-1960.* U of North Carolina P, 2010.

Smith, Andrew. *Eating History: 30 Turning Points in the Making of American Cuisine.* Columbia UP, 2009.

Stern, Alexandra M. "Responsible Mothers and Normal Children: Eugenics, Nationalism, and Welfare in Postrevolutionary Mexico, 1920-1940." *Journal of Historical Sociology*, vol. 12. no. 4, December 1999, pp. 369-97.

Stoller-Conrad, Jessica. "Long Before Social Networking, Community Cookbooks Ruled the Stove." *NPR* 20 July 2012, www.

npr.org/sections/thesalt/2012/07/18/156983942/long-before-social-networking-community-cookbooks-ruled-the-stove. Accessed 26 July 2021.

Treviño, Roberto. "Prensa y patria: The Spanish-Language Press and the Biculturation of the Tejano Middle Class, 1920-1940." *Western Historical Quarterly*, vol. 44. no. 4, November 1991, pp. 451-472, JSTOR, www.jstor.org/stable/970986.

Voss, Kimberly Wilmot. *The Food Section: Newspaper Women and the Culinary Community*, Rowman & Littlefield Publishers, 2014.

Adelina "Nina" Otero-Warren: A Nuevomexicana in Suffrage, Politics, and Letters in the Early Twentieth Century

ANNA M. NOGAR
University of New Mexico

Among early feminist figures in United States history, Nuevomexicana Adelina "Nina" Otero-Warren (1881-1965) stands out. Otero-Warren's advocacy for women's right to vote in New Mexico was highlighted through the 2020 suffrage centenary. It will be recognized throughout the United States via a series of quarters issued by the US Mint recognizing important women in United States history.[1] Otero-Warren was the first Hispana to run for Congress and held significant positions in the New Mexico state government before and after her candidacy. Otero-Warren's civic and literary influence is frequently invoked in scholarship on New Mexico and Nuevomexicano public memory: a state historical marker near her birthplace of Los Lunas, NM, underscores her substantial political legacy, and a mural in downtown Albuquerque illustrates her advocacy for women's suffrage.[2] As an educated, engaged, bilingual Hispana, Otero-Warren experienced New Mexico's transition from nineteenth-century territory to a twentieth-century state firsthand, participating as an activist, political candidate, and author in that extraordinary milieu. Her life and work offer a window into the unique positionality that she—and many

Nuevomexicanos of her era—occupied, even as she negotiated and shifted the parameters of the societies in which she moved. This essay looks beyond the contours of Nina Otero-Warren's biography to reframe the critical narrative of how she was understood in her time through an examination of the periodical and popular cultural production about her. In addition, I rethink her sole book publication, *Old Spain in Our Southwest* (1936) in light of Otero-Warren's career of advocacy for Nuevomexicanos in the public sector, examining how the text corrected erroneous ideas about New Mexico and its people prevalent in the government institutions and Anglophone worlds in which Otero-Warren often moved.[3]

Otero-Warren's recent appeal to historians has made her a feature of new scholarship on suffrage, which focuses on her as a racially inflected point of articulation between national and local efforts to secure the right to vote for women.[4] Such studies look to the institutional records of suffrage organizations and contemporaneous, primarily Anglophone periodicals to unearth the important linkages connecting the National Women's Party to Otero-Warren and other New Mexican suffrage advocates. This approach, however, overlooks the conversations occurring simultaneously among Nuevomexicanos regarding her family's history, the idea of women's suffrage, and Otero-Warren's political activities. This discourse frequently took place in Spanish and/or in the Hispanophone press, speaking to the majority New Mexican population. These conversations reflect a view of her that is not available in English-language sources but is essential to understanding how the Nuevomexicano population perceived her. This essay therefore draws from both Spanish- and English-language sources in discussing Otero-Warren to more thoroughly contextualize Nuevomexicano conceptualizations of her and her work.

Otero-Warren's biography presents a significant challenge to research, as access to primary materials is limited. While Charlotte Whaley's 1994 biography draws on some published sources,[5] much of the information about Otero-Warren that Whaley uses derives from personal interviews Whaley conducted with the members of Otero-Warren's extended family, which are not publicly available. To my knowledge, open archives of Otero-Warren's papers and personal effects are few, a condition that demands consideration of other types of primary sources, such as those used here.

A limited corpus of non-biographical secondary scholarship focuses on Otero-Warren as a literary figure, examining *Old Spain in Our Southwest* in the context of contemporaneous Nuevomexicana writers such as Cleofas Jaramillo and Fabiola Cabeza de Baca Gilbert.[6] As the analysis presented here argues, the cultural content of *Old Spain in Our Southwest* filters through the lens of Otero-Warren's intimate knowledge of the cultural and political stakes at play for Nuevomexicanos of the early twentieth century. Her book conserves and projects particular aspects of Nuevomexicano life, history, and culture as much for her own Nuevomexicano community as for the Anglophone communities Otero-Warren continuously educated about New Mexico over her lifetime.

Although Otero-Warren's memoir-style publications other than *Old Spain in Our Southwest* are few (she published at least one short work of cultural biography, "My People," in *Survey Graphic* in 1931), this does not mean that she left no other written intellectual record. As might be expected given her many civic positions, a portion of Otero-Warren's writing consists of official documents and governmental reports, many of which remain to be located and examined.[7] An example of such writing is "Teaching English to Non-English Speaking Adults," a twenty-one-page pamphlet Otero-Warren created for the Works Progress Administration (WPA) in her capacity as State Supervisor of Literacy Classes.[8] The document showcases the socially and linguistically attuned content she created for administrative purposes, addressing the needs of the Nuevo-mexicano population she served through leadership and civic roles.

A Nineteenth-Century Nuevomexicano Family Legacy in His-panophone Popular Song

A descendant of the Luna and Otero families from the Río Abajo region south of Albuquerque, both sides of Otero-Warren's family had long been involved in New Mexico politics and governance. She was born to Eloisa Luna, whose family traced its history in New

Mexico to the late sixteenth century, and Manuel B. Otero, whose father Manuel Antonio Otero had purchased half the Baca Land grant in Estancia, New Mexico. Together, Eloisa and Manuel B. Otero had three children, Eduardo, Nina, and Manuel. Tragically, the youngest of the siblings was born a mere month after the elder Manuel's death at the hands of land squatter and millionaire James Whitney. Whitney shot Otero in the neck as he asked Whitney to leave his lands in 1883. While a wounded Whitney was spirited away by his family members and freed on bail, a pregnant, nineteen-year-old Eloisa was left to welcome her husband's corpse. Whitney was later acquitted and left the state without significant consequences, much to the sorrow and anger of Otero-Warren's family and community.

The murder of Otero-Warren's father was recounted in popular songs in Spanish, expressing a specifically Nuevomexicano perspective of the injustice suffered by the Otero and Luna families, an injustice shared to varying degrees by many other Nuevomexicano families. An *indita* documented by Donald Chávez y Gilbert and Enrique Lamadrid, and sung in 1956 by Edwin Chávez Berry, detailed the confrontation. According to Otero-Warren's friend, author Erna Fergusson, the song was attributed to Casimiro Luján of Torreón, New Mexico, and was sung to Eloisa Luna Otero herself by Luján. The indita opens by plaintively stating Manuel B. Otero's right in claiming his property and naming the crime of his murder: "Ay indita de Don Manuel B/ residente de La Costancia [sic] / por defender tus derechos/ tu sufriste muerte sin causa" (Chávez y Gilbert). A verse from the *indita*, narrated in the voice of a dying Manuel B. Otero, emphasizes these sentiments: "Ante Dios pongo mi queja/ y al Supremo Tribunal/ que se ha de andar mi querella/ ante una corte marcial/ que mi muerte fue sin causa/ y mi derecho legal" (Chávez y Gilbert). The picture the *indita* paints is of profound wrongdoing to the Otero and Luna families, specific in its details, but reflective of similar suffering endured by the Nuevomexicano community.

The wrongdoing committed against Otero-Warren's family was not readily forgotten in Nuevomexicano collective memory: Fergusson sampled a second song about Manuel B. Otero's murder and published it decades after the events themselves, suggesting that it was still readily accessible in the 1940s. This song, by Plácido Romero of Peralta, New Mexico, describes Manuel B. Otero's murderer Whitney as "a coward, a Texas robber and a murderer who devils await in hell which is the place (la estancia) for him" (Fergusson 43). The lyrics of both Spanish-language songs illustrate how Otero-Warren and her family were imagined within the Nuevomexicano community in the late nineteenth century and in the years to come, when this critical contextualization would intertwine with Otero-Warren's own political persona.

Contemporaneous nineteenth-century English-language newspaper reports suggested that Whitney was justified in his actions assaulting and killing Manuel B. Otero; however, the resistive story the Spanish-language press and the songs told rang true to the experiences of loss and trauma Nuevomexicanos experienced. Folklorist Carmella Scorcia Pacheco observes of the corrido form that it "traditionally documented and reinterpreted conflict . . . In New Mexico, much of the oral lore focuses on social injustices suffered by the people; consequently, corridos are a popular means of political conveyance" (Scorcia 375). The songs about her father's death framed how Otero-Warren was later seen as a public figure and political candidate in a poignant, powerfully understandable and resonant way for Nuevomexicanos. She was a person who had suffered firsthand what many Nuevomexicanos themselves endured and who would therefore (it was hoped) represent their well-being and interests as a leader. Although studies of Otero-Warren typically link her political acumen and success to her family's ongoing participation in New Mexican politics (Cahill 235 noting the nineteenth- and twentieth-century Hispanic land dispossession that was rampant during her life (Whaley 1-2),[9] these characteristics alone do not tell the whole story of how and why Spanish-speaking New Mexicans so extensively supported Otero-Warren's ideas and political candidacy. These Spanish-language songs help complete this picture.

Otero-Warren's family moved from Los Lunas to Santa Fe, and she attended school at St. Vincent's Academy in Albuquerque, and then Maryville College in Saint Louis, returning home in her teenage years.[10] After many years of informal political involvement in Santa Fe (her cousin Miguel A. Otero served as territorial governor) Otero-Warren began to engage in civic and political activity, including volunteering for suffrage organizations and chairing the Child Welfare Department in Santa Fe. In 1907, when property rights for women in New Mexico were usurped by new American-influenced laws imposed on the territory,[11] Otero-Warren ensured that she and her sisters' interests were protected through trusts established from her mother Eloisa Luna's estate (Whaley 71).

Nina Otero-Warren: Advocate for Women's Suffrage in New Mexico

By the time Otero-Warren was in her mid-thirties, she had separated from her husband, US Cavalry officer and bigamist Rawson D. Warren (Whaley 65) and was living again in Santa Fe. She was visible in a variety of public positions in New Mexico and had taken on leadership roles, including election to three terms as Superintendent of Public Schools for Santa Fe County beginning in 1918.[12] Her gender and political and social prominence made her the target for national organizations advocating for women's right to vote, including the National American Woman Suffrage Association and the Congressional Union. By 1915, many states had granted women state-level voting rights, but New Mexico had not done so, and a national movement to amend the Constitution that would guarantee women the federal right to vote was advancing briskly. Otero-Warren was already involved with the National Association of Women's Clubs, which had lobbied unsuccessfully for women's right to vote. She soon became a primary point of articulation between national suffrage organizations, in particular the Congressional Union, and advocacy efforts in New Mexico for organizing advocates and lobbying elected officials to support women's enfranchisement.[13] Otero-Warren's work in this regard, in particular her relationship to suffrage efforts carried out by contemporaneous women of color, has most recently been revisited by historian Cathleen Cahill, who notes that the NAWSA and CU viewed Otero-Warren as an essential asset not only for her bilingualism, but also because she could recruit other Nuevomexicanas to the suffrage cause. Congressional Union organizer Ella St. Clair Thompson wrote about the participation of Otero-Warren and other Nuevomexicanas such as Aurora Lucero and Mona Baca in New Mexico: "They say it is very difficult to get the Spanish ladies out, but as I have one on the program to speak *in Spanish* [Otero-Warren], I think they will come-and their husbands as well" (Cahill 144). Thompson's remark reflects an awareness from the outside of the importance of self-recognition among Nuevomexicanos, a recognition that would extend to Otero-Warren's later political activities.

On the ground in New Mexico, Otero-Warren successfully parlayed her own political experiences and leveraged her knowledge and connections to effect change. Whaley explains:

> That considerable arm-twisting on the part of Nina and others was having a positive effect on the New Mexico legislators in Washington was evident. She had brought to the battle her knowledge of the bureaucracy learned at an early age from her stepfather and uncles. (84)

Otero-Warren's promotional work was superb, though she was fighting against established opponents within the state, including Thomas B. Catron, the one-term New Mexico senator and land thief who rebuffed the discussion of suffrage entirely.[14] Regardless of how helpful the expertise of male family members might have been, Otero-Warren herself was the political actor in this effort, her extensive labors the fruit of her determination and her successes deriving from it.

Otero-Warren and her suffrage colleagues were unsuccessful in seeing the state pass its suffrage legislation; in 1917, the state legislature voted down women's right to vote on a state level again, this time by a narrow margin of four votes (Whaley 85). Undeterred, Otero-Warren continued to lobby state legislators and congressmen, becoming more confident and effective. Whaley reports that the political work of suffrage engaged Otero-Warren, perhaps laying the groundwork for her future political candidacy: "Nina had discovered the joy and drama of revolutionary politics and of breaking down stereotypes and in the process, she had learned to trust her own strength and judgment" (87). Through Otero-Warren's suffrage liaisons in Washington, DC, she observed firsthand that women in other states were not hesitating to run for office as soon as the opportunity was made available. She learned during a 1918 visit that Montanan Anne Martin planned a Senate run, perhaps planting the seed of federal office in Otero-Warren's mind (Cahill 193).

With the advent of World War I, suffrage voices nationwide took on a different timbre, as many activists, including Otero-Warren, assumed multiple civic roles in addition to their advocacy of suffrage. With Erna Fergusson and Alice Corbin Henderson in New Mexico, Otero-Warren collaborated in local war efforts, including the Red Cross in Santa Fe County, War Bonds, and other causes (Whaley 89).

In June 1919, the Congress of the United States of America passed the Nineteenth Amendment to the Constitution, guaranteeing women the right to vote. This amendment required ratification by thirty-six states to be enacted as law, and Otero-Warren again put shoulder to the wheel in New Mexico to campaign for its passage. Although approval of the constitutional amendment passed the NM House, it failed in the Senate, where a substitute referendum for suffrage advocates was proposed (Whaley 94). Returning to lobbying efforts, they were fearful that similar referenda would be successful in other states, delaying or nullifying ratification, so Otero-Warren and her colleagues redoubled their efforts. In February 1920, both houses of the New Mexico State Legislature voted to ratify the Nineteenth Amendment. New Mexico was the thirty-second state to vote in favor of amending the Constitution for women's suffrage, and in 1920, it became so for women throughout the United States.

Hispanophone voices in New Mexico negotiated these major political changes in the newspapers and through oral forms. "El corrido de la votación," a corrido about women's suffrage in New Mexico, has only recently been rediscovered (2019) from a 1937 WPA collection[15] and in a 2004 recording shared among the women of a San Cristóbal, NM family (Scorcia 394). Scorcia Pacheco argues that the corrido's satirical narrative voice is that of a woman, reminding the community—specifically, other women, or the "comadrita" addressed

in the song—of the resistance they had faced in claiming
enfranchisement through voting. The 2004 recording of the corrido by
Quirina Córdova, a version she inherited from her grandmother Isabel
Córdova, highlights the impact of women getting out to vote: "El día
de las elecciones/ todos los hombre se unieron,/ de ver votar las
mujeres/ que llamaban la atención" (400). This version also
specifically mentions women's suffrage organizations ("un club de
señoras"), presumably those such as the CU and NAWSA with a
presence in New Mexico, and connects them with women running for
political office: "Ya se juntan las mujeres/ hacen un club de señoras,/
cambean sus candidatas,/ también pa'gobernadora" (Scorcia Pacheco
400). The 1937 corrido alludes to women running for office in
relationship to gaining the right to vote ("Ya se juntan las mujeres/ Y
hacen un flux de Señoras/ Nominan sus candidatas/ también de
gobernadoras" 402) and imagines a world in which women win their
contests: "Ganaron sus candidatas/ Secretarias, jueces de paz/ Reciben
sus oficinas/ Suspiran por las demás" (402). These early (and ongoing)
Nuevomexicano visions of suffrage and women running for office
undoubtedly inflected how the Spanish-speaking community
understood Otero-Warren's endeavors to secure women's right to vote
and, later, her efforts as she ran for political office.

New Mexican newspapers observed that apart from achieving
voting rights for women, suffrage campaigners lobbied for and
succeeded in seeing passed other vital pieces of legislation in the
state asserting women's rights and providing them with protections.
The Carlsbad Current reported on January 9, 1920, that in addition
to bringing about the successful ratification of the suffrage
amendment, Otero-Warren and others had accomplished equally
significant advances for women and children.

> Mrs. Lindsey, Mrs. A. A. Kellam, and Mrs. Otero-Warren
> served in turn as Chairmen of the legislative department of
> the State Federation of Women's Clubs and aided by the
> interested women of the state, succeeded in securing some
> excellent legislation. The laws secured the raising of the age
> of consent, the repeal of the act which permitted the husband
> to dispose of community real estate without the consent of

the wife, the creation of juvenile courts, the act providing for
the care of dependent and neglected children, the creation of
the Child Welfare and Girl's [sic] Welfare boards. ("New
Mexico Women Public Life")

Having amply proven her political expertise through these
actions and through her suffrage work, Otero-Warren awaited the
1921 amendment to the New Mexico State Constitution, which
permitted women to hold public office (Whaley 94-5). With its
passage, she ran for a Congressional seat and became the first
Hispana candidate for Congress in the history of the United States.

"Candidata republicana para el Congreso, 1922"

Otero-Warren's first challenge lay within the Republican party,
as she campaigned in the primary against incumbent Néstor
Montoya. Montoya was a prominent political figure in New Mexico
and the owner and editor of the Spanish-language newspaper *La
Bandera Americana*. Otero-Warren stumped from county to county
and announced her candidacy in various newspapers, including in
the Republican-leaning *La Revista de Taos* on August 25, 1922,
where she expressed her policy goals in Spanish for the majority
Hispanophone population:

> Si soy electa, me esmeraré en el representar consistentemente
> los intereses de el pueblo de Nuevo México con especial
> atención al Proyecto de Reclamaciones: las cédulas de tarifa;
> la extensión de necesarios créditos a rancheros y creadores
> de Ganado; la justa liquidación de la deuda que las naciones
> les deben a aquellos que las defendieron durante la última
> Guerra. ("Lanza su candidatura la Sra. Otero-Warren")

Otero-Warren's assertion of her positions on questions important to
Nuevomexicanos were made clear for the paper's readers: both local
issues (land reclamation, taxation, ranching and livestock credits)
and global ones (international World War I debts) she would
undertake as a federal official representing New Mexico.

The candidacy statement describes other aspects of her platform, specifically those promoting the education and the well-being of children and families. These objectives included appealing to the Federal government for support for the state in "progresar en materias de educación y en materias de salud y en el bienestar de la niñez" and developing child labor laws "para hacer efectiva la legislación de la labor de los niños" ("Lanza su candidatura la Sra. Otero-Warren"). She closes by gracefully acknowledging the honor that her nomination (and election) would bring, and her intention to do well by the people of New Mexico as an elected official of the state: "Si soy la escogida de la Convención republican para esta oficina, consideraré aquello un alto honor y una oportunidad para el servicio" ("Lanza su candidatura la Sra. Otero-Warren"). Otero-Warren won the Republican primary and began her campaign against John Morrow, the Democratic candidate for the Congressional seat, as observers soon noted.

Otero-Warren's candidacy as a woman drew interest from outside the state, and she was grouped in national media with other women campaigning for federal office. An article in the September 15, 1922, *Omaha Bee* discusses Otero-Warren's primary victory over Montoya, calling New Mexico the latest state to "wheel into line" by advancing a female candidate for Congress. The news piece praises Otero-Warren for her victory over Montoya, commenting that

> Her compelling victory is notable because of the admitted popularity of the man she defeated. He was elected to Congress two years ago by the largest plurality ever given a candidate for the office in New Mexico, and the selection of Mrs. Otero-Warren is therefore the more impressive. ("Woman Keeps on Coming")

The news note closes with high hopes for her victory in the Congressional election, referencing not only her gender but also her Spanish bilingualism, which is described positively in this instance:

> It is not unreasonable to expect that Miss Alice [Alice Mary Robertson, Congresswoman from Oklahoma and the second

woman elected to Congress] will not be lonesome in the next congress, for she will have a colleague not only of her sex, but speaking as well the language of the great southwest." ("Woman Keeps on Coming")

This contextualization of Otero-Warren on the national stage, reflecting on how she would be seen as a representative of the new state of New Mexico and as a bilingual woman, was a major topic of conversation in the local Hispanophone and Anglophone press. As her early accomplishments indicate, there were plenty of reasons why Otero-Warren's candidacy received broad support across Nuevomexicano political groups and populations.

Similar to the *corrido del sufragio*, which reflected on the shifting roles of women in New Mexico resulting from efforts by Otero-Warren and others, her candidacy for Congress occasioned a lyric intervention in Spanish, meant to communicate political advocacy within the Hispanophone community. A political poem in support of Otero-Warren written by fellow Nuevomexicano Felipe M. Chacón provides a fascinating look into how her supporters in New Mexico perceived her and backed her candidacy.[16] The poem was published in *La Bandera Americana* in 1923, though it is likely that it was also published earlier, during her candidacy.

Because the poem is in Spanish, certain elements, such as Otero-Warren's gender, are implicit in the words themselves, as in the poem's subtitle, which reads "Candidata republicana para el Congreso, 1922," or "Woman Republican Candidate for Congress, 1922." The poem expresses unequivocal support for Otero-Warren, as it implicitly acknowledges the women's suffrage efforts that preceded her nomination and women's fundamental equality with men in matters of governance: "Nacida en el sufragio igual al hombre,/ Pero en lo espiritual, más elevada." Otero-Warren's candidacy is described in the second stanza: "El mundo avanza con la idea humana/ y nacen nuevas cosas en la vida;/ hoy refleja la luz de mañana/ En otra esfera la mujer nacida (*El feliz ingenio neomexicano* 116). Perhaps referencing her previous political and civic work, the poem praises Otero-Warren's accomplishments, completed "en pureza moral . . . y la tierra va bien en su jornada"

(116). Indeed, the poem posits a great deal of progressive pride in Otero-Warren's candidacy, asserting that her election as a woman would reflect well on New Mexico and Nuevomexicanos: "Cubrirá Nuevo México de Gloria/Poniendo una mujer en el Congreso" (116). Chacón's poem closes with another shout of support for Otero-Warren from the progressive quarter "Un brindis de alegría/Placer del progresivo ciudadano" (117), a greeting from "un pueblo soberano" (117), or the Nuevomexicano community to whom the poem is directed.

As in Chacón's poem, *La Revista de Taos* advocated for Otero-Warren's candidacy as the Republican candidate for Congress. Not only does the newspaper name her many civic and political positions, it comments explicitly on her involvement in the advancement of suffrage in New Mexico, as "presidenta de los Clubs de Federación de Mujeres del Estado durante la campaña a favor del sufragio de la mujer en Nuevo México, gracias a cuyos esfuerzos se debe el triunfo en el Estado de esta medida" ("Sra. Adelina Otero-Warren para el Congreso"). The article asserts that Otero-Warren's proven past leadership leaves no doubt as to her future abilities in high office, and specifically talks about her as a female congresswoman who

> demostraría que la energía, la dignidad, la inteligencia o sabiduría no son solo propias del varón hispano sino de la MUJER de esta raza [. . .] el triunfo de la señora Otero-Warren es necesario para el más grande orgullo de Nuevo México y de la raza Hispana, especialmente al referirnos al sexo mujeril que debe ver en el triunfo de Nina Otero-Warren una de sus mayores glorias. ("Sra. Adelina Otero-Warren para el Congreso").

The newspaper's support of Otero-Warren was based on party and gender. It contested detractors who worked against her candidacy by characterizing her short-lived marriage as a negative characteristic.

After a vigorous campaign crisscrossing the state, documented in local papers such as *The Spanish American*, *Revista de Taos* and *El Nuevo Mexicano*, Otero-Warren lost the election to the Democratic candidate by a small margin (approximately 9%). Otero-Warren's campaign was a vital proving ground, as she was "the first woman to challenge an all-male political system, and that year the Democrats elected a governor, James Hinkle, and most of the state officials" (Whaley 98). As political historians of New Mexico observe, the 1922 election marked the beginning of a move of many New Mexicans towards the Democratic party and away from Republican alliances.

Though the loss must have come as a disappointment to Otero-Warren, she did not rest for long, nor did she run again for federal office, though she helped her brother Manuel Otero run for governor in 1924 (he lost by less than two hundred votes to his Anglo Democratic opponent) (Whaley 99). In fact, she continued to enact her many different facets: advocating for educational reforms for adults and children in New Mexico, buying a homestead property outside of Santa Fe and operating it with her companion Mamie Meadors, and continuing as the heart of her family's home in Santa Fe, where her numerous siblings, their children and her stepfather lived. One of Otero-Warren's half-sisters, Estella Bergere, married the conservationist Aldo Leopold, whose knowledge of New Mexican wildlife arose in part from the Otero-Luna family's long acquaintance with the place.[17] Once Otero-Warren's Las Dos homestead was established in the mid-1930s, and with the encouragement of friends in Santa Fe, she undertook a new type of endeavor: penning her cultural memoir, *Old Spain in Our Southwest*.

Educating Through the Published Word: Old Spain in Our Southwest

Otero-Warren's book treated daily life, stories, and practices from the time of her childhood in Los Lunas, reflecting the Nuevomexicano voices that had narrated these important moments and whose message she would reshape for English-dominant audiences. *Old Spain in Our Southwest* is a fascinating compilation attending to many different topics. It was positioned as a bulwark of selective cultural representation at a historical moment when Nuevomexicano local history and cultural practices perched on the precipice of erasure, edged out of the record and public space under the pressure of American influence: a situation Otero-Warren acutely realized through her many interactions and public roles.[18] Her book allowed her to correct misinformed, ill-intentioned, or simply erroneous information about New Mexico and its Indo-Hispano citizenry. She accomplished this by incorporating historical reflections, presented through the lens of Spanish colonial history in New Mexico (which includes at times the exclusivist and racial problems found in other borderlands writing of the epoch), in order to create space for Nuevomexicanos in the history of the place. These are followed by descriptions of day-to-day life in late nineteenth-century New Mexico, including celebrations ("saints' days and feasts"), and concepts of specific value to Nuevo-mexicanos. For example, Otero-Warren's description of water displays her understanding of its particular meaning in New Mexican life and culture and attempts to make that meaning legible for others:

> Water actually means the livelihood of the people, not only food, the product of gardens and fields, but all that their surplus may be exchanged for . . . so water is carefully guarded and saved . . . . There is little wonder that the Saints are taken into the fields that they may intercede for the farmer and that God, in His mercy, may send rain. Water is sacred indeed! (61).

Otero-Warren translates for non-natives to New Mexico the vital notion that, for Nuevomexicanos, water is not a commodity; it is central to life in all its facets, revered and held to a higher value than resources that can be bought and sold.

Otero-Warren turns her attention to details of life and space recognizable to Nuevomexicanos, including explanations of place names, the history of the religious statue La conquistadora, who she calls "Our Lady of Victory" (and which is now known as Nuestra Señora de la Paz), and information about schooling and educational organization in early New Mexico, but which would not be imme-diately obvious to an outsider. The book's final chapter recounts songs and stories from New Mexico's past, quoting Chilean Nobel

Prize-winning poet Gabriela Mistral in citing examples from New Mexico's *trova* of ballads and verse and folk stories.

The sparse literary scholarship on *Old Spain in Our Southwest* has primarily recovered and historically contextualized the text, drawing attention to contemporaneous works by Nuevomexicana authors and the text's shortcomings. Literary scholar Tey Diana Rebolledo's foundational study compared Otero-Warren's writing to that of two other Nuevomexicana authors of the epoch who engaged in similar projects of recollection and preservation: Cleofas Martínez Jaramillo and Fabiola Cabeza de Baca Gilbert. In Rebolledo's analysis, all three women participated in what she termed the "cultural flourishing of the Northern New Mexico literary scene" (200); this reading reinserted them into literary conversations from which they had been excluded, primarily for the "Spanish" identifiers they used in their writing. More recently, and building from Rebolledo's premises, Vanessa Fonseca-Chávez critically observed that Otero-Warren and her contemporaries represented a New Mexican history and culture that "succeeded in rejecting Indigenous history" (70). These critical approaches provide a rich point of departure for contemporary analysis of *Old Spain in Our Southwest*. However, a consideration of the work in light of Otero-Warren's long career in public works—a career in which she continuously advocated for nuevomexicano's fundamental rights in contexts where her audience had little idea of New Mexican history, language and culture, and perhaps little incentive to learn about it— provides insight into how and why she writes what she does.

The section "A Little History" implicitly illustrates the arguments about New Mexico and its people that Otero-Warren no doubt frequently addressed in her dealings with Anglo newcomers and powerbrokers across the territory/state. Its three parts can be read inversely as responses to mainstream hegemonic pressures to erase Nuevomexicano legacy and, by extension, the political agency in the early twentieth century. "Our Lady of Victory" asserts the 1609/1610 establishment of Santa Fe—far predating the arrival of the Mayflower and eastern United States colonial history as it was understood when Otero-Warren wrote—and in doing so, challenged the notion of New Mexico as a tabula rasa awaiting eastern colonization. Aside from outlining charming and historical anecdotes about extant Spanish and Indigenous language names for places, "Spanish Place Names" tacitly argues against their eradication and replacement with American names, a fear that had long plagued Nuevomexicanos as the removal of the name for the place itself— New Mexico—was at one point proposed as a condition for statehood, as Gabriel Meléndez has shown.

Finally, as superintendent and in subsequent educational roles, Otero-Warren spoke to the learning requirements of Nuevomexicanos (as her WPA writing attests), correcting misperceptions about education in New Mexico. "Early Schooling in New Mexico" unwrites the propaganda that New Mexicans were uneducated prior to American intervention. Complicating previous readings of *Old Spain in Our Southwest*, the chapter asserts that the earliest schools in New Mexico were Native: "The first schoolhouse in this New World was an Indian *estufa* . . . the youth of the tribe, or of the clan, gathered in this room to be instructed in their traditions, the significance of their dances and social practices" (103). The chapter elaborates the many different types of teaching and learning that occurred in New Mexico during the colonial period (including the establishment of public schooling by the Mexican government in 1822), not only providing a contestatory genealogy of education, but also emphasizing the ongoing importance of teaching and instruction, connecting it to the time period in which she wrote: "Today if one visits a mountain community, one finds the children in an adobe school building being taught the subjects now requiring report cards; and their parents in a setting of their own making, still performing the same tasks, uninterrupted for the past two hundred and forty years" (110). Otero-Warren's experiences in the political realm translated into how and what she wrote in *Old Spain in Our Southwest*.

In the book's glossary, Otero-Warren's bilingualism and awareness of her readers' probable unfamiliarity with Spanish terms manifest in the expressions and terms she records and explains. She decodes lexical regionalisms in her explanation of "Gallina de la tierra" as the local word for turkey[19] (189), and clarifies intersections

between Spanish and English, as in "¡Ay, pópe!" which she explains
means "There, puppy!" (187). She articulates common expressions
such as "Ni con jabón de la Puebla" to say something so dirty that
not even a town whose claim to fame was making soap (La Puebla)
could clean it (190), and "Tan tonto como un burro" (192). Otero-
Warren also divulges the humor that typifies Nuevomexicano life, as
in the conclusion of the story "The Beggar" or the explanation of the
origin of the name for Garrapata canyon near Taos, NM. That
lightness distinguishes her from her contemporaries, whose memoirs
lack the carefully aimed buoyancy that Otero-Warren projects in *Old
Spain in Our Southwest*. This patient decoding of Spanish and
bilingual terms and the sublety and humor Otero-Warren
implements may be read as strategies to draw in readers who were
unaware or misinformed about New Mexican life, culture, and
language. By using humor, Otero-Warren defuses some of the
tension that she was well aware perpetually simmered beneath the
surface of interactions between Nuevomexicanos and those
unfamiliar with New Mexico. Through *Old Spain in Our Southwest*,
Otero-Warren undercuts and rewrites the outsider narratives about
New Mexico she had come to know during her years of civic and
political activity in a divided post-territorial New Mexico and resets
the starting points for future policy and public works affecting
Nuevomexicanos.

A Multifaceted Conclusion

Nina Otero-Warren was the matriarch of a family in which she had
no children of her own; she successfully helmed her real estate business
and was a lively presence on Santa Fe's increasingly heterogeneous
social scene well into the twentieth century. An image from the New
Mexico State Historical Archives shows Otero-Warren in 1949 at a
costume party she hosted at the former Magoffin home in Santa Fe, a
site on the historical Plaza which would soon become a hotel parking
lot for tourists. The theme party was styled as a nineteenth-century
gambling salon, evoking New Mexico's Spanish, Mexican, and
Territorial epochs, and Otero-Warren dressed up as Doña María
Gertrudis de Barceló, known as La Tules.[20] A powerful, independent

social figure of the nineteenth century well known to Nuevomexicanos, La Tules would undoubtedly have required explanation to many of Otero-Warren's guests. Ever the teacher and activist—perhaps especially among those who would shape New Mexico's future social and political landscape—Otero Warren educated others about Nuevomexicano histories and of the political activities in which they had long engaged, even as she remained rooted in a Nuevomexicano sensibility, language- and historical consciousness.

Works Cited

Cahill, Cathleen. *Recasting the Vote: How Women of Color Transformed the Suffrage Movement.* U of North Carolina P, 2020.

Chávez y Gilbert, Donald. "Indita de Manuel B. Otero." *Terra Patre Farm and Ranch: Cowboy History.* terrapatrefarms.com/wp-content/uploads/2021/01/CH7.pdf. Accessed 17 April 2023.

Davidson, Margaret Garcia. "Borders, Frontiers and Mountains: Mapping the History of "U.S. Hispanic Literature." *Reading the West: New Essays on the Literature of the American West,* edited by Michael Kowalewski, Cambridge UP, 1996, pp. 177-196.

Fergusson, Erna. "The Ballad of Manuel B." *Murder and Mystery in New Mexico.* Albuquerque, Merle Armitage Editions, 1948, pp. 33-48.

Fonseca-Chávez, Vanessa. *Colonial Legacies in Chicana/o Literature and Culture:Looking Through the Kaleidoscope.* Tucson, U of Arizona P, 2020.

"Lanza su candidatura la Sra. Otero-Warren." La Revista de Taos, August 25, 1922. chroniclingamerica.loc.gov. Accessed 5 January 2020.

Massmann, Ann M. "Adelina 'Nina' Otero-Warren: A Spanish-American Cultural Broker." *Journal of the Southwest,* vol. 42. no. 4, 2000, pp. 877-96.

Meléndez, Gabriel. "Nuevo México By Any Other Name: Creating a State from an Ancestral Homeland." *The Contested Homeland,* edited by Erlinda González-Berry and David Maciel, U of New Mexico P, 2000, pp. 143-68.

"New Mexico Women Public Life." *The Carlsbad Current,* January 9, 1920. *Chronicling America,* chroniclingamerica.loc.gov. Accessed 10 January 2021.

Nogar, Anna M. and A. Gabriel Meléndez. *El feliz ingenio neomexicano: Felipe M. Chacón and Poesía y prosa.* U of New Mexico P, forthcoming.

Nogar, Anna M. and Enrique Lamadrid. "*Nuevomexicano* Cultural Memory and the Indo-Hispana *Mujerota,*" *Journal of the Southwest,* vol. 58. no. 4, 2016, pp. 751-80.

Otero-Warren, Adelina. "My People." *Survey Graphic,* 1931. Reprinted: *The American Mosaic: The Latino American Experience,* ABC-CLIO, 2020, latinoamerican2.abc-clio.com/search/Display/1366966. Accessed 25 Nov. 2020.

_____. *Old Spain in Our Southwest.* 1936. Sunstone P, 2006.

_____. "Teaching English to Non-English-Speaking Adults." Federal Works Agency Collection, Special Collections Library and Archives, Albuquerque Public Library, Albuquerque, NM, July 22, 2021.

Ponce, Merrihelen. *The Lives and Works of Five Hispanic New Mexican Women Writers, 1878-1991.* Southwest Hispanic Research Institute, 1992.

Rebolledo, Diana. Nuestras mujeres: Hispanas of New Mexico, *Their Images and Their lives,* 1582-1992. El Norte Publications/Academia, 1992.

Salas, Elizabeth. "Adelina Otero-Warren: Rural Aristocrat and Modern Feminist." *Latina Legacies: Identity, Biography and Community,* edited by Vickie Ruíz and Virginia Sánchez Karrol, Oxford UP, 2005, 135-47.

Scorcia Pacheco, Carmella. "Voces Nuevo Mexicanas: Power, Gender, and Recovery of 'El Corrido de la Votación' for the Centennial Celebration of New Mexico's Suffrage Movement." *New Mexico Historical Review,* vol. 95. no. 4, 2020, pp. 373-408.

"17 Women Elected as County School Superintendents." *The Spanish American,* November 27, 1920. *Chronicling America,* chroniclingamerica.loc.gov. Accessed 10 January 2021.

"Sra. Adelina Otero-Warren para el Congreso." *La Revista de Taos*, September 22, 1922. *Chronicling America*, chroniclingamerica. loc.gov. Accessed 5 January 2020.

Whaley, Charlotte. *Nina Otero-Warren of Santa Fe*. Sunstone P, 2007.

"Woman Keeps on Coming." *Omaha Bee*. September 15, 1922. *Chronicling America*, chroniclingamerica.loc.gov. Accessed 5 January 2020.

Appendix

A la señora Adelina Otero-Warren
— Candidata Republicana para el Congreso, 1922.
Felipe M. Chacón (1924)

Ceñida está tu frente de laureles,
Y tu nombre de honores irradia;
Hoy se asoma tu estrella en los dinteles
De la aurora triunfal de un nuevo día.

El mundo avanza con la idea humana
Y nacen nuevas cosas en la vida;
Hoy refleja la luz de la mañana
En otra esfera la mujer nacida.

Nacida en el sufragio igual al hombre,
Pero en lo espiritual, más elevada;
En pureza moral labra su nombre
Y la tierra va bien en su jornada.

Aquesta evolución tan meritoria,
Marcando el alto paso del Progreso,
Cubrirá Nuevo México de gloria
Poniendo una mujer en el Congreso:

Habilidosa, competente, honrada,
De alma gentil, de corazón sincero,
¡Héla ahí, la del pueblo proclamada,
La dama típica, Adelina Otero!

Vástago noble de español linaje,
Y más aún, americana pura,
Pero ¡qué importa el exterior ropaje
Del que amerita distinguida altura!

No es exclusiva la grandeza humana,
Que no limita con nación ninguna;
Del alto Cielo su poder dimana
Y a quien le place su belleza aduna.

Mas no es esta lisonja que motiva
El servil interés del egoísmo,
Que sólo encierra mi intención altiva
Teñir en la Justicia un idealismo.

¡Salud! ¡Salud! Un brindis de alegría,
Placer del progresivo ciudadano,
Os manda junto con la trova mía,
¡El saludo de un pueblo soberano!

PART IV
RADICAL LATINA'S POLITICS

Luisa Capetillo, Free Love and the *Falda-Pantalón*

CHRISTOPHER CASTAÑEDA
California State University, Sacramento

"The human being by nature is an anarchist . . ."
Luisa Capetillo, *Mi Opinión. Sobre las libertades,
derechos y deberes de la mujer*,
([San Juan, P.R.]: The Times Pub Co., 1911), p. 151

*"I am fighting for the time when we can all
go down Fifth Avenue in overalls."*
"No Volunteers for Trousers," *The Kansas City Times*, July 1,
1912

One sunny summer day in 1912, Luisa Capetillo (1879-1922)—identified in the US press as the "Porto Rican Jeanne D'Arc"—strolled down New York City's Fifth Avenue. She created quite a stir, not because the public knew who she was, certainly the vast majority of those who saw her had never heard her name, but because of her clothing. She was dressed, according to a reporter on the scene:

. . . in a trouserette costume of the sensational sort guaranteed to stop traffic on any thoroughfare and which she is trying to have the local suffragettes adopt as their political dress and symbol of emancipation. It consists of a dainty lace and linen coat full length thrown over striking bloomers, which reach from an inch or two above the ankle to the waist.

And when she reached 52nd Street, "the crush of carriages, taxis and limousines became so great that a policeman had to ask her to pin down the front of her coat as far as her knees. . . ." Threatened with detention, Capetillo complied.[1] This performance likely received the attention she had desired, perhaps even more than expected, as versions of this event were reprinted in newspapers throughout the United States, including those in Kansas City, Chicago, San Francisco, and Hot Springs, Arkansas.

Line drawing of Luisa Capetillo. Source: *The Kansas Weekly Capital*, July 11, 1912; Photo of Luisa Capetillo in her falda-pantalón. Source: *The Richmond Palladium and Sun-Telegram*, July 1, 1912; and Luisa Capetillo close-up. *The San Francisco Examiner*, July 7, 1912.

Capetillo had begun wearing pants well before arriving in New York in 1912. She had already adopted this politically and socially provocative style of dress in Puerto Rico as part of a strategy to promote and demonstrate the gender equality for which she so fervently fought. And then, in 1915, three years *after* the New York episode, she repeated this performance in Havana, resulting in her famous arrest and brief detention. While the Havana incident is a well-known highlight of Capetillo's activism, it should be emphasized that the New York episode occurred first and on the mainland; it is historically noteworthy for that reason. In fact, six years later, in 1918, when Capetillo made a return visit to New York, Bernardo Vega met her and described her as having arrived in New York "from Havana, where she had created a scandal by showing up in the streets dressed in culottes, which only the most advanced women at that time dared to wear." Little did he seem to know that Capetillo had created a bigger scandal on the very streets of Manhattan six years earlier.[2]

This essay focuses on Luisa Capetillo's life and writing during the years 1911 to 1913, when she was already receiving publicity in Puerto Rico for wearing pants, and then traveled to New York City where she wrote essays on free love that Jaime Vidal, the Catalan émigré anarchist, printed in his anarchist periodicals. While there is much unknown about Capetillo's life during her first trip to New York, her public appearance on Fifth Avenue and the essays she wrote that year for Vidal's periodicals provide important insight into the development of her anarcho-feminist ideas. It is clear that Capetillo's views on gender equality, love and sex were deeply influenced by her personal experiences, as well as the lives of her parents, in combination with the knowledge she had gained from the wide-ranging and radical literature to which she was exposed growing up in Arecibo, Puerto Rico.

Formative Years: Anarchism & the falda-pantalón

Capetillo's formative years were well documented by Norma Valle-Ferrer in the biographical study, *Luisa Capetillo, Pioneer Puerto Rican Feminist*.[3] For the purposes of this essay, a brief review of Capetillo's youth and early adulthood is helpful in establishing prominent themes that deeply influenced her adulthood and anarchist views.

She was born on October 28, 1879, in Arecibo, Puerto Rico. Her father, Luis Capetillo Echevarría, was an immigrant from the Basque region of Spain. Her mother, Luisa Margarita Perone (later changed to Perón), had emigrated from France. Luis and Margarita never married, but they lived together for a time and had one child, Luisa, who was baptized but did not become a practicing Catholic.[4] Although Luis' family was wealthy, the family fortune passed to his sister. He nevertheless exuded a sense of privilege, even though he had to work to support himself. Capetillo's progressive-minded parents, particularly her mother, nurtured and encouraged her love of literature, learning, and progressive thinking. In her home, she had access to a wide variety of books on science and philosophy, among other subjects; she became an avid and passionate reader. Her father's knowledge and interest in working-class movements and anarchism certainly piqued Capetillo's imagination. At some point during her youth, Luis left his wife and daughter, never to return home.[5] Margarita continued to work as a domestic, sometimes accompanied and assisted by Capetillo.

When Capetillo was eighteen years old, she developed a romantic relationship with Manuel Ledesma. He was the progeny of a wealthy and aristocratic family for whom Capetillo's mother had been working. Luisa and Manuel also never married, but they lived together for a brief time. Two children came quickly. Manuela was born in 1897 and Gregorio in 1899. However, as noted by historian Nancy Hewitt, "both children lived with Luisa's mother while Luisa moved between her household and that of the Ledesmas."[6] Luisa's passionate romance with Manuel would not continue as he eventually resumed a prestigious and bourgeois lifestyle reflecting his privileged background. Hewitt explained that: ". . . [Luisa] was clearly disappointed and disillusioned by his embrace of social property . . . [and] she used her experiences in this relationship to fuel her feminist critiques of traditional forms of marriage, motherhood, and the family."[7]

As a young adult, Luisa worked as a journalist and union organizer.[8] She joined *La Federación de Torcedores de Tabaco* (FTT), an affiliate of *La Federación Libre de Trabajadores* (FLT), and began labor organizing. She also found success as a *lectora* (reader), reading out loud to cigar makers in Arecibo factories; a profession she would continue throughout her life. Labor organizing required frequent travel, and she "became immersed in the radical politics . . . in Puerto Rico and . . . throughout the Caribbean." Capetillo's mother continued to care for her children while she was on the road.[9]

At this time, Capetillo wrote *Ensayos libertarios* (1907), and she dedicated it to both male and female workers.[10] As carefully narrated by Lisa Sánchez González, these years marked "Capetillo's entry into the public scene of politics" and the development of her anarcho-syndicalist agenda.[11] She also engaged in another romantic relationship, this time with a married pharmacist, and became pregnant with her third child, a son named Luis born in 1911. The father never acknowledged Luis as his son, and this experience certainly amplified Capetillo's resentment of men who enjoyed intimate relationships with women before leaving them and their children behind; Capetillo's mother also helped raise Luis.

This same year, 1911, Capetillo published *Mi opinión*, her first major book on feminist theory.[12] Significantly, she included an essay titled "Free Love" by Madeleine Vernet, a French teacher and libertarian who in 1906 had established an orphanage for workers' children. Vernet's pronouncements that "Love should not be confused with marriage" and "Love has to be completely free; no law, no morality can rule over it . . ." clearly reflected Capetillo's deep interest, if not experiences, in the dynamics of intimate relationships and romantic commitment.[13] And the dedication page of *Mi opinión* is illuminating. It identified those who were most important to her: the people of Puerto Rico, the workers of the world, her children, "A TI" [it is unclear from the text who this is] for whom I have sighed and sigh . . .", and to her mother who "never imposed on me or obligated me to think according to tradition. And you allowed me to inquire freely, only reproaching me about what you thought were exaggerations, without violating me." Capetillo's mother remained deeply committed to supporting her and her children throughout her life.[14]

In a brief preface to *Mi opinión*, dated October 1, 1910, Capetillo explained that her motivation for writing the book was simple: to tell the truth. She acknowledged that some people thought her ideas were merely "utopian," but she explained that it was wrong to believe that a worthy yet difficult to achieve goal should be discredited as being simply "utopian." She craftily pointed out that the desire for financial success, for example, could be called utopian in this sense, but that had never stopped prospective entrepreneurs from establishing new businesses and ventures. She therefore reasoned that fighting for equality and liberty and striving to empower and improve the lives of the working class was not just utopian but a profoundly worthy endeavor and commitment.

Capetillo's preface to *Mi opinión* also reinforced her primary objective: to write about the condition of women. She explained that she had long desired to express her opinion about women's lives in their diverse forms and had studied them and the typically meager freedoms women had historically enjoyed, so she had dedicated herself to confirming that women ". . . are an important factor in human civilization . . . [worthy of] full liberty."[15] Capetillo stated: "We are going to begin narrating the enslavement of women in marriage. . . . The consequence of their misery is reflected in their children." And she pondered about the best methods for teaching children and husbands about the plight of the enslaved wife and mother.[16] Interestingly, Capetillo recommended as literary evidence of women's powerful historical influence the book *Galería histórica de mujeres célebres* by Emilio Castelar. He had been President of the first Spanish Republic whose own book, *La abolición de la esclavitud*, had years earlier contributed to the successful efforts to end slavery in Puerto Rico.[17]

Capetillo also wrote about pants as a representation of gender equality. In *Mi opinión*, she highlighted their importance, symbolically and practically. "This custom of wearing pants," she wrote, "adapts perfectly to the era of female progress."[18] In introducing the importance of pants, she referred to Marius de Zayas, the Mexican caricaturist, illustrator, and art dealer who had moved to New York City in 1907. Capetillo cited a comment by Zayas in relation to theatrical performances that demonstrated "the superiority of women over men." Capetillo declared that Zayas *had not* fully acknowledged the important new trend of women wearing pants in those performances. She argued that once pants were worn, there could be no return to dresses; women could wear pants effectively and attractively in theater and dance, and therefore women should be able to wear pants in all aspects of daily life.[19]

Capetillo may have also been aware of the nineteenth-century dress reformers who believed that "trousers represented physical freedom, and [that] some women imagined being freed from societal restraints as well."[20] For her part, Capetillo emphasized that pants, or the pant-skirt as it was often termed, were simply more comfortable than women's standard dress, and that they could be worn in any kind of profession and, theoretically, anywhere. She also pointed out that women's dresses were unhygienic . . . they carried and propagated germs and dirt, collecting more of the same as they dragged along the ground. In her characteristically observant and sharp-witted way, Capetillo finally pointed out that women had legs just like men and why shouldn't women be able to cover them individually just like men?

In Puerto Rico, after publication of *Mi opinión*, Capetillo began to publicly perform this idea. In 1911, a newspaper article titled "La 'jupe-culotte,'" suggested that Capetillo's interest in pants was based on the orientalist themed "harem pantaloons" created by French fashion designer Paul Poiret that had debuted in 1911. Capetillo responded to this suggestion by defending her own use of what she referred to as the "falda-pantalón." "I am not trying to dress in fashion," she stated, "but rather to dress in the most comfortable and hygienic way in accord with this era of freedom." Indeed, for Capetillo the falda-pantalón represented the perfect mixture of new fashion, hygiene, and freedom from traditional formulas of dress.[21]

A few months later in August 1911, in a theatrical review of the performance "La Bella Carmela," the writer noted a scene that included the "falda-pantalón" which was coldly received by the audience. The writer identified Capetillo as the one responsible for this "mess."[22] Three months later, in November 1911, another newspaper report explained that Capetillo had recently begun to increase her "number of public shows" in Mayaguez. These "shows" consisted of Capetillo wearing an unusual "falda-pantalón." Apparently, there was a "public uproar" that included curious children following through the streets "the fearless and frustrated cheerleader of a '*demodé*' outfit.[23] Capetillo responded that while this criticism had effectively discouraged other women from wearing the "falda-pantalón," she would continue the practice on her own. It is worth considering that as a cigar factory reader and labor organizer, wearing pants would also have been more hygienic (as she often claimed) and practical.

New York City & Jaime Vidal: 1912

Soon after publishing *Mi opinión*, Capetillo traveled to New York City. She arrived in the Spring of 1912. Due to a lack of extant documents, it is not clear with whom in New York she might have been in contact, but as Hewitt has written, "it was in New York City that she first experienced the excitement generated by an international community of anarchist and socialist labor activists."[24] It is my belief that Capetillo had already been in touch with Jaime Vidal, who at that time was an editor of *Cultura Obrera*, the Spanish-language anarcho-syndicalist newspaper published in that city.[25]

Soon after her arrival, she penned a brief essay titled "Mi Primera Impresión," dated May 15, 1912, for *Cultura Obrera*. In it, she expressed her initial views of New York City, not by simply describing her new urban surroundings, but by posing three questions addressed to her Puerto Rican compatriots:

1) Why having so many millionaires, is there so much misery?
2) Why having so many carriages and automobiles going through areas where the poor live and where so many children play around, there have not been more accidents?

3) [point three was not numbered in the essay, which seems to have had some lines cut off] And why aren't washrooms required in 2ⁿᵈ and 3ʳᵈ-class restaurants and cafes like they are in the first-class ones?[26]

These queries reflect her astute observations about a densely populated urban area, full of automobiles and eating places, and the social dynamics and consequences of living in such an environment.

In the same issue of *Cultura Obrera*, an announcement appeared for a new anarchist paper, *Brazo y Cerebro*, to be edited by Jaime Vidal. He stated in the notice that "our initiative of publishing a magazine dedicated to spreading anarchist ideas with the pencil and the pen has been seconded and supported by various friends from different countries. . . ."[27] He included excerpts from letters written by Fernando Tarrida, Carlos Malato and Fermín Sagristá, an artist and friend of Vidal who would contribute artwork and drawings to this new journal of "art, science and literature." The announcement also stated that $58.56 had been raised to support *Brazo y Cerebro's* publication. Significantly, Capetillo was listed as the first contributor, having donated $1.00.[28]

The first issue of *Brazo y Cerebro* appeared on June 22, 1912, and the editorial address was 270 West 4ᵗʰ Street. According to an updated listing of financial contributors that appeared on the periodical's last page, a total of $114.32 had been raised. Most donations were in amounts of $.25 each. They came from many locations, primarily from New York but also from Ybor City, Boston, Chicago, Los Angeles, and Kyle, Texas, among others. Again, Capetillo was one of the donors, along with Pedro Esteve, the lead editor of *Cultura Obrera*; Juan Martínez, *Brazo y Cerebro's* treasurer; Maximiliano Olay, who recently arrived in Ybor City and who years later would write anarchist essays against fascist Spain; Juan Vilariño, who assisted Vidal's journalist endeavors; Agustín Castañeda, *El Despertar's* former administrator and treasurer of the "Spanish Pro-Revolution Committee"; and "un hambriento," among others. [29] Although it's difficult to determine with certainty how many women had contributed funds to this paper, it is clear that

Capetillo was one of the very few female contributors of either funds or essays.

It was later that same month, on June 28, 1912, that the "Porto Rican Jeanne D'Arc" strolled down Fifth Avenue in her unique "trouserette."[30] According to the reporter on the scene, Capetillo had "arrived in this city last week with the avowed declaration that she was going to awaken New York to a real sense of freedom in politics, dress and matrimony. And apparently she has started."[31] The report continued: "When Miss Capetillo left her new residence at 724 Lexington Avenue the coat was allowed to fly with the winds. At Fifty-second street the crush of carriages, taxis and limousines became so great that a policeman had to ask her to pin down the front of her coat as far as her knees at least or else he would have to call another sort of conveyance and put the matter of progressive feminine styles up to higher authorities. So Miss Capetillo pinned it down. But she still had her ideas."[32]

Apparently, Capetillo's brave performative call-to-action did not garner much support. One brief follow-up newspaper article stated simply: "So far no women have volunteered services for [the] army of Luisa Capetillo, Porto Rican Joan of Arc, who plans to free women from bondage of skirts."[33] Another article quoted Capetillo as stating:

I believe in love but I don't believe in marriage. The American woman is under the spell of matrimony. The wedding ring is the symbol of her slavery. Real love ends with death, but it is difficult to find real love the first time. Divorce is the same as trial marriage. If you go around in swishy skirts you will get the swishy skirt attitude. I am fighting for the time when we can all go down Fifth Avenue in overalls.[34]

Although there is scant documentation about Capetillo's life in New York City during 1912, she continued collaborating with Vidal. In addition to small donations for *Brazo y Cerebro*, she contributed essays, including one for its second issue dated October 22, 1912, the lead essay of which, "Anarquismo," was penned by Emma

Goldman. Capetillo's contribution was "Femeninas—en pro de la mujer."

Capetillo began her essay by describing the total subservience to men that women had traditionally suffered—indeed, the following passage might well have been a description of her mother's life or her own:

> For and through generations, women give away their beauty, youth, health, happiness, and even their own life. Women give guidance, solace, temperance, happiness, and pleasure to men, as mothers, companions, sisters, and friends. However, they are relegated to oblivion as simple objects of pleasure, machines to make children, and domestic slaves . . . this is the situation of Latina women, especially in all Spanish-speaking countries."[35]

She continued to describe the typical life of a woman, in relation to a man: "She puts on makeup, adorns herself with jewels, excessively deforms her body with the use of a corset, does a thousand silly things, becomes a fashion mannequin, and all of this because she believes she will attract men with these games of disguise."[36] Capetillo understood that a woman's attempt to make herself more sexually attractive following patriarchal standards was in fact counter to the idea of free love. These themes can be found in many of her essays and dramas including, among others, "Cómo se prostituyen las pobres" and "La corrupción de los ricos y la de los pobres o cómo se prostituye una rica y una pobre."[37]

It is clear in Capetillo's writing that her anarchist views, her attempt to dismantle authority and hierarchy, were directed at patriarchy and the society that created and reinforced it. In this same essay, she described scenes where men would come home from work, or from wherever, only to scare their children and then demand sex from their wives. And she asked how children created through such acts of forced intimacy, or "débito conyugal," could be considered children of love. Consequently, she looked forward to the day when women would be emancipated from the clerical tutelage that enforced such marriages, and when reason and conscience guided relationships.[38]

Capetillo did express confidence in the ability of women, freed from oppressive and legalistic relationships, to create wonderful and nurturing environments for children: "Each home will be a school . . . and fraternity will be the unique law that overwhelms our hearts." She concluded this essay with an appeal to all women: "Oh, women, the humanity's happiness is in your hands, take a book, and be friends, mothers and teachers of our children! What a beautiful truth!"[39] This passage, in particular, seems to allude to Capetillo's own childhood, nurtured by her own mother and the books that surrounded her.

Brazo y Cerebro appeared in print only twice. Vidal had encountered resistance from New York postal officials including a demand, to which he did not agree, to translate certain essays into English, although the exact circumstances of the paper's demise remain uncertain.[40] However, the specific problems confronting *Brazo y Cerebro* did not prevent Vidal from establishing an alternative paper to take its place. He was then, and had been for several years, in contact with the Mexican revolutionary Ricardo Flores Magón and the *Partido Liberal Mexicano* (PLM) in Los Angeles. They published their own periodical, *Regeneración*, that also reported on Vidal's forthcoming new "radical and anti-parliamentarian labor paper."[41] Vidal determinedly moved forward with *Fuerza Consciente* which first appeared on March 15, 1913. The inaugural issue began with an essay explaining the periodical's purpose: "'Fuerza Consciente' symbolizes the new man and new ideas. It is Anarchy, in which each individual is the center of the universe, with a positive right to his full development."[42] Capetillo published an essay in the second issue of *Fuerza Consciente*. Interestingly, Vidal printed one of his own, about class conflict, in the exact same position on the facing page as Capetillo's article. Her essay, "Por La Libertad Femenina" began with an entreaty for women to literally "wake-up": "When women realize that they should not be something sold, or obtained, for the highest price; when they are not rented like furniture . . . Then mothers will say to their daughters: join freely with whomever you prefer, without fear, and fulfill the natural law."[43]

It must be emphasized that men wrote virtually all the essays in these periodicals, with the notable exceptions of Emma Goldman and Luisa Capetillo. The typical reading audience was undoubtedly dominated by men as well, but they sometimes served as "readers" in their own homes and through such readings would expose their family to these periodicals and essays. Indeed, Capetillo's essays on free love were directed to men and women. She strongly promoted the belief that women and men are equal and that they should be able to satisfy all of their needs by right and freely. She stated that sexual relations are a natural and logical result of being in love: ". . . with love comes sexual pleasure among both sexes, a logical consequence and complement, and something very natural and necessary . . ."[44]

Capetillo also insisted that women should free themselves from the belief that sex is shameful. She pointed out that women typically believe—and are taught to believe—that sex is not good, pure or necessary—in fact, that sex is like a criminal act—and that by consequence of this perspective, women allow men to control and dictate sexual relations. At the same time, she observed, women typically refuse to have intimate relations with men unless a man agrees to marry. For Capetillo, this was an important issue because a woman might deny her own natural sexuality in order to force a marital union that might not, in the end, be based on love. And then, Capetillo reasoned, men would turn to other women, or to prostitutes, in whom they had no interest other than sex. Ultimately, Capetillo suggested that if women allowed themselves the liberty of "free love," everyone and society as a whole would be the better for it. "Therefore, women," she wrote, "be generous and brave, do not throw men into a life of vice because of your selfishness and for an incorrect concept of purity and chastity. Be pure and chaste loving freely, without contracts or hypocrisy, as nature consents. Spontaneous and natural love, to be truly love, needs to be free."[45]

This issue of *Fuerza Consciente* (August 9, 1913) which would be the last one published in New York, also included a brief unsigned essay about attempts by "authorities" in Rochester, Pennsylvania;

Chicago, Illinois; and Richmond, Virginia to regulate the way women dressed. . . . . Although making exceptions for dresses of "high-fashion" including the "falda transparente" and the "falda cortada" . . . . The essay concluded by noting that: "The world progresses, and there is nothing more natural than women's style of dress, that in truth they need to emancipate themselves from the uncomfortable and antihygienic dress."[46] Although the essay has no signature, it had Capetillo's markings.

On the Road Again

During the summer of 1913, Vidal decided to move from New York to Los Angeles, and he took *Fuerza Consciente* with him. He departed New York for good, presumably fed up with hostile treatment from local postal authorities; he was also attracted to the community of Mexican revolutionaries in Los Angeles. He traveled with Josephine Cipresso, his partner and a recently arrived Italian immigrant with whom he had one child, and the Spaniard José Vilariño, who was then serving as the business manager for *Fuerza Consciente*.

Vidal made the long trip on the North Western Railway during September 1913. It was during this trip that his strong intellectual bond with Capetillo became clear. She had asked Vidal to write the prologue for the forthcoming second edition of *Mi Opinión*, and he agreed to do it on the train ride west.[47] Titled "Dos Palabras" [Two Words] Vidal's prologue was dated September 28, 1913. He began his essay recounting that "Mi querida hermana Luisa Capetillo" had asked him to write a preface as he was preparing his move to California, so he was writing it now. He complimented Capetillo on "her beautiful and profound work" about the "sexual problem" that she had published in *Brazo y Cerebro* and *Fuerza Consciente*. Describing Capetillo as "one of the most independent and free women of the "raza hispano-americana," he explained that she dealt directly with issues related to free love that Anglo-Saxon writers ignored.

Vidal claimed that the idea of free love had always been part of the philosophy of anarchism; it was an intrinsic element in the anarchist project to emancipate humans from all forms of authoritarianism. But Vidal acknowledged that "slavery in the home" was an ongoing and unacceptable form of tyranny. Undoubtedly reflecting Capetillo's influence, Vidal made the point—somewhat unusual in much writing on free love in the male-dominated anarchist press—that it was not only the bourgeoisie, or "men of high social position," who took advantage of women in the home but even those who had been "disinherited" and otherwise opposed social and economic exploitation and tyranny, who in their own homes sometimes made their wives and children suffer. Vidal emphasized the importance of true equality and freedom from all oppression, and he concluded this preface with the desire that Capetillo's "regenerative work" be fruitful and intense.[48]

About one week after writing this essay, Vidal finally arrived in Los Angeles. "We have had the pleasure of meeting at the offices of *Regeneración*," wrote this paper's editors. Vidal also confirmed in the article that he would continue publishing *Fuerza Consciente* in Los Angeles.[49] The following issue of *Regeneración* (Oct. 11) included a brief notice that Vidal was preparing the third issue of *Fuerza Consciente* to be published on October 13, the anniversary of Spanish educator Francisco Ferrer's martyrdom. He had been executed in Barcelona four years earlier under the false charge of inciting the bloody *Semana Trágica* riots of 1909.

In the meantime, Capetillo had relocated as well, this time from New York City to Ybor City, Florida, and she continued to send essays to Vidal. Her next article again appeared on the facing page of one by Vidal that was titled "Prohibición y educación." Capetillo's essay, "Femeninas por la justicia," had been written in Ybor City and was dated October 16, 1913.[50]

Capetillo continued the theme of free love, but she clarified some of her earlier writing. This essay, clearly addressed to men, began abruptly and to the point: "Don't believe friendly supporters of free love that free love is about you persuading inexperienced young girls to give themselves to you, and later abandon them pregnant." Capetillo stated sarcastically that in this case, men should first warn women that they planned to leave them with a "remembrance" of their intimacy and without support. In fact, she wrote, "this is simply an abuse," and worldly men of vice should instead find women like them and not innocent young girls.[51] She repeated this theme later in the same essay, reminding my "esteemed friends" that "it is not my intention to promote free love so that you can surprise ignorant girls, humiliating them." Men should use the ideas of free love to make women free and happy, "but not for five minutes. . . ." Men must understand that if they do not actually love and desire a woman, they should not "possess her."[52]

According to news reports from Tampa, Capetillo departed for Cuba on December 21, 1913, after living in Ybor City for about one year, working as a cigar factory reader and giving "frequent street orations." She reportedly travelled to the island with the express purpose of "dissiminating [sic] the doctrine of free love."[53] Vidal himself had moved once again, along with *Fuerza Consciente*, from Los Angeles to San Francisco.

Capetillo's final essay for Vidal, "Educación Femenina," was dated January 7, 1914. It was an appeal for education, particularly to women who "have to direct the generations, entrusted to your care." In some respects, Capetillo provided her most philosophical view about life in the following passage asking women to:

> Learn and understand everything that is most essential for the knowledge of life, in accordance with natural laws. Also, know the reason for things, their origin and development, according to scientific and non-religious observations. To be educated is to be wise."[54]

Capetillo pointed out that many people considered themselves to be educated if they had learned a profession, but she observed that these individuals might actually "have no concept of the world . . ." It is the "great maternal mission," therefore, to "form the senses and direct our children's intelligences." She extolled the value of natural law, of nature and the interconnectedness of all living beings:

> It is therefore necessary, women, that you study Nature, and free yourself from religious dogmas and lies. True religion is about loving the neighbor and not about praying to images. Prepare yourselves to be free so that you freely educate your children, and create a new humanity.[55]

Now living in Havana, Capetillo continued her feminist activism. On July 24, 1915, she was famously arrested in Havana for causing a disturbance while walking down the street wearing pants.[56] While this event has been remembered as one of Capetillo's most transgressive public performances, it is clear that wearing pants was already a well-established theme in her crusade for gender equality and equal rights. Indeed, Capetillo's highly publicized, but otherwise largely ignored, street performance three years earlier on New York's Fifth Avenue was the moment when she most brazenly and publicly challenged gender norms in the United States.

During the years 1911 to 1913, Capetillo had ventured beyond Puerto Rico, first to New York City, then Ybor City and finally to Havana. This was a tour during which she performed, wrote, lectured to cigar makers and gave public talks. In a series of essays for Jaime Vidal, she challenged women to be fully aware of, and true to, their individual rights, personal freedoms, and sexual desires. Later in 1913, she clarified her message by including a strong reproach to men who took advantage of women, something she knew about all too well. Free love did not mean that men were at liberty to take advantage of women and then abandon them and their children.

The desire to educate men and women about gender equality, free love and sexuality was powerful in Capetillo. Her views, writings and actions were clearly anarcho-feminist and consistent with, if not even more advanced, than contemporary anarchist thought. At the same time, she fought against the ways in which men—even those who identified as anarchists—tried to demean and disempower women's equality and sexuality. During her own life, she sought to be, for both women and men, a powerful, thoughtful, and resourceful role model for equality; she wore pants to publicly express her ideas about freedom, and she wrote essays to explain them.

Loud, Hidden Voices of the Revolution: Reynalda González Parra, Organized Labor, and *Feminismo Transfronterizo*

SONIA HERNÁNDEZ
Texas A&M University

"Grab your red *rebozo* and join the fight"
Reynalda González Parra, "¡Al Abordaje!" *Germinal*
(Tampico, Tamaulipas) June 14, 1917

Five years after the breakout of the Mexican Revolution, Reynalda González Parra, a young educator and writer from the border state of Chihuahua, left the Mexican capital and headed toward the Gulf of Mexico port of Tampico. As revolutionary factions led by *caudillos* (strongmen) and rebels fought over the strategic oil-rich fields of Tampico located near the Pánuco River extending toward the *faja de oro negro* in Veracruz, a group of idealists and pragmatists influenced by anarchism, put these ideas to practice to wage their own revolution. González Parra formed part of this corpus of activists, and theirs would be a "true" revolution, separate from what they considered a bourgeois revolution now led by regional *norteño* elite, Venustiano Carranza. As González Parra wrote in 1917 in the anarchist newspaper *Germinal*, "grab your red *rebozo*," she urged women to follow the red, anarchist path, to "join the fight," to bring about equality for *all* workers.[1] While state-

sanctioned violence and press censure at the behest of Carranza
stifled a 'true' revolution as envisioned by this smaller, more radical,
yet equally powerful segment of revolutionary Mexico, their ideals
and histories left an imprint on numerous communities. Of particular
significance, but not fully examined, was the gender equality that
this more radical, anarchist vision could potentially yield. González
Parra was among these anarchist visionaries who dreamed of an
equitable world to which all women and men could aspire. González
Parra swam with so-called big fish—Jacinto Huitrón and Ricardo
Treviño; her writings appear alongside giants like Ricardo Flores
Magón. Yet, despite her loud, public voice in a visionary world of
gender, labor, and racial equality, free of national boundaries and
religious impositions, her voice remains largely hidden.[2]

Historians have expended energy examining the rise of the 1912
Casa del Obrero Mundial (COM)—the House of the Global
Worker—as the earliest and most radical embodiment of anarchism
in Mexico. With few exceptions, the literature on the COM's
influence on the Gulf of Mexico region has centered on male
workers and male thinkers within the context of anarchism and its
more structured form, anarcho-syndicalism, which privileged the
labor union outside of the bounds of the state.[3] This essay builds
upon this historiography but centers on a crucial voice in the history
of anarcho-syndicalism and the COM and the emergence of
transnational feminism within this wing of the labor movement. It
seeks to underscore the voice and actions of Reynalda González
Parra, a relative unknown in the historiography of labor, the
Mexican Revolution, and the greater history of intellectual exchange
along the US-Mexican borderlands. By doing so, the gendered and
transnational dimensions of greater revolutionary Mexico come to
the fore and expose hidden voices and lived experiences of women
who shaped the course of democratization in profound ways.

An emerging Feminismo Transfronterizo: *Anarchist and Feminist Linkages*

Since the early nineteenth century, women have participated in
various efforts to increase their opportunities in education, welfare,

health and sanitation, and labor rights. By mid-century, women had also formed part of delegations to some of the first regional and national labor congresses in Mexico, and by 1891, they called for suffrage. However, it was not until the turn of the twentieth century that a more structured, cohesive agenda centered on women's labor issues emerged. As ideas about the social welfare of workers began to circulate in sites around the globe that underwent industrialization, a gradual opening took place in labor organizations and their print propaganda in which women's issues were included. An open call for women to "join the struggle" to usher social and political change in Mexico as early as 1901 helped create a viable opening for women's increased involvement in labor matters. In the north, in San Luis Potosí, anarchists, including Ricardo Flores Magón and Camilo Arriaga met in what became the first Liberal Congress that led to the establishment of the *Partido Liberal Mexicano* (PLM). The PLM advocated the overthrow of Mexican dictator Porfirio Díaz, promoted worker autonomy and women's labor protections, and sought an end to child labor, among other progressive causes.

While riddled with gendered assumptions and normative expectations for both women and men, an anarcho-feminist discourse on women's rights emerged during the years leading up to the Mexican Revolution. Anarcho-feminism differed in three basic ways from a mainstream *feminismo* embodied in a women's rights agenda that had, by the early twentieth century, distinguished itself by prioritizing women's suffrage. First, Mexican anarcho-feminism within organizations such as the PLM and the COM was not pre-occupied with suffrage as its main goal. Second, anarcho-feminists opted for direct action and protests resembling communist-based women's organizing and were not hierarchically organized. It differed from communist organizations as it rejected any affiliation with a political party. Third, while anarcho-feminism resonated with the emerging privileging of maternalism/motherhood in the revolutionary rhetoric espoused by the Carranza government and his successors, anarcho-feminism differed, distinguishing its revolutionary motherhood through its rejection of clericalism and affiliation to a religious institution; it underscored revolutionary motherhood to serve the women themselves, not the interests of the nation-state. Lastly, it envisioned both a class-less and nation-less collective of women and men as an alternative to socio-economic and political inequalities, which industrial capitalism further exacerbated. Anarchist beliefs, at least as framed and explained by thinkers that came to fill the pages of the Tampico anarchist press, including González Parra, critiqued the plight of workers and the institutions that perpetuated gender hierarchies despite claims about women's societal value.

González Parra was among these early thinkers and pioneers who pushed the boundaries of anarchist thought to make room for women in the broadest sense. She was introduced to anarchist thought via the COM and its newspapers, including the ideas of Francisco Ferrer i Guardia, Teresa Claramunt, and Ricardo Flores Magón, among others. Her writings in the Tampico press, while not extensive, circulated within and beyond Mexico's borders, and her actions in Tampico and Mexico City concerning labor organizing are noteworthy. These fragments of her lived experiences help us trace how her *feminismo* was anchored in anarchism and reflected her thoughts on the role of collective action despite geo-political borders. Her *feminismo* was *transfronterizo* in thought and action despite the lack of evidence of her migration across geo-political borders. Her ideas represented an avant-garde thinking because she took normative gendered expectations and reframed them to reflect a new understanding of women's place in society. Her *feminismo transfronterizo* was an activism that "reconceptualized location," promoting the nation-less anarchist vision, while advocating for women's equality. While González Parra moved in labor circles in Tampico, her local community formed part of the larger US-Mexican border ambit, "historically a crossroads of political, economic, and social ideological exchange."[4]

While González Parra left a mark in the history of revolutionary Mexico and in the emergence of feminist/s discourse, there is little scholarship on her contributions. However, a growing literature in history and related fields on the idea of revolutionary motherhood and transnational feminisms helps to better contextualize González

Parra's lived experience. As scholars Pilar Melero and Emma Pérez note, border women had contributed their ideas about women's advancement influenced by *magonismo* and had applied those ideas to respond to socio-economic and political developments in their local communities.[5]

Gender ideals in this corner of the world took on a transnational character that mirrored both United States and Mexican heteronormative conceptions of the family unit and both were sites of a gendered and racialized hierarchy. Claiming motherhood thus formed part of a larger feminist political strategy to address "problems of racism and poverty," as well as claim equal status, as historian Gabriela González has written.[6] Motherhood then operated as an identity that could be used for self-empowerment and to deal with unfavorable living and working conditions. For working-class women and those concerned about labor issues such as González Parra, their identity as women was informed by their class position and limited access to economic resources.

While the gender ideals that dictated norms for Mexican women in places like Texas and northern Mexico were framed in nineteenth-century concepts of domesticity, the Mexican Revolution provided an opening to include women's political and social issues, as scholar Clara Lomas has shown. In short, based on my analysis of González Parra's writings, this gradual reconfiguration of gender which Lomas, Pérez, and González have explained correlates with González Parra's ability to enter a labor activist world, still overwhelmingly occupied by men.[7]

Unlike other prominent labor leaders, we have limited biographical data on González Parra. She was most likely born in 1878 in Casas Grandes, Chihuahua and sometime between her childhood and early adult years moved to Mexico City.[8] Little is known about her childhood, but she soon began working as an organizer and educator for the COM in Mexico City. González Parra contributed her thoughts in at least seven commentaries published in two anarchist newspapers, *Germinal* and *Tribuna Roja*, and likely her writings were re-printed in other newspapers either in Mexico or abroad, as this was commonplace in the anarchist press. An examination of González

Parra's writings, mostly in the form of editorial commentaries on the question of equality, women's rights, and workers' rights provides a window into her philosophy. Her presence in the press is noteworthy as only a handful of women's writings appear in either of these newspapers during the 1910-1920 period.

COM-sponsored *Germinal* and *Tribuna Roja* functioned as early vehicles by which women like González Parra shared their goals and aspirations. Founded in 1912, the COM was run by railroad worker and activist Jacinto Huitrón and colleagues, including Manuel Sarabia. The year it was founded, the COM proceeded to put to practice the ideas of Alella native Francisco Ferrer i Guardia, among others, to provide the theoretical foundation for their collective organizing. Working alongside González Parra was Adolfo González, Paula Osorio Avendaño, Genoveva Hidalgo, and an engineer named Manuel Velasco. Together they offered a hands-on approach to an education modeled after the ideas of Ferrer emphasizing individuals' ability to think in a rational, non-dogmatic and non-clerical way to achieve full liberty. After Spanish authorities executed Ferrer in 1909, supporters and like-minded activists did not let his philosophical worldview die; they carried the mantle setting up reading groups to discuss Ferrer's work, organized labor collectives bearing his name, and established *escuelas racionalistas* modeled after his *talleres* or workshops in Spain. In basic terms, his pedagogical framework proposed free thought based on rational ideas and not on the teachings of the Church (Catholicism) nor the state. This was the foundation for true freedom. It also envisioned an education for girls and boys in equal terms; both were entitled to the same theories and practices during their formative years to transform them into full-fledged individuals.[9] While the idea of gender educational equality was not new in Mexican circles, the COM took it a step further and applied a hands-on approach and structured their organization to achieve gender parity. The COM team regularly met to discuss teaching lessons and field trips, including site visits to nearby textile factories operating thanks to the labor of many of their fellow COM members.[10] Ideas about worker autonomy and worker dignity popularized by Magón and PLM colleagues complemented the *racionalista* approach adopted by COM members. These ideas featured in the anarchist press appealed to workers because they emerged as a response to the Porfirian industrial capitalist project.

As industrial capitalism proliferated in the capital, women's labor became more conspicuous in sectors defined as light industries, including textiles and food factories catering to the labor and demographic changes. On the eve of the COM's founding, at least 35% of the labor force in Mexico City was female; *obreras* labored in textiles, food preparation establishments, candy shops, *tabacaleras*, and related industries.[11] Women's presence as *obreras* and particularly as *madres obreras* forced society to see them as members of a rapidly growing working-class community.

This changing labor landscape increased the presence of women in organized labor and activists like González Parra helped organize *obreras*. González Parra worked to organize seamstresses and bottling factory workers who then joined the ranks of the COM.[12] The COM became one of the first labor-based collectives to welcome women constituents who found a welcoming space to share their labor grievances and hopes for a better livelihood.[13]

Figure 1. "Casa del Obrero Mundial" (COM) members, Mexico City, ca. 1912. Courtesy: Fototeca, Instituto Nacional de Antropología e Historia.

González Parra was one of six teachers at the COM's *escuela racionalista*. She shared the responsibility of guiding close to one hundred pupils. She and her colleagues took children attending the COM-sponsored school to nearby cultural sites including historic

Xochimilco, acknowledging the cultural and indigenous heritage of the Mexican labor force. Curricular highlights included a workshop about the effects of industrialization on the Mexican industrial labor force. Both boys and girls were presumed equal, and each lesson plan privileged this fundamental principle. While the *racionalista* model dealt with more than gender equality, at least in Mexico, as historian Ana Ribero Carbó explains, these ideas were adopted by the COM and helped transform it into "a site for the exchange of libertarian ideas, geared toward an emergent syndicalist movement which sought to prepare men and women in the struggle for a world that embraced solidarity, just and equal and one not to prepare them to compete with one another in the labor market . . ."[14] The COM did not replicate Ferrer's ideas verbatim, but it nonetheless ushered its own brand of anarcho-feminist syndicalism inspired by Ferrer.[15]

Beyond Rhetoric: Feminismo Tranfronterizo

As a full-fledged Revolution raged in the countryside and urban centers, the COM continued its mission and other branches emerged. Among the largest and most successful branches of the COM was the collective in Tampico, of which González Parra was a co-founder. With support from various regional groups from different trades and those that "had been affiliated to or supported both the IWW and the PLM," the Tampico COM quickly recruited members.[16] It enlisted women and men from artisan trades, including laundry workers, food vendors, tailors, bakers, oil workers, printers, chauffeurs, stone-masons, and carpenters. The Tampico COM operated as an umbrella organization to which smaller anarchist groups and unions affiliated and formed the crux of the radical, working-class arm of organized labor in the region compared to mutual-aid organizations and socialist groups of the region, such as the *Gremio de Alijadores* (Dockworkers' Union), that later became affiliated with the revolutionary state.[17]

The Tampico COM, founded in October 1915, emerged as a strong collective of labor activists. Members set up reading circles to discuss Ferrer's writings, re-print Magón's critiques, and re-printed essays written by Russians Peter Kropotkin and Emma Goldman, and *norteño* Librado Rivera, among others. They came together to analyze recent news stories featured in the anarchist press, celebrate the birth of an 'obrero' child, share book citations, or organize letter-writing campaigns to free detained political prisoners.[18] The COM branch also endorsed direct-action strategies such as labor strikes via *Germinal* and *Tribuna Roja*, its main newspapers in the Gulf of Mexico region. Many of its news stories were reprinted in other Mexican newspapers and in the international anarchist press.

While in Tampico González Parra participated in a COM-sponsored labor conference. The *Segundo Congreso Obrero Regional* took place on October 13, 1917, in tribute to Ferrer, whom Spanish authorities executed on that day eight years prior. The *Congreso* transpired despite President Carranza's purging of anarchists affiliated with the COM and affinity groups. Labor collectives and its delegates, including González Parra, stuck to the plan and attended.[19] The tense environment overshadowed the solemn occasion to honor Ferrer as conference participants remained on guard.

Calls for global solidarity with workers from various parts of the world figured prominently in the conference's resolution. The urgency of transnational collaboration was invoked because members pledged how "an insult to one [worker] is an insult to all [workers]," which echoed similar proclamations throughout the world by organizations such as the IWW. Other principles advocated by attendees included "*organización sindical*" or "organizing through unions," as the "most efficient medium" by which "the proletariat could reach its goals."[20]

Two resolutions adopted in the *Segundo Congreso Obrero* stood out in their boldness given the time period. These reflected the larger gendered concerns of Tampico members like González Parras. One resolution gave the "right to workers to avoid unlimited procreation when this place[d] economic threats on their livelihoods," reflecting larger concerns over reproductive rights. Another resolution, appearing as point number six of ten, "recommended all labor organizations and *grupos educativos*, etc., carry and promote an active propaganda to encourage women's education and women's organizations as well as that of the peasant and all of the workers who need to be in contact with the centers of propaganda and collectives."[21] González Parra's participation as a delegate shifted the conversation to include such provisions. She appears as the lone female delegate endorsing and signing the resolutions among thirty-four male delegates at the convention. The resolutions concerning gender issues reveal the extent to which labor activists concerned themselves with matters that were *obrera*-based, but with broad relevancy to all workers.

González Parra's activist participation in the *Congreso* reflected her deep commitment to the gendered concerns within the growing labor movement. While she lauded women's reproductive capacity, she nonetheless couched it within an anarchist framework. In "A la Mujer," in *Germinal*, she reminded her readers that "women [are] evolving and [now she] occupies her place . . . and sees her actions and claims her right to educate herself, to learn and then use her strength to launch that final blow that will change the course of things, create a new path . . ." She further politicized women's reproductive capacity by urging them to "emancipate yourselves, because then you will produce free children and you will have contributed to the reconstruction . . . of a new society . . ."[22] But, her revolutionary motherhood would not serve the interests of the new revolutionary regime. For González Parra individuals such as Carranza had failed the real revolution. Instead, because this vision served the very ideals for which anarchists had risked their lives, it would bring about a new cadre of revolutionary thinkers that would ultimately transform society not by implementing yet another government to represent the nation-state, but by self-governance in a collective trans-border world void of any class distinction. It was a motherhood that served the interests of the women themselves and their communities, not the state. That made her ideas about motherhood radical because they deviated from the state-promoted rhetoric.

González Parra's *feminismo transfronterizo* reflected her own concerns about the more significant transformations unfolding in her environment and her ideas about how best to effect change. She understood the place of organized labor and particularly the place of the organizations supporting workers in gendered terms. She made sense of the COM as a mother guiding a family but refracted through anticlericalism. She urged colleagues not to "make the COM into the type of family that blindly follows God." She wrote, "do not make the *Casa del Obrero*, [which is] our common and loving mother, into what Catholics do . . . to the family . . . they tie it to God." She continued explaining how belief in God created a false dichotomy that, at its core, destroyed the very foundation of the family. She argued that the COM had to, at any cost, avoid acting like God, "God . . . either loves his children or throws them into that so-called hell." According to González Parra, the true revolutionaries had to reject this false dichotomy to achieve real liberty and equality and in this way, her rejection of a man-made religion captured the secular revolutionary spirit framing anarchist views.[23] She was not against family in the cooperative-egalitarian sense of the term but in her opinion, the family who blindly followed religious doctrine was doomed and more importantly, it was the structuring of family via religion that helped to breed inequality within the home.

González Parra's message of privileging motherhood from a radical political perspective, albeit in a heteronormative context in and outside of the home, stood in stark contrast to some of her colleagues' superficial calls for gender equity. COM-sponsored newsletters and newspapers such as *Ariete* published pieces by COM members whose gender equity message fell short. Leobardo Castro in "*La Infancia en la Casa del Obrero Mundial*," praised the work of COM educators such as González Parra's in the "first ever school of rational thought."[24] He boasted that these "*compañeritos nuestros*," many of whom were the children of COM members who toiled in the factories, could begin a new life with the real knowledge needed to fight inequalities. However, as he closed his message about the need to send children to the new COM-sponsored *Escuela Racionalista*, he exclaimed, "*¡Las madres a sus deberes domésticos; los padres a los sindicatos, para ser Fuertes; y los niños, a la escuela racionalista de la Casa del Obrero Mundial!*"[25] Thus, while COM supporters promoted rhetoric of gender equality, too often, those same progressives replicated the old domestic-private/public sphere that contradicted the very message that an anarchist *feminismo transfronterizo* sought to convey.

In other commentaries González Parra published, she further urged women to join the proletariat uprising. She promoted the goals of the anarcho-syndicalist movement and of all the COM branches, publicly underscoring the issues that mattered most to *obreras*, which included good wages to sustain themselves and their families, fair working conditions, gender equity within and beyond labor collectives, and reproductive rights. The COM held "conferences on labor issues" and "conferences focused on labor unionism among women."[26] In "¡Al Abordaje!" published that same year, González Parra exclaimed in detailed prose, "don't you hear the shots from the gun-fire, those outrageous screams, the groans from the *hijos del pueblo* (the children of the people) who lay on the ground, their bodies pierced with bullets, not from enemies but from brothers who have been lost since childhood? Rise up! Join the multitude who enraged have now clenched their fists!" She continued, "grab your red *rebozo*/shawl and join the fight," and exclaimed, ". . . if you are not yet sick from the incense and the falsity of glorious promises have not yet driven you crazy . . . if you feel like a man at least once in your lifetime, then brandish the axe of vengeance and fight with a raucous voice, all aboard!"[27] González Parra's writings reflected her belief in gender equity with her own biases about men's comportment. She urged men to act like 'real men', thereby using the old masculine trope as the normative standard to measure all men. While González Parra vocalized her commitment to gender equality, her *feminismo* also echoed or reinforced normative behavior for men.[28]

Figure 2. Reynalda Gonzalez Parra, lone female delegate at the Segundo Congreso Obrero held in Tampico, 1917. Image available on the internet and included in accordance with Title 17, Section 107.

As González Parra's writings invoked her revolutionary motherhood within an anarchist framework, it too invoked the belief in a community of workers beyond geo-political borders taking on a transborder or *transfronterizo* character.[29] Her ideas and written thoughts in *Germinal* and *Tribuna Rojo* reached audiences across the border in Texas, both big and small and reflect larger, extra-local imperatives that concerned all workers. Yet, González Parra never quite lost focus on the local conditions, she linked more significant developments to her community to make sense of socio-economic and political developments. Similarly, her writings were shared with foreign audiences as these anarchist newspapers circulated beyond Mexico.[30]

Germinal featured commentaries submitted by fellow COM supporters within Mexico and throughout Texas. Clippings of specific *Germinal* news stories and, at times, entire issues made their way across the Río Grande folded neatly into the correspondence destined to PLM-based groups in Texas. In this way, via literature the ideas of women like González Parra reached distant places with the potential to influence other women and men.

Small towns across Texas such as Buda and La Coste as well as budding urban centers like San Antonio, Houston, and Dallas served as the home of a variety of labor-based groups, including IWW, PLM, and clubs affiliated to the Texas Socialist Party learned about developments in the port of Tampico. Other news that traveled with migrants searching for employment opportunities in Tampico's oil sector made its way via correspondence and newspaper sharing. Editorials on workers' conditions from Havana, for example, reprinted from *El Productor Panadero* appeared in Germinal and reached audiences in Texas. Other news farther afield from Barcelona's *Tierra y Libertad* featuring women's conditions in factories added to the diverse coverage offered by the small but influential anarchist Tampico press. Donations, big and small, from diverse organizations as well as funds from the local labor collectives from the port sustained the overall operation of the small press. Relying on collective sharing and word-of-mouth propaganda became crucial to women's continued public presence in the world of labor activism.[31]

The re-circulation of newspapers and re-prints of stories helped to spread the COM's reach within and beyond Mexico and resulted in the establishment of reading groups and labor collectives in Texas. Further north in San Antonio, Texas, a Ferrer-inspired collective had emerged with substantial female participation, including Isaura Galván who later served as *Germinal's administradora* during González Parra's activist days in Tampico. Responding in good part to the increase in the number of wealthy exiles tied to the old Porfirian regime who had made their home in San Antonio, the new group emerged to continue the struggle abroad. Embracing ". . . anarchist centers' [concerns]," Galván and thirty-eight other individuals, including thirteen women, formed this collective during the spring of 1915. The group adhered to "the widening of the ideals of freedom" and critiqued how San Antonio had become "a nest of the Mexican plutocracy" and sought to "enter the struggle for existence . . . making the fight of other anarchist centers our own and those to come throughout the continent."[32] Other like-minded collectives set up shop in Texas and maintained ties to the Tampico COM and other affinity groups.

Via the re-printing of news stories, commentaries, and other writings by anarchists such as González Parra, anarchism slowly spread throughout the city and countryside within and beyond Mexico. Despite its limitations and riddled with its own gendered biases, the COM and its media outlets had proven a crucial base in which González Parra engaged and promoted a *feminismo transfronterizo* that envisioned a better future for all workers, including women.

González Parra politicized and radicalized the idea of motherhood to claim women's autonomy, independence, and full liberty to serve her own interests and benefit her community, not to serve as a pawn of the state or any political entity.[33] In this way, her *feminismo* took on a *transfronterizo* character and privileged motherhood that was both revolutionary and anarchist.

By the early 1930s, the idea of the revolutionary mother as a true citizen of the new Mexican state—synonymous with the Calles Administration and subsequent presidencies—quickly became a manipulative trope used to integrate women into a new post-Revolutionary state. Yet, such revolutionary motherhood was more rhetoric than reality. However, González Parra's *feminismo transfronterizo* remained a vibrant, loud reminder of the diversity within organized labor, which the subsequent revolutionary regimes could not completely erase. Her voice is a testament to women's direct role in paving a rugged, albeit uneven, long path toward the democratization of Mexico, of which anarcho-feminist ideas formed part. These echoes remain within and well beyond the country's geopolitical borders despite the revolutionary government's intent to silence the most radical wing of the labor movement and despite the lack of scholarship on one of the most dynamic anarcho-feminists of the early twentieth century.[34]

Works Cited

Archival
Archivo General de la Nación, Mexico City (AGN)
Fondo: Magonistas Revoltosos (MR)
Universidad Autónoma de Tamaulipas (IIH-UAT)
Instituto de Investigaciones Históricas-Archivo Histórico,
Fondo: Esteban Méndez Guerra
Hemeroteca Histórica
Archivo Librado Rivera y Los Hermanos Rojos, *www.libradorivera.com* (ALR-HR)
Archivo Histórico de Tampico Carlos González Salas (AHT) Fondo: Presidencia
Sterling C. Evans Library, Texas A&M University (College Station)
Hispanic American Historical Newspapers

Newspapers
¡Luz! (Mexico City)
Ariete: Revista Sociológica (Mexico City)
Regeneración (Los Angeles)

Revolución (Los Angeles)
Germinal: Periódico Libertario (Tampico)
Sagitario: Mensual Sociológico (Villa Cecilia)

Secondary Works

Adelson, Leif, "Historia social de los obreros industriales de Tampi co, 1906-1919." PhD Dissertation, El Colegio de México, 1982.

Alcayaga Sasso, Aurora Mónica, "Librado Rivera y Los Hermanos Rojos en el MovimientoSocial y Cultural Anarquista en Villa Cecilia y Tampico, Tamaulipas, 1915-1932," Tesis Doctoral, Universidad Iberoamericana, 2006.

Barry Carr, "The Casa del Obrero Mundial, Constitutionalism and the Pact of February 1915," edited by Elsa Cecilia Frost, et al (eds), *El trabajo y los trabajadores en la historia de México.* México, Tucson: El Colegio de México, U of Arizona, 1979.

Castañeda, Christopher J. and Montse Feu, eds. *Writing Revolution: Hispanic Anarchist Print Culture and the United States, 1868-2015.* U of Illinois P, 2019.

Cole, Peter, Stuthers, David, and Zimmer, Kenyon. eds. *Wobblies of the World: A Global History of the IWW.* Pluto P, 2017.

Fernández Aceves, María Teresa, Carmen Ramos Escandón, Susie Porter, coord. *Orden Social e identidad de género: México, siglos XIX y XX.* Guadalajara: Universidad de Guadalajara, 2006.

Hart, John Mason, *Anarchism and the Mexican Working Class.* Austin: U of Texas P, 1978.

Hernández, Sonia, "Revisiting *Mexican(a)* Labor History through *Feminismo Transfronterista*: From Tampico to Texas and Beyond, 1910-1940" *Frontiers: A Journal of Women Studies*, Transnational Feminism Special Issue, vol. 36. num. 3, 2015, pp. 107-136.

____. "For a Just and Better World": *Engendering Anarchism in the Mexican Borderlands, 1900-1938.* U of Illinois P, 2021.

Huitrón, Jacinto. *Orígenes e historia del movimiento obrero en México.* Editores Mexicanos Unidos, 1974.

Kanellos, Nicolás, "Spanish-Language Anarchist Periodicals in Early Twentieth-Century United States," in *Protest on the Page.* U of Wisconsin, 2014.

Lomas, Clara, "The Articulation of Gender in the Mexican Borderlands, 1900-1915," edited by Ramón Gutiérrez and Genaro Padilla, ed. *Recovering the U.S. Hispanic Literary Heritage.* Arte Público P, 1993.

Las mujeres en la revolución mexicana: biografía de mujeres revolucionarias. INEHRM, 1992.

Lau, Ana y Carmen Ramos. *Mujeres y Revolución: 1900-1917.* INEHRM, 1993.

Lear, John. *Workers, Neighbors, and Citizens: The Revolution in Mexico City.* U of Nebraska P, 2001.

Melero, Pilar. *Mythological Constructs of Mexican Femininity*, 1st edition. Palgrave, 2015.

Oikion Solano, Verónica. *Cuca García (1889-1973): Por las causas de las mujeres y la revolución.* Colegio de Michoacán; Colegio de San Luis, 2018.

Olcott, Jocelyn. *Revolutionary Women in Post-Revolutionary Mexico.* Duke UP, 2006.

Pérez, Emma. *The Decolonial Imaginary: Writing Chicanas into History.* Indiana UP, 1999.

Porter, Susie. *Working Women in Mexico City: Public Discourses and Material Conditions, 1879-1931.* AUP, 2003.

Ribera Carbó, Anna. La Casa del Obrero Mundial: Anarcosindicalismo y revolución en México. México: INAH, 2010.

____. "Mujeres Sindicalistas: Las Trabajadoras de la Casa del Obrero Mundial (1912-1916). Una aproximación a las fuentes para su estudio," file:///C:/Users/soniah/Downloads/Dialnet Mujeres Sindicalistas LasTrabajadoras DeLaCasaDelObre-1256568.pdf [accessed October 1, 2019].

Shaffer, Kirwin, "Freedom Teaching: Anarchism and Education in Early Republican Cuba, 1898-1925," *The Americas*, 60. 2, October 2003, pp. 151-183.

Josefina de la Grana's Letters to the Editor: A Window into her Activism in Tampa, Florida

ANA VARELA-LAGO
Independent Scholar

In a letter to the editor of the *Tampa Morning Tribune* on the importance of defending freedom of speech in radio broadcasting, Josefina de la Grana revealed her own experience with censorship. It was 1934, and a Unitarian minister had invited her to participate in a forum on religion at a local radio station to speak on "the religion of a reformer." "I am no reformer!" de la Grana replied. "In fact I detest the whole tribe for they actually believe that our capitalist system is fundamentally sound! I am a radical." The minister encouraged her to change the title to "the religion of a radical," but the program never aired. As de la Grana explained, some "mysterious manipulation" prevented the broadcast. When the minister, outraged by the censorship, protested the violation of her constitutional rights, de la Grana observed: "You are free to say what you please if your ideas agree with those of the powers that be, otherwise—well—some accident will always happen to delicate mechanisms!" ("Radio").

Fortunately, censorship did not interfere—or not as fully—with the dissemination of de la Grana's ideas in the printed press. Over three hundred of her contributions to the correspondence sections of Tampa's two leading dailies survive.[1] As Karin Wahl-Jorgensen argues, letters to the editor represent "a rich source of vernacular

207

social and political history" (v). They illustrate "dominant debates or prevailing public opinion in a particular time and place." Equally important, they provide "access to the voices of individuals and groups who have been marginalized in historical accounts" (vii). In de la Grana's case, these documents are particularly relevant because they are one of the few sources available to scholars in an otherwise slim historical archive. This article uses two decades of de la Grana's letters to the editor as a window into Tampa's vernacular history and the history of Latin women's activism.

Like other women of her generation, de la Grana participated in various social, cultural, and civic organizations. She was also a committed feminist and socialist. In Tampa, as in most of the American South, associations were structured along gender, racial, and ethnic lines. De la Grana's background and outlook shaped her efforts to bridge some of those fractures. As a college-educated "white" woman she was welcomed in several of Anglo Tampa's organizations. As a "Latin" married to a Spanish cigar worker, her voice often supported Tampa's immigrant community.[2] As a feminist and a socialist, she advocated for the rights of women and workers. In the 1930s, de la Grana was remarkably active beyond her letter writing. She ran for mayor of Tampa as a Socialist in 1931, worked as a labor organizer for the Cigar Makers' International Union, and supported the Spanish Republic during the Spanish Civil War—a defining political moment for Tampa's Latin community.

Despite her very public activism, de la Grana's name is absent, or appears only briefly in the scholarly record. This article begins the task of recovering both her writings and her biography. It brings to light de la Grana's upbringing in New Orleans, her formative years as a student at Newcomb College, her move to Tampa in 1914, and the transnational connections of her family. This, in turn, contextualizes her activism, primarily in the 1930s, when her identity as a Latin, a woman, and a socialist came together in the life and work of this self-proclaimed radical.

Family Roots and Upbringing: The Making of a "Newcomb Girl."

Josefina de la Grana was born Josefina Díaz Cannere on February 12, 1888 in Camargo, in the Mexican state of Tamaulipas, across the border from Texas. She was the first child of Pablo Díaz, a Cuban physician, and Margarita Cannere.[3] A few years after her birth, the family moved to New Orleans. Josefina attended the Guillot Institute for Girls, excelling in French, literature, and music. In one of her letters to the editor of the *Tampa Daily Times,* she reminisced about her childhood literary ambitions. Describing her experience reading *Jane Eyre* with her best friend, she wrote: "We both aspired to become writers someday in the golden future" (*"Havana"*).

After graduating from Guillot, in 1905, Josefina enrolled in Newcomb College, the women's college affiliated with Tulane University. There she continued her studies in literature and French and, by her senior year, was vice-president of the French Club (*"Cerclé"*). At her graduation ceremony, Josefina received an award for the best French essay (*"Fair"*). Another essay was awarded a literary prize by L'Athénée Louisianais and earned her a mention in Ruby Van Allen Caulfeild's book *French Literature of Louisiana.*[4]

Josefina's language skills would prove valuable when she moved to Tampa, a multiethnic environment where English shared space with other languages, particularly Spanish and Italian. A letter by Louise Pearce to the *Tampa Morning Tribune* describing her visit to the county farm (a charitable institution that included a hospital and asylum) illustrates this:

> On a recent call at the county farm with Mrs. J. de la Grana. Down a corridor came Tillie, jabbering to herself. To Tillie's delight, Mrs. de la Grana joined her in French. To an aged woman sitting all alone, Mrs. de la Grana spoke in Spanish. How ardently the old creature seized her hand as she responded. Writhing upon a bed and moaning, was a pitiful wreck. To her, Mrs. de la Grana spoke Italian. The moaning ceased as she eagerly replied in the same tongue. I wish that I could speak and write three foreign languages and English, as eloquently, as correctly, as Mrs. de la Grana.

Modern languages were part of the liberal arts curriculum in many women's colleges at the turn of the twentieth century, but this visit reveals another important component of Josefina's Newcomb education—a progressive brand of civic engagement.

Like other Southern women's colleges, Newcomb sought to reconcile "the traditional icon of the Southern Lady with the end-of-the-century New Woman" (Watts 80). As Trent Watts argues, the "Newcomb girls" did not radically challenge the main tenets of Southern culture, but the college's rhetoric was "often distinctly progressive" (91). Students were exposed to the social reform movements of the time, like suffrage or public health reform, and had the opportunity to meet some of their leaders, like Jean Gordon or Eleanor McMain. Faculty and alumnae provided important models of female civic engagement and social activism. Josefina no doubt learned those lessons.

The class of 1909, Josefina's graduating class, became the exemplar of a "modern" Newcomb education. In 1908, the senior class embarked on a program of reform meant to create a more meaningful collegiate experience. Women's suffrage and women's rights permeated the calls for reforms. In 1909, the Newcomb College Equal Suffrage League invited suffragist Maud Wood Park to campus. Women's suffrage was also one of the topics in the debate program. Students used the new literary magazine *The Arcade* to argue for Newcomb female representation on the Board of Administrators of Tulane University and to demand that Newcomb female faculty receive equal pay with their male counterparts (Tyler 306, 309). Scholars have shown how these "Newcomb girls" engaged in and led various important social and civic movements in New Orleans and elsewhere (Tucker and Willinger). Josefina Díaz, too, would carry her Newcomb experience to Florida and leave her mark there as a defender of women's rights and other progressive movements striving to change Southern (and American) society.

The Move to Tampa: From Josefina Díaz to Mrs. J. de la Grana

In 1914, Josefina's family relocated to Tampa where Pablo Díaz's siblings and mother lived. Originally from Cuba, the Díaz family had joined thousands of their compatriots in Key West and Tampa when cigar manufacturers moved their factories there in the late nineteenth century to avoid social and political unrest in the island. Cuban émigré communities in the United States would become instrumental in supporting the struggle for national independence culminating in the Spanish-Cuban-American War of 1898 (Poyo; Lazo).

The first immigrant settlement, east of Tampa, was built in 1885. It was named Ybor City after Vicente Martínez Ybor, a Spanish cigar manufacturer who received enticements from the newly created Chamber of Commerce to bring his factory to the then sleepy town of seven hundred inhabitants. Ybor City's booming success led a decade later to the development of another "cigar city," West Tampa (Mormino and Pozzetta; Méndez). As cigar factories multiplied, the towns became magnets for an assortment of businesses that catered to the cigar workers. Josefina's uncles, Máximo and Manuel, were among those pioneering entrepreneurs.

When the first trees were felled to build Ybor City, Máximo Díaz was already an established pharmacist in Key West. As Tampa's immigrant enclave grew, he moved the family there. Manuel Díaz had lived in Tampa in the 1890s but later moved to New Orleans. It was there that he married Mary Cannere, the sister of Josefina's mother, in 1897. By 1906, the couple had settled in West Tampa, where Manuel ran a pharmacy. Also in Tampa lived Josefina's aunt, Aurora Salas, and grandmother Micaela Díaz.

The first two decades of the twentieth century brought a formidable expansion of the cigar industry and a significant increase in immigration to Tampa. Latin became the term used to refer to the Cubans, Italians, and Spaniards that settled in the city. Afro-Cubans had to negotiate a difficult line between their Latin identity and the rigid strictures of racial identity in Jim Crow Florida (Greenbaum; Grillo). Mutual aid societies became a defining feature of Tampa's immigrant enclaves. Their striking clubhouses, among the most prominent buildings in the city, offered education, sociability, and entertainment to thousands of members. The immigrant architectural landscape also included hospitals and cemeteries. By 1914, when

Josefina moved to Tampa, there were five such Latin mutual aid societies.[5] A variety of smaller mutual aid organizations, local clubs, masonic lodges, and labor unions enriched the social, cultural, and political life of these immigrant communities (Mormino and Pozzetta).

Censuses and Tampa city directories indicate that Josefina, now in her twenties, lived in the family home in the relatively affluent and English-speaking neighborhood of Hyde Park. Her brothers began professional careers as dentists, but her work is harder to pin down.[6] Newspaper notices mentioned her participation in several social events—playing the piano at meetings of the Tampa Music Club ("Tampa"; "Music"), singing in the Friday Morning Musicale Chorus ("Big Circus"), and attending gatherings organized by the Ladies' Section of the Centro Español ("La Sección"). As the local press coverage of these events illustrates, while Josefina participated in both worlds (Anglo and Latin) the two remained somewhat separated. Terese Volk Tuohey has documented these divisions and argued that clubs like the Friday Morning Musicale, which appealed to middle-class women, recruited primarily women "from a white, Protestant background" (7). After World War I, this segregation began to change, but Josefina was often the only woman with a Latin name in the (non-immigrant) organizations she joined.[7]

Life changed significantly for Josefina in the 1920s. In 1923 her mother died. In the summer of 1925, her father too passed away. A few months later she married José de la Grana, a Spanish cigar selector, and moved to West Tampa. It was then that she started to develop a more public persona. Mrs. J. de la Grana became her signature as she began to express her views in the correspondence columns of Tampa's Anglo press. *The Tampa Morning Tribune* and *The Tampa Daily Times* were the two leading Tampa newspapers, their foundation dating back to the 1890s. Until 1933, most of de la Grana's letters appeared in the *Times*. In 1933, the *Times* was sold, and the new owners virtually eliminated the correspondence section. From then on, de la Grana's letters were published in the *Tribune*. (Table 1).

Mrs. J. de la Grana's Activism

Journalism scholars have called attention to the role of letters to the editor as "tools of citizenship" (Cavanagh 89), contributing to the creation of a public sphere that fosters civic engagement. In theory, the correspondence section was open to all readers, but in reality, it represented a minority of the population, "a small group of literate readers brave enough to express their views" (Perkins et al. 52). Within this group, the typical letter-writer has been described as "middle-aged or older, male, well educated, with an above-average income and frequently conservative in politics" (Pedersen 25).

This profile applied to Tampa as well. An analysis of the correspondence columns of the *Tampa Daily Times* in April 1927, the month before de la Grana's first letter appeared in the newspaper, shows that out of a total of eighty-four letters published that month, only seven (eight percent) were signed by authors identified as women.[8] As a Latin woman with socialist and feminist leanings, de la Grana was very much in the minority, but her intellect and powerful writing style impressed other contributors, even those who disagreed with her. A Methodist pastor with whom she debated religion and science wrote: "She has certainly evidenced a wide range of reading. It is a pleasure to exchange ideas with such" (Palmer). The correspondence section provided de la Grana a venue to voice grievances and a tool for self-expression and civic engagement. Her letters often appealed to a broad concept of rationalist humanism and supported initiatives that would open opportunities for a wider representation of the public—including women, minorities, and the working class—in democratic life.

Women's Rights

A college graduate and member of the Tampa chapter of the American Association of University Women, de la Grana was deeply interested in women's education. As a progressive, she was also alarmed by efforts to control the readings and the experiences women would have access to in college. In one of her letters, she denounced the Purity League's attempts to monitor the books faculty and students were allowed to discuss at the State College for Women in Tallahassee. "It is incredible that these 'dear pastors' should have the nerve and audacity to flagrantly attack the inalienable rights of freedom of thought and freedom of worship guaranteed by the American constitution," she wrote ("Calls"). De la Grana also condemned the Women's Christian Temperance Union's attempt to ban tobacco, which they saw as a particularly bad habit for young women. She decried the imposition of Christian morality on others, arguing that it thwarted the freedom that was "liberating all women from age-old repressions, shackles, and taboos." Exposing the WCTU's ignorance of, or obliviousness to, local conditions in Tampa, de la Grana also reminded her readers of the economic impact that such a ban on tobacco would have on a city whose main industry was cigar making ("Evolution").

De la Grana extolled women's desire to learn and to become a force of good. "The audiences that eagerly throng the halls to hear lectures on health, science, art, etc., are made up mostly of women," she wrote. When a male writer warned that white women were "destroying America" because they "[kept] company with foreigners" and went "crazy over every new religion, or new love colony, as every new dress they see" ("Whooper"), de la Grana expressed surprise that what she saw as the "modern assertion of woman's personality" was for this man "just craziness." "The womanhood of today enthusiastically responds to every noble influence in her effort to learn how to use the life forces in a conscious responsible way," she explained ("Women and 'Foreigners'").

De la Grana's emphasis on women's education also translated into a call for political participation. In 1929 the *Tampa Daily Times* ran an article on the opinions of three women on the topic of women and politics. Mrs. Clare Ogden Davis, author and newspaperwoman who had been the personal secretary to the first female governor of Texas, Miriam A. Ferguson, claimed that women were unfit for politics. Mrs. Roy Frierson, introduced as "head of the women's representative club of Tampa," advocated for women in politics but believed that they needed more time to learn its ways. De la Grana, described as a "member of the local league of Women Voters," argued that women should dismantle the "man-made machine" of politics and begin to express themselves. "The economic influence of women is going to transform everything, and the future will hold very definite things for women in politics," she concluded ("Women Differ").

While de la Grana did not specify what women's politics would look like, her trajectory and statements in the 1930s illustrate some of her views on the topic. As the ravages of the Great Depression on the working class became more apparent, and her own involvement with socialism grew stronger, de la Grana's criticism of conservative women's movements grew louder. When the chair of the Woman's National Committee for Law Enforcement visited Tampa to defend Prohibition, de la Grana suggested that the group "devote their efforts to secure for every under-privileged American child—the sons and daughters of the unemployed and of those who are earning 'starvation wages,' simple human rights such as abundant food and decent homes to live in" ("Suggesting"). She argued that "organized women power" should be used "in the cause of justice and humanity" and hailed the work of women like Mrs. Gifford Pinchot (first lady of Pennsylvania, supporter of the National Association for the Advancement of Colored People and advocate of women's rights and labor unions) as a model of women's activism ("Mrs. Pinchot"). While often critical of President Roosevelt's policies, de la Grana admired his wife. "[I] consider her the best and greatest woman in the world," she wrote to one of Mrs. Roosevelt's detractors in 1939, "and I should like to see her occupy and grace the Presidency of the United States" ("Mrs. Roosevelt").

Crossing Boundaries and A Call for Political Representation

De la Grana's activism came to fruition at a time when, as historian Nancy Hewitt states, "Tampa's 'New Women' wielded their skills and resources developed over the previous decades to forge stronger interracial and interethnic alliances" (249). While racial, ethnic, and class identities still shaped women's engagement in African-American, Latin, and Anglo communities, the 1920s and 1930s opened new opportunities for them to cross and redefine some of those boundaries.

De la Grana's public and political engagement during this time exemplifies this boundary crossing. She was involved in several organizations (Tampa Psychology Club, Tampa Drama Center League, Tampa Little Theater, Florida Archeological Society) that attracted a predominantly Anglo, middle-class membership, but she also championed initiatives that benefited the working-class Latin community. In 1928, for example, de la Grana wrote to the *Tampa Daily Times* about the (mis)management of funds by the board of Tampa's public library and argued that the board owed an explanation to the citizens, and particularly to the Latin community, "one-third of the white population of the city," who despite paying taxes "have never, up to the present time, been honored with the privilege of being represented on the sacred library board" ("Concerning"). A year later she was named to the board. De la Grana and her husband also contributed to creating the Jose Martí library in Ybor City. The institution honored the leader of Cuban independence who had spent time in the 1890s among Florida's Cuban émigré communities fundraising for the revolution in which he lost his life in 1895. Housed at Ybor City's Labor Temple (*Centro Obrero*), the cigar workers union hall, the library served the immigrant population with books in English, Spanish, and Italian ("Jose Marti").

Another aspect of de la Grana's boundary crossing was her use of the letters to the editor to address some of the stereotypes about the "Latin race" prevalent in the Anglo community. In 1930, she wrote of the "Nordic" myth that portrayed Latins as "noisy [...] very excitable, unruly, indolent, incapable of good government—generally inefficient" ("Latin"). She challenged this myth with letters describing the achievements of the different Latin mutual aid societies (Centro Español, Centro Asturiano, Círculo Cubano), hailing them as examples of civic activism that was a testament to the power of workers' cooperation. De la Grana also relayed the experience of attending a lecture delivered by Catalan writer and politician Pere Corominas in Ybor City. "Here was a 'Latin,'" she explained, "with a trained, logical 100 per cent efficient mind . . . a living encyclopedia of stupendous culture, cool, collected, free from passion and prejudices calmly discussing before an audience composed largely of 'workers' who listened spell-bound to his discussions of abstruse, vital intellectual subjects which are generally reserved for our best universities." She praised the audience as much as the speaker: "a large audience of more than 600 persons . . . delighted with the 'feast of reason and the flow of soul' which the newly organized Latin cultural society makes possible" ("Latin").

Corominas' visit to Tampa illustrates another important dimension of crossing boundaries—the transnational networks that kept Tampa's Latin immigrant community connected to the world. As Spain grappled with the end of the seven-year dictatorship of General Primo de Rivera, pro-Republican intellectuals sought the support of the diaspora in bringing about a change of regime. Corominas was on a lecture tour in Cuba when the *Sociedad Hispano-Cubana de Conferencias* and the *Frente Único de Acción Republicana* (both recently created) invited him to speak in Ybor City. In April 1931, a few months after Corominas' visit, the success of the Republican coalition in municipal elections led to the fall of the Bourbon monarchy and the proclamation of the Republic, to the delight of Tampa Latins. The 1930s, however, would put to the test the power of popular democracy both in Spain and Tampa.

The proclamation of the Republic in Spain coincided with de la Grana's affiliation with the Socialist Party, which was being reorganized in Florida after its demise in the 1920s following the repression triggered by the Red Scare after World War I. Communism was also making inroads in Tampa at the time. Apparently, de la Grana considered joining the Communist Party but decided against it (Edson). Like many voters in Tampa, she had denounced the city's infamous political machine. Indeed, her very first letter to the *Tampa Daily Times*, in the midst of a heated debate about municipal reform, had been about her opposition to the continuation of a commission form of government (which limited the representation of workers, immigrants, and African Americans) and her support for the election of councilmen by wards (Kerstein 52-71). She condemned the white municipal primaries that disenfranchised African-American voters and called for the abolition of poll taxes, which hindered voter participation and encouraged political corruption. As she wrote in one of her letters, "we need a complete revision of our election laws . . . to give back to the people the power usurped by grafting politicians" ("Purification").

Those shady electoral practices, the successful example of municipal socialism in Milwaukee (Wisconsin) and Reading (Pennsylvania), and the encouragement of friends and fellow socialists persuaded de la Grana, in 1931, to present her candidacy for mayor of Tampa, challenging the winner of the white municipal primary. With no budget, no campaign, and only a few weeks to share her message with potential voters de la Grana's chances to win were slim, but when a *Tampa Morning Tribune* editorial questioned her decision, she replied that she believed that her candidacy would allow "all those who clamor for a change . . . to register their protest, whether they believe in socialism or not" ("Not 'Unfortunate'").

The protest vote did not materialize. Several factors contributed to this outcome. First was the entrenched power of the traditional parties, which made it almost impossible for an independent candidate to challenge the political machine. De la Grana's participation in the white primary meant that her name would not appear on the ballot in the general election. Instead, voters had to write in her name next to an "X." But that was also subject to manipulation. After the election, one of the official observers claimed that many votes that had been clearly intended for her had not been counted because voters had used a slightly different version of the name (for example, Mrs. De la Grana, instead of the sanctioned "Mrs. Josephine de la Grana") or had used the proper name but did not include the "X" next to it (Lansdowne).[9]

Lack of grassroots support and the appeal of the Communist party also played a role in the socialists' poor results. *La Gaceta,* Tampa's Spanish daily, called de la Grana's choice as the socialist candidate "a grave mistake." Reminding his readers that she had voted in the Democratic primary, the editor declared her "evolution" to socialism too sudden ("Chungas" October 23, 1931). Following socialist defeats in Tampa and Reading, he punned that the "Socios listos" (smart fellows) were ill-prepared to defend the interests of the working class ("Chungas" November 5, 1931). The Communist party came to fill this void in the 1930s, organizing actively among immigrant and African-American workers.

As historian Sally Miller contends, the Socialist party conceived of the worker primarily as a white male and did not seem to consider the significance of gender, race, and ethnicity in the experience of American labor. A letter from the party's secretary in Florida reporting on events in Tampa illustrates the different approach of communists and socialists regarding African-American and Latin workers. "The Communists have been very active here recently among the Latin people in the cigar factory districts also among the Negroes," he wrote. Then he explained: "Anyone who knows anything of the psychology of the Southern people knows that the quickest way to kill any effort to organize and benefit the working people is to start an agitation among the Negroes and the foreign element. No movement could possibly win without the support of the native whites, and once we have enough of them with us the others will quickly fall in line" (Edson). Indeed, the rise of organized labor led to a swift response by Tampa's political elite, a "reign of terror" (Brenner and Winthrop) that included deportations and vigilante violence, tactics rooted in the region's past response to so-called radicals and outside agitators (Ingalls).

Workers' Rights and the Antifascist Struggle

De la Grana's defeat in the mayoral election did not temper her political activism. As secretary of the Socialist party in Tampa, she led a campaign to disseminate its program and increase its membership using various tools. For example, she organized monthly public meetings where topics such as "What is socialism and what can we do to promote socialism?" were discussed by members and guest lecturers ("Socialists"). She echoed her message through the media, speaking on "Woman under Socialism" on the local radio station ("To Discuss"). She used her letters to the editor to support Socialism and denounce Tampa's corrupt politicians. While still small in numbers, by 1935 the Florida branch had the largest party membership in the South, with the Tampa chapter providing most of its leadership (Ingalls 252).

With other socialists and progressives, de la Grana supported the program of the Modern Democrats. This new group had emerged to challenge the power of the established hierarchy and aimed to clean up local politics. Again, an independent challenged the Democratic candidate in a mayoral race. Although like de la Grana in 1931, the candidate lost, the threat of a progressive coalition was considered serious enough that a few weeks after the election, a meeting of the group was broken by the police and members of the Ku Klux Klan. Three of the men were kidnapped, flogged, tarred, and feathered. One of them, Joseph Shoemaker, the leader of the Modern Democrats, was tortured so severely that he died a few days later (Ingalls 182-4). The *Daily Worker* headlined one of its articles on the murder "Woman Escaped Tampa Torture" and reported that de la Grana had received calls to entice her to attend the meeting where the men had been captured (Jameson).

The flogging case and the repression of labor organizers shone a national spotlight on Tampa's corrupt political machine. Norman Thomas (the leader of the Socialist party) and Earl Browder (leader of the Communist Party) visited the city, and William Green (president of the American Federation of Labor) threatened to move the national convention from Tampa if those involved in Shoemaker's murder were not persecuted. De la Grana too denounced the killing of Shoemaker, the activities of the Ku Klux Klan, and the actions of "the beneficiaries of the present system," who, most expected, would not punish the criminals ("Blinders").[10]

By 1936 de la Grana was also working as a special organizer of the Cigar Makers' International Union (affiliated with the American Federation of Labor) and wrote letters on labor topics, one declaring the sit-down strike "the most efficient weapon ever invented by the working class!" ("For the Sit-Down"). Some of her articles, calling on workers to organize, appeared in Tampa's Spanish daily *La Gaceta* ("La organización"). In July 1936, de la Grana was one of the speakers at a rally in Ybor City to "Free Tom Mooney"—a socialist labor leader who had been wrongly imprisoned for over two decades ("Nine"). A month later, she and her husband were among the signatories of a letter to the Tampa city council requesting the use of the municipal auditorium for an event where Earl Browder, the Communist candidate for the presidency, would speak. Browder's visit caused further violence from the KKK and a new round of denunciation by progressive organizations in the press ("Use").

In the summer of 1936, another event began to take prominence on the front pages of newspapers worldwide: the Spanish Civil War. Like most Spanish immigrant communities in the United States, the one in Tampa supported the Spanish Republic against the forces of General Franco and his allies, Fascist Italy and Nazi Germany (Varela-Lago "From Migrants"; Feu). Several Tampa Latin men volunteered to fight in Spain and joined the International Brigades. Still, most of the support for the Republic came from *la retaguardia* (the rearguard), as *La Gaceta* titled its column on the activities of the Latin community (Tignor; Varela-Lago "¡No Pasarán!").

De la Grana threw herself into this effort. She was one of the speakers at the first mass meeting of the Committee for the Defense of the Spanish Popular Front that gathered over one thousand people in Ybor City's Labor Temple weeks after the start of the conflict ("La asamblea"). She also helped organize a mass demonstration from the Latin quarter to City Hall to protest the bombing of civilians in Guernica by the German Condor Legion. De la Grana was a member of delegations charged with speaking to the mayor and the cigar manufacturers about the event and meeting with the Red Cross and other organizations to encourage them to join ("Se efectuará"). The brainchild of female workers at one of the cigar factories, the community soon embraced the march, with newspapers reporting five to seven thousand participants. De la Grana praised the work of the women who had protested "the outrage committed on childhood and womanhood." She encouraged "every organization of women in Tampa and the United States" to do the same ("Women Protest").[11]

A keen observer of the international situation, de la Grana used her letters in the *Tampa Morning Tribune* to provide readers with a different perspective on events in Spain. She took issue with the characterization of the government of the Spanish Republic as "Red" and "communistic" by Arthur Brisbane, the famous journalist whose syndicated column appeared in the paper. She accused Brisbane of deliberately misrepresenting the truth about the conflict in Spain to the American people ("Spain's Government"). She denounced Great Britain, France, and the Soviet Union for supporting the "infamous non-intervention neutrality agreement," which she defined as an attack "against a noble brave people who had the nerve to resist fascism" ("Superior"). She applauded the "glorious story" of the American volunteers of the International Brigades who "beat back the Moors [Franco's Moroccan troops] at Teruel annihilating Franco's squadrons" ("In Spain"). She condemned the killing of the Nye resolution (requesting the lifting of the arms embargo against Republican Spain) and the influence over the State Department of Catholic American supporters of Franco who "[believe] that the inadequately unarmed (sic) Spanish people fighting for a legally constituted democratic government should continue to be murdered by the fascists" ("Sacred"). Despite the efforts of its supporters, the "neutrality" of the democracies sealed the fate of the Spanish Republic.

The Spanish Civil War ended with Franco's victory on April 1, 1939. World War II began a few months later. In the following years, de la Grana's presence in the press waned. However, she continued to share her views about America—"Intolerance, persecution, the stirring of the dangerous fires of racial prejudice, is the opposite of our ideal of true Americanism" ("The American")—and about the importance for democracy of supporting a strong labor movement. As war raged through Europe she proclaimed, "the organized labor movement is one of the strongest bulwarks of democracy," and reminded her readers that "the first thing that a dictator does in assuming power is to deprive the workers of the right to organize, of the right to free assembly and of the right to strike" ("Labor"). Addressing critics who called the closed shop "undemocratic" she referred to those who refused to join unions but did not refuse to enjoy the benefits of labor won by others, as "shirker[s] and traitor[s] to democracy" ("Shirker").

De la Grana must have taken solace in the fact that Florida, which she had once described as "a conservative, almost feudal Southern state" ("Orchids") was represented in the Senate by Claude Pepper, one of the most prominent liberals in the Democratic party, nicknamed by his detractors "Red Pepper." In her last letter to the *Tampa Morning Tribune,* de la Grana praised the senator for his stance in support of legislation to improve working conditions and strengthen the power of labor unions. "It takes 'guts' to speak the truth," she wrote. "It takes courage to be a true American" ("Bouquet").

By the time de la Grana died in 1952, a few days short of her sixty-fourth birthday, Claude Pepper had been defeated for a third term in the Senate and the progressive causes that she had fought for were being muzzled in the stifling environment of the Cold War and McCarthyism. Her own activism as a writer, feminist, socialist, advocate for workers, and community organizer was also forgotten. There is still much that we do not know about de la Grana's life, but her letters to the editor can help us begin to recover her voice. They became an important tool in her efforts to change the world. Through de la Grana's letters we also recover an important chapter of Tampa's vernacular history in the 1920s and 1930s—the history of progressive men and women who fought to defend the rights of women, immigrants, and workers and to support the international struggle against fascism.

Year of Publication	*Tampa Times*	*Tampa Tribune*
1927	8	0
1928	13	0
1929	21	0
1930	50	3
1931	35	7
1932	41	0
1933	15	3
1934	0	14
1935	0	5
1936	0	13
1937	0	22
1938	0	13
1939	0	14
1940	0	7
1941	0	10
1942	0	5
1943	0	1
1946	0	1
Total Number of letters	183	118

Table 1. Letters to the editor signed by "Mrs. J. de la Grana" in the *Tampa Daily Times* and the *Tampa Morning Tribune* (1927-1946).

Works Cited

Manuscript Collections

Edson, M. E. Letter to Socialist Party National Headquarters. 29 November 1931. Socialist Party of America Papers, Correspondence and General Records, 1897-1960. Microfilm.

Newspaper Articles and Letters to the Editor
LG = La Gaceta
TDT = Tampa Daily Times
TMT = Tampa Morning Tribune

"Big Circus Pleases a Very Large Crowd." *TMT*, 1 December 1917, p. 5.
"Chungas y no chungas." Editorial. *LG*, 23 October 1931, p. 1.
"Chungas y no chungas." Editorial. *LG*, 5 November 1931, p. 1.
de la Grana, Mrs. J. "Women and 'Foreigners.'" Letter. *TDT*, 16 February 1928, p. 5.
_____. "Concerning the Library." Letter. *TDT*, 20 July 1928, p. 6.
_____. "Calls Purity League Ridiculous." Letter. *TDT*, 28 August 1928, p. 6.
_____. "Evolution Emancipating Women." Letter. *TDT*, 27 November 1928, p. 6.
_____. "Havana Interests and Our Races." Letter. *TDT,* 17 May 1929, p. 6.
_____. "Latin and Nordic." Letter. *TDT*, 4 December 1930, p. 6.
_____. "Suggesting to Mrs. Peabody." Letter. *TDT*, 9 April 1931, p. 4.
_____. "Mrs. Pinchot's Fearless Courage." Letter. *TDT*, 18 June 1931, p. 4.
_____. "Not 'Unfortunate.'" Letter. *TMT*, 21 October 1931, p. 6.
_____. "Purification of Ballot First Step." Letter. *TDT*, 8 January 1932, p. 6.
_____. "Negroes and Primaries." Letter. *TDT*, 8 October 1932, p. 6.
_____."La organización, el arma más poderosa." *LG,* 1 April 1936, p. 4.
_____. "Radio Freedom." Letter. *TMT,* 15 July 1936, p. 4.
_____. "Spain's Government." Letter. *TMT*, 21 August 1936, p. 8.
_____. "Women Protest." Letter. *TMT*, 8 May 1937, p. 8.

____. "For the Sit-Down." Letter. *TMT*, 11 May 1937, p. 6.

____. "Superior England." Letter. *TMT*, 14 June 1937, p. 4.

____. "Blinders." Letter. *TMT*, 27 July 1937, p. 4.

____. "In Spain." Letter. *TMT*, 19 February 1938, p. 6.

____. "Sacred Opinion." Letter. *TMT*, 19 June 1938, p. 8.

____. "Mrs. Roosevelt." Letter. *TMT*, 8 April 1939, p. 8.

____. "Orchids for Pepper." Letter. *TMT*, 11 August 1939, p. 8.

____. "The American Way." Letter. *TMT,* 14 November 1940, p. 8.

____. "Labor a Bulwark." Letter. *TMT*, 16 April 1941, p. 8.

____. "Shirker and Traitor." Letter. *TMT*, 22 May 1941, p. 8.

____. "Bouquet to Pepper." Letter. *TMT*, 3 June 1946, p. 4.

"Fair Newcomb's Brows Hooded." *Times-Picayune.* 19 May 1909, p. 4.

Jameson, Jack. "Shoemaker Named Klan Killers; Woman Escaped Tampa Torture." *The Daily Worker,* 31 March 1936.

"Jose Marti Library To Be Opened Sunday." *TDT,* 31 March 1928, p. 3.

"La asamblea de anoche en el Centro Obrero." *LG,* 14 August 1936, p. 1.

Lansdowne, Robert. "Variable Name." Letter. *TMT*, 13 November 1931, p. 8.

"La Sección de Damas del Centro Español." *Bohemia,* 30 December 1916.

"Music Club Meeting." *TMT*, 26 March 1917, p. 7.

"Nine Speakers Talk on 'Free Mooney' Program in Ybor." *TMT,* 28 July 1936, p. 7.

Palmer, O. Sewell. "The Only Hope." Letter. *TDT*, 9 December 1927, p. 11.

Pearce, Louise. "Visit to County Farm." Letter. *TMT*, 18 June 1937, p. 10.

"Se efectuará el Jueves la Gran Manifestación de protesta por el asesinato de mujeres y niños." *LG,* 4 May 1937, p. 3.

"Socialists Will Meet." *TDT,* 25 January 1933, p. 11.

"Tampa Music Club." *TMT*, 9 December 1916, p. 8.

"To Discuss Socialism." *TMT,* 16 July 1935, p. 11.

"Use of Auditorium is Requested for Communist Speaker." *TMT,* 26 August 1936, p. 3.

Whooper, John. "The Wrecking Crew." Letter. *TDT*, 11 February 1928, p. 7.
"Women Differ Regarding Political Place and Achievements of Sex." *TDT*, 22 July 1929, p. 4.

Secondary Sources

Baxley, John Hood, et al. *Oaklawn Cemetery and St. Louis Catholic Cemetery: Biographical & Historical Gleanings.* Tampa, 1991.
Brenner, Anita, and S. S. Winthrop. *Tampa's Reign of Terror.* New York: International Labor Defense, 1933.
Caulfeild, Ruby Van Allen. *French Literature of Louisiana.* New York: Columbia University, 1929.
Cavanagh, Allison, and John Steel, editors. *Letters to the Editor. Comparative and Historical Perspectives.* London: Palgrave Macmillan, 2019.
Cavanagh, Allison. "Letters to the Editor as a Tool of Citizenship." Cavanagh and Steel, pp. 89-108.
"Cercle Français de Newcomb." *Jambalaya* [Tulane Yearbook], vol. xiv, 1909, p. 273.
Feu, Montse. *Fighting Fascist Spain. Worker Protest from the Printing Press.* Chicago: U of Illinois P, 2020.
Greenbaum, Susan D. *More Than Black. Afro-Cubans in Tampa.* Gainesville: UP of Florida, 2002.
Grillo, Evelio. *Black Cuban, Black American. A Memoir.* Houston: Arte Público P, 2000.
Hewitt, Nancy A. *Southern Discomfort: Women's Activism in Tampa, Florida, 1880s-1920s.* Chicago: U of Illinois P, 2001.
Ingalls, Robert P. *Urban Vigilantes in the New South. Tampa, 1882-1936.* Gainesville: UP of Florida, 1993.
Kerstein, Robert. *Politics and Growth in Twentieth-Century Tampa.* Gainesville: UP of Florida, 2001.
Lazo, Rodrigo. *Writing to Cuba. Filibustering and Cuban Exiles in the United States.* Chapel Hill: The U of North Carolina P, 2005.
McNamara, Sarah. "Borderland Unionism: Latina Activism in Ybor City and Tampa, Florida, 1935-1937." *Journal of American Ethnic History*, vol. 38, no. 4, 2019, pp. 10-32.

Méndez, Armando. *Ciudad de Cigars: West Tampa*. Tampa: Florida Historical Society, 1994.

Miller, Sally M. "For White Men Only: The Socialist Party of America and Issues of Gender, Ethnicity, and Race." *The Journal of the Gilded Age and Progressive Era*, vol. 2, no. 3, 2003, pp. 283-302.

Mormino, Gary R, and George E. Pozzetta. *The Immigrant World of Ybor City. Italians and Their Latin Neighbors in Tampa, 1885-1985*. U of Illinois P, 1987.

Pedersen, Sarah. "Speaking as Citizens: Women's Political Correspondence to Scottish Newspapers, 1918-1928." Cavanagh and Steel, pp. 25-48.

Perkins, Stephynie C., et al. "Letters to the Editor in the *Chicago Defender*, 1929-1930: The Voice of a Voiceless People." Cavanagh and Steel, pp. 49-68.

Poyo, Gerald E. "With All, and for the Good of All." *The Emergence of Popular Nationalism in the Cuban Communities of the United States, 1848-1898*. Duke UP, 1989.

Tignor, Lisa. "La Colonia Latina: The Response of Tampa's Immigrant Community to the Spanish Civil War." *Tampa Bay History*, vol. 12, no. 1, 1990, pp. 19-28.

Tucker, Susan, and Beth Willinger, editors. *Newcomb College, 1886-2006. Higher Education for Women in New Orleans*. Louisiana UP, 2012.

Tuohey, Terese V. "'The Study of Music in All its Various Branches': The Friday Morning Musicale of Tampa, Florida." *Research Perspectives in Music Education*, vol. 18, no. 2, 2016, pp. 2-18.

Tyler, Pamela. "Hilda, Martha, and Natalie. Newcomb's Furies." Tucker and Willinger, pp. 303-19.

Varela-Lago, Ana. "¡No Pasarán! The Spanish Civil War's Impact on Tampa's Latin Community, 1936-1939." *Tampa Bay History*, vol. 19, no. 2, 1997, pp. 5-35.

____. *Conquerors, Immigrants, Exiles: The Spanish Diaspora in the United States (1848-1948)*. 2008. U of California San Diego, PhD dissertation.

_____. "From Migrants to Exiles: The Spanish Civil War and the Spanish Immigrant Communities in the United States." *Camino Real*, vol. 7, no. 10, 2015, pp. 111-128.

Walh-Jorgensen, Karin. Foreword. Cavanagh and Steel, pp. v-x.

Watts, Trent. "What Makes a 'Newcomb Girl'? Student Culture in the Progressive Era." Tucker and Willinger, pp. 80-96.

AKA Frances: Francisca Flores and the Radical Roots of Chicana Feminism in California

PABLO LANDEROS

*Francisca Flores is believed to be the most dangerous and
who, in all probability, should be interned in the event of war.*
—FBI report[1]

Writer, publisher, and organizer Francisca Flores is widely recognized as a modern voice for "La Nueva Chicana" in the 1960s. Yet, very few people know that her activism in the 1960s and 1970s was the culmination of decades of addressing issues of race, class, and gender that impacted the Chicana/o community in Southern California. Most scholars see Flores as a member of the "Mexican American generation," who bridged the generation gap to mentor young women encountering barriers to leadership in the Chicano Movement. However, the story is far more interesting than that: by the time Flores established Comisión Femenil (1970) and the Chicana Service Action Center (1972), her radicalism had already spanned four decades, and included years of work with the Communist Party USA (CPUSA) in San Diego and Los Angeles. This prehistory makes Francisca Flores an important figure not just for Chicana feminism, but also for the history of the Mexican American Left. Indeed, Flores' involvement in the CPUSA in California supports Maylei Blackwell's assertion that there are histories of the Left in Mexican-American communities that are yet to be explored:

> Although the rise of the New Left in the 1960s is often tied to the activism of red diaper babies, there needs to be further historical study of the role that Mexicans in the United States played in left politics throughout the twentieth century. (Blackwell 49)

Therefore, by the 1960s, we find that Chicana feminism was influenced by multiple socio-political concerns of the mid-twentieth century such as war, labor exploitation and unionism, segregation, ethnic identity and culture affirmation, women's political participation, and advocating for equality.[2]

Much has been written about Flores' political activism in the post 1960s era, yet very few scholars have touched on her CP involvement. Utilizing her Federal Bureau of Investigation (FBI) record, I uncovered a past that has never been researched before. I build upon other studies of the Left to illuminate how Flores' early work with the CPUSA informed the intersectional Chicana feminist praxis she articulated in the 1970s. In his book *Sojourning for Freedom*, Erik McDuffie provides a parallel frame of analysis, noting how the origins of black feminism, and what scholars now define as "triple oppression," were first explicitly articulated by black CPUSA members well before the advent of second wave feminism (McDuffie 4). Though McDuffie notes that many women would never have used the term "black feminist" during the 1940s or 1950s, they were nevertheless addressing issues that would become the cornerstone of Black Feminism in the 1960s and 1970s (McDuffie 4). Similarly, Flores' political involvement in the CPUSA—her study of Marxism and the economic status of Mexican Americans, and particularly her advocacy of race and gender equality within the Party—undoubtedly pushed her to think about how racism, sexism, and labor exploitation were interlinked, an ideological framework that that would come to inform her work with Comisión Femenil and the Chicana Service Action Center in the 1970s.

The Birth of Her Causa

Born in December 1913 in Old Town San Diego, Francisca Flores was the daughter of Vicente and Maria Flores, who were both from Coahuila, Mexico.[3] Her parents' experiences reflect the struggles of many Mexican nationals who came to the United States to flee the repressive conditions that they faced in Mexico. Western economic imperialism and the consequent Mexican Revolution caused many to migrate to the United States.[4] Once in the United States, Flores' father, Vicente, obtained employment as a "prodder in a slaughterhouse" while her mother, Maria, "labored in various food-processing industries as a cook and union shop steward" (Escobedo 214). Adding to the economic challenges the Flores family faced in San Diego, Francisca contracted tuberculosis at the age of fifteen, causing her to lose a lung and spend eleven years in a sanitarium.[5]

During her time in the sanitarium, Flores gained valuable knowledge by immersing herself in conversations with Mexican nationals who had actively participated in the Mexican Revolution, an experience that shaped her political consciousness by introducing her to "radical ideas and writings of revolutionaries like Enrique and Ricardo Flores Magon" (Meares). This experience and knowledge became instrumental as it helped build her political identity.

Within this space, Francisca helped form *Hermanas de la Revolución Mexicana* (*Hermanas*), a group that fostered a gendered Mexican national identity within the United States (Flores, "Francisca" 1). Historian Cynthia Orozco has observed that Mexican women nationals frequently created women's auxiliaries or independent women-only mutual aid organizations due to their exclusion from male-dominated organizations (Orozco 71).[6] *Hermanas,* however, moved beyond just a social group, becoming a space to address politics and activism. When Flores heard about the low wages the nurses received at the sanitarium, she organized a strike. On the day she was released, she put theory into practice and jumped on the picket line to support her caretakers (Meares). The eleven years that Francisca Flores spent in the sanitarium were critical to her political formation and her radicalism. Indeed, she would apply what she learned from her revolutionary education and her organizing on behalf of women and workers to her political activities with the Communist Party in the 1930s and 1940s.

Life in the Communist Party

Francisca Flores' emergence from the sanitarium in the latter part of the 1930s coincided with a high point in the Communist Party's interest in Mexican Americans. Chicano labor activist Bert Corona has noted that the Party was quite active in the *barrios* during the Depression. They worked on multiple issues, including the desegregation of schools and public facilities, obtaining relief aid, and preventing the deportation of Mexicans during the 1930s. (García, *Memories* 126-7)[7]

In the 1930s, the CPUSA abandoned a Bolshevik style revolution and embraced New Deal liberalism emphasizing progressive reforms that included coalition building with industrial unions, liberals, students, and cultural organizations, in turn creating an American version of communism (Weigand 21). By developing strong ties with different ethnic groups and women, the CPUSA hoped to build a larger base that welcomed race solidarity among people of color while fighting for ethnic/gender liberation and continuing the struggle against class exploitation. By the mid-1930s, the Party encouraged members to work with ethnic organizations to build support for Communist programs, which included promoting the history and culture of people of color. They also called for organizing women's councils and neighborhood committees and publishing a women's magazine, supporting women's access to free and legal birth control and abortion, and promoting the CPUSA Woman's Charter (1936), which advocated for equality at the workplace yet protected women from the most hazardous and exploitable types of labor (Weigand 22-4). Interlinking the struggles for racial equality and labor unionism as a common cause, the CPUSA successfully recruited Mexican-Americans and Latino organizers throughout the 1930s.

Flores joined the San Diego region Communist Party in 1939 (*Flores*).[8] Like other Mexican Americans, Francisca Flores saw communism as a way to challenge the racism and labor exploitation that kept Mexican Americans subordinated in the United States. Flores immersed herself in the CPUSA, focusing on organizing and recruiting new members into the party. She worked largely under the radar of the FBI and was not a target of investigation until 1940, when she was elected to the Branch Finance Committee on April 13, 1940 (*Flores*).[9] In 1940, undercover FBI agents observed that Flores attended nine meetings, some of which were accessible to CPUSA members only (*Flores*).[10] She also attended meetings and events regularly throughout Southern California in the early 1940s, such as the May Day parades in Tijuana, Mexico, which linked an international workers movement on both sides of the US/Mexico border.

The surveillance of Francisca Flores indexes the beginning of a wave of repression of activists on the Left that would find its culmination in the Red Scare of the 1950s. The passage of the Voorhis Act of 1941, which required left-leaning political activists, particularly those in the Communist Party, to register with the federal government, made them targets in a time of war, hindering their political activities (*Flores*).[11] In fact, with the entrance of the United States into World War II on December 8, 1941, Flores' classification status changed to "dangerous, to be considered for custodial detention" (*Flores*).[12] During this period, the FBI's surveillance of Flores increased to the point that multiple informants focused on her daily activities, even following her to social events like "a buffet supper at the home of an undercover agent because there were . . . other well-known Communist members in the area" (*Flores*).[13] This high level of surveillance demonstrated the potential threat the FBI believed her to be.

Rethinking the Mexican-American Left

As a result of her recruitment work for the CPUSA and her relationships with other activists of the era, Flores often worked with grassroots organizations that focused more directly on race. One such organization was *El Congreso*, which forcefully advocated for the rights of the Spanish-speaking population within the United States.[14] Flores worked closely with *El Congreso,* researching reports for the San Diego Branch activities (*Flores*).[15] She also worked with other labor unions, such as the United Cannery, Agricultural, Packing, and Allied Workers of America (UCAPAWA-CIO), and was even "offered an important position" in the organization (*Flores*).[16] In 1943, she joined the "Sleepy Lagoon Defense Committee . . . who fought for the release of twelve Mexican American young men wrongly convicted of murder" (Ruiz and Sanchez 234). Although these political involvements seem to suggest a shift toward greater concern for Mexican-Americans, Flores actually worked to connect Mexican-Americans' racial and ethnic struggle to class struggle as defined by the CPUSA. In 1948, Flores became involved in the Asociación Nacional Mexico-Americana (ANMA), which included labor and CPUSA activists. She attended ANMA's founding convention, served as an elected committee member, and became the organization's secretary (Flores).[17] In doing so, she linked communist ideology to the struggle for racial equity, a connection which further developed in the 1960s with the rise of the Civil Rights Movement.

These connections to early Mexican-American labor/civil rights organizations made Flores an important asset to the CP, particularly in its efforts to draw more Mexicans and Mexican-Americans into the Party. Though the CPUSA had a major interest in increasing Mexican and Mexican-American participation, their recruitment efforts often lacked the enthusiasm that Flores envisioned. Historian Mario T. García has argued that skilled labor organizations often ignored Mexican migrant workers because they believed that such laborers understood their time in the US to be temporary and that they hoped to return to their homeland. However, many migrant workers participated in labor struggles when their economic interests were at stake, which tended to be sporadic or circumstantial (García, *Mexican Americans* 175-6). And while the CPUSA had adopted a more liberal New Deal platform in the 1930s, a significant number of Mexican-American workers saw trade unions as the best avenue towards integration into American society. Flores, a person who wore many hats, navigated between these two spaces, and used her skills to help organize Mexican and Mexican-American workers. In truth, she became an important recruiter for the CPUSA during this period, sharing literature within the Mexican-American population in places such as Logan Heights, which had a high Mexican and Mexican-American population (*Flores*).[18] As she moved up within the Party's hierarchy, the FBI began to see Flores as a key figure in the San Diego County CP. By the mid-1940s, the FBI sought to collect "handwriting specimens" and photographs of Flores, a testament to the increased surveillance of her political and personal activities (*Flores*).[19]

Gender, Race, Class & Identity in the CPUSA

Flores flourished personally in the CPUSA yet, as a woman of color, she faced a glass ceiling within the Party structure. The FBI reported that although Flores had never had any "disciplinary action taken against her, she was denied leadership on several occasions without being called in for discussion" (*Flores*).[20] Despite this systematic exclusion from leadership, Francisca Flores took on many active roles and often represented the Party in organizing spaces. She was named a member of the Executive Committee for the Logan Heights Section; was appointed the Director of the CPA Literacy Department; and was assistant manager of the Community Book Center; was elected to the Branch Finance Committee; gave speeches at different meetings; and served as a delegate, just to name a few of her roles. And though her marriage to LaVerne Lym, who was "the Communist Party Chairman for San Diego County and was manager of the International Book Store in the city of San Diego," which certainly opened doors for her, it was her initiative that pushed Francisca Flores to inform and educate herself in CPUSA ideology and become indispensable to its aims (*Flores*).[21]

According to internal CPUSA documents collected by the FBI, Flores "was not politically developed" enough to be a leader in the Mexican-American community (*Flores*).[22] However, a close examination of documents within her FBI file indicate a very different story. In multiple examples, we see that she was invited to different groups, such as the *Congress of American Women* and the *American Jewish Labor Council,* to address the status of Mexican Americans, indicating that she became an important voice of her community. In addition, she was very vocal when addressing political matters and advocated action when necessary. At a Communist Political Association (CPA) meeting, she called for all her comrades to write to the San Diego mayor and attend the city council meeting to voice their concerns regarding the lack of implementing "price ceilings" during the war (*Flores*).[23] Other times, after WWII, she stated that "if it were not for the need of the world to build and borrow and buy from America, 'we' would go ahead and have the revolution, whether peaceful or otherwise, on any bright tomorrow" (*Flores*).[24] Her rhetoric tended to be more radical than others as she called for direct action and advocated for revolution.

In fact, being involved in so many different organizing spaces allowed Flores to be aware of the global and imperial dimensions of the oppression that Mexican Americans faced both in the community and the workplace. In a speech given at a CPUSA meeting in late 1945, one source noted that Flores criticized the role of US and British monopolies in places such as "China, Egypt, the Middle East and the Netherlands Indies," asserting that they were interfering with these areas' internal affairs in ways that amounted to the colonization of people of color (*Flores*).[25] In another speech, she examined the relationship between growers and immigration authorities, arguing that they allowed Mexicans to enter orchards illegally to harvest crops and then paid them substandard wages (*Flores*).[26] Flores saw a connection between the global economic interests that caused people to migrate and the formation of an ethnic underclass in the US. This connection was undoubtedly shaped by her personal experiences (at home and in the sanitarium) and by her activism within grassroots Mexican-American organizations.

Throughout the 1940s, Flores came into her own politically, putting her energy towards the organization of Mexicans and Mexican Americans within the CPUSA and working towards inclusiveness of other ethnicities. She translated many CPUSA publications from English into Spanish for distribution amongst the Spanish-speaking population in Los Angeles and became a vocial advocate for the Mexican-American community (*Flores*).[27] On October 27, 1949, Flores was introduced as a "Mexican American leader in the struggle for civil liberties and as the secretary of the Mexican American Commission of the Communist Party" for a radio show called *Pension, Minorities, and Civil Rights* on radio station KLAC (*Flores*).[28] Though there was not much information as to what took place, Flores was well aware of the plight of Mexican-Americans. In addition, this did highlight how Mexican-Americans were taking a much more active role in addressing issues that they saw as important rather than accepting a top-down approach from the Party.

Flores too had undergone a metamorphosis within the CPUSA, reflected in her changing name. During her days in the sanitarium, she was known by her Mexican name, Francisca. As the years progressed, she embodied the cultural shifts that happened to many Mexican-Americans of this generation. Chicano historians have argued that many Mexican-American youth in the 1920s and 30s "expressed pride in their US citizenship and had a desire to be accepted as first-class Americans" (García, *Mexican Americans* 8). This is indicative in her name as it morphed from Francisca to Frances reflecting the acculturation of this generation. In the FBI's collection of Flores' handwritten letters, we see her sign her name as Frances showing that she herself adopted this transition of her name (*Flores*).[29] In addition, aliases Flores adopted when she went underground, including "*Lavern*," "*Val*," and "*Eva*,"[30] would conform to this cultural shift often sounding like Americanized names or like a variation of her husband's name, LaVerne Lym (*Flores*). It was not until the late 1950s, when she left the CPUSA to focus more exclusively on Mexican-American causes, that she reverted to *Francisca* (Buelna 225).

Going Underground

In the midst of McCarthyism and the "Red Scare," Flores, who was now in her late thirties, simultaneously embraced CPUSA teachings and went underground. According to sources, the FBI lost track of Flores for twelve months during this period, and so we are left with a general and inconclusive record of her location and actions. It is significant to note that fifty-plus undercover agents had not heard about her whereabouts for months at a time.

Flores' husband told an undercover FBI agent that Francisca was at a hospital suffering from tuberculosis. However, on December 19, 1952, the FBI reported that they "searched the San Diego Tuberculosis records but failed to find anything, which forced them to try to locate her back in Los Angeles" (*Flores*).[31] As the FBI frantically searched for Flores throughout the Southwest, informants provided little useful information about her whereabouts. For example, one agent overheard that Flores had talked to her husband, but nothing was confirmed. Other sources indicated that the CPUSA loaned Flores 300 dollars but had no idea where the money went. Others suggested that she could be in Arizona, but her exact location was unknown (*Flores*).[32] Sources indicate that the FBI searched for family members, such as her mother and brother, to re-establish a connection with her. For one year (1953), her FBI record indicated Frances Flores as "MISSING" with no known addresses (*Flores*).[33] With no viable leads, the pictures that the FBI had taken and the writing samples they had collected in the 1940s became very instrumental in uncovering her location.

As months passed, new information emerged about a woman named "Val." By July of 1953, the name "Val" appeared next to an initial "F" on the CPUSA payroll. With this new information, the FBI sought to collect handwriting samples to determine "Val's" identity. With a collection of letters that seemed either coded or provided very little insight into her actions in the CPUSA underground, the FBI successfully determined the identity of "Val" as Francisca Flores (*Flores*).[34] During this time, the House of Un-American Activities Committee (HUAC) issued a "subpoena . . . but the FBI felt that it would jeopardize the underground penetration of Los Angeles" (*Flores*).[35] At least from the eyes of the FBI, they viewed Flores as an important figure that could provide valuable information either on the CPUSA or on her relationship with other higher CPUSA comrades. As more letters emerged with names that were not familiar to FBI informants, and with the disappearance of "Val," the FBI was back to square one in its search for Flores.

Although more letters were obtained, they tell us very little about the type of "work" Flores was engaged in while she was underground. One letter, presumed to be from Flores, discussed "problems" with the leadership in addressing political issues within the Communist Party, but it is left unclear what these problems were (*Flores*).[36] Rather, what we see from these personal letters is a sense of the political climate of the 1950s, where HUAC's political persecution of CPUSA members was taking its toll. Flores stated that there "was a great deal of unclarity as they must safeguard the leadership" (*Flores*).[37] She continued her underground work under a new alias and, by December 1953, reliable sources indicated that Flores had changed her name to "Eva."

Flores reemerged from the CPUSA underground by the middle of 1954. Although the FBI records do not indicate her role in the underground, in July 1954 they noted that her status was designated as "1 ½," an organizational level between the open and underground CPUSA apparatus, using security measures of the underground but having daily operational contact with the open Communist Party (*Flores*).[38]

While some CPUSA members viewed Flores as "intellectually underdeveloped" in the 1940s, after she emerged from the underground in the mid 1950s Flores moved toward a more instrumental role in critiquing and developing Party ideology in Los Angeles for Mexican Americans.

Bringing Race to the Forefront of Struggle

After her reappearance in 1954, Flores began teaching Marxist-Leninist Communism in the Mexican-American community. Sources indicated that she also became active in a "new level of leadership designed to facilitate CPUSA day to day guidance . . . for assignments to the California State CPUSA organization" (*Flores*).[39] In the beginning, she taught courses for the CPUSA from her home, focusing on Marxist literature, such as the *Communist Manifesto* and *Dialectical and Historical Materialism* (*Flores*).[40] While the goal was to recruit Mexican Americans into the Communist Party, Flores tried to align communist ideology and race. By the mid-1950s,

Flores taught courses focused on the "Mexican people, their problems, and their struggles" (*Flores*).[41] Sources indicate that the courses were offered to the public and that "communism would not be discussed" (*Flores*).[42]

Already in her forties, Flores' political focus shifted in this period, and race began to supersede class struggles. This is reflected in the courses that she taught throughout the decade, which showed a gradual shift from communism to Mexican-American history (*Flores*).[43] Since Marxist theory does not take ethnic culture as a central unit of analysis, Flores sought to reconcile this within her courses.[44] For example, her course "Mexican-Americans in the Struggle for Democracy" began with the Mexican Revolution and addressed "practical problems of organizing among Mexican-Americans" (*Flores*).[45] Flores' emphasis here on the Mexican Revolution (rather than the US-Mexico War) as a starting point suggests that she saw the revolutionary period as a pivotal historical moment when the forces of Western economic imperialism had created a mass displacement of Mexican nationals and set the stage for the development of a Mexican-American underclass in the US. Offering a bottom-up analysis of Mexican-American history, Flores continued to increase enrollment into the Communist Party in Southern California. In addition to making critical links between race and class in her courses, Flores also argued that to have a strong Communist movement in the Mexican-American community, the CPUSA had to allow Mexican Americans to maintain and celebrate their culture since it played a very intricate role in their daily lives. In the late 1950s, the CPUSA sponsored *Cinco de Mayo* celebrations, which fostered Mexican-American culture, and allowed the Party to disseminate information to increase Mexican-American participation (*Flores*).[46] This cultural shift continued as the East Los Angeles division contemplated whether to continue with the CPUSA or to separate. Flores stated in 1956 that "it was 'now or never' to start the Mexican people to move 'en masse'" maybe not away from the CPUSA but if it had to, then so be it (*Flores*).[47] For Flores, this would lead her to question her commitment to the CPUSA, but it would also forecast a movement based on ethnic pride that challenged perceptions of Mexican-American passivity.

While Mexican-American participation in the CPUSA had steadily increased from the early 1930s to the late 1940s, by the mid-1950s, when Flores reemerged from the underground and began teaching classes, there were clear indications that contradictions within the CPUSA around the Party's position on race/ethnicity were at a breaking point. Although the CPUSA felt that Mexican Americans did not experience the same type of discrimination as African Americans and assumed that they would assimilate without conflict, Mexican Americans felt otherwise. They fought within the Party to integrate the needs of the Mexican American. This led to the formation of the Cuauhtemoc Club, Zapata Section, (Mexican Commission), which connected their struggles to other historical underclass movements in Mexican history. Francisca Flores would eventually become the leader of the Mexican Commission on October 4th, 1955 (*Flores*).[48] The group recommended that the CPUSA increase outreach and recruiting of Mexican Americans, expand on the Spanish section of the *Daily People's World*, address historical awareness of Mexicans and Mexican Americans within the CP, implement courses on Marxism, develop organizing skills in multiple industries, along with increasing civic education to Mexicans (Buelna 126-7). This was an essential step in both trying to advance race issues within the CPUSA and creating a space for Mexican-American members to address issues that reflected their concerns. Given her extensive experience with the Party, Flores had her vision of what direction the CPUSA should take to include Mexican Americans and sought to advocate for Mexican-American leadership at the County Convention of the CPUSA CP in Los Angeles in 1956 (*Flores*).[49]

By 1957, Flores began to indicate an internal struggle in the Los Angeles CPUSA, and many members questioned whether to continue their activism openly as communists or to remain quiet as in the past (*Flores*).[50] Flores seemed exhausted with the Communist Party's refusal to address Mexican-American participation, and she had continuously challenged the CPUSA to help the Mexican-

American community, to little effect. This criticism was evident in her complaint about the *People's World*, the West Coast communist newspaper, which, to her, seemed as a "'rehash' of old news" (*Flores*).[51] By March of 1958, Flores argued that the party was at a crossroads in the United States and in June of that year she, along with other members of the East Los Angeles Communist Party, signed a letter tendering their resignation . . . from the CPUSA on the ground that the present CPUSA could not carry out the decision of the sixteenth National Convention to overcome dogmatic issues and find a way to merge Marxism with an indigenous American socialist movement. She concluded that there was not one idea presented that was less than thirty years of age. (*Flores*)[52]

At the 16th National Convention in February of 1957, the debate centered on what direction the CPUSA should undertake, particularly after Nikita Khrushchev's statements about Stalin's abuses.[53] Even before the meeting, the Mexican Commission "advocated that the National Convention set up a special commission to give attention to the problems of the Mexican people in the Southwest" (*Flores*).[54] Due to a job commitment, Flores could not attend the National Convention; however, when she met with the Mexican Commission, she "commented on a resolution that had passed and stated that she could no longer stay in the CP" (*Flores*).[55] Though the file does not specify which resolution Flores opposed, Ralph Cuaron, a comrade of the Mexican Commission that attended the National Convention, addressed his concern to the group regarding the Party's "weak and noncommittal stance on the role of minorities within the party" (Buelna 152). By 1962, Flores openly stated that the CPUSA did not do enough for the Mexican-American community, and, therefore, she felt that "she could do more . . . outside the party by participating in legitimate political and community matters in the East Los Angeles area" (*Flores*).[56] Though her disillusionment with the Communist Party is palpable in this statement, it is clear that as a result of her work for the party in the 1950s Flores possessed a body of knowledge in political theory and community organizing, which she could use to far more significant effect in grassroot movements outside the Party.

As the 1960s loomed, Flores became a target of CPUSA members. One source indicated that multiple CPUSA comrades who called to testify before HUAC were also hated by Flores, which led some to believe that Flores was an FBI informer. Thus, some CPUSA members disassociated themselves from her altogether (*Flores*).[57] Ben Dobbs, who was labor secretary of the CPUSA in Los Angeles, stated that "Frances . . . had done everything possible to wreck the Party" (*Flores*).[58] Other party members wanted Flores to distance herself from the CPUSA. One such person was Rose Chernin who was unhappy that Flores was attending the Women's Peace Conference in Mexico in April of 1960 because she was "not a recognized leader in the community and that she was a disruptive force wherever she went and was creating dissension among people" (*Flores*).[59] Though Chernin tried to discredit her by stating that she had "confused opinions," Flores was, by all accounts, deeply respected amongst Mexican-American CPUSA membership and in her community. While some American communists could not envision the new direction of activism that was taking shape in the early 1960s, Flores was able to evolve politically and thus stay relevant, a fact amply demonstrated by the significant role she played in the Chicana/o Movement that was just around the corner.

When Flores and the CPUSA parted ways, FBI surveillance of her daily activities declined and her classification of "Detcom was . . . deleted in as much as Flores held no position of leadership in any organization" (*Flores*).[60] Ironically, the FBI was so consumed with the singular threat of communism that they overlooked the significance of Flores' political training as she became involved in other movements taking shape in the early 1960s. Indeed, she was part of a larger exodus from the CPUSA that would contribute both leadership and political thought to the rising ethnic community-based movements of the 1960s. Her break from the Communist Party enabled her to turn to a new political praxis that emphasized race and gender as central areas of analysis, even as it incorporated class and labor exploitation into a powerful analytic framework.

Conclusion

This perspective on the early political life of Francisca Flores sheds new light on the experiences and ideas that shaped her later activism. As Anna Nieto Gomez (who considers Flores one of the most significant mentors of Chicanas in the 1960s) notes, Flores was shaped by a very basic principle of "making her community a better place" (Gomez 35). Her lived experience as the daughter of working-class Mexican immigrants in San Diego and her early education in Mexican radicalism while at the sanitarium would profoundly influence her worldview. Later, her participation in the CPUSA taught her about the fight for economic social justice. Although she was not a high-profile national leader in the Communist Party, Flores was well respected and did become a vital voice for the Los Angeles chapter and utilized her skills as an organizer to encourage greater Mexican-American inclusion into the Party. While involvement in the CPUSA allowed Flores the opportunity to develop as a political force within the Mexican-American community, participating directly in community organizing sharpened her perspective on the contradictions in Party ideology and practice. As she educated herself and developed as an activist within the CPUSA and grassroot organizations, Flores sought to reconcile the intersectionality of race, class, and gender, particularly as she experienced them in the Communist Party. Utilizing the tools gathered in her long political journey—from Marxist-Leninist frameworks of class struggle to racial and gender analyses—Flores contributed instrumentally to the development of *la nueva Chicana*.

Works Cited

Blackwell, Maylei. *Chicana Power! Contested Histories of Feminism in the Chicano Movement.* U of Texas P, 2012.

Buelna, Enrique M. *Chicano Communists and the Struggle for Social Justice.* U of Arizona P, 2019.

Escobedo, Elizabeth. "Flores, Francisca." *Notable American Women: Completing the Twentieth Century.* Edited by Susan Ware and Stacy Braukman, Harvard UP, 2004.

Flores FBI File 1128474-000. Edited by Federal Bureau of Investigations, Comisión Femenil Mexicana Nacional, CEMA 30, Department of Special Collections, UC Santa Barbara Library, University of California, Santa Barbara.

Flores, William. "Francisca Flores Eulogy May 1, 1996." Box 24, Folder 19. Comisión Femenil Mexicana Nacional, CEMA 30, Department of Special Collections, UC Santa Barbara Library, University of California, Santa Barbara.

García, Mario T. *Memories of Chicano History: The Life and Narrative of Bert Corona.* U of California P, 1994.

____. *Mexican Americans: Leadership, Ideology, & Identity, 1930-1960.* Yale UP, 1991.

McDuffie, Erik. *Sojourning for Freedom: Black Women, American Communism, and the Making of Black Left Feminism.* Duke UP, 2011.

Meares, Hadley. "Activist and Journalist Francisca Flores is a Chicana Hero Every Angeleno Should Know." *Los Angeles Magazine,* 26 Nov. 2018, www.lamag.com/citythinkblog/francisca-flores.

NietoGómez, Anna. "Francisca Flores, The League of Mexican American Women, and the Comision Femenil Mexicana Nacional, 1958-1975." *Chicana Movidas: New Narratives of Activism and Feminism in the Movement Era.* U of Texas P, 2018.

Orozco, Cynthia. *No Mexicans, Women, or Dogs Allowed: The Rise of the Mexican American Civil Rights Movement.* U of Texas P, 2009.

Ruiz, Vicki and Virginia Sanchez. *Latinas in the United States.* Indiana UP, 2006.

Weigand, Kate. *Red Feminism: American Communism and the Making of Women's Liberation.* John Hopkins UP, 2001.

PART V
RECLAIMING COMMUNITY,
RECLAIMING KNOWLEDGE

Mujeres y mártires: Cristero Diaspora Literature

ANITA HUIZAR-HERNÁNDEZ
Arizona State University

In the aftermath of the Mexican Revolution (1910-1920), a group of Catholics who rejected Mexico's secularization took up arms against the newly-formed government in what is known as the Cristero War (1926-1929). The Cristero War has received far less attention than the Mexican Revolution; the War was for many years considered taboo as both the Catholic Church and the Mexican state maintained a long silence on the topic.[1] Nevertheless, the impact of the Cristero War on Mexicans was severe, inciting enough violence to prompt many Cristeros to seek shelter across the border in the United States.

Such was the case for María de la Torre, a Mexican woman from Zacatecas whose family was closely connected to the Cristero cause. María de la Torre was the oldest of eight children and the only daughter of Ignacio de la Torre Berumen and María Uribarren Velasco (J. l. de la Torre 1, 3). The deeply Catholic and conservative De la Torre family opposed the Mexican Revolution, which cost Ignacio de la Torre "all his possessions, farms, lands and fortune" (5). As strong supporters of the Cristero War, the De la Torres earned the suspicion of the Mexican government, which began surveilling their homes in Tampico and San Luis Potosí. Aware of the danger they faced in Mexico, in 1927 the De la Torre family decided to seek refuge across the northern border, settling in Nogales, Arizona ("Familia de la Torre").

Once in the United States, María de la Torre, like many other exiled Cristeros, turned to writing to document her experience of the War. Instead of focusing on her family's forced migration, however, María de la Torre recorded another personal loss—the execution of her former suitor, a Cristero fighter named Fidel Muro. Between 1933 and 1934, María De la Torre compiled a thirty-four-page *Álbum sobre la vida y muerte de Fidel Muro* [Album of the life and death of Fidel Muro], combining poetry, prose, images, and objects to commemorate Muro's martyrdom on behalf of the Cristero cause. Today, the unpublished *Álbum* forms part of the University of Arizona's *De la Torre Family Papers* archival collection, which documents the family's transnational ties to the Cristero War.

In this essay, I approach María de la Torre's *Álbum* not as an isolated archival text, but rather as a nexus between two bodies of literature that have not as yet been in dialogue with one another—Literature of the Cristero War and Latino/a literature.[2] Literature of the Cristero War has long played an important testimonial role, filling the void left by official historical narratives that elided the War and enjoying commercial success more or less continually from the time of the War itself to the present day (Ruiz Abreu 22-5). Though long overlooked by literary critics, there is now a growing body of scholarship on Literature of the Cristero War that has begun to document its role in bringing to light the violence and suffering that the War caused within Mexico (Ruiz Abreu 18; González Luna 102).[3] Nevertheless, as María de la Torre's *Álbum* attests, literary representations of the Cristero War did not stop at Mexico's borders. The Mexicans who settled in the United States explicitly to flee anti-Catholic persecution, what historian Julia Young calls the "Cristero diaspora," continued to grapple with the War and its meaning through writing in exile (7). They did so in private documents, in Cristero-specific publications, and within the pages of non-Cristero Spanish-language newspapers.[4] As such, they became part of the development of Latino/a literature in the United States. The specific contours of their influence, however, have largely gone unexplored.

First in Mexico and then in the United States, the Cristeros' religious identity positioned them on the margins of modernity. What they were marginal to, however, was very different in each nation. In Mexico, the modernity the Cristeros attributed to the Mexican Revolution was grounded in what they condemned as a violent secularization that betrayed the fundamentally Catholic base of Mexican cultural and political identity. The stakes were as high as the sacrifice required, as the Cristeros saw their cause as nothing short of the salvation of Mexico. Once in the United States, the modernity the Cristeros encountered was grounded not in secularization but rather in the racialization of religious difference. Though the Cristero diaspora continued to target their critique at Mexico and its anticlerical laws, that critique took on new resonance as it joined a longstanding resistance to US Anglo-Protestant hegemony and the anti-Mexican discrimination it promoted. Cristero thought became fundamental to the elaboration of "México de afuera," an idea cultivated within and disseminated through some Spanish-language outlets "in which it was the duty of the individual to maintain the Spanish language, keep the Catholic faith and insulate their children from what community leaders perceived as the low moral standards practiced by Anglo-Americans" (Kanellos 37). When viewed transnationally, Cristero diaspora literature highlights the crucial role religion played in consolidating early-twentieth-century US and Mexican national identities, dramatizing the intertwined politics of modernization, assimilation, and racialization and their impact on Latino/a communities.

In what follows, I closely read María de la Torre's *Álbum* as an example of how Cristero diaspora literature both participates in and complicates our understanding of early twentieth-century Latino/a literature. I engage a transnational and feminist reading of the *Álbum* to bring to light how the story of sacrifice that it tells is inevitably transformed by the displacement that story prompts and the women that it impacts. In particular, I focus on how two of the most salient characteristics of Literature of the Cristero War, the prominence of women protagonists and the emphasis on martyrdom, are destabilized when taken up in a diasporic context. In the *Álbum,* the central yet circumscribed role of women within the conflict begins to break down, as a return to previous expectations regarding gender roles no longer seems plausible. Similarly, the celebration of martyrdom sombers when extended beyond the national context, making the nationally-oriented salvation Cristero martyrdom promises inaccessible. In both cases, the *Álbum* makes legible the impact of the Cristero War beyond the borders of Mexico. Here I build on the work of Yolanda Padilla, who has called for "a transnational optic that emphasizes margins, borders, and migrations" to read the Literature of the Revolution in a way that interrupts "the nation-state's totalizing narratives" (Padilla "Literary Revolutions" 335). For Padilla, it is precisely "the dispossessed" who "constitute narrative *openings*— their experiences of dislocation and migration are the starting points from which to engage the revolution's meanings" (335). Following Padilla, I propose that centering migrants and migration within the Literature of the Cristero War is a necessary first step in unraveling the totalizing narratives promoted by Mexico, the United States, and the Cristeros themselves, each of which serves to obscure the War's full impact.

A transnational reading of the Literature of the Cristero War restores the migrant experience within what Ángel Arias Urrutia has called the "herida abierta" caused by the historical silencing of the conflict (231). Arias' invocation of an "herida abierta" recalls Gloria Anzaldúa's characterization of the US-Mexico border as "*una herida abierta* where the Third World grates against the first and bleeds," inadvertently drawing the borderlands and its literary production into his depiction of the history of erasure surrounding the Cristero War (25). The full extent of the loss alluded to in the *Álbum* and its impact on Latino/a literature can be apprehended within this expanded definition of a transnational wound.

Modern *mujeres*

Though the focus of the *Álbum* is, as the title attests, *la vida y muerte de Fidel Muro*, Muro's life story takes shape through the eyes of two women. The first is María de la Torre, the compiler of the *Álbum* and Muro's former sweetheart. The second is Sor María

Guadalupe Muro, Fidel Muro's sister, a nun whose account of her brother's martyrdom forms the narrative center of the *Álbum*. The prominence of women within the *Álbum* is not unusual for texts depicting the Cristero War. Unlike Literature of the Revolution, from its earliest iterations, Literature of the Cristero War featured women's role in the conflict (Vaca 21; Arias Urrutia 112; León Vega 430).[5] Women's literary significance is attributable to their historic centrality to the War's action and their importance within its ideological foundation. As Álvaro Ruiz Abreu remarks, "La mujer es el pilar sobre el que se edificó una buena parte del edificio cristero; fiel a su causa, su hombre y su iglesia, la mujer que retrata el relato cristero suele ser justa, virgen y mártir" [The woman is the pillar on which a good part of the Cristero edifice is erected: faithful to her cause, her man and her church, the woman that the Cristero story portrays is typically just, a virgin, and a martyr] (159). In an ironic twist, during the Cristero War, Mexican Catholic women became the foundation of an armed political uprising. Canonical examples of novels that feature Cristeras include Jorge Gram's *Héctor* (1930), Fernando Robles' *La virgen de los cristeros* (1934), and Jesús Goytortúa Santos' *Pensativa* (1945).[6] Though the perspective each text takes vis-à-vis the War differs markedly, women are central to the action that unfolds in all cases.[7]

The *Álbum* is notably distinct from these other texts, however, in that it not only features women but is also told from their perspective. As Agustín Vaca clarifies, "Al igual que la mayoría de las obras historiográficas y de los testimonios, las novelas [de la Literatura de la Guerra Cristera] son un producto en el que predomina la óptica masculina" [Like the majority of the historiographies and testi-monios, in the novels (of the Literature of the Cristero War) the masculine optic predominates] (25). An exception is Elena Garro's *Los recuerdos del porvenir* (1963), though unlike the aforementioned texts, it was written many years after the conflict ended. As a document authored by women and produced contemporaneous to the War itself, the *Álbum* stands in unique contrast to these other literary representations of the women of the Cristero War. It is not surprising, then, that the images, objects, poetry, and prose that María de la Torre and María Guadalupe Muro contribute to the *Álbum* together defy the geographic, literary, and ideological boundaries typically associated with the Cristero War and its literary representation.

In the *Álbum*, María de la Torre challenges the restrictions that limited women's autonomy by rewriting her love story with Fidel Muro. In a shocking fragment of a letter she wrote but did not send to the priest Felix Rougier, De la Torre explains how her family forced her to end her relationship with Muro before his martyrdom because he was a "pobre carpintero de educación y posición social inferiores a la mia [sic]" [poor carpenter whose education and social position were inferior to my own] (26). The separation from Muro torments De la Torre. Even after her family moves to Nogales, Arizona she remains devastated by the loss of Muro in her life and resentful of her family. She even goes so far as to say "perdí la piedad por que [sic] todo me parecia [sic] hipocresia [sic], sentí dentro de mí despecho, odio, quise abandonar mi casa de cualquier manera y si hubiera podido quitarme la vida!!!" [I lost piety because everything seemed to me to be hypocritical, I felt spite, hate, I wanted to abandon my house somehow, and if I had been able to, I would have taken my own life!!!] (28-29). Though confessions of a temporary loss of faith are not uncommon in Cristero narratives, they are typically prompted by external adversity, namely government persecution, and not the antagonism of fellow Cristeros. By including this internal tension within her *Álbum*, De la Torre reveals how Cristeros were not insulated from broader debates about the changing role of women in society. To the contrary, as Barbara Miller explains, the exceptional space of the Cristero War accelerated those changes as "the church, the very institution which sanctified the role of women as custodians of the family's morals, gave women the opportunity to move out of their sphere of influence into the 'male' world of violent confrontation" (322). Though this was a temporary opportunity prompted by extraordinary circumstances and the Church later "compelled [women] to return to their 'proper' role once the crisis had passed," Miller suggests that the expanded opportunities that the Cristero conflict afforded to women initiated an irreversible undermining of traditional gender norms (322-3).

For María de la Torre, writing about Fidel Muro's death provides her an opportunity to undermine her family's objections to their relationship. Upon finding out that Muro was executed, De la Torre writes, "senti [sic] como transformado mi corazón, y perdoné las ofensas que habia [sic] recibido en casa por que [sic] por primera vez, sentí vergüenza de mi pequeñez ante tan alto ejemplo de generosidad y de nobleza" [I felt like my heart was transformed, and I forgave the offenses that I had received in my home because for the first time, I felt ashamed of my smallness in view of such a great example of generosity and nobility] (5). She finds comfort when she learns that he was, in fact, killed on the Feast of the Assumption, as she had previously prayed to the Virgin Mary to take Muro to heaven, and portrays his martyrdom as an answer to her prayers. She writes, "Vi clara y patente la protección de la Sma. Virgen que recojió nuestras lágrimas, que recojió nuestra pena, que oyó mis ruegos, pues se lo llevó al cielo en su dia [sic]" [I saw clear and evident the protection of the Virgin Saint who collected our tears, who collected our pain, who heard my pleas and took him to heaven that day] (5). The union indicated here by the use of first-person plural, as De la Torre describes herself and Muro sharing the same tears and pain, is underscored by the marital imagery she uses in both the dedication and closing of the *Álbum* to describe their continued connection. In the dedication, she writes:

A Fidel Muro. A él dedico éste humilde album [sic] que el cariño y el dolor de su novia ha coleccionado, como un homenaje a su generosa vida y a su heróica muerte y que las lágrimas con que ha sido mojado, se conviertan en los nudos de un lazo que nos una en el cielo. Maria de la Torre Nog. Ariz 1933. (2)

[To Fidel Muro. To him, I dedicate this humble album that his sweetheart's affection and pain have collected, as an homage to his generous life and his heroic death. I hope that my tears that have wet it will turn into the knots of a bow that will unite us in heaven.]

The image of a "lazo" uniting them here recalls a wedding ceremony that, despite not happening on earth, nevertheless is realized in heaven. De la Torre again invokes marital language in a letter she includes towards the end of the *Álbum*, addressed to Muro "en el 6° aniversario de su muerte" [in the sixth anniversary of his death] in which she defiantly asks, "¿quién puede separar lo que Dios ha unido?" [who can separate what God has joined?] (32). It is through writing, then, that María de la Torre is able to make peace with Fidel Muro's sacrifice as a Cristero fighter and her own sacrifice as a dutiful Cristera daughter.

Before and after De la Torre reimagines her romance with Muro, within the *Álbum* she includes visual and poetic fragments that underscore the Cristero War's long reach beyond Mexico's borders. She begins with a series of images and objects that refract the visual landscape of the Cristero War through her position within its diaspora. Captionless photographs of María de la Torre, Fidel Muro, and other Cristeros as well as postcards depicting the penitentiary at San Luis Potosí where Fidel Muro was held prisoner and *la Virgen de Guadalupe* appearing to Juan Diego allude to the battle the Cristeros waged to realize their vision of a Catholic nation. The cost of that battle is hauntingly referenced in two pages containing unexplained objects: scraps of sullied white and black cloth and a dried flower tied with a red bow. These personal mementos, so private that they are presented without context, are lovingly pre- served behind clear plastic sheets. Are these the clothes of Fidel Muro? A flower exchanged between lovers? Whatever their specific referents, their inclusion in the *Álbum* points to the enduring wounds that the War caused participants on all sides, both those who stayed in Mexico and those who sought refuge abroad.

In addition to images and objects, De la Torre also bookends the *Álbum* with *modernista* poetry, thereby linking the Cristero War to a broader hemispheric literary exchange. She uses Mexican writer Amado Nervo's "Ofertorio" as an epigraph and includes Uruguayan poet Raquel Sáenz's "Sed" among the *Álbum*'s final pages. Both poems include a first-person poetic voice that laments the loss of love. In Nervo's poem, the speaker addresses God, describing the pain he experiences due to the death of his lover (1). In Sáenz's poem, the speaker addresses a former lover, describing the "sed" [thirst] she experiences after denying him a kiss (31). The resonance between De la Torre's own story and those of the speakers in the poems is obvious, yet her decision to include them in her *Álbum* suggests two unexpected connections. Though critics have disparaged Literature of the Cristero War for favoring religious didacticism over aesthetics, De la Torre's inclusion of *modernista* poetry indicates first that she had some knowledge of literary movements; and second that she was in tune with their movement across borders. As John Alba Cutler has shown, in the early twentieth century *modernista* poetry often appeared in the pages of Spanish-language newspapers in the United States, where it became part of a broader conversation about Latino/a identity and its relationship to both the United States and Latin America.[8] It is very possible that De la Torre encountered both Nervo's and Sáenz's poems not in Mexico, but rather in the pages of these US-based Spanish-language periodicals. Regardless of how De la Torre encountered the poems, her reprinting of them in the *Álbum* puts Cristero diaspora literature in direct conversation with Latino/a print culture. This connection is significant, as Cristero diaspora literature's rejection of both Mexican and US modernity complicates our understanding of how Latino/a print culture grappled with what Cutler calls "doubled coloniality," or "the way that US Latinos identified with the history of Latin American modernity, while finding themselves marginalized, dispossessed, and exploited by US modernity" ("Latinx Modernism" 578).

In addition to *modernista* poetry, in the *Álbum* De la Torre also reprints an article written by Fidel Muro's sister, María Guadalupe Muro, to explain in detail what befell Fidel Muro after he and De la Torre parted ways. Like María de la Torre's *Álbum*, María Guadalupe Muro's "MAS [sic] MARTIRES [sic] EN MEXICO [sic]! . . . LA HEROICA MUERTE DEL JOVEN FIDEL MURO" [MORE MARTYRS IN MEXICO! THE HEROIC DEATH OF THE YOUNG FIDEL MURO] has its own transnational publication history.[9] Muro indicates that she wrote her essay in Mexico, signing it "S. Luis Potosí 5 de Diciembre [sic] 1928" [San Luis Potosí

December 5, 1928]. Though there is no indication that either Fidel Muro or his sister María Guadalupe Muro ever left Mexico, De la Torre notes that she reprints the text from volumes 16 and 17 of the April 1929 *Revista Católica*, a Catholic weekly published in El Paso, Texas that was founded prior to the Cristero War but vocally supported the Catholic revolutionaries once the conflict began (De la Torre 9; Young 65).[10] Cristero diaspora literature found a ready home in the *Revista,* which had defended the centrality of the Catholic faith to Mexican immigrant identity for many years. Other Spanish-language periodicals did not share this view, including Laredo's *La Crónica*. The two papers maintained a public feud, publishing editorials decrying one another decades before the Cristero War began. Within this context, the publication of "MAS [sic] MARTIRES [sic]" in the *Revista* demonstrates that the debates over the role of Catholicism in Mexico were not separate from similar concerns in "México de afuera."

In telling the story of her brother's life, glimpses of María Guadalupe Muro's own life become visible as well. "MAS [sic] MARTIRES [sic]" is the first narrative-driven introduction to the man whose life and death are the *Álbum*'s stated focus and the only introduction to his sister, who was herself an active part of the Cristero resistance as well. Within the narrative, María Guadalupe Muro reveals a key fact about her involvement in the Cristero War: her role as a nun. Her vocation comes to light in a letter she sends to her brother to let him know that she has been taken prisoner. She writes:

> Cuando nos cogieron presas a nosotras por el hecho de ser religiosas, le escribí diciéndole; "Hermano, no te apueres [sic] por mí, ni tomes parte en cosa alguna, por que [sic] se [sic] te descubren, yo te complico; mejor déjame, al fin que a mí no me pueden quitar la vida, puesto que soy mujer; y si te encarcelan a ti, no conviene, por que [sic] tu puedes trabajar mucho en la causa y yo de nada sirvo." (16)

> [When they took us prisoners because we were nuns, I wrote to him saying, "Brother, do not worry about me, or take part in anything because if they discover you, I complicate things

for you; it is better to leave it be since they cannot take my life since I am a woman; and if they imprison you, it is a problem, because you can work much more for the cause and I am useless.]

María Guadalupe Muro's self-effacing letter expresses expected deference to her brother and is far from a feminist statement. Nevertheless, her words register the degree to which women, particularly members of Catholic religious communities, were not immune to danger and simultaneously did not shy away from risk during the Cristero War. Miller writes about the Mexican nuns who became "the object of government persecution" and "were forced to go underground" during the Cristero War (313). In some ways, the threat they faced was even greater, as they were often the targets of rape at the hands of Mexican soldiers (Miller 313).

María Guadalupe Muro's statement also alludes to how choosing the life of a nun allowed women an acceptable pretext to gain a certain degree of autonomy from men. Through being married to Christ, nuns notably avoided being married to men, sidestepping the aforementioned challenges that women like María de la Torre faced. In her letter to her brother, despite professing humility, María Guadalupe Muro encourages Fidel Muro to leave her free of his care. Just as Fidel Muro was willing to become a martyr for the cause, so too was María Guadalupe Muro prepared to suffer because of her professed faith. Despite her respectful claim that "yo de nada sirvo" [I am useless], it is clear that she was, independent of her brother, an active protagonist in the story of the Cristero War (16).

Mártires migrantes

Though all the contents of the *Álbum* commemorate Fidel Muro's martyrdom, the details emerge most clearly in "MAS [sic] MARTIRES [sic]." Part-testimonio and part-hagiography, Muro's narrative bears witness to a life otherwise elided by the official historical record. In this way, María Guadalupe Muro's text exemplifies one of the key characteristics that defines Literature of the Cristero War generally: a hyper awareness of its role as a counter to the pervasive historical silence surrounding the war and its victims (Arias Urrutia 120; Ruiz Abreu 22-3; Naranjo Tamayo 73; González Luna 102). This sensibility is clear from the title, an emphatic cry for recognition and remembrance. From start to finish, "MAS [sic] MARTIRES [sic]" builds a case for "LA HEROICA [sic] MUERTE DEL JOVEN FIDEL MURO" to be counted among those other brave Cristeros who made the ultimate sacrifice as martyrs to the cause.

María Guadalupe Muro attributes her brother's martyrdom to his involvement in "la Liga," or the *Liga Nacional Defensora de la Libertad Religiosa* [National Religious Freedom Defense League], an important Cristero organization that was heavily involved in coordinating the armed resistance to Mexico's anticlerical government (Young 25). Nearly all the essay is focused on Fidel Muro's work for *la Liga*. After providing a few basic biographical details about her brother's early life on page 1, by page 2, María Guadalupe Muro shifts to describing her brother's decision to join *la Liga*, which he explains as a conscious choice to likely die a martyr. He tells his sister, "te hago saber que soy de la Liga de Defensa Religiosa, y no es muy remoto que tenga que morir en el campo de batalla o fusilado" [I'm letting you know that I am part of the Religious Defense League, and it is not unlikely that I will have to die on the battlefield or by firing squad] (20). Her response underscores the likelihood of her brother's eventual martyrdom, as she depicts herself in Mass the following day offering her brother "a Dios como víctima de su gloria" [to God as a victim for his glory] (20).

Fidel Muro's sacrifice for the cause is not, however, limited to his death. As in other narratives of martyrdom, "MAS [sic] MARTIRES [sic]" describes in great detail the torments he suffers prior to his eventual execution.[11] These include various periods of imprisonment, such as when he is tortured so severely that he is left unable to walk (21). Another time, the soldiers hang him from his fingers until they begin to decompose, "pero sin conseguir con ésto [sic] que denunciara a persona alguna" [but without getting him to denounce anyone else] (22-3). Importantly, Fidel Muro never gives away another Cristero, defying the tortures inflicted by the authorities at every turn. When not in prison, his suffering continues as he experiences severe and constant hunger completing his clandestine work for *la Liga* (23).

After these visceral descriptions of the physical suffering Fidel Muro endures during his life, the final pages of the essay are dedicated to the story of his death. On July 19, 1928 when his guarantor and daughter are imprisoned because of their association with Muro, he decides to present himself to the authorities to secure their freedom despite knowing that it will almost certainly lead to his own death (17-18). After nearly a month in prison, on August 15, 1928 he is killed by firing squad (21). María Guadalupe Muro describes him in his moment of death as "extendiéndo [sic] sus brazos en cruz y al grito de 'Viva Cristo Rey'" [extending his arms forming a cross with his body and shouting 'Long live Christ the King'], the rallying cry of Cristero fighters (21).

In keeping with the generic expectations that accompany narratives of martyrdom, María Guadalupe Muro concludes with miraculous details about her now-deceased brother.[12] At first, his body does not bleed while he remains under government custody, but once released, "empezó a correr sangre en abundancia, enteramente líquida y roja. A las treinta y cinco horas despues [sic] de muerto, la sangre corría en mayor abundancia" [blood began to pour in abundance, entirely liquid and red. Thirty-five hours after his death, his blood flew even more.] (21-2). When María Guadalupe Muro arrives at the place where they are keeping her brother's body, she perceives the miraculous circumstances and addresses him as a martyr, saying "Martir [sic] de Jesucristo, acuérdate que en el mundo has dejado una patria que sufre, a tus padres y a mí" [Martyr of Jesus Christ, remember that in this world you have left a nation that suffers, your parents and me] (22). Her explicit recognition of her brother as a martyr is then affirmed by the behavior of others who come to view his body, which she describes as "enteramente flexible y de color bonito" [entirely flexible and of a beautiful color], as they "recogieron su sangre en algodones, en flores y pañuelos, llamándolo el mártir zacatecano" [collected his blood with cotton, flowers, and handkerchiefs, calling him the Zacatecan martyr] (22).

Throughout these descriptions of her brother's life and death, María Guadalupe Muro connects her brother's story with other narratives of martyrdom, one of the most fundamental tropes of the Cristero movement and its literary representation. Martyrs were extremely important to Cristeros, both during and after the War. As Young explains, "In the popular Catholic tradition, martyrdom is especially valued, since those who are killed because of their faith are believed to ascend straight to heaven and become saints, where they can intercede directly to God for those on earth, as well as grant the prayers of their faithful" (167). For the Cristeros, all "the people who were killed by federal troops during the War were martyrs, regardless of whether they were officially declared to be so by the Catholic Church" (167).[13] María Guadalupe Muro's account of her brother's martyrdom joins this larger Cristero tradition, turning to writing to honor a life that was otherwise absent from the official historical record (or lack thereof) of the conflict.

In Literature of the Cristero War, martyrs are foundational to challenging the hegemony of the Mexican nationalism promoted by the Revolution. As Ruiz Abreu explains, "La literatura cristera ha construido sus propios mitos, su propia visión de la historia de México y la ha edificado sobre las ruinas de la Guerra, sus apóstoles y sus mártires, sus víctimas y sus verdugos" [Cristero Literature has constructed its own myths, its own vision of the history of Mexico and it has built on the ruins of the War, its apostles and its martyrs, its victims and executioners] (22). The *Álbum* clearly participates in this alternate myth-making, proposing Muro and the Cristero men and women who fought alongside him as the foundation of a different sort of nation-building. Their collective martyrdom, as Ana María González Luna argues, "es vivido como una gracia y como el medio de hacer que avance la salvación de México" [is lived as a grace and as the means to advance the salvation of Mexico] (104). Their martyrdom resolves the problems Cristeros attributed to Mexico's modernization, that is to say, its secularization, doubly promising both spiritual and national salvation.

Resolution is more elusive, however, when this nationally-oriented martyrdom is translated beyond the bounds of the nation-state. As discussed previously, both María De la Torre's *Álbum* and

María Guadalupe Muro's narrative within it were written or circulated in the United States. For the Cristero diaspora, the US represented a temporary reprieve from the immediate danger they faced. However, migration did not shield them from persecution entirely. To the contrary, maintaining a fiercely Mexican Catholic identity in a dominantly Anglo Protestant country invited new kinds of discrimination.

Though neither De la Torre nor Muro speaks directly to this situation, when their words are read alongside the larger body of Latino/a literature from the time period, the double displacement of Cristeros as exiles from their native Mexico and members of a marginalized community within the United States becomes clear. A few months after María Guadalupe Muro's "MAS [sic] MARTIRES [sic]" appeared in *Revista Católica*, the paper included a 2-page spread titled "EL PROPAGANDISTA CATOLICO [sic]," [THE CATHOLIC PROPAGANDIST] which warned "Hispanoamericanos" [Hispanic Americans] to wake up and not succumb to "el Protestantismo Sajón" [Saxon Protestantism]. The article then goes on to list the number of "Protestantes" [Protestants] and "No Protestantes" [Not Protestants] in each US state (including the District of Columbia) and notes that "los Estados en que más abundan los protestantes, son también los más atrasados y en los que más predomina la ignorancia religiosa, los linchamientos, etc" [The states in which Protestants are most abundant, are also the most backward and those in which religious ignorance, lynchings, etc. predominate] ("EL PROPAGANDISTA CATOLICO"). The racialization of religious identity is unambiguous, as the article casts Protestantism as not only "Sajón" [Saxon] but also associates it with the regions of the country that are the most "atrasados" [backwards], where "linchamientos" [lynchings] prevail. The paper specifies that the two-page text is also available for purchase as a separate pamphlet and implores readers to buy as many copies as possible to share with their communities. That there was a need for such a pamphlet points to the magnitude of the pressure on Latino/a communities to assimilate through religious conversion, which *Revista católica* in no uncertain terms casts as a loss not only of religious but also cultural identity.

Against this backdrop, Cristero diaspora literature serves as an important link between the ways religious affiliation interpellated national identity in early-twentieth century Mexico and the United States. Through their writings, the Cristero diaspora brought the concerns they carried from the War with them across the border. In so doing, they expanded the geographic, literary, and ideological boundaries that had already come to define the Cristero War and its literary representation. They also introduced those expanded stakes into the broader context of Latino/a print culture, shaping its development in ways that become visible through a transnational and feminist analysis of their writing.

Works Cited

Anzaldúa, Gloria. *Borderlands/La frontera: The New Mestiza.* 3rd edition, Aunt Lute Books, 2007.

Arias Urrutia, Ángel. *Cruzados de novela: Las novelas de la guerra cristera.* Eunsa, 2002.

Bantjes, Adrian A. "The Regional Dynamics of Anticlericalism and Defanaticization in Revolutionary Mexico." *Faith and Impiety in Revolutionary Mexico*, edited by Matthew Butler, Palgrave, 2007, pp. 111-30.

Brickhouse, Anna. *The Unsettlement of America: Translation, Interpretation, and the Story of Don Luis de Velasco, 1560-1945.* Oxford, 2014.

Cutler, John Alba. "Rubén Darío, Latino Poet." *English Language Notes,* vol. 56, no. 2, 2018, pp. 71-89.

____. ""At the Crossroads of Circulation and Translation: Rethinking US Latino/a Modernism." *Modernism/modernity,* 3. 3 (2018) https://doi.org/10.26597/mod.0069.

____. "Latinx Modernism and the Spirit of Latinoamericansimo." *American Literary History*, vol. 33, no. 3, 2021, pp. 571-587.

"De la Torre family papers, 1874-2003 (bulk 1910-1946)." *ArizonaArchives*, www.azarchivesonline.org/xtf/view?docId=ead/.uoa/ UAMS online 420.xml. Accessed 30 January 2021.

De la Torre, José Luis. *From Sonora to Heaven: Biography of His Excellency Vicar General of the Archdiocese of Hermosillo, Sonora, Monsignor Ignacio de la Torre Uribarren.* Guayabera P, 2013.

De la Torre, María. *Álbum sobre la vida y muerte de Fidel Muro.* 1933. Box 2, Folder 8. MS 420 De la Torre family papers, 1874-2003 (bulk 1910-1946). University of Arizona Special Collection, University of Arizona, Tucson, AZ, January 30 2021.

"EL PROPAGANDISTA CATOLICO." *Revista católica,* El Paso, TX, 14 July 1929.

"Familia de la Torre." *La Vida Fronteriza: Church, Economy and Daily Life—Excerpts from the De la Torre Family Papers.* University of Arizona Special Collections, speccoll.library. arizona.edu/online-exhibits/exhibits/show/delatorre/familia-de-la-torre#top. Accessed 30 January 2021.

González Luna, Ana María. "La literatura de la Cristiada: Una visión apocalíptica de la historia de México." *Altre Modernità*, no. 1, 2013, pp. 100–11.

Kanellos, Nicolás with Helvetia Martell. *Hispanic Periodicals in the United States, Origins to 1960: A Brief History and Comprehensive Bibliography.* Arte Público P, 2000.

León Vega, Margarita. "Las mujeres como agentes en dos novelas de tema cristero." *La memoria cultural acerca de la Revolución Mexicana, la Guerra cristera y el cardenismo*, edited by Ute Seydel, Universidad Nacional Autónoma de México, 2018, pp. 427-454.

Meyer, Jean. *The Cristero Rebellion: The Mexican People Between Church and State, 1926-1929.* Cambridge, 2008.

Miller, Barbara. "The Role of Women in the Mexican Cristero Rebellion: Las señoras y las religiosas." *The Americas*, vol. 40, no. 3, 1984, pp. 303-23.

Naranjo Tamayo, Omayda. "*Pensativa* de Jesús Goytortúa Santos: Imagen y representación de la mujer Mexicana en la novela de tema cristero." *Relaciones*, vol. 31, no. 123, 2010, pp. 59-83.

Olivera de Bonfil, Alivia. *La guerra cristera: Aspectos del conflicto religioso de 1926 a 1929.* Instituto Nacional de Antropología e Historia, 1966.

Padilla, Yolanda. "The 'Other' Novel of the Mexican Revolution." *Bridges, Borders, and Breaks: History, Narrative, and Nation in Twenty-First-Century Chicana/o Literary Criticism,* edited by William Orchard and Yolanda Padilla, U of Pittsburgh, 2016, pp. 63-79.

_____. "Literary Revolutions in the Borderlands: Transnational Dimensions of the Mexican Revolution and Its Diaspora in the United States." *The Cambridge History of Latina/o American Literature,* edited by John Morán González and Laura Lomas, Cambridge, 2018, pp. 334–52.

Ruiz Abreu, Álvaro. *La cristera: una literatura negada (1928-1992).* Universidad Autónoma Metropolitana, 2003.

Ryan, Steven P. "Revista Católica." *Handbook of Texas Online,* www.tshaonline.org/handbook/entries/revista-catolica. Accessed 30 January 2021.

Thiébaut, Guy. *La contre-révolution mexicaine à travers sa littérature.* L'Harmattan, 1997.

Vaca, Agustín. *Los silencios de la historia: las cristeras.* El Colegio de Jalisco, 1998.

Young, Julia G. *Mexican Exodus: Emigrants, Exiles, and Refugees of the Cristero War.* Oxford, 2015.

Mujeres vascas en Estados Unidos, 1850-1950: La formación de una comunidad

KOLDO SAN SEBASTIÁN
Estudioso Independiente

William A. Douglass y Jon Bilbao recuerdan que "el inmigrante vasco más característico del oeste americano fue durante mucho tiempo el joven varón soltero"[1]. La emigración a los estados del este siguió el mismo patrón, y la mayoría de los emigrantes eran marinos mercantes y muchos estaban casados. Conseguían la nacionalidad con facilidad y ello propiciaba la reunificación familiar o bodas con paisanas en el nuevo país[2]. Así, no es hasta la llegada de las mujeres cuando puede hablarse de una comunidad vasca en Estados Unidos. Bilbao, refiriéndose entonces a los vascos del oeste, señalan que, durante el siglo pasado (s. XIX) eran más los que volvían al País Vasco que los que se quedaban. En cambio, en los últimos sesenta años ha ocurrido todo lo contrario. Ello se ha debido principalmente a la emigración de la mujer vasca. Los tenderos, los patronos de borregas, el ranchero, estaban ya en posición de formar un hogar. Por otra parte, los hoteleros necesitaban chicas para atender a sus clientes, especialmente en época de Navidad. Y estas chicas (. . .) pasaban en poco tiempo de criadas a esposas de rancheros, tenderos u hosteleros (. . .) Es entonces cuando comienza la verdadera colonización vasca de estados como Nevada y Idaho[3], los nuevos

267

matrimonios construyen su rancho y el pastor se convierte no solo en pastor de borregas sino en agricultor [4].

La venida de mujeres vascas se acentuó especialmente después de la guerra hispanoamericana (1898). Durante los primeros años del siglo XX y hasta 1922 la comunidad vasca aumentó rápidamente. Algunos agentes de emigración o "enganchadores" en el País Vasco y hoteleros vascos en Estados Unidos "organiz[aron] expediciones de criadas vascas para las pensiones de pastores" [5]. La "importación" de solteras vascas se convirtió como veremos en un buen negocio para los hoteleros. Era una forma de atraer a sus establecimientos clientes solteros. Aunque, claro, no todas llegaban como criadas. A pesar de la importancia de la mujer en la constitución y consolidación de la comunidad, sorprende que no haya recibido atención académica. De acuerdo con Sydney Sthal Wimberg, una de las grandes especialistas norteamericanas en la cuestión, "el estudio de la inmigración ha sido distorsionado y empobrecido por la omisión de los estudios sobre la transición a la vida en Estados Unidos" [6]. Existen diferentes estudios sobre mujeres inmigrantes pertenecientes a minorías: irlandesas, japonesas, chinas, mexicanas, puertorriqueñas, noruegas, judías . . . en los Estados Unidos que muestran el recorrido historiográfico pendiente para el caso de las vascas.[7] Gloria Totoricagüena afirma que las vascas "han sido omitidas en los primeros estudios sobre inmigración o se han percibido únicamente junto a los hombres que han emigrado" [8]. La antropóloga Teresa del Valle asienta que "la emigración de las mujeres vascas se ha relegado al silencio" [9].

No abunda la literatura sobre la mujer vasca en los Estados Unidos. Uno de los pocos ensayos relevantes es el de Marie Pierre Arrizabalaga, *Las mujeres pirenaicas y la emigración en el siglo XIX*[10]. Asun Garikano incluye el capítulo ("Emakumeak ere joan ziren Amerikerara": "Las mujeres también fueron a América") en su libro sobre los vascos del oeste[11]. Joan Errea publicó *My Mama Marie* sobre su madre [12]. Otros son *Catherine Etchart: A Montana Love Story*, de Monique Urza[13], o *The Basque Hotelera: Implications for A Broader Atudy*, de Jerónima Echeverría[14]. Un punto de vista más contemporáneo lo encontramos en Janet C. Inda. *Basque Sheepherders Daughter* [15]. También hay algunas referencias en algunos recetarios de cocina vasca publicados en Estados Unidos en los que se cuenta la historia de las cocineras que los inspiraron[16].

El origen de las mujeres

La mayor parte de las mujeres vascas que emigraron a Estados Unidos procedía de entornos rurales tradicionales. Su vida giraba en torno a la granja (caserío: baserri), el grupo que comprendía un hombre activo (etxeko jauna: el señor de la casa), su mujer (etxeko andrea: mujer de la casa), sus hijos, sus parientes y/o los consanguíneos solteros de los cónyuges[17]. El etxeko jauna era nominalmente la primera autoridad[18] y las funciones económicas de etxeko andrea complementaban las de etxeko jauna. Su finalidad fundamental consistía en la acertada gestión del ciclo doméstico. Como la etxeko andrea realizaba la mayor parte de las transiciones económicas que afectaban al grupo, casi siempre llevaba el control del dinero y no era raro que el etxeko jauna pidiera a su mujer el dinero que necesitaba[19].

Hay algo más: la casa (caserío, etxe, baserri) la heredaba el primogénito, lo que lógicamente refuerza la autoridad de etxeko jauna. El sistema de herencia evitaba la división de la propiedad hecho que, en la mayor parte de los casos, por el tamaño de ésta, la llevaba a la ruina[20]. La mujer podía heredar la casa. En este caso, la autoridad estaría también encarnada por la etxeko andrea y su marido entonces no tendría mayor importancia que la de otro miembro de la casa[21].

Como resalta la etnógrafa Amaia Mugika Goñi, hubo un tiempo en el que el matrimonio, en general, era de conveniencia, con la firma de un contrato en cuyas capitulaciones se especifican las respectivas aportaciones de los contrayentes y las servidumbres para con la casa (etxe) (padres, hermanos, criados) y, por supuesto, la dote[22]. En muchos casos, las capitulaciones y el sistema de dotes se extendió a las mujeres que se casaban para ir a las Américas[23].

Leonard Kasdan señala que, en algunas comunidades vascas del Pirineo, mientras que los varones jóvenes emigraban, las mujeres quedaban "para casa", para atender a las personas mayores y a esperar que regresase algún emigrante con cierta fortuna para casarse con él[24]. El retornado, bien se quedaba en el lugar, o regresaba con su esposa al lugar al que había emigrado. Pero, también hubo mujeres que llegaron desde zonas urbanas. Así, por ejemplo, entre 1895 y 1924, emigraron al oeste americano unas doscientos mujeres de Lekeitio, un pueblo de pescadores de la costa de Bizkaia[25]. La mayoría se instalaron en Boise, Idaho, y sus alrededores. Otras lo hicieron en Oregón y en el norte de Nevada y muy pocas en California[26]. La mayor parte de las mujeres de las comunidades vascas del este de Estados Unidos proceden de los pueblos costeros de la Bizkaia oriental, eran vascoparlantes y tradicionales.

La etxekoandre se encargaba de la administración del hogar y del cuidado de los hijos mientras el hombre estaba en la mar. Pero la mujer también trabajaba fuera de casa —en las fábricas de conservas, cosiendo redes, como criadas— lo que le daba cierta independencia económica. De hecho, la mujer vasca ha trabajado fuera de casa —en su inmensa mayoría como criadas— desde tiempos inmemoriales. William Douglass habla de las jóvenes de Etxalar que iban a trabajar a hoteles de la Cote Basque y de las de Aulestia-Murelaga que iban a trabajar como criadas. También eran mujeres solteras de Etxalar las que iban (a pie) a trabajar en la cosecha de trigo de la Navarra media[27]. Los ejemplos se multiplican en todo el País Vasco.

Algunas de aquellas muchachas llegaron hasta París. La antropóloga Monique Selim estudió la emigración a París de muchachas de Barcus-Barkoxe, Soule-Zuberoa y menciona que no todas emigraban por razones económicas. Había quien huía del duro trabajo en su casa (granja) o, simplemente, en busca de independencia. Viviendo lejos, no se veían obligadas a seguir con las restrictivas y tradicionales normas de su sociedad[28]. Algunas de aquellas mujeres emigraron a Estados Unidos. Algunas pudieron financiar en parte su viaje a Estados Unidos, como lo hizo Anuntzi Amías Jayo, de Boise. Ello les dio una mayor libertad frente a otras que tuvieron que retornar íntegramente el importe del viaje y otras deudas[29].

Estados Unidos, destino de emigrantes

Hasta la segunda mitad del siglo XIX, la emigración vasca se dirigió, sobre todo, a la América Latina independiente, y, en menor medida, a Cuba y Filipinas, que todavía eran colonias españolas. Los primeros en llegar fueron los vascofranceses en la década de los

1830[30]. Luego, los vascos de España. La inestabilidad política y los conflictos armados en las nuevas repúblicas y la aparición de oro en California hizo que los vascos comenzaran a dirigirse hacia el oeste. La emigración se intensificó tras la Guerra de Secesión (1861-1865). Procedían, en su mayoría, de las provincias pirenaicas. Entre 1872 y 1892 se intensifica la emigración desde los Bajos Pirineos —departamento en el que se encuentra el País Vascofrancés— al oeste americano. Por lo que se refiere a los vascos de España, la emigración se intensificó tras la Tercera Guerra Carlista (1872-1876). Durante casi un siglo, los vascos del este se dedicaron mayoritariamente al pastoreo de ovejas. Entre los del este, por el contrario, eran mayoritariamente marinos mercantes.

La aparición de oro en California marcó una nueva etapa que ha sido estudiada con detalle y maestría por W.A. Douglass y J. Bilbao en su *Amerikanuak. Basques in New World* [31]. La mayor parte de estos "forty-niners" (los del 49) llegaron desde los países del Cono Sur, navegando desde Valparaíso. Las noticias de California se expandieron con tanta fuerza que algunos incluso viajaron a aquel lugar "doblando" el Cabo de Hornos. En este periodo llegaron asimismo algunas mujeres vascas y, en 1866, Juan Miguel Aguirre, de Etxalar, abrió con su esposa Martina Lavayen, el primer hotel vasco con su frontón en San Francisco. Aguirre llamó a emigrar a su sobrino Juan Miguel Arburua que se casó en San Francisco con Josefa Lavayen, sobrina a su vez de Martina, a quien había llamado su tía.

Sabemos que las mujeres vascas que emigraron a los países del Cono Sur (Argentina, Uruguay y Chile) se emplearon como cama-reras, costureras, nodrizas y cocineras. Estas últimas, en hoteles y fondas, pero no en el campo, donde los cocineros eran solo hom-bres[32]. Como veremos, las que emigraron más tarde a Estados Unidos realizaron los mismos trabajos, aunque sí cocinararon en los ranchos y campamentos ovejeros. En los hoteles y restaurantes del este, por el contrario, son mayoritariamente los hombres quienes cocinan (eran cocineros de barco).

Las primeras vascas contemporáneas, como ha quedado dicho, llegaron al oeste en los días del gold rush, pero otras lo hicieron directamente desde Europa"³³. Un primer grupo estaba formado por continentales (francesas) y peninsulares (españolas). Algunas son mujeres cuyos maridos se encontraban ya en California, eran pastores. Miles de vascos se dedicaron a esa actividad, aun cuando sus empleos en su país de origen no tenían que ver —o tenían que ver poco— con el mismo. En realidad, eran carpinteros, canteros, pescadores, . . . pero acabaron en las montañas o en los desiertos del oeste rodeados de centenares de ovinos sin más compañía que la de sus perros y la soledad. Una vida que se convierte en epopeya en el clásico de Robert Laxalt, *Sweet Promised Land* (1957). El protagonista, el padre de del autor, se casó con una vasca cuando él ya "era rico en ovejas"³⁴. También en el oeste se localizaron comunidades de marinos en Los Ángeles-San Pedro, Monterey, San Francisco, Seattle o Columbia británica.

Pero, en algunos rincones del país, surgieron comunidades de marinos que regentaron pensiones, restaurantes, y clubes sociales, predominantemente en ciudades como Nueva Orleans, Boston, Filadelfia y, sobre todo, Nueva York. El Centro Vasco-Americano de la ciudad de Nueva York (hoy, Euzko Etxea), ya centenario, fue fundado por marinos. La vida de los vascos de esta última ciudad quedó reflejada en la novela de Nea Colton, *The Rivers are Frozen* (1942)³⁵. En ambos casos, los trabajos que realizan pastores y marinos son estacionales y les obliga a pasar tiempo en pensiones (boarding houses, ostatuak u hotelak, en lengua vasca). Garteiz, un avispado hotelero vasco de Nevada, bautizó su hotel como "un hogar lejos del hogar" (home away from home)³⁶. Desde los primeros días del siglo XX, comenzaron a llegar las esposas e hijos de los pioneros.

En busca de una mujer trabajadora

Cuando el emigrante (pastor o marino) decidía asentarse y quedarse en el país, pensaba en que necesitaba una mujer que cumpliera las funciones de la etxekoandre tradicional. Además, para un emigrante un divorcio era una tragedia (suponía dividir lo que tan duramente le había costado ganar). Así que había que organizar una boda. La primera opción era una paisana, acostumbrada al trabajo duro desde niña —por lo que no protestaría por las duras condiciones de la emigración— y que, por cuestiones religiosas (eran católicas), no se divorciaban. En los primeros tiempos, fueron muchos los que viajaron al País Vasco en busca de una esposa que se encargase del hogar, criar los hijos, hacer la compra de provisiones, cocinar y lavar la ropa de los hombres (en los ranchos) y, en ocasiones, cultivar una pequeña huerta, así como cuidar de gallinas y conejos.

En el este, además de atender a su familia, trabajaban como domésticas, en labores de limpieza en hoteles. Algunos no conocían a la mujer con la que iban a casarse: habían dejado el pueblo cuando estas eran unas niñas, o no habían nacido aún. O, simplemente, buscaban jóvenes casaderas en un pueblo vecino. Otros fueron a buscar o llamaron a las novias que había dejado en el su país de origen. Los hubo, en un porcentaje menor, que llamaron a sus esposas e hijos. También están los casos de los que se casaron a distancia, a través de casamenteros profesionales, por poderes, con auténticas desconocidas. Pero, para casarse con una paisana (hasta, por lo menos, la generalización de los hoteles vascos) se necesitaba dinero, así que muchos optaron por buscar mujeres que se cumpliesen los requisitos: trabajar y no divorciarse. No era tarea fácil, pensando en el tipo de trabajo que realizaban y que los pastores, en general, residían en lugares aislados y donde no había concentraciones de vascos. Muchos vascos, como segunda opción se casaban con católicas que, por lo menos (al menos en principio), tampoco se divorciaban. Estos se casaron con mexicanas, sobre todo, en Arizona, New México, sur de Nevada o California. En el este lo hicieron con españolas (asturianas y gallegas, en un porcentaje alto) y, sobre todo, con puertorriqueñas.

Flora Alzola Barainka, una de mis bisabuelas paternas, nació en la casa Etxebarri de la anteiglesia (aldea) de Bedarona en Bizkaia el 23 de noviembre de 1880. Sus padres eran agricultores arrendatarios (la casa y las tierras no eran suyas). Siendo una niña, la enviaron a servir a una casa burguesa de Bilbao donde aprendió castellano y ahorró algo para el arreo[37]. A finales del siglo XIX y principios del XX, numerosos jóvenes de Bedarona habían emigrado a Estados Unidos. En 1899, su hermano menor, Nicanor, se fue por primera vez a Idaho. Melitón Bengoechea Anduiza, mi bisabuelo, nació asimismo en Bedarona (casa Zarakondegi-goikoa), el 11 de febrero de 1868. Con trece años se embarcó como grumete y, luego, como cocinero, en una goleta, y tras más de diez años en la mar, en 1893 se fue a Estados Unidos llamado por su hermano José que había prosperado como ganadero en Nevada —que llegó a ser el ovejero más rico de Idaho hasta que se arruinó. José, aparte, ya estaba con el otro hermano, Gabriel.

No les iba mal y los hermanos Bengoechea pensaron que uno de ellos debía casarse. Necesitaban una mujer capaz de atender la "casa" (aunque ésta fuese una tienda de campaña) y cocinase y lavase la ropa de los hombres: la de los hermanos y la de los pastores que trabajaban para ellos. Preferían que esa mujer fuese vasca campesina, estaban acostumbradas al trabajo duro y tenían fama de buenas administradoras. Los hermanos financiaron el viaje del más joven, Melitón. La guerra hispano-norteamericana retrasó el mismo. Tras el final de la contienda, Melitón (que, en aquel momento, tenía treinta y dos años) se fue a Bedarona en busca de la esposa que necesitaban. Las guerras y la emigración habían vaciado de varones jóvenes y casaderos los pueblos y aldeas de los contornos por lo que abundaban las mujeres solteras. Eligió a Flora de dieciocho años. La tradición familiar dice que la seleccionó entre un grupo de chicas reunidas en la cocina de una casa del pueblo. El 14 de mayo de 1900, se firmaba el contrato matrimonial ante el notario de Gernika Pedro Pascual de Areitio y Asua, sometidas las capitulaciones al Fuero de Bizkaia. Al convenio, Melitón aporta 20,000 pesetas-oro en ovejas "que posee en Estados Unidos". Los padres de Flora aportaron una dote de 2,750 pesetas y otras 550 pesetas más para el arreo[38]. El 26 de mayo, días después de su boda católica en la iglesia de Bedarona, Melitón y Flora Bengoechea embarcaron en Le Havre a bordo de "La Bretagne", llegando al puerto de Nueva York, el 3 de junio de 1900, entre los dos traían 230 dólares y declararon tener domicilio propio en Boise (Idaho). Se instalaron en Bruneau, condado de Owyhee.

En los primeros meses, mientras Melitón estaba en el monte con las ovejas, Flora se empleó como criada en un rancho de la zona (el Tindall Ranch). Luego, se mudó a una casa pequeña, poco más que una modesta choza, donde Flora se encargaba de las labores domésticas, además de cocinar y encargarse de la ropa de los hermanos Bengoechea, como ha quedado dicho, también se encargaba de la ropa de los pastores vascos que trabajaban para ellos en el "campamento". Durante el invierno, Flora atendía a los demás pastores vascos de Bruneau. Aún no se habían generalizado los "hoteles vascos". Eso sí, les cobraba unas monedas por su trabajo con las que compraba alimentos, mantas y material de costura en Mountain Home, el pueblo más cercano. El invierno del 1900 fue especialmente duro para la joven ya que, además, estaba embarazada. Muchos años después, contaba que, para conseguir agua, Melitón, su marido, debía romper el hielo de una laguna cercana con un hacha. El 21 de marzo de 1901, nacía en Bruneau la primera de sus hijas, Flora, convirtiéndose en quizá la primera mujer vasca nacida en el estado de Idaho. La noticia apareció recogida en un diario local.[39] El matrimonio tuvo dos hijos más: Luis (Boise, 31 de enero de 1903) y Balbina (Boise, 6 de enero de 1906). Los tres hijos fueron bautizados en la catedral de Boise, dado que era el único templo católico que había en los alrededores.[40] La vida de Melitón se repartía entre el monte y el rancho. Mientras tanto, en 1901, junto a su hermano José, inició los trámites para conseguir la nacionalidad. En 1906, había concluido los trámites. En el censo de 1910, ya aparece como ciudadano.

Las criadas

La institución vasca más persistente en los Estados Unidos han sido las pensiones, pequeños hoteles, boarding houses (ostatuak, en lengua vasca), que se extendían por los estados del oeste y, en menor medida, en algunas ciudades del este, especialmente Nueva York. Durante décadas, además de hogar y lugar de descanso, fueron centros de reunión, de contratación de hombres, de organización de bodas, de celebración, de asistencia mutua . . .[41] Jerónima Echeverria resalta que "la mayor parte de las jóvenes vascas que viajaban al oeste de Estados Unidos para reunirse con vecinos y familiares en las pensiones habían preacordado un empleo en los ostatuak. En general, se encargaban de cuestiones domésticas: limpiar cocinar, servir. (. . .) Una gran mayoría de esas mujeres encontraron a sus maridos mientras trabajaban en los ostatuak o mientras asistían a bailes y funciones sociales allí"[42]. Muchas de las mujeres (y también algunos niños) que emigran a Estados Unidos lo hacen siguiendo una vieja costumbre vasca. Para aligerar la carga de una familia, los padres enviaban a sus hijos e hijas a trabajar como criadas a otra casa "tripa-truke" (hand to mouth). Es decir, no tenían salario. Recibían un regalo anual y algo de ropa. Muchas realizaban trabajos extra para poder ahorrar algo.

Como hemos visto, los hoteles vascos se convirtieron en agencia de inmigración para mujeres solteras (y, de paso, en una agencia matrimonial). Generalmente, eran las "hoteleras" quienes se encargaban de ambas labores. Estas recababan información sobre jóvenes solteras en sus pueblos y aldeas. Por ello, en la mayor parte de los casos, son paisanas o parientes de la hotelera las que llegan a Estados Unidos. Como señala Mary Grace Paquette está en los comienzos de "migraciones a gran escala de vasco-franceses y vasco españoles a Kern County, en 1893"[43]. Eva Hunt Dockery afirma que, a finales de 1909, residían unos 6.000 vascos en Idaho. En el cómputo, solo unas doscientos mujeres, "y a ninguna chica le estaba permitido permanecer mucho tiempo soltera, ante tal cantidad de pretendientes"[44]. Cuando la periodista intentó fotografiar a las diez jóvenes que acaban de ser "importadas" por Benito Arego, la esposa del hotelero se lo impidió: "Eran chicas muy bonitas, y podrían irse tan pronto como pudiesen, pero si se publicaba una foto en la que apareciesen todas a la vez ella no podría emplearlas en su casa, los vascos llegados de todos los rincones del país asaltarían la casa y ella las había traído para que le ayudasen en la pensión"[45]. El trabajo de aquellas muchachas era extenuante. Marie Jeanne Goyenetche, de Banka, por ejemplo, "se levantaba a las cuatro de la mañana y muchas veces seguía trabajando a las 12 de la noche. (. . .) Tenía que cocinar tres comidas al día, trabajaba de camarera (maid) del hotel y ayudaba a la dueña a hacer la compra. Por esto, le pagaban treinta dólares al mes, más alojamiento y comida"[46]. Cuando Marie Jeanne logró pagar el dinero que le había prestado su hermano para el viaje, entonces llegó el momento de casarse.

Precisamente, Benito Arego protagonizó un caso que define cómo trabajaban algunas jóvenes en los *ostatuak*. Anastasia Arriandiaga "Ana" tenía catorce años cuando sus padres la enviaron a Boise a servir como criada a la pensión de Arego. Habían llegado a acuerdo con él por ser del mismo pueblo, Elantxobe. El trato era que le pagaría 5 dólares al mes hasta satisfacer los gastos del viaje (que eran de 150 dólares). Las condiciones de trabajo eran durísimas y, además, según comentó la joven a su hermana, sufría malos tratos. El cuñado de la joven, José Alastra, copropietario del Howell Spring Valley Ranch, se reunió con Arego para llegar a un acuerdo que permitiese "liberar" a Ana. El hotelero se negó y el caso acabó en los tribunales. La joven —que temía que aquello perjudicase a sus padres— pudo abandonar su trabajo tras pagar la cantidad adeudada[47]. Jerónima Echeverria recoge asimismo el ejemplo de Margarita Aramayo, de Ondarroa. Esta última había llegado a Boise en 1918 para trabajar como criada en el hotel de Barbero. Había acordado con ella un sueldo de 18 dólares al mes, cantidad que nunca recibía porque se retenía para pagar la deuda de su viaje[48]. El 6 de febrero de 1919 se casó en Boise con Marcelino Osa, de Ibarrangelua. Como hemos visto, esta especie de "compra de libertad" acabó en algún momento ante los tribunales del estado.

La endogamia, cemento de la comunidad

La mayor parte de los pioneros vascos —con algunas excepciones— de quienes se tienen noticias se casaron con paisanas que residían en California antes del comienzo de la Guerra de Secesión. Con alguna excepción, la mayoría de las novias son vascofrancesas. Asimismo, muchos inmigrantes prósperos buscaban casar a sus hijas con vascos. John B. Edlefsen señalaba que solo el 10 por ciento de los vascos estaban casados antes de dejar el País Vasco: "De aquellos que estaban casados antes de emigrar, la mitad llegó sin sus familias. En muchos casos, la familia era llamada para reunirse con el hombre al cabo de un año o dos, o el marido viajaba a su país de origen y regresaba con su familia a su hogar en Estados Unidos"[49]. En el mismo estudio se señala que solo en el 5 por ciento casos la boda es con una mujer no vasca.

Sin embargo, el 60 por ciento de la segunda generación se casaba con no vascas[50]. Los mismos datos se repiten en lugares como Stockton como constata Carol María Plagiarulo[51]. El proceso de formación de las primeras familias vascas de Nueva York es similar al de otros núcleos de la diáspora, dándose además altos grados de endogamia en la primera generación. Hay algunos casos sorprendentes en Nueva York. Hay varios ejemplos de bodas entre vascos hasta cinco generaciones.

Identidad y lengua materna

Si, como hemos señalado, no puede hablarse de comunidad vasca sin mujeres vascas, estas se convirtieron en parte esencial de transmisión de una identidad propia en los Estados Unidos. Transmitieron la lengua; sin embargo, se da un hecho interesante que es común a otras minorías. La mujer vascoamericana fue creando formas culturales nuevas y símbolos que sus hijos y nietos estaban convencidos que procedían del país de origens.[52] Mercedes Fernández-Martorell lo llama "recreación de la identidad" a la que se suman los nacidos en Estados Unidos.[53]

Señalan Douglass y Bilbao que, "la especialización laboral de los vascos del oeste en la industria ovina ha influido considerablemente sobre su vida religiosa. (. . .) en la mayoría de los casos, su modelo de asentamiento disperso impidió la creación de feligresías dominadas por los vascos". Según Adrian Gachiteguy[54], muchos se limitaban a asistir los principales días festivos, como las Navidades, la Pascua de Resurrección y la Asunción, mientras que otros solo iban a la iglesia para asistir a una boda o a un funeral. Un porcentaje más elevado de mujeres mantuvo una residencia permanente en las ciudades o en las proximidades y su implicación en las actividades religiosas locales fue mucho mayor. Hasta cierto punto, sin embargo, los vascos de ambos sexos se muestran algo reticentes en convertirse en fieles activos dentro de las comunidades católicas 'norte-americanas'. Esto se ve claramente en la persistencia y en el interés por traer sacerdotes vascos a Estados Unidos para que ejercieran su ministerio entre los vascos del oeste americano"[55].

Quizá el idioma fue uno de los problemas que debían resolver los emigrantes. Muchos vascos no sabían más que su lengua propia. Muchas mujeres no tenían el mismo problema porque, además de haber asistido durante más tiempo a la escuela, habían trabajado como criadas en casas en las que solo se hablaba castellano o francés. Algunas, sobre todo las de la zona fronteriza eran, además, trilingües (vasco, español y francés) en el momento de emigrar. Hay quienes emigraron desde zonas no vascófonas en las que solo se hablaba español porque se había perdido la lengua propia. El diario *The New York Times* se hizo eco de las dificultades de los agentes de inmigración para entenderse con un grupo de ciento —cincuenta emigrantes vascos (el número más alto de vascos que se recordaba en Ellis Island) que viajaban a Idaho, Nevada y Montana. La situación se salvó gracias a la intervención de un oficial de un vapor que estaba fondeado cerca. Los emigrantes le hablaban en euskera, él traducía al castellano y un tercero lo hacía al inglés. Al final, todos los vascos pudieron desembarcar.[56]

Maria Ocamica, casada con Pedro Corta y, luego, con su hermano Justo, pasó casi setenta años en Estados Unidos (mayoritariamente en Oregon) y nunca habló otro idioma que el vasco como recordaba su hija Eugenia en una entrevista. Esto, por ejemplo, forzó a sus hijos a utilizar la lengua vasca toda su vida[57]. Hoy parece aclararse la importancia de la mujer en la transmisión de la lengua propia a las generaciones de vascos nacidos en la diáspora.

Mujeres maltratadas, promesas rotas

Como hemos señalado, una de las razones por las que los pastores se casaban con mujeres vascas era porque éstas no se divorciaban. Sin embargo, lo hicieron. José Mendiola había llegado al país en 1893 y, cinco años más tarde, en 1898, se casó en Nevada con Isabel Malaxechevarria y con la que tuvo un hijo, Frank. El hombre abandonó a su esposa e hijo y la cosa acabó en divorcio. Los términos del mismo no debieron de gustar al pastor, porque, en 1903, José fue declarado culpable por un jurado del condado de Humboldt, Nevada, y condenado a un año de cárcel tras intentar asesinar a su esposa[58]. Anna Etchegaray, una costurera de Urepel, en la Navarra francesa, llegó a Stockton en junio de 1908. Como tantas otras jóvenes vascas, había acordado casarse con Jean (John) Mentaberry, de Baigorri, un pueblo cercano al suyo, que había prosperado como ganadero en California. Según el acuerdo, Anna no tendría que trabajar más allá de las labores domésticas habituales. Pero, Mentaberry no cumplió el acuerdo y la obligó a trabajar fuera del hogar. Durante un tiempo, trabajó como sombrerera y, más tarde, como gobernanta en un domicilio privado. El marido se quedaba con el dinero que ganaba. Harta, en 1911, llevó a Mentaberry a juicio, solicitándole 10.000 dólares por perjuicios morales: sentía que "le había roto el corazón"[59].

El 8 de julio de 1917, Lorenza Gabica, de cuarenta y tres años, mató en Nampa, Idaho, a su marido Juan Calzacorta, con quien se había casado en 1909, poniendo así fin a un calvario de malos tratos y amenazas del marido hacia la mujer. Durante el juicio, Lorenza declaró que, durante años, su esposo le había maltratado, "algo a lo que no están acostumbradas las mujeres vascas". La noche de autos el marido llegó a la casa y le dijo a su mujer que tenía veinticuatro horas para irse, mientras cargaba su revólver de seis tiros. Al mismo tiempo, dejó su rifle a los pies de la cama. Entonces se fue. Regresó sobre las ocho de la tarde, diciendo a Lorenza "ha llegado tu última hora". Y volvió a irse. A su regreso, volvió a insultarla y maltratarla, arrojándola al suelo. Fue allí donde la mujer pudo hacerse con el revólver y disparó sobre su marido que falleció en el acto. Un testigo de apellido O'Donnell declaró ante el juez que el vasco le había dicho que iba a matar a su mujer, a sus hijos y a su cuñado John Gabica (el hermano de Lorenza), y que amaba a otra mujer. En el juicio, Lorenza, que solo hablaba euskera, tuvo como intérprete a Frances Jayo, de Boise. El jurado solo tardó doce minutos en declararla inocente, al haber actuado en defensa propia. En 1930, Lorenza seguía viviendo en Nampa con sus tres hijos[60].

Las que regresaron: "amerikanas"

Para el emigrante, de cualquier tipo, no hay nada peor que regresar a casa "con las manos vacías". Hay que llevar algo por poco que sea. Entre los retornados del Oeste americano, muy pocos llegaron con "las manos vacías". Los fracasados preferían no regresar.

Con los ahorros, "rescataron" caseríos y granjas (arrendados durante generaciones pasando a su propiedad), construyeron casas o crearon pequeños negocios e industrias que ayudaron a la economía de algunos pueblos.[61] A los retornados desde Estados Unidos, se les conoce como "amerikanuak" ("amerikanos"). Tanto en el País Vasco de España como en el de Francia.

Muchos de los emigrantes regresan con sus mujeres e hijos nacidos en Estados Unidos. Una vez instaladas las familias, la esposa y los hijos se quedaban en el país de origen, mientras que el hombre regresaba a Estados Unidos a ocuparse de sus negocios (generalmente, ovejeros) que había dejado en manos de algún socio. Pasados los años, cuando los hijos varones nacidos en América llegaban a la edad militar emigraban para evitar ser reclutados por el ejército español o francés. Mientras que la madre y las hijas se quedaban en el país de orígen. Incluso, se dieron asimismo casos en los que no volverían a reunirse. También eran comunes los casos en los que el hombre dejaba a su esposa e hijos y después de regresar a Estados Unidos, desaparecía, formando en ocasiones una nueva familia.

Apenas un año después de llegado al País Vasco y arreglado los asuntos relacionados con la compra del terreno y construcción de la casa. Muchos pastores dejaban a sus familias en el Viejo País y regresaban a Estados Unidos donde tenían sus rebaños. Muchos tardaban años en regresar. En algún caso esperaban y/o patrocinaban el viaje de sus hijos varones. Se debe al caso de que los varones de la familia estaban todos en la emigración mientras que las mujeres se quedaban solas.

La suerte de las viudas era diversa. Al fallecer el marido, muchas no tenían los medios para viajar de regreso al viejo país, quedando incluso en una situación de desamparo. Algunas volvieron a casarse, abundaban quienes lo hicieron con cuñados, con paisanos solteros de mucha edad o con hombres de otros orígenes puesto que quedarse solas suponía la indigencia. En 1906, Melitón Bengoechea decidió regresar al País Vasco con su mujer y sus hijos. Junto a otro pastor, Juan Iturraspe Uberuaga, se construyó una casa y compró unas tierras en el barrio de Kurtziaga-Arropain, de Ispaster, a menos de un kilómetro del centro de Lekeitio. En Estados Unidos, Melitón enfermó de fiebres tifoideas, falleciendo el 11 de enero de 1911, y fue enterrado en Mountain Home. Flora, su viuda, administró durante años los negocios de su marido desde Lekeitio (con ayuda de parientes).

La preocupación de Flora fue la educación de sus hijos. Algo bastante común entre muchos retornados. Las hijas, Flora y Balbina, fueron internas a un colegio de monjas de Durango. A Luis no le gustaba estudiar. Prefería corretear por los montes cercanos antes que ir a la escuela. Se acercaba el momento de ser llamado a filas. Su madre se entrevistó con el alcalde de Lekeitio para saber qué ocurriría si su hijo era reclutado. Generalmente, los hijos de una viuda no ingresaban en el ejército. Pero, Flora era considerada como una "amerikana" rica, sus hijas recibían educación en un colegio de señoritas y era notorio que Luis no hacía nada para ayudar a la economía familiar, así que debería incorporarse a filas. La madre tomó la decisión de muchos "amerikanos" que habían vuelto al viejo país: enviar a su hijo (a quien ya no volvería a ver) a Estados Unidos.

A modo de conclusión

Aunque solo un 30 por ciento de los inmigrantes vascos fueron mujeres, a ellas se debe la formación y consolidación de la comunidad. Transmitieron la identidad (costumbres, tradiciones, actitudes) y, por supuesto, la lengua. Durante décadas, las mujeres vascas fueron mano de obra barata en régimen de explotación (y en algunos casos de sumisión). Están documentados números casos de incumplimientos y de malos tratos. Aquellas mujeres —muchas de las cuales vivían solas y aisladas durante parte del año— tuvieron que ganarse el respeto, más allá de lo que imponía la tradición. Asimismo, no se puede olvidar la situación de indefensión y precariedad económica en que quedan numerosas viudas, algunos con hijos menores, que no tuvieron medios para regresar a su país de origen. Queda pendiente seguir el rastro de las vascas en Estados Unidos para documentar cómo negociaron el poder sobre ellas en la casa, los negocios y la comunidad. En particular, nuevas investigaciones podrán resolver cómo colaboraron entre ellas o con mujeres que hablasen español o francés en Estados Unidos.

"We Were Always Chicanos," or "We Did it Our Way": Situated Citizenship in the Equality State

VANESSA FONSECA-CHÁVEZ
Arizona State University

> "I don't like being put on a back burner.
> We want what they have."
> —Annie Vigil Mejorado

This essay begins with a quote by Annie Vigil Mejorado, a Chicana whose family moved from northern New Mexico to Wyoming in the 1950s, well after Wyoming was established as an Equality State and as one that was the first to champion women's suffrage by allowing women to vote in 1869 when Wyoming was still a territory. Annie's quote is significant in that, although she is a woman and a citizen/resident of Wyoming, her statement contradicts the notion that Wyoming is equal in the treatment of all its citizens— "We [Annie's Chicana/o community] wanted what they [Anglo residents of Riverton, Wyoming] had" (Herrera). And what they had was paved streets, curb and gutter, and the necessary environmental infrastructure that kept their communities safe. This essay interrogates notions of equality and citizenship, particularly for Chicanas/os in the Equality State. I draw from Annie and her younger sibling Susana Vigil's archives,[1] which document a more than ten-year community struggle with the city of Riverton,

Wyoming, to improve the hazardous and environmentally unsafe conditions of the South Park Barrio.[2] Though Wyoming is not a location upon which scholars have mapped Chicana activism, uncovering this archive adds to our understanding of not only migration patterns of Mexican origin communities, but it also undercuts a territory and state ethos that was built on the notion of afforded rights to its citizens, thereby demonstrating that equality and accountability to its citizens, although desired by the South Park Barrio community, was hard fought and never guaranteed, at least not in a conventional way.

This essay privileges stories and community organizing efforts of Chicana residents of the South Park Barrio in Riverton, Wyoming, to advocate on behalf of their community, one that often suffered disproportionately from a lack of access to essential community services. I argue that their role as community activists and archivists who employed myriad forms of Chicana *movidas* demonstrated a sustained commitment to Chicana/o activism that remains a palpable example of how Chicanas/os mobilized in non-traditional spaces. At the same time, their activism elucidates the extent to which they were keenly aware of their positionality within a state that is over-whelmingly white and one that historically has failed to extend equality and fairness to Chicana/o communities as well as other marginalized populations. As their oral histories and archives will demonstrate, these Chicanas mobilized their community to advocate for improved neighborhood conditions. They exhibited a commitment to community justice and fairness through the contestation of regional politics, thereby recognizing how situated citizenship affected their lived experiences.

I draw from the work of Natasha Behl, whose concept of *situated citizenship* provides a framework for understanding the contradictions of democracy when considering the intersections of social relations. Though Behl's research focuses on the gendered dynamics of democratic India, situated citizenship helps think about how Chicanas/os have experienced unequal citizenship in Wyoming both during the territorial and statehood periods. When this concept is extended to the context of Wyoming, it makes evident that citizenship is more than simply a legal term or status. For Behl, "situated citizenship highlights how citizens understand and experience the promises of formal equality" (4).

What I hope to offer here is an intimate look at a historical moment in the 1970s and 1980s that demonstrates the ways in which Chicanas challenged notions of gender and ethnic equality and fairness in Riverton, Wyoming, an unlikely place to uncover historical moments of Chicana activism. Even though each of these individuals had voting rights in their city as citizens of the United States, they often were outvoted on issues important to their livelihoods. In other words, they experienced what Behl calls, "exclusionary inclusion" (5). Their community concerns were often dismissed in ways that countered notions of equality and, in turn, mobilized to challenge the ways they felt excluded in a state that was premised on equality. Despite these trials, Chicanas led the charge to negotiate their power and place in Riverton, Wyoming, by utilizing the same rhetoric intended to exclude them.

Alongside Behl's concept of situated citizenship, a framework of *movidas* allows us to chart small and larger processes of activism that Annie, Susana, and their Chicana/o community of Riverton, Wyoming, utilized to draw attention to the inequities they faced as citizens of a predominantly white community. In the introduction to *Chicana Movidas: New Narratives of Feminism in the Chicano Movement*, Dionne Espinosa, María Cotera and Maylei Blackwell offer a way to track these politics and strategies:

> Mapping movidas is a mode of historical analysis that allows us to chart the small scale, intimate political moves, gestures, and collaborations that reflect the tactics women used to negotiate the internalities of power within broader social movements. It identifies how they tracked and negotiated multiple power scales within their homes, communities, organizations, social movements, and dominant society (11).

Espinosa, Cotera, and Blackwell highlight four types of *movidas* that are central to the collection of scholars in their anthology. While not all these *movidas* are central to Annie and Susana's activism, I came to learn of their stories through Memory *movidas*, namely oral history interviews. As Espinosa, Cotera, and Blackwell note, memory *movidas* allow Chicanas to make sense of the structures that produce inequalities and invisibility for brown bodies, particularly Chicanas (Espinosa, et al.). This frame helps elucidate the meaning of Annie and Susana's activism, which included their oral history narratives, their extensive archives, the documentation of an important community event in 1986, and the organizing strategies which utilized a reciprocal community approach. Memory *movidas* work in tandem with situated citizenship, particularly for women, as Behl's work shows how "women negotiate, navigate, and resist exclusionary inclusion in these different domains" (5).

Annie and Susana's archive provides a counternarrative engaged in a "practice of historical recuperation" as a central element to memory *movidas*. In reflecting on the kind of work ethic that Annie, Susana, and their community embodied as an economically displaced population in their home state of New Mexico, I am struck by the fact that they essentially came to Wyoming to work. The ethos connected to physical labor, displacement, and the desire to build a future perhaps motivated their *movidas* in Riverton and made them aware of their situated citizenship. I'd like to suggest, however, that this ethos drastically contrasts the bootstrap mentality that Wyoming embodies—a historically white state that has embraced this moniker as a badge of individualism. Instead, we can look to Chicano and Nuevomexicano writer Rudolfo Anaya, who utilizes a community principle of reciprocity he refers to as "a pura pala." He writes, "A pura pala is a nuevomexicano chant, a mantra, a song sung on the way to work. Hard work" (xviii). I map the *movidas* of the Chicana/o community of Riverton thinking about their activism as communally minded hard work, thereby resisting western ideals of individuality. The key difference is that their work is rooted in a land-based community/shared responsibility to each other rather than individual work for individual gain. Equality, thus, isn't about individual people being equal to other individuals—or perhaps this is too limited of a view. Rather, it is about the overall structural health of the community, the very premise by which Riverton Chicana/o residents express their situated citizenship. Their archive is documentary evidence that recoups silenced memory and utilizes tactics of remembrance, or memory *movidas*, to contextualize prevailing notions of equality, and provides first-hand accounts of what Michael D. Aguirre frames as migrating politics, that is, "the moves were embodied by a repertoire of experience from which they drew to maneuver through different arenas . . . Their becoming Chicana was rooted in their early lives in the Southwest" (179). Thus, Annie and Susana's family migration from northern New Mexico comprised a particular social consciousness and work ethic that they carried with them to Wyoming. Doing this allowed them to recognize the ways in which they could contest their situated citizenship by utilizing cultivated tools of resistance.

The oral histories discussed in this chapter were conducted as part of the FMT project, which was created to document the migration and lived experiences of Hispana/o New Mexican, or Manita/o, communities who left their home state to pursue economic opportunities.[3] In doing so, they created a vibrant Manita/o diaspora that extends to nearly every state in the United States. In 2015, the FMT team arrived in Riverton, Wyoming, to conduct oral history interviews with the Chicanas/os who migrated to Wyoming from rural communities in northern New Mexico, namely around the Taos and Las Vegas areas.[4] This migration pattern was the product of a changing social and economic structure in the US Southwest brought forth by US colonization in the nineteenth century. These were the same communities that became unequal citizens of the United States following the signing of the Treaty of Guadalupe Hidalgo in February of 1848. In the first half of the twentieth century, Chicana/o families hailing from northern New Mexico traveled along what has been termed by Levi Romero and myself as the Manito Trail, a migration corridor extending from New Mexico through Colorado and into Wyoming. Drawn to the prospects of employment in the sugar beet fields, railroad, sheepherding industry, or mines, many Hispano males left their home abodes in search of work. As census data shows, continued economic opportunity in Wyoming resulted in more family units, rather than single males, migrating to the state. Eventually, families began to settle down and build new lives.

The FMT project outlines the historical migration patterns of Manitas/os, or Hispanic New Mexicans, to the state of Wyoming and draws from census data, oral history interviews, and other archival materials to trace the contributions to the territorial and statehood economies of Wyoming beginning in the mid nineteenth century.[5] As a recovery project, FMT is attentive to recuperating this important archive, while also bringing to light the patterns of discrimination and racism that characterize and highlight the unequal treatment and tensions Chicanas/os experience in the Equality State.

Wyoming sits on the ancestral homeland of the Eastern Shoshone, Cheyenne, Arapaho, Sioux, and Crow tribes. With a significant Anglo population, Wyoming's extension of equality is rooted in settler colonialism and was a direct benefit to white women in the late nineteenth and early twentieth century. While Chicanas/os have never accounted for more than fifteen percent of the state's total population, their participation in the formation of the state's major economies (agriculture, mining, railroad) is notable.[6] Annie and Susana's family, too, is part of this story, as their migration to Wyoming is an example of a larger scale migration of New Mexicans who moved north to find employment.

To demonstrate how situated citizenship affected Chicanas/os in the state of Wyoming, I utilize archival materials and oral histories of Chicanas/os who migrated from New Mexico in the early 1900s and who currently reside in Riverton, Wyoming, a town located in West Central Wyoming with a population of approximately 11,000. Riverton is an interesting place to untangle the experiences of marginalized groups. As a predominantly white community, it is a contested borderland located next to the Wind River Reservation, home to Eastern Shoshone and Northern Arapaho tribes. Though the focus of this essay is not on the racialized and gendered citizenship of these tribes, it is important to recognize that multiple ethnic groups have experienced varied levels of exclusion within the territory and state of Wyoming.

Though Chicanas from New Mexico, like Annie and Susana, migrated at an early age to Wyoming with their parents or later with their partners, they quickly established systems of support and coupled this with educational endeavors that allowed them to enact a social justice consciousness. In 2015 as part of the FMT project, Levi Romero and I interviewed Annie, a Manita/Chicana born in 1942 in Cimarrón, New Mexico, a rural community located in the northern part of the state. Her family moved to Wyoming in 1950 to work in the wheat fields by traveling from Cimarrón by bus to Ratón, then by train to a small burg named Bonneville, Wyoming, five miles north of Shoshoni. They were met by beet farmer Joe Appelhans, who transported them in his truck to his farm. This was part of a larger network established by farmers to transport laborers to Wyoming. Annie recalls that her family did not work in the wheat and, later, sugar beet fields for very long because they did not want to do that type of work. When the family moved to Riverton, Wyoming, her dad and older brother were hired by the City of Riverton to do construction. Annie and her family joined other Manita/o families on the south side barrio of Riverton, a neighborhood that fostered a sense of Manita/o, Chicana/o identity and community, and one that was largely neglected by the city.

When interviewing Annie, I was particularly struck by her use of the word Chicana when referring to her identity. Aware of the precarity of racialized identities and politics in the state of Wyoming, I asked Annie about her experiences in school, and she recounted that although she did not remember much, she recalled that there were many Chicana/o kids her age and that she did not have any friends outside of the barrio where she lived. Annie's simultaneous experiences of isolation from the larger city of Riverton and her sense of community within the South Park Barrio illustrate the very palpable dynamics of Manita/o—and Chicana/o—existence throughout the state of Wyoming and frame her later activist struggles. The title of this essay, "We were always Chicanos" was Annie's expression of individual and communal identity and highlights the ways in which Annie's political consciousness shaped her ability to advocate for her community.

Annie stayed in the barrio throughout her childhood and adolescent years. She married her husband, Arthur Mejorado, a Mexican migrant farmworker from Texas who later worked for a major oil company for twenty-two years and retired as a foreman at age fifty-five. They made the barrio their home in the late 1960s. This was precisely the period in which Wyoming was preparing to celebrate the hundred year anniversary of women's suffrage. Annie described her house as, "a tiny house as big as a living room, no indoor plumbing—definitely not a toilet inside. The lady next door would leave us a little bit of water inside the buckets so you could prime it [the pump]. And then, for electricity we ran the extension cord all the way from our house, across two lots to my brother's home" (Annie). Annie didn't say at this moment that she viewed this as something necessarily or inherently unfair or unequal. It was common, in fact, for the barrio residents to rely on one another to obtain access to basic services, such as water and sewer. This was part of the communal survival strategies for the South Park Barrio residents, though it soon became clear to me that this was not something Annie was willing to tolerate for very long.

In her interview, Annie discussed, among other things, her early years in the barrio and her transition to another part of Riverton later in life. Her current residence had all the basic amenities she lacked in her childhood and during her early years of marriage. She stated proudly that these things took patience and hard work and commented that younger folks should not expect to have everything right away. Indeed, she imparted a more powerful message than what I had realized at that moment. After we spoke about family recipes, photos, and a community quilt gifted to her mother in a raffle, she recalled a time in her life for which she was particularly proud.

Annie counts as one of the greatest achievements of her life a more than ten-year struggle with the city of Riverton, Wyoming, to bring essential sanitation services and paved roads to the South Park Barrio. She notes, "And I tell you, one of the most . . . I think the biggest accomplishment that we had . . . the whole area where I used to live that we call the barrio . . . we fought and fought and fought 'cause the city was neglecting us as far as sewer, paving, and all that stuff" (Annie). She follows by saying, "I had them fight with the city forever, forever, to put a sewer" (Annie). Annie frames her participation in this moment as a communal struggle, but her use of the personal "I" in her narrative situates her as a leader who rallied the collective. As a Chicana from New Mexico who witnessed social injustices within her community, Annie "mobilized to imagine and enact collective social change" (Espinosa, et al. 4) using various tactics and strategies, or *movidas*. When viewed alongside historical trajectories of Chicana/o movement politics, Annie's politics of resistance is situated within the same time frame as the larger Chicano movement (1960s-1980s) but happens in a geographical space largely unknown to movement politics of this time period. Her activism, thus, can be framed within current and historical scholarship about Chicanas/os who mobilized around issues of social justice and traces the journey for Chicanas/os in Riverton to contest popular notions of fairness and equality.

Riverton, let alone the state of Wyoming, has never been viewed as a likely place for Chicana/o activism, although it was not far from Denver, Colorado—the center of various Chicana/o youth movements during the height of the Chicano movement. What is clear, however, is that Wyoming was a hostile state for ethnic minorities, and this highlights the ways their situated citizenship affected their daily lives. Trisha Martínez notes that "common to the experience of other communities of color, Latinos in Wyoming were forced to deal with processes of assimilation, legal exclusions, limited citizenship opportunities, and other daily forms of discrimination" ("Politics" 109). Various individuals interviewed as part of the FMT project commented on the difficulties in obtaining housing in white neighborhoods throughout the state, which almost always led them to ethnic havens on the south side of town. Even though these neighborhoods were connected by cultural and racial heritage, they often were neglected by city and town officials due to existing racist sentiments that contradicted social constructs of equality and citizenship in the town of Riverton and the state of Wyoming.

Annie does not descend from a long line of Chicana activists, but she has always possessed the ability to react to her environment and took the steps necessary to correct what she viewed as unfair and unequal treatment. From her childhood through her early years of marriage, she was acutely aware of what the residents of Riverton had in relation to South Park Barrio residents. Because of this consciousness, she recognized her individual and communal situated citizenship and strategically used *movidas* to right what she viewed and experienced as a social inequity that city officials refused to remedy.

In 1975, after various petitions by South Park Barrio residents to the city of Riverton were denied, they were encouraged to apply for a Community Development Block Grant, an initiative created through the Community and Housing Development Act of 1974. This modified the Housing Act of 1937 to create Section 8 housing and allowed communities to apply for grants through the US Department of Housing and Urban Development. Communities often were in regional competition for the grants and needed the support of local city officials to move anything forward.

Annie and Susana's archives include, among other items, two applications for the Community Development Block Grant that were submitted in 1975 and 1982, respectively. In the first community hearing to discuss the grant on November 29, 1975, more than ninety percent of the attendees were from the South Park Barrio and voiced concerns over the lack of fire hydrants in the neighborhood, improper sewer drainage systems, unpaved and dusty roads, and overgrown vacant lots. Some residents testified that they had lived in the South Park neighborhood for fifty years and had never seen a road grader come down their street. Though many individuals, including then-Riverton Mayor Bill Moffat, openly voiced their support for the barrio community, others were hesitant to back an initiative to improve the lives of barrio residents. In a *Riverton Ranger* article from 1975, City Councilman Lynn Coleman asks, "Can the people [in this area] afford to hook up on water and sewer tap? If not, it's no use in creating this beautiful thing if people can't participate" (Ward n.p.). This rhetorical move by Coleman suggests that low-income communities, albeit citizens, were not deserving of basic city services that have significant environmental and health impacts.

Ultimately, the block grant submitted by barrio residents in 1975 was denied and residents were told that their requests were not a high enough priority. This did not deter Annie and her community, however. Between 1975 and 1985, the barrio residents submitted seven different funding applications, including another major Community Development Block Grant requesting basic upgraded facilities to their neighborhood, assistance for low-income and predominantly minority families to improve the quality of their environment, foundation improvements that would result in development and redevelopment of their neighborhood, and the elimination of blighted conditions in the area, each one of them resulting in no funding. Adam Herrera notes that although the city slowly created fire infrastructure and put in sewer lines, by 1986 the South Park Barrio was the only neighborhood in Riverton without paved roads.

Annie reached out to and inspired other Chicanas in the barrio to gain momentum. Her younger sister, Susana, grew up watching her older brothers and sisters involved in community work. Susana, then Susan Vigil Lawson, was a student at the University of Wyoming working on her bachelor's degree in social work and was taking a class on Community Organization at the time. Susana was involved with El Movimiento Estudiantil Chicano de Aztlán (MEChA) for three years and served as president of the organization from 1986-1987. According to Antonio Ríos-Bustamante, "The influence of the Chicano movement reached into Wyoming from Colorado . . . Students at the University of Wyoming in 1972 formed a student group, the Chicano Coalition. The group, eventually called MECHA (sic), held a Chicano conference" (8). Susana, then, had access to academic and community-based models that afforded herself and her community multiple strategies of collaboration and mobilization.

Annie, Susana, and their sister-in-law Helen Vigil were the primary movers and shakers of what would become the South Park Paving Project. As a younger sibling, Susana noticed from an early age the different *movidas* that Annie and Helen used in the barrio. One of the most salient characteristics of Annie's activism is her ability to be a model to younger generations and the hope she

294 Vanessa Fonseca-Chávez

inspires in the continuity of community work. Susana witnessed the organizing strategies of her older sibling and was motivated to join the efforts. For Susana, it was not difficult to see the urgency of their cause. She notes, "I got involved because I wanted to. My sister Annie was the main instigator of the project and my sister-in-law Helen. They came and asked me to help. Just the fact that the rest of the town had paving and when you hit the barrio, there was no paving, no sidewalks, no curb and gutter. And that, in itself, seemed wrong" (Herrera).

As one of the oldest neighborhoods in Riverton, the South Park Barrio represented a community of residents bonded in a spirit of resilience and resistance. Regarding their more than ten-year struggle to receive basic city services, Annie commented, "It just got me angry that we were being left in the dark ages. I don't like being put on the back burner. We want what they have" (Herrera). Annie's lived experiences highlight Behl's assertion that situated citizenship is a "situated social relation" (3). In other words, Annie was keenly aware of the ways in which unequal citizenship was extended to the South Park Barrio and was intent on challenging and shifting those dynamics. She was tired of the rest of the city being upgraded, while they had petitioned numerous times for the same services, only to be refused each time.

In 1986, Annie and Susana approached the city of Riverton in hopes that it would help to pay for the necessary materials to pave their streets. The city agreed to pave the roads but told residents that they would have to pay for and construct their own curbs and gutters. Annie quickly mobilized the community and approached her brother Emilio Vigil. While the men agreed to do the physical labor, the women discussed how they could help. The work would not have been possible without the women's organizing efforts and their culinary labor, nor would it have been successful without the skills of the men, who had extensive experience working in construction. Annie notes that everyone operated as a team and worked nonstop until it was done. Throughout the city, many residents and companies rallied around the barrio by donating cement, tools, food, and even beer. When the project was completed, Emilio Vigil commented that all the important people (including the mayor) showed up, while many of the people who executed the physical labor were notably absent. This was not out of disinterest in their accomplishment but, rather, a particular *movida* enacted by the barrio residents to demonstrate that they would not celebrate the performative aspect of inclusion.

While city officials attended a neighborhood celebration to signal notions of hard work linked to the bootstrap mentality in the state of Wyoming, the struggle leading to this moment was more complex. That is, while the city largely was not willing to engage in how the denial of various requests and funding opportunities as "non-priority" issues may suggest a deep-rooted social inequity/inequality problem in the town of Riverton and throughout the state of Wyoming, they were quick to celebrate their successes because South Park Barrio residents found a way to persevere, despite failed attempts to hold city officials accountable to its citizens. In a *Riverton Ranger* article from 1986, Bob Peck writes that because of the labor that South Park Barrio residents contributed, "[City] officials *probably* have new respect and admiration for citizens who are willing to help themselves" (Peck; emphasis mine).

Wyoming historian Phil Roberts observes that "[t]here is little satisfaction provided by the contradictions of equality in theory and equality in fact. Even casual knowledge alerts the least observant that equality is hardly closer today than it was in the last century" (Roberts). Roberts expounds on the tension between Wyoming's cowboy mentality and its state motto, The Equality State. Though the image of the lone cowboy on a bucking horse is but a myth, for many in Wyoming it promotes ideas of overcoming struggle to build character, or a bootstrap mentality. Whether the state of Wyoming is rooted in equality or in an ethos of rugged individualism, recognizing both as a moniker of a nostalgic era is important. Annie's archive demonstrates that Chicanas/os were never part of that visionary past. Even in its moment of origin, the "Equality State" was unequal in granting all people of color the same rights as white citizens. Wyoming's cowboy mentality is a perfect illustration of this tension.

The recuperation of this story first came through Annie's testimonio, a memory *movida* that provided the narrative framing of her
archive. As a community leader and organizer, she was careful in
documenting what transpired from the time she arrived in Riverton
in 1950 and walked us through newspaper clippings, family photos,
home movies, and a scrapbook titled South Park Paving Project. It
was through these memory *movidas* that we were able to reconstruct
the activist backgrounds of the Chicana/o community of Riverton
and to assess not only what the story was but how the story was
being told by various participants. By recognizing the contradictions
exposed through their situated citizenship, Chicanas/os in Riverton
organized and mobilized the community. They engaged in work that
was reciprocal to call out various injustices and to support one
another over a period of more than ten years, though this support has
not dwindled since that time. This resulted in the completion of a
community project that, ultimately, improved the health and
environmental conditions of their barrio.

In 2016, with the help of the Following the Manito Trail team, the
South Park Barrio residents gathered in the neighborhood park to
celebrate the thirtieth anniversary of the South Park Paving Project.
To no one's surprise, Annie was the main organizer of the event,
sending out invitations, organizing games, and reminding everyone
in attendance of the importance of setting examples for younger
generations and what it means to engage in community. And in the
background, on a small screen and as a reminder of their communal
struggles, was the home movie that Annie filmed in 1986,
documenting the day-in and day-out activities of the barrio residents
who labored to create a safer neighborhood for themselves and their
families.

While Wyoming's promises of equality premised by the passing
of women's suffrage in 1869 signaled a larger movement within the
United States to recognize the voting privileges and voice for
women, it was not a promise made to those who lived within the
territory but who were denied citizenship. In Annie's case, not even
citizenship would guarantee that her community would be safe from
racialized and gendered hostilities, a sentiment she feels even

today—nearly seventy years after her family arrived in Wyoming. Notwithstanding, Annie's community is proud of the work it accomplished. This was evident as we walked the streets of the South Park Barrio to reminisce about the earlier years of the barrio, sat on the front porch of Emilio and Helen Vigil's home to hear stories of comunidad and resilience, and spoke with younger generations of barrio residents who fondly remembered how their parents, aunts, and uncles advocated and labored to do the reciprocal work necessary to improve their lives and the lives of future generations of South Park Barrio residents.

The archival footage from Annie's 1986 home video, which appears in Adam Herrera's Riverton Paving Project documentary, ends with Susana and Annie in the South Park Barrio. Susana is filming as she asks Annie what she thinks about the project so far. Drawing from the lyrics from Frank Sinatra's song entitled "My Way," Annie proudly exclaims that the barrio theme song was "We did it our way," taking the individual *I* to the collective *we* as a sign of a particular community ethos. Susana responds by singing "they said it could not be done," before Annie evokes another popular song, this one by the Beatles—"I get by with a little help from my friends" (Herrera). In this moment, both Annie and Susana contested a work ethic built on ideas of rugged individualism so deeply ingrained in the American West. Instead, they demonstrated that community, friendship, and working together were *movidas* of resistance and paramount to their success and their survival in the South Park Barrio.

Did the efforts of this community come to gain what Annie had hoped for? Did South Park Barrio residents effectively strategize to not be put on the back burner and did they get "what *they* had?" This essay has demonstrated that, via situated citizenship and various *movidas*, the Chicana/o community of Riverton, Wyoming, led by Annie, Susana, and Helen were able to challenge an ethos of equality and citizenship that they found unsuitable for their livelihoods. They moved themselves from the back burner to achieve the kind of equality they deserved, while exposing the "contradiction between expressed commitment to equality and the lived reality of inequality"

(Behl 5). While feelings of discrimination and racism continue to exist in Wyoming for marginalized communities, this important archive is an opportunity to reflect on how women's suffrage in Wyoming was premised on particular social locations—and how Chicanas spoke back to these exclusions through organized strategies of resistance. By looking closely at Chicana-led activism in Riverton, Wyoming, I have demonstrated how Chicana activism disrupted and mapped upon the Wyoming landscape another way to conceptualize the perceived benefits of women's suffrage, granted in 1869 in the territory of Wyoming, by centering the experiences of Chicana activists and their communities in the Equality State.

Works Cited

Aguirre, Michael D. "Excavating the Chicano Movement: Chicana Feminism, Mobilization, and Leadership at El Centro de la Raza, 1972-1979." *Chicana Movidas: New Narratives of Activism and Feminism in the Movement Era*, edited by Dionne Espinoza, et al. U of Texas P, 2018, pp. 174-188.

Anaya, Rudolfo. "Querencia, Mi patria chica." *Querencia: Reflections on the New Mexico Homeland*, edited by Vanessa Fonseca-Chávez, et al. U of New Mexico P, 2020, pp. xiii-xxii.

Behl, Natasha. *Gendered Citizenship: Understanding Gendered Violence in Democratic India.*Oxford UP, 2019.

Billock, Jennifer. "Women Have Been Voting in Wyoming for 150 Years, and Here is How the State is Celebrating." *Smithsonian Magazine.* 7 June 2019, www.smithsonianmag.com/travel/women-voting-wyoming-150-years-here-how-state-celebrating-180971263/. Accessed 15 Dec. 2020.

Cobos, Rubén. *A Dictionary of New Mexico and Southern Colorado Spanish.* Revised and Expanded Edition, Museum of New Mexico P, Santa Fe, 2003.

DiGrappa, Emy. "Renee Laegried: The Right to Vote Was Their Most Radical Demand." *First But Last* podcast, Wyoming Humanities 11 Dec. 2019, www.thinkwy.org/first-but-last/renee-laegried. Accessed 29 Jan. 2021.

Espinoza, Dionne, et al., eds. *Chicana Movidas: New Narratives of Activism and Feminism in the Movement Era*. U of Texas P, 2018.

First But Last. Podcast. Wyoming Humanities, 2019. www.thinkwy.org/podcasts. Accessed 29 Jan. 2021.

Fonseca, Vanessa. "'Donde mi amor se ha quedado:' Narratives of Sheepherding and Querencia along the Wyoming Manito Trail." *Annals of Wyoming: The Wyoming History Journal*, vol. 89, no. 2/3, 2017, pp. 6-12.

Herrera, Adam, producer. "Riverton Paving Project." *Following the Manito Trail*, 2017, www.manitotrail.com. Accessed 29 Jan. 2021.

Lovata, Troy. "Making Heritage and Place on the Trees: Arborglyphs from Latina/os in Wyoming." *Annals of Wyoming: The Wyoming History Journal*, vol. 89, no. 2/3, 2017, pp. 113-122.

Martínez, Trisha Venisa-Alicia. "Living the Manito Trail: Maintaining Self, Culture, and Community." *Dissertation*. University of New Mexico, 2019.

____. "The Politics of Space, Community, and Identity: Mexican Ballet Folklórico in Cheyenne, Wyoming." *Annals of Wyoming: The Wyoming History Journal*, vol. 89 no. 2/3, 2017, pp. 107-112.

Martínez, Trisha Venisa-Alicia and Vanessa Fonseca-Chávez. "Finding and Building Community on the Manito Trail." *Western Lands Western Voices: Essays on Public History in the American West*, edited by Gregory E. Smoak, U of Utah P, pp. 85-100.

Vigil Mejorado, Annie. "Oral History Interview." *Following the Manito Trail*, conducted by Levi Romero and Vanessa Fonseca. 2015.

Morris, Katy. "'More Reputation Than She Deserves:' Remembering Suffrage in Wyoming." *Rethinking History: The Journal of Theory and Practice*, vol. 21, no. 1, 2017, pp. 48-66.

O'Connor, Sandra Day. "The History of the Women's Suffrage Movement." *Vanderbilt Law Review*, vol. 49, 1996, pp. 657-1577.

Peck, Bob. *The Riverton Ranger*. 1986.

Redwine, Augustin. 1979. "Lovell's Mexican Colony." *Annals of Wyoming: The Wyoming History Journal*, vol. 5, num. 1/2 , 1979, pp. 26-34.

Ríos-Bustamante, Antonio. "Wyoming's Mexican Hispanic History." *Annals of Wyoming: The Wyoming History Journal*, vol. 73, num. 2, 2001, pp. 2-13.

Roberts, Phil. "Equality State or Cowboy State-and What About the Miners?: An Essay." *Wyoming Almanac and History of Wyoming*, 2014.wyomingalmanac.com/wyoming_history/cowboy_state_equali ty_state_2014_version. Accessed 15 Dec 2020.

Romero, Levi. "Following the Manito Trail: A Tale of Two Querencias." *Querencia: Reflections on the New Mexico Homeland*, edited by Vanessa Fonseca-Chávez, et al. U of New Mexico P, 2020, pp. 308-324.

Vigil, Susana. "Oral History Interview." *Following the Manito Trail*, conducted by Vanessa Fonseca and Adam Herrera. 2016.

Vigil Mejorado, Annie. "Oral History Interview,". *Following the Manito Trail*, conducted by Levi Romero and Vanessa Fonseca. 2015.

Ward, Karen L. *The Riverton Ranger*. 1975.

Western, Samuel. "Hispanic Wyoming: A Shift from Agriculture." *WyoFile: People, Places, & Policy*. 2011, www.wyofile.com/hispanic-wyoming-01. Acessed 15 Dec. 2021

List of USLDH Grants-in-Aid (2020-2023)

One of the most significant outcomes of the US Latino Digital Humanities Center has been the USLDH-Mellon grants-in-aid program. The USLDH center has awarded and administered over twenty competitive grants-in-aid scholars to faculty and advanced graduate students and community members to develop digital skills and projects.

The awardees conduct research in US Latino studies in any discipline of the humanities between the Colonial period to 1980; include archival materials in English or any Hispanic language; and publish Phase 1 of a DH project (visualization, mapping, text mining or analysis, data curation and/or text encoding) and an academic article on their research analysis and/or protocols.

This program builds on the early years of the Recovery program grants-in-aid awards (182) that not only provided a research corpus but also built the new field known as Recovering the US Hispanic Literary Heritage by publicizing the need for research and opportunities for support as well as identifying the potential members of the new discipline. The results of the grantees' research also provided some of the publications of Recovery and university presses around the nation. These publications were also used to secure promotion and tenure for several scholars. USLDH has revived this program to, likewise, create a core constituency of data, professionalize the field, produce digital publications and disseminate research.

2023-2024

- Gabriela Barrios (University of California, Los Angeles), Sonia Del Hierro (Rice University), and Sophia Martinez-Abbud (Rice University), *Señora Power: A Chicana Mapping Project*

- Maribel Bello (University of Houston), *The Cristino Garza Peña Papers: From U.S. Expulsion to Leadership in Rural Mexico*

- Maya Chinchilla, MFA (Independent Scholar), *Precursors of leadership to the Central American Solidarity Movement in the United States*

- Marisa Hicks-Alcaraz, PhD (University of Illinois, Urbana-Champaign), *Reclaiming Film Histories of the U.S. Civil Rights Era: The Latina Film Recovery Project*

- Mary Okin, PhD (Independent Scholar) with Olivia Bowman, BA, *March With Us! Lessons in Activism from San José State*

- Paloma Vargas Montes, PhD (Tecnológico de Monterrey), *The Indigenous Episteme of the Borderlands: Conquest, Acculturation and Permanence*

- Omaris Z. Zamora (Rutgers University-New Brunswick) and Keishla Rivera-Lopez (Princeton University), *DominiRicanDH*

2021-2022

- Caroline Collins, PhD (University of California, San Diego), *Black and Brown California: A Media Archeology of Raciality, Colonialisms, and Identity in Alta California.*

- Erendina Delgadillo (Oakland Museum of California) and Osa Hidalgo de la Riva, PhD, *The de la Riva Family Herstory Project.*

- Veronica Durán (University of Nebraska-Lincoln), *(Re)Discovering* Carrascolendas*: The Aida Barrera Digital Project.*

- Cristina Pérez Jiménez, PhD (Manhattan College) and J. Bret Maney, PhD (Lehman College, CUNY), *The Latino Catskills.*

- Lilia Raquel Rosas, PhD (University of Texas at Austin), *Tejana Historias: Indigenous Indentations and Transfrontera Transformations through a Visual Chronology.*

- Hinda Seif, PhD (University of Illinois at Springfield) and Diana Solís (Teaching artist: Changing Worlds, Urban Gateways, National Museum of Mexican Art), *Pilsen's Festival de Mujeres: Digital Windows to 1970s Mexicana-Chicana & Latina Queer Feminisms in Chicago.*

- Tomás F. Summers Sandoval, Jr., PhD (Pomona College) *The Barrio in Vietnam.*

- Josephine S. Talamantez (Chicano Park Museum and Cultural Center) and Alberto Pulido, PhD, (University of San Diego) *The Logan Heights Archival Project.*

- Martin Tsang, PhD (University of Miami) and David Fonte-Navarrete, PhD (Lehman College, CUNY), *Beyond the Archive: A Collaborative Research-Based Digital Edition of Música de los cultos (ca. 1956), the Cabrera-Tarafa Collection of Afro-Cuban Music.*

2020-2021

- Tessa Córdova, Ph.D., University of New Mexico, *The Enriqueta Vásquez Digital History Project*

- Ana María Díaz-Marcos, Ph.D., University of Connecticut, *Hispanic Antifascism and Feminism in* La Voz *(New York, 1937-1939)*

- Montse Feu, Ph.D. and Jenny Patlan, Sam Houston State University, *Fighting Fascism: Workers' Visual Print Culture in US Spanish-language Periodicals*

- Sarah Rafael García, Founder of Barrio Writers and LibroMobile, *Modesta Ávila: Obstructing Development Since 1889 (MAOD)*

- Claire Jiménez, University of Nebraska-Lincoln, *The Puerto Rican Literature Project*

- Joshua Ortiz-Bacó, University of Texas at Austin, *Unearthing Brazilian, Cuban, and Puerto Rican Abolitionism in the 19th Century US Press*

- Cristina Ramírez, Ph.D., University of Arizona, *Recovering Barrio Rhetorics: A Discursive and Historical Remembering of Chicana Border Writer Ramona González*

Editors and Contributors

Editors

Montse Feu is an Associate Professor of Spanish at Sam Houston State University. She researches historical US Hispanic antifascism and US Hispanic periodicals at large. She is the author of peer-reviewed articles and books, including *The Antifascist Chronicles of Aurelio Pego. A Critical Anthology* (2021); *Fighting Fascist Spain. Worker Protest from the Printing Press* (2020); and *Correspondencia personal y política de un anarcosindicalista exiliado: Jesús González Malo (1943-1965)* (Universidad de Cantabria). Feu has co-edited *Serving Refugee Children: Listening to Stories of Detention in the USA* (2021) and *Writing Revolution: Hispanic Anarchism in the United States* (2019). She is the curator of *Fighting Fascist Spain— The Exhibits*, an interpretative digital archive with the mission to curate, interpret, and make accessible US Hispanic antifascist print culture.

Yolanda Padilla is Associate Professor in the School of Interdisciplinary Arts and Sciences at the University of Washington, Bothell. She is the co-editor of two volumes: *Bridges, Borders, and Breaks:*

History, Narrative, and Nation in Twenty-First-Century Chicana/o Literary Criticism (University of Pittsburgh Press, 2016) and *The Plays of Josefina Niggli: Recovered Landmarks of Latina Literature* (University of Wisconsin Press, 2007). Her essays on borderland literature and print culture have appeared in venues such as *New Centennial Review*, *Women's Studies Quarterly*, *English Language Notes*, *Aztlán,* and the volumes *Open Borders to a Revolution* (2013) and *The Cambridge History of Latina/o Literature* (2018).

Contributors

Esmeralda Arrizón-Palomera is an Assistant Professor of English at the University of Illinois, Chicago. She specializes in US Latinx and African American Literature and culture with a focus on race, gender, and migration. Her current book project, *The Coloniality of Citizenship and the Turn to the Undocumented in Feminist Thought*, studies the work the undocumented immigrant, whose presence and absence, has enabled in feminist history, theory, and literature from the mid-nineteenth century to the late-twentieth century. Her work has been supported by the Ford Foundation and published in *Aztlán: A Journal of Chicano Studies*, *Latino Studies*, *MELUS*, and *DreamersAdrift*.

Ayendy Bonifacio is an Assistant Professor of English at the University of Toledo. He writes and teaches about American literature and culture, Latinx studies, and print culture from the nineteenth century to the present. He is currently at work on a book titled *Newspapers and the Poetics of Paratextuality (1855-1901)* that sits at the intersection of periodical studies and nineteenth-century poetry. His research is published and/or forthcoming *in American Periodicals*, *Prose Studies*, *American Literary Realism*, *The New Times*, *ASAP/Journal*, *J19*, *The Black Scholar,* and other scholarly and public-facing venues.

Christopher J. Castañeda is Professor of History at California State University, Sacramento. His publications include *Americanized Spanish Culture: Stories and Storytellers of Dislocated*

Empires, co-edited with Miquel Bota (Routledge, 2022) and *Writing Revolution: Hispanic Anarchism in the United States*, co-edited with Montse Feu (University of Illinois Press, 2019). He also wrote "'Yours for the revolution': Cigar Makers, Anarchists, and Brooklyn's Spanish Colony, 1878–1925," in *Hidden Out in the Open: Spanish Migration to the United States (1875–1930)* co-edited by Phylis C. Martinelli and Ana Varela-Lago (University Press of Colorado, 2018).

María Cotera is an Associate Professor in the Mexican American and Latino Studies Department at the University of Texas. Her first book *Native Speakers: Ella Deloria, Zora Neale Hurston, Jovita González, and the Poetics of Culture* (University of Texas Press, 2008) received the Gloria Anzaldúa book prize in 2009 from the National Women's Studies Association. Her edited volume (with Dionne Espinoza and Maylei Blackwell) *Chicana Movidas: New Narratives of Feminism and Activism in the Movement Era* (University of Texas Press, 2018) has been adopted in courses across the country. She is director of the Chicana por mi Raza Digital Memory Project, an online interactive collection of oral histories and archives documenting Chicana Feminist praxis from 1960-1990.

Martha P. Cotera is a founder of the National Women's Political Caucus, Texas Women's Political Caucus, Partido Raza Unida, the Center for Mexican American Studies at UT Austin, and a community advisor and advocate for forty years to establish the Mexican American and Latino Studies Department. Martha was also instrumental in designing and establishing the Mexican American Library Program at the Benson Latin American Collection where she was a consultant for archives acquisitions, from its inception to 2010. Currently, she serves as a national advisor for the Chicana por Mi Raza Digital Memory Project. Martha's publications include numerous bibliographies on Mexican American and Latina/o topics, also *Diosa y Hembra: History and Heritage of Chicanas in the US* and *The Chicana Feminist*. Martha has been honored with the prestigious OHTLI Award from the Mexican government, the highest honor for immigrant advocacy.

Vanessa Fonseca-Chávez is an Associate Professor of English and Associate Dean of Diversity, Equity, and Inclusion in the College of Integrative Sciences and Arts at Arizona State University. She is the co-editor of *Querencia: Reflections on the New Mexico*, published in 2020 with the University of New Mexico Press, and the author of *Colonial Legacies in Chicana/o Literature and Culture: Looking through the Kaleidoscope*, published in 2020 with the University of Arizona Press. Fonseca-Chávez is the co-director of the Following the Manito Trail project and the co-editor (with Yvette Saavedra) of the *BorderVisions* book series with the University of Arizona Press.

Inés Hernández Ávila is Professor of Native American Studies at the University of California, Davis and a scholar, poet, and visual artist. She is Nez Perce, enrolled on the Colville Reservation, Washington, and Tejana. She is one of the six founders of the international Native American and Indigenous Studies Association. Her research focuses on the national movement of indigenous writers in Mexico, especially poets in Chiapas, and the influence of ancient Nahuatl philosophy on contemporary Chicana/indigenous creative expression. She is co-editor, with Norma E. Cantú, of *Entre Guadalupe y Malinche: Tejanas in Literature and Art* (University of Texas Press, 2016).

Sonia Hernández is a Chancellor EDGES Fellow and Associate Professor of History at Texas A&M University. She is the author of the award-winning *Working Women into the Borderlands* (Texas A&M, 2014) and *For a Just and Better World: Engendering Anarchism in the Mexican Borderlands* (University of Illinois, 2021). Her work has appeared in *Frontiers: A Journal of Women Studies*, *LABOR: Studies in Working-Class History of the Americas*, and her research has been supported by Humanities Texas, National Endowment for the Humanities, and the Fulbright Foundation. She is a founding member of the public history project 'Refusing to Forget,' which seeks to bring public awareness of early twentieth century anti-Mexican violence. She is currently working on a book which revisits the near-lynching attempt of Gregorio Cortez in 1901 in central Texas from a gendered and transnational perspective.

Anita Huizar-Hernández is an Associate Professor of Spanish in the School of International Letters and Cultures at Arizona State University. Her research and teaching focus on the relationship among narrative, identity, and place in the archival traces of the US-Mexico borderlands and beyond, bringing historical intent to contemporary questions about racial justice and belonging. She is the author of *Forging Arizona: A History of the Peralta Land Grant and Racial Identity in the West*, which recovers a nineteenth-century con artist's attempt to claim ownership of a substantial portion of the newly acquired US Southwestern territories through falsifying archival records.

Pablo E. Landeros is a history instructor for the Maricopa County Community College District (MCCCD) in Phoenix, Arizona. He received his Ph.D. from the University of California, Santa Barbara in History (2013) focusing on Chicana feminism in the 1970s. He was raised in Pacoima and Paso Robles, California, which influenced his interest in Chicana/o identity. Currently, he teaches a plethora of courses including Chicana/o Studies, Women's, and Medieval History.

Paul Losch holds a Master of Arts in Latin American Studies from the University of Florida and a Master of Library Science from Florida State University. He has been the Field Director of the Library of Congress Overseas Operations Office in Rio de Janeiro since 2020. Prior to this position, he was a Latin American and Caribbean Collection librarian at the University of Florida.

Anna NietoGómez is a Chicana feminist activist scholar. She published the first Chicana feminist newspaper, *Hijas De Cuauhtémoc*, and the journal *Encuentro Femenil*. She was the first to teach Chicana Studies from 1972-1976 at California State University at Northridge, and in 1976 she created the "Chicana" slide show, a history of la Chicana. NietoGomez adapted the script for *Chicana*, the first Chicana film, which was directed by Sylvia Morales in 1979. Alma M. Garcia published her other works in *Chicana Feminist*

Thought (1997) and Espinoza, Cotera, and Blackwell published her latest work in *Chicana Movidas* (2018).

Anna María Nogar is Professor of Hispanic Southwest Studies in the Department of Spanish and Portuguese at the University of New Mexico. Her scholarship includes the prizewinning texts *Quill and Cross in the Borderlands: Sor María de Ágreda and the Lady in Blue, 1628 to the Present* (2018), *A History of Mexican Literature* (2016), and *Sisters in Blue/Hermanas de azul* (2017), as well as *Colonial Itineraries of Contemporary Mexico* (2014). In 2021, she published *El feliz ingenio neomexicano: Felipe M. Chacón and Poesía y prosa,* on the nineteenth-century Nuevomexicano poet Felipe Maximiliano Chacón. She is an editor of the forthcoming volumes *A History of Mexican Poetry* and *A History of the Mexican Novel.*

William Orchard is Associate Professor of English at Queens College, CUNY, where he teaches Latinx literature, queer studies, and visual culture. He is the co-editor of *Bridges, Borders, and Breaks: History, Narrative, and Nation in Twenty-First-Century Chicana/o Literary Criticism* (University of Pittsburgh Press, 2016) and *The Plays of Josefina Niggli* (University of Wisconsin Press, 2007). He has recently completed a monograph titled *Graphic Educations: The Lessons of Latinx Comics* that is forthcoming from the University of Arizona Press. His essays have appeared in *Aztlán, Women's Studies Quarterly, ASAP/J, Post-45 Contemporaries,* and *CENTRO Journal.*

Monica Perales is Associate Professor of History and the Director of the Center for Public History at the University of Houston. Her first book, *Smeltertown: Making and Remembering a Southwest Border Community* (University of North Carolina Press, 2010), received the Kenneth Jackson Award for Best Book in North American Urban History from the Urban History Association. She also co-edited *Recovering the Hispanic History of Texas* (Arte Público Press, 2010). Her current research explores Mexican-American women, labor, and foodways in the US Southwest in the twentieth century.

Samantha M. Rodriguez is a History and Humanities Professor at Houston Community College. She served as the NACCS—Tejas Foco Co-Chair (2019-2021) and the NACCS Chicana Caucus Co-Chair (2014-2016). Rodriguez is a co-founder and member of Más Que Tres, a Chicana Collective that addresses the core topics of feminism, health, empowerment, race, and justice. Rodriguez's research has been featured in *¡Chicana Movidas!: New Narratives of Activism and Feminism in the Movimiento Era!* (University of Texas Press, 2018) and *Civil Rights in Black and Brown: Histories of Resistance and Struggle in Texas* (University of Texas Press, 2021). She is working on a monograph that leverages oral histories to examine the ways Tejanas balanced a commitment to gender liberation and ethnic self-determination within the broader nexus of the Chicana/o Movement, the Black Power Movement, and the mainstream Anglo Feminist Movement.

Koldo San Sebastián is a journalist and a historian. He is a former member of the Advisory Board of the Basque Studies Center of the University of Nevada-Reno. He is Lecturer and director in summer courses on emigration in Basque Country University. His items of interest: Spanish Dictatorship (1937-1977): *Euskadi, dos años de impaciencia* (1978), *Crónicas de postguerra* (1981), *Los años :oscuros* (2019). Exiles. *El exilio vasco en Venezuela* (1992), *El exilio vasco en América* (2014), *Las cenizas de Gernika* (2023). Emigration & Diaspora*: Los vascos en México* (1992), *Origen de la comunidad vasca en México* (1997), *Basques in the USA* (2015), *Newyorktarrak. La comunidad vasca de Nueva York* (2016), and *Un idioma en la maleta* (*sobre la lengua vasca en la emigración*) (2022).

Evelyn Soto is Assistant Professor of English and American Studies at Sam Houston State University. Her research and teaching interests bring together hemispheric literary studies, Latinx studies, and histories of race to understand how revolutionary imaginaries emerged from the fissures of colonial conflict in the long nineteenth-century. She is currently at work on a first book titled *Tainted Translations: Early Latinx Political Imaginaries and Trans-*

American Empire. Her research projects have been supported by the Mellon Foundation, the Social Sciences Research Council, the American Council of Learned Societies, and the César Chávez Fellowship at Dartmouth College.

Ana Varela-Lago received her PhD from the University of California, San Diego with a dissertation titled "Conquerors, Immigrants, Exiles: The Spanish Diaspora in the United States (1848-1948)." She is an independent scholar and author of several publications on the Spanish immigrant experience in the United States. She co-edited, with Phylis C. Martinelli, *Hidden Out in the Open: Spanish Migration to the United States (1875-1930) (2018)*.

Stalina Emmanuelle Villarreal lives as a rhyming-slogan creative activist. She is a Generation 1.5 poet (mexicanx and Xicanx), an essayist, a translator, a sonic-improv collaborator, and an instructor of Creative Writing. She co-authored an article with a historian in the book *Chicana Movidas* (University of Texas, 2018). Her poetry can be found in the *Rio Grande Review, Texas Review, Spoon River Poetry Review, The Acentos Review, Defunkt Magazine*, and elsewhere. She has published translations of poetry. Her debut hybrid collection *Watcha* is forthcoming from Deep Vellum Publishing. She is the recipient of the Inprint Donald Barthelme Prize in Poetry.

ENDNOTES

The Practice of Latina Feminist Recovery

[1]For more on the history of the Recovery Project, see Kanellos and Aranda.

[2]While some would argue that the term "Latina" is anachronistic when applied to historical periods prior to the mid-twentieth century, Jesse Alemán compellingly asserts that "the term *Latino* is not an anachronism but a marker of nineteenth-century transnationality" (2016, "Forgotten" viii).

[3]For a discussion of transnationalism and Chicana/o/x literature, see Orchard and Padilla.

[4]Lazo identifies the Recovery Project's archival collections as "migrant archives" (2009, " Migrant Archives" 47-50).

[5]Calls for a move beyond recovery or that question the value in studying women's literary and other cultural histories often arise during informal conversations or in meetings rather than in print, as attested to by Looser. Harris' essay suggests as much given that it starts with the question "What do critics mean when they use the phrase post-recovery?" without naming the critics—she takes it as a given that her readers are familiar with this position. For examples of publications that raise doubts about the continued value of feminist recovery work, see Poovey and Marsden. Marsden does end her article with suggestions and a more positive view of the future of such recovery work. Coates and Dippold use the phrase "beyond

recovery" not in the sense of rejecting traditional recovery paradigms, but rather to "complicate the binaries of lost and found, absent and present" by exploring the possibilities of allowing absences to speak when one cannot find archival traces (209).

[6]See Foster ("Preface" 2006) for an engaging discussion of the benefits that come with recovering texts that raise unanswerable questions and cannot easily be situated in existing frameworks.

[7]See Alarcón for an analysis of how white feminism challenged the centered subjectivity of white men only to claim that positionality for white women and a consideration of the alternatives presented by radical Chicana feminists Cherríe Moraga, Gloria Anzaldúa, and other contributors to *This Bridge Called My Back*.

[8]González's book was in progress when Castañeda referred to it in her article, and was subsequently published with the title *Refusing the Favor: The Spanish-Mexican Women of Santa Fe, 1820-1880*.

[9]See, for example, Gruesz and Lazo.

[11]For a fascinating discussion of development if Chicana History, see Castañeda, Emma Pérez, and Deena Gonzáles (Castañeda 2014, 273-90)

[12]For another example of the use of "memory work" to uncover Chicana feminist activism during the movement, see Blackwell

[13]Dworkin y Méndez and Lugo-Ortiz identify challenges and future directions for the Recovery Project in their 2006 essay that we believe are still relevant today (14-17)

Citizenship, Suffrage, and the (Un)making of the Mexican-American Woman Citizen in María Amparo Ruiz de Burton's *Who Would Have Thought It?*

[1]See, for example, De la Luz Montes (1998), Rivera (2006), Soares (2009), Hernandez-Jason (2010).

[2]For example, in *The Chicana Feminist* (1977), Martha P. Cotera identifies Mexican women's activism in the late nineteenth century and the early twentieth century as part of Chicanas' feminist heritage. Cotera does not mention Chicana feminism's relationship to the US women's movement prior to the 1960s and 1970s. Cotera, moreover, proposes that "Anglo feminism has had little to do with the development of the Chicana" and rejects the "Anglo woman's chauvinistic attitude" she describes as Anglo women's intent to liberate themselves and then "liberate Chicanas, Blacks, and all the women in the world" (8, 17). For a longer discussion of Chicana feminism's relationship to white feminism, see Cotera (1980), García (1997), and Moraga et. al (2015).

[3]These are my translations of Ruiz de Burton's letters. See *Conflicts of Interest* (2001) for original text in Spanish.

[4]For more on the framing of the women's movement as the "other Civil War," see Clinton (1999) and Stanton et al. (2017).

[5]National Women's Rights Conventions in the United States began in 1850 and continued through 1860. The reasons for their suspension in 1857 are unclear.

[6]Susan B. Anthony, Elizabeth Cady Stanton, and Matilda Joslyn Gage compiled the first three volumes of the *History of Women's Suffrage,* which covered thirty-seven years, beginning in 1848. Volume I was published in 1881.

[7]The 1872 lawsuit began a formal disarticulation of suffrage from legal citizenship. The 1872 decision on *Minor v. Happersett* was appealed in the Missouri Supreme Court in 1873 and in the United States Supreme Court in 1874; it was decided that US citizenship did not guarantee women the right to vote.

[8]In 1872, Virginia Woodhull published an article in her newspaper about an adultery scandal involving prominent members of the abolition and suffrage movement. For more on the publication of this article and its aftermath, see Shaplen (1954).

[9]Frances D. Gage wrote the most well-known version of Sojourner Truth's speech twelve years after the second National Women's Rights Convention. Gage's recollection first appeared in the *New York Independent* on April 23, 1863 and was included in the first volume of the *History of Women's Suffrage*. A different account of Sojourner Truth's appearance at the 1851 woman's convention was offered by Rev. Marius Robinson in the *Anti-Slavery Bugle* on June 21, 1851. For all versions of Sojourner Truth's speech, see www.thesojournertruthproject.com/.

[10]For a longer discussion of the legal incorporation of Mexicans into the United States, see Richard Griswold del Castillo (1990), Haney López (1996), and Martha Menchaca (2011).

[11]For a longer discussion on the role of African American women in the women's movement see Terborg-Penn (1998). For a longer discussion on the role of Native American women in the women's movement see Roesch Wagner (2001).

[12]At times, Magoffin's racist descriptions of Mexican women overlap with equally racist descriptions of Native American women. For a longer discussion of Anglo-American women's misconstructions of Native American women and their effect in the treatment of Native American women in the United States, see Emmerich (1991) and (1993).

[13]See the American Equal Rights (AERA) proceedings in Stanton et al. (2017) for more on these criticisms.

[14]This is my translation of a line from a Spanish-language letter written by María Amparo Ruiz de Burton in New York to Mariano Guadalupe. The letter is dated February 15, 1869, just months before the American Equal Rights Association met in New York City and dissolved into two separate women's rights organizations. See *Conflicts of Interest* (2001) for original text in Spanish.

[15]Racial provisions for citizenship in the United States changed over time. The Fourteenth Amendment of 1868, for example, extended citizenship to black men and black women. The citizenship status of people who were neither black nor white was less clear. Mexicanos, for example, had to prove their whiteness by distancing themselves from Indigeneity and Blackness, or at least prove that they were part of the group of Mexican citizens to whom the Treaty of Guadalupe Hidalgo promised citizenship and property rights in the United States.

Translating the Tapada's Veil in *Who Would Have Thought it?*

[1]The majority of historical and cultural studies of tapadas in the Americas focus on their popularity in Lima, Peru, but evidence suggests that it was more widespread in the Spanish colonies including Mexico, Chile, and possibly other regions. See Marco Antonio León León, "Entre lo público y lo privado: acercamientos a las *tapadas* y *cubiertas* en España, Hispanoamérica y Chile."

[2]While most descriptions of the *manto* describe it as a mantle to cover the face, Hall describes it in his journals as a second petticoat used for the one-eyed style of *medio ojo*: "The Manto, or cloak, is also a petticoat, but, instead of hanging about the heels, as all honest petticoats ought to do, it is drawn over the head, breast, and face, and is kept so close by the hands, which it also conceals, that no part of the body, except one eye, and sometimes only a small portion of one eye, is perceptible" (83).

Aurora Mena and *The Pearl Key*: Unlocking the Meaning of a Mambisa's Story

[1]The digitized book may be found at ufdc.ufl.edu/AA00061841. The University of Florida's copy is very brittle, is missing the back cover, and has only been used for occasional exhibits and for digitization. The acidic paper and inexpensive binding used were not favorable for long-term preservation. Another copy was held at a Texas library but is no longer

available. It is likely that at least one copy eventually reached Cuba, because bibliographer Carlos M. Trelles was aware of the work and its author and made some very brief mention in his surveys of books from and about Cuba. A physical description of *The Pearl Key* appears in his *Bibliografia del siglo XIX* (Matanzas, 1915, vol. 8, p. 146) and, in his *Biblioteca Histórica Cubana Vol. 1* (Matanzas, 1922), there appears among some notes about authors, "Aurora de Mena (1896) es una separatista cubana" (490). Her only publication listed is *The Pearl Key*, in English.

[2]The college's annual report for 1894-1895 justified the hiring the new instructor as follows: "Our near proximity to the people of Mexico, Central America, and the West Indies, and the rapidly increasing commercial and social relations between these countries and our own, led us to believe that instruction in the Spanish tongue should become an important part of our College work. We therefore secured a lady from Havana, whose training in the best schools of that city and whose experience as a teacher of her native language had proven her ability as an instructor." Mena taught Spanish in Lake City for two years, and then from about 1896 to 1900, in Jacksonville and Tampa, where she participated in the political, religious, and labor organizations of the local Cuban communities. The college was also one of the advertisers that supported the publication of *The Pearl Key*.

[3]The author would like to thank Richard Phillips, Dr. E. Haven Hawley, and Dr. Efraín Barradas, all of the University of Florida, for their encouragement in pursuing this research. Any shortcomings are my own.

[4]"Acuerdos de las Sufragistas." *Diario de la Marina* 27 July 1922; "Spanish Instructress: Secretary of the Cuban Junta Will Teach Spanish in Tampa." *Tampa Weekly Tribune*. 29 December 1898.

[5]The Vance Printing Company mainly produced works underwritten by others, such as tourism promotion materials, official state publications, and creative works by local authors. The attractive front cover features the Cuban flag, and a small note that the book had been registered at the Jacksonville post office so that it could be distributed by mail at a discounted rate.

[6]"Souvielle, Mrs. E.M.," *Herringshaw's Encylopedia of American Biography of the Nineteenth Century* (Chicago, American Publisher's Association, 1899, p. 872).

[7]The statement that Mena had left Cuba "about a year ago" (circa 1895) may have been intended to make her account seem timelier, but Mena herself mentions that, at the time of writing the book in 1896, she had already spent six years in the US (34).

[8]The character Matagás is based on a real bandit of Matanzas by that

nickname, who did, in fact, join the rebel army (Schwartz, 110-111). According to Dabove, the bandit figure appeared in Latin American literature of the nineteenth century as an alternative, sometimes dangerous and sometimes welcome, to modern society. The figure of the indigenous "noble savage" was another such device, symbolizing a rejection of the corrupt Old World (Sebreli). According to Jameson, a common theme in the literature of many countries emerging from colonial rule has been the "national allegory," in which characters stand for distinct groups constituting the nation. It is significant that Mena leaves the Afro-Cuban population unrepresented in this scene, perhaps to avoid offending the sensibilities of her US readers.

[9]Mena and Torres took each other to court, and eventually Mena was arrested on charges of slandering the judge's wife. The Tampa cigar workers took up a collection for Mena's legal defense, apparently because Mena had assisted them as their representative to the press during their strike in July 1899. The *Tribune*, while generally sympathetic to Mena, tended to make light of the legal battle with brief comments such as "In the Miss DeMena case, the lawyers were unable to prove a misdemeanor" (21 October 1899, p. 4).

[10]Mena, like Cisneros, became a US citizen but returned to Cuba after independence. The paths of the two authors, Mena and Cisneros, apparently crossed in Jacksonville in 1898, after the US entered the war in Cuba. Mena was teaching Spanish to US Army officers there, and Cisneros was accompanying her husband, a Cuban-American aide to General Fitzhugh Lee. This is indicated in a brief note appeared in the *Ocala Evening Star* of July 15, 1898. "Miss Pearl Mann is in Jacksonville teaching General Lee and staff Spanish and Mrs. Carbonel [sic], nee Miss Cisneros, English. She is stopping with Miss A.D. Mena, formerly teacher of Spanish in the Lake City College, under whom Miss Pearl acquired the language that she speaks so fluently."

[11]"Cuban Patriot" (*Boston Daily Advertiser*, 1900), "Life of Tragedy" (*Boston Globe,* 1906). The newspapers in Boston repeated stories about Mena from *The Pearl Key* and added to her biography with exploits resembling those of Cisneros and of Clemencia Arango, another *mambisa* who enjoyed celebrity in the US press.

[12]"Dr. Sargent's Work," *Cambridge Tribune*, 18 Sept. 1909. The album is among Eliot's papers at Harvard, along with a signed handwritten note from Aurora Mena. An item in a Cuban teachers' magazine entitled "La Señorita Mena en Harvard" noted with pride that the Cuban flag and national anthem had been honored at the presentation, and that she had represented her colleagues and the country well.

[13]"La Escuela Décima Séptima," *Diario de la Marina*, March 1903;

Gutierrez, Tomás Servando, "Noble Inteligencia," *DIario de la Marina*, 8 March 1911, 11; Mendoza, Miguel Angel. "Habaneras," *Diario de la Marina*, 1909; "Las Escuelas de Sagua la Grande," *Instrucción Primaria*, 30 January 1910, pp. 141-43. "En la Exposición Nacional," *La Lucha*, 7 February 1912.

[14]*Diario de la Marina*, 3 June, 1921. Even after her official retirement (*Diario*, November 23, 1923, p. 14), Mena continued to be interested in physical education. She prepared a physical education manual that was discussed at the 1926 national meeting of school superintendents. "Reunión ordinária de la Junta de Superintendentes de Escuelas," *Diario*, 7 Feb 1926, p. 7. No copies of that manual have been located, and it is not clear if the manuscript was published.

[15]*The Nashville Tennesseean*, August 19, 1897, contained a brief mention of the book as being on sale in the Women's Pavilion of the Centennial Exhibition, which indicates that it was being marketed specifically to US women.

[16]*Boletín oficial de la Oficina Nacional de Invenciones, Información Técnica y Marcas*, 1910, p. 228.

[17]In 1935, Mena signed a petition calling on the government to pay teachers' pensions, according to "Los Retirados Escolares Afirman...," *Diario de la Marina*, 29 August 1935, 3. She would have been seventy-four at that time. We do not have information about her death. Del Corral writing about her innovative mining operation, mentions her as "ya desaparecida" in 1943 (37).

[18]"Unsatisfactory Affair," *Cambridge Tribune* (1906). Mena's remarks were translated and condensed by others.

María Cristina Mena and The Masturbating Boy

Thanks to Yolanda Padilla for urging me to return to this essay, whose first iteration was as a conference paper for the 2006 Recovering the US Hispanic Literary Heritage Conference in St. Louis. Thanks also to Renee Hudson for incisive feedback on a late draft of this essay.

[1]As Sedgwick explains, the paper became notorious when Roger Kimball plucked its title from an MLA program as an example of the degradation of US humanities scholarship. In *Tenured Radicals*, Kimball calls the essay "a founding document in the annals of 'Queer Theory'" that "does not raise one's hopes for responsible pedagogy" (7, 300). Given that the essay wasn't published until after the appearance of *Tenured Radicals*, it seems likely that Kimball didn't actually read the essay and just used the essay's catchy title as fodder for caricaturing his political opponents.

[2]Sedgwick further notes that "it is through gay and lesbian studies that the skills for a project of historicizing any sexuality have developed; along with a tradition of valuing nonprocreative forms of creativity of pleasure; a history of being suspicious of the tendentious functioning of open secrets; and a politically urgent tropism toward the gaily and, if necessarily, the defiantly explicit" (821). One way, then, of seeing this reading of Mena's work is as a queer extension, via a centering of nonprocreative sexual acts, of some earlier work that focused more on gender and the heterosexual romance.

[3]An early dismissal of Mena's work appears in Raymund Paredes' important 1978 essay "The Evolution of Chicano Literature," in which he praises her as a "talented story-teller" while also describing her work as quaint local color fiction that "tended toward sentimentalism and preciousness" (85).

[4]In the first story, the Indian Petra alters her appearance with the face powder and rouge she discovers in a vanity set. An incriminating birth mark is removed by a surgeon in "The Vine Leaf," while the last story features an unmarriageable older sister whose visage is transformed by cosmetic surgery.

[5]Sheffer detects an incest plot in "Doña Rita's Rivals," in which the Doña Rita positions herself as a rival for her son's love. The story describes her as a "coquette" as she attempts to seduce her son to divert his attention from the woman that he loves (73). Similar structures also appear in "The Emotions of María Concepcion," in which the title character is enlisted by her father to be his caretaker in opposition to her erotic investment in a visiting bullfighter, and in "John of God, Water Carrier," in which the eponymous character raises a young orphan to become his wife, resulting in an unnerving slippage between sibling and erotic love in their exchanges with each other.

[6]There have been numerous essays on this topic and others that note the significant exclusion of blackness in mestizaje's imaginings of the future. The canonical piece on mestizaje's erasure of indigeneity in the context of Latinx and Chicanx studies is Maria Josefina Saldaña-Portillo's "Who's the Indian in Aztlán?"

[7]See Doherty's introduction to *The Collected Stories of Maria Cristina Mena* and Tiffany Ana López's "Tolerance for Contradictions."

[8]Interestingly, Popo is the same age that Mena was when she fled Mexico to live with family friends in New York City.

[9]See, for example, George Mosse's *Nationalism and Sexuality: Respectability and Abnormal Sexuality in Modern Europe* and Michel Foucault's *History of Sexuality: An Introduction, Volume 1.*

¹⁰Sheffer also sees an allusion to Shakespeare's *Romeo and Juliet* in Mena's story "Doña Rita's Rivals," which, in its opening pages, features star-crossed lovers, one of whom commits suicide because the relationship was forbidden by her love's mother. The story "The Son of Tropics" (1931) makes reference to *Julius Caesar*, who the young revolutionary refers to as he plots his revenge against Mexico's rich landowners.

¹¹This, of course, refers to Act 1, Scene 2 of Shakespeare's *The Tempest*, when Caliban declares: "You taught me language; and my profit on't / Is, I know how to curse. The red plague rid you / For learning me your language!"

¹²On the significance of Retamar's resignification of Caliban for Latin American, Hemispheric, and Latinx Studies, see José David Saldívar's chapter, "The School of Caliban," in *Dialectics of Our America*. Ricardo Ortíz's "Revolution's Other Histories" supplements Saldivar's chapter, critiquing the homophobia in Retamar's essay as well as the elision of sexuality in Saldívar's chapter.

¹³Pratt also sees the short story as having a connection to journalism, in contrast to the novel's origins in travel writing and history (190-1). Because of this connection, the short story is more associated with craft and commerce, while the novel is absorbed into a discourse about art and genius. On the significance of Mexican-American novels of the Mexican Revolution, see Yolanda Padilla's "The Other Novel of the Mexican Revolution."

A Forum on Chicana Memory Work, Past, Present, and Future: Nuestras Autohistorias

¹Cotera, "Invisibility is an Unnatural Disaster," *SAQ*, 796.

²For Anzaldúa, this process was central to the development of a "New Mestiza Consciousness" that could better navigate the ambiguities and contradictions of "life at the crossroads." Anzaldúa, Gloria. *Borderlands/ La Frontera*. Aunt Lute Books, 1987, p. 104.

³Jacques Derrida and Eric Pedowitz. *Archive Fever: A Freudian Impression*. Chicago: University of Chicago Press, 1996.

⁴Inés Hernández-Ávila, "Manifesto de Memoria: (Re)Living the Movement Without Blinking," *Chicana Movidas: New Narratives of Activism and Feminism in the Movement Era*, eds. Dionne Espinoza, María Eugenia Cotera, and Maylei Blackwell. Austin: University of Texas Press, 2018, 374.

⁵Lee Maracle, *Memory Serves: Oratories*, ed., Smaro Kamboureli. NeWest Press, 2015, 54. Maracle uses the term throughout the collection of essays, but she explains the term on page 54.

[6]N. Scott Momaday, *The Names: A Memoir* (New York: Harper & Row Publishers, 1976, 63.

[7]Monica Muñoz Martinez, "The Injustice Never Leaves You: Anti-Mexican Violence in Texas Kirkus Review of Books, July 1, 2018, www.kirkusreviews.com/book-reviews/monica-munoz-martinez/the-injustice-never-leaves-you/. Accessed on 11 August 2021.

[8]Samantha Rodriguez and Stalina Emmanuelle Villarreal, "María Jiménez: Reflexiones on Traversing Multiple Fronteras in the South" in *Chicana Movidas: New Narratives of Activism and Feminism in the Movement Era*, eds. Dionne Espinoza, María Eugenia Cotera, and Maylei Blackwell. Austin: University of Texas, 2018, 278-279.

[9]Rodriguez and Villarreal, "María Jiménez: Reflexiones on Traversing Multiple Fronteras in the South," 277.

[10]Rodriguez and Villarreal, "María Jiménez: Reflexiones on Traversing Multiple Fronteras in the South," 278.

[11]Stalina Emmanuelle Villarreal, "Breath Distress" (unpublished manuscript, July 13, 2019), Microsoft Word file.

[12]Robert D. Bullard, "Environmental Justice in the 21st Century: Race Still Matters," *Phylon* 52, no. 1 (Summer 2015): 76.

[13]Villarreal, "Breath Distress".

[14]Ibid.

Gertrudis Gómez de Avellaneda and Puerto Rico's Colonial Press

[1]Carmen Bravo-Villasante, *Una vida romántica: la Avellaneda* (Madrid: Instituto de Cooperación Iberoamericana, Ediciones Cultura Hispánica. 1986), 57-58.

[2]Jacques Derrida, *Margins of Philosophy*, translated by Alan Bass, (Chicago: The University of Chicago Press, 1982), 11.

[3]Jacques Derrida, *Positions*, translated by Alan Bass, (Chicago: The University of Chicago Press, 1972), 41.

[4]Walter Mignolo, *The Darker Side of Western Modernity: Global Futures, Decolonial Options* (Durham: Duke University Press, 2011), 2-3.

[5]Mignolo, *The Darker Side of Western Modernity*, xii.

[6]Beth Miller, "Gertrude the Great: Avellaneda, Nineteenth-Century Feminist, *Women in Hispanic Literature: Icons and Fallen Idols*, "(Berkeley: University of California Press, 1982), 203.

[7]Miller, "Gertrude the Great," 203.

[8]Catherine Davies, "Founding-Fathers and Domestic Genealogies: Situating Gertrudis Gómez De Avellaneda," *Bulletin of Latin American Research* 22, no. 4 (2003): 423.

[9]Davies, "Founding-Fathers," 423.

[10]Albin, Corbin, and Marrero-Fente, "A Transnational Figure," 75.

[11]Anna Brickhouse, *Transamerican Literary Relations and the Nineteenth-Century Public Sphere. Cambridge Studies in American Literature and Culture*, (Cambridge: Cambridge University Press, 2009), 173.

[12]Davies, "Founding-Fathers," 429.

[13]In 1836, *La Gazeta* replaced the "z" in its title with a "c." The new title remained until *La Gaceta*'s final issue in 1902. This is the title I use in my analysis.

[14]*La Gaceta de Puerto-Rico,* July 28, 1846.

[15]This poem was read by Ms. Avellaneda to the Dukes of Montpensier on the occasion of her highness Doña Luisa Fernanda's birthday, and the next day the Princess and the Prince sent the poet a rich gift consisting of a beautiful case with a rich jewel of shiny pearls and rubies of exquisite work. "Serenata," April 20, 1858.

[16]See Juan Nicasio Gallego's introduction of Avellaneda's *Poesías* (1841) for one example.

[17]*La Gaceta de Puerto-Rico,* May 14, 1861. Translator: Ayendi Bonifacio.

[18]Antonio s. Pedreira, *El periodismo en Puerto Rico. Bosquejo histórico desde su iniciación hasta el 1936.* Tomo 1. Monografías de la Universidad de Puerto Rico. Serie A. Estudios Hispánicos. Núm. 3.

[19]Chronicling America Database, Library of Congress, *La Gaceta de Puerto-Rico*.

[20]See, Bonifacio, Ayendy, "Se habla Español": Hispanophone-Merchant Advertisements in José Ferrer de Couto's *El Cronista* (1878). *American Periodicals: A Journal of History and Criticism*, vol. 30, no. 2, 2020, 118-121.

[21]Kirsten Silva Gruesz, *Ambassadors of Culture: The Transamerican Origins of Latino Writing*, (Princeton: Princeton University Press, 2002), 20.

[22]Literary News.

[23]"Noticias Literarias," *El Boletín mercantil de Puerto Rico*, September 22, 1871. "La única de las escritoras de la escuela analítica sentimental que tiene alguna semejanza con la Sra. Gómez de Avellaneda, es miss Mulock, porque, llevada de su instinto vigoroso, refiere los aconte-

cimientos con desembarazado y firme estilo, comenta con sobriedad, no abusa demasiado del análisis filosófico." In 1871, this excerpt was also reprinted in *La Revista de España*.

[24]"Noticias Literarias," September 22, 1871. "Esta creación de la fantasía popular, hábilmente reproducida por miss Mulock, vino a nuestra memoria como delicada analogía de naturalezas femeniles, al leer La flor del ángel de la Sra. Gómez de Avellaneda, flor del Deva, muy semejante en forma a una abeja."

[25]"Noticias Literarias," September 22, 1871. "Las mujeres comprenden y sienten más delicada e intensamente que los hombres estas fantásticas ilusiones de la musa de las montañas, y la Sra. Gómez de Avellaneda nada tiene que envidiar en esta parte a la imaginación soñadora de las razas septentrionales."

[26]"[Sand] can't never dispense with her insane systematic designs, usually so uncertain, that even [Pierre-Joseph] Proudhon, who is certainly not scrupulous and skittish in matters of daring and innovation, condemns with energy and even distaste her fierce desire for feminine emancipation without restraint and without measure, and all the inevitable consequences of this *rebellious bacchante* philosophy using the violent expression of Proudhon, namely: the absolute equality of both sexes; freedom in love, the ban on marriage; or in other words, envy and hatred of men, and spontaneous debasement of women" ("Noticias Literarias," September 22, 1871).

[27]"Noticias Literarias," September 22, 1871. "La Sra. Gómez de Avellaneda es novelista y no propagadora de arriesgadas y ambiciosas doctrinas; no desnaturaliza la novela ni el drama, convirtiendo estos géneros literarios, destinados al culto y honesto recreo de las gentes, en órgano de trastornos y agitación moral."

[28]"Noticias Literarias," September 22, 1871. "La moral de las leyendas y novelas de la Sra. Gómez de Avellaneda es franca, resuelta y sana, la cual ofrece de suyo el estudio sincero de la naturaleza humana, sin barruntos de doctrina social y sin melindres de forma."

[29]"Noticias Literarias," September 22, 1871. "Las mujeres . . . cultivan su entendimiento y ayudan, en las letras o en las artes, a la civilización general y al lastre de su patria."

[30]Dixa Ramírez, *Colonial Phantoms: Belonging and Refusal in the Dominican Americas, from the 19th Century to the Present* (New York: New York University Press, 2018), 38.

[31]Ramírez, *Colonial Phantoms*, 38.

[32]Ramírez, *Colonial Phantoms*, 36.

[33]*El Boletín mercantil de Puerto Rico*. February 1, 1873. "Es verdad! ¡El cuerpo de la que fue Gertrudis Gómez de Avellaneda descansa en un nicho del Cementerio de la sacramental de San Martín, de Madrid!"

[34]*El Boletín mercantil de Puerto Rico*. February 1, 1873. "Quien fue la Avellaneda?" "La Avellaneda, en vida, había poseído . . . fuerza de atracción: talento, hermosura, riqueza, posición social; su sexo la ponía fuera del alcaneo del tiro de la opinión política, que todo envenena . . ."

***Entre la plancha y la página*: Early Twentieth-Century Mexican Food Work and the Spanish-Language Press in Two Texas Cities**

[1]See Castillón (2014).

[2]See Ramos (2009); García (1991; 1981); Perales (2010).

[3]I am grateful to Dr. Nicolás Kanellos for his insight on the history of *El Continental*. Personal email communication with the author, 16 July 2021.

[4]Barragán Goetz (2020). In one El Paso barrio, nearly 50 percent of residents had some literacy, per the 1920 U.S. Census. See Perales, *Smeltertown*, 166.

[5]See Baeza Ventura (2001); Feu López (2015); Barrera (2008-2009).

[6]See Rebecca Sharpless (2010); Engelhardt (2011); Inness (2006); Counihan (2009); Abarca and Carr Salas, (2016).

[7]See Muncy (1991); Perales (2012), 146-163; Sánchez (1994); Stern (1999); Stephanie Mitchell and Patience A. Schell, eds. *The Women's Revolution in Mexico, 1910-1953*. Lanham, MD: Rowman and Littlefield, 2006.

[8]See National Institute of Food and Agriculture, "Cooperative Extension History," National Institute of Food and Agriculture, nifa.usda.gov/cooperative-extension-history; Jessica Mudry, "Quantifying the American Eater: USDA Nutrition Guidance and a Language of Numbers," in *Food as Communication, Communication as Food*, ed. Janet M. Cramer, Carlnita P. Greene, and Lynn M. Walters. New York: Peter Lang, 2011, 235-54.

[9]See Marchand (1985).

[10]On the class-based discourse of respectability, see Garza-Falcón (1998).

Adelina "Nina" Otero-Warren: A Nuevomexicana in Suffrage, Politics, and Letters in the Early Twentieth Century

[1] See US Mint Press release: www.usmint.gov/news/press-releases/ mint-announces-additional-honorees-in-american-women-quarters-program (9 June 2021). The entry on Otero-Warren reads: "Adelina Otero-Warren—a leader in New Mexico's suffrage movement and the first female superintendent of Santa Fe public schools."

[2] In Los Lunas, New Mexico, an Official Scenic Historical Marker (established by the New Mexico Historic Preservation Division) is dedicated to Nina Otero-Warren. The roadside sign outlines her accomplishments and co-locates her life accomplishments in the historic Luna family settlement. A mural on 2nd Street and Central in Albuquerque bears the message "Free exercise of religion; Freedom of speech and of the Press; The right to assemble and to petition the government" and "The right of all citizens to vote regardless of race, color or gender." The colorful artwork, covering a full building wall, features three large figures, and a woman teaching children and holding a newspaper whose banner reads "Free Press." The three figures each bear an attribution explaining their relationship to the mural's themes: Miguel Trujillo ("Native American Vote"), Witter Bynner ("Free Expression") and Nina Otero-Warren ("Votes for Women").

[3] Otero-Warren, Adelina. *Old Spain in Our Southwest*. 1936. Sunstone Press, 2006.

[4] Cathleen Cahill, *Recasting the Vote: How Women of Color Transformed the Suffrage Movement*.

[5] Whaley, Charlotte. *Nina Otero-Warren of Santa Fe*. Santa Fe: Sunstone Press, 2007.

[6] The pioneering work of Diana Rebolledo helped establish Otero-Warren, Jaramillo and Cabeza de Vaca Gilbert as important early twentieth-century writers of New Mexico, and this work continues to be developed by Elizabeth Salas and Vanessa Fonseca-Chávez, among others.

[7] Merrihelen Ponce's *The Lives and Works of Five Hispanic New Mexican Writers* provides a useful bibliography of primary sources of this nature, including Otero-Warren's professional writing on issues relating to bilingual education, bilingual literacy, and her work with the WPA.

[8] This text is archived in the Special Collection of the Albuquerque Public Library.

[9] As Cahill notes in *Recasting the Vote*, "Despite deep anger in New Mexico, a judge released Whitney on bail and allowed him to leave for

California . . . Indeed, in this period, the courts were systematically favoring Anglo challenges to Hispanic land grant claims . . . This assault on Hispanic land ownership and political power was an unavoidable fact of life among Hispanos in the New Mexico Territory. The need to protect their rights framed every other political issue" (48).

[10]Eloisa Luna Otero later remarried and had nine children during her marriage to Alfred Bergere.

[11]Scorcia Pacheco traces this property-rights change to the 1907 passage by the New Mexico Territorial Legislature of "An Act in Relation to Property Rights of Husband a Wife," commenting that this act "granted all community property acquired after marriage to the husband" (385). Aware of the legacy left to her full siblings, through the estates of her father Manuel B. Otero and of her mother Eloisa Luna, and of her mother's estate (shared with her half siblings) that greatly eclipsed Alfred Bergere's economic contribution to the second marriage, Otero-Warren acted quickly to protect the interests of the women of the family.

[12]*The Spanish American*, 27 November 1920. For an accounting of Otero-Warren's accomplishments during her twelve-year tenure as Super-intendent of Santa Fe schools, see Salas, 138.

[13]Historian Ann M. Massmann framed Otero-Warren's role as that of a cultural broker between Nuevomexicano and Anglo communities in New Mexico: "Adelina 'Nina' Otero-Warren presents a unique perspective as a woman who not only balanced, but expanded her positions in the two cultures, primarily by utilizing the power structures with which she had become familiar. Her life shows how traditional Hispano or 'native' New Mexican culture and modern American culture and institutions inter-acted."

[14]Cahill writes of the intervention with Catron that "The women present were likely not surprised, since these assertions echoed sentiments Senator Catron had shared many times. He would continue to resist woman suffrage to the very end of his term, introducing an anti-suffrage statement into the Senate just a few weeks before leaving office as a final insult to the women of New Mexico" (145-6).

[15]"In 2019 a group of Albuquerque High School students, mostly girls, began researching suffrage movements for their National History Day 2020 projects, which led CSWR archivist Nancy Brown-Martínez to the WPA file." (Scorcia Pacheco 394)

[16]For more on Felipe M. Chacón, including his 1924 collection of creative writing in which the poem dedicated to Otero-Warren was published, see

El feliz ingenio neomexicano: Felipe M. Chacón and Poesía y prosa (Anna M. Nogar and A. Gabriel Meléndez, University of New Mexico Press 2021).

[17]Leopold, author of *A Sand County Almanac* (1949), was one of Otero-Warren's favorite in-laws: "Of her brothers-in-law, Aldo Leopold was the one Nina thought 'walked on water'" (Whaley 191). Leopold's conservation efforts are memorialized in an urban open space in Albuquerque's Rio Grande Valley, the Aldo Leopold Forest: www.cabq.gov/parksandrecreation/open-space/lands/aldo-leopold-forest

[18]A comparison of *Old Spain in Our Southwest* and *My Life on the Frontier* (1935) by Otero-Warren's cousin Miguel Otero can be found in Margaret García Davidson, "Borders, Frontiers and Mountains: Mapping the History of 'U.S. Hispanic Literature.'"

[19]The suffix "de la tierra" means "of the land" and originally referred to animals and plants originating in the Americas that had no counterpart in Europe. In some places, the colonial-era term remains in common use.

[20]See Nogar and Lamadrid for a literary-historical exploration of New Mexican mujerotas including La Tules.

Luisa Capetillo, Free Love and the *Falda-Pantalón*

[1]I wish to thank the editors, Montse Feu and Yolanda Padilla, as well as an anonymous reader for their excellent comments and suggestions. "It Did Not Work," *The Topeka State Journal*, June 28, 1912. Note: the photo of Luisa Capetillo reproduced in Norma Valle-Ferrer, *Luisa Capetillo, historia de una mujer proscrita*. Río Piedras, PR: Editorial Cultural, 1990, p. 130, dated circa 1918 appears to be the same photograph of Capetillo taken in New York during the summer of 1912. Also, see the line drawing in *Kansas Weekly Capital*, July 11, 1912, 1 that also appears in Valle-Ferrer's book.

[2]César Andreu Iglesias, ed. *Memoirs of Bernarndo Vega: A Contribution to the History of the Puerto Rican Community in New York*. New York: Monthly Review Press, 1984, 107.

[3]Valle-Ferrer, *Luisa Capetillo, Pioneer Puerto Rican Feminist* (New York: Peter Lang, 2006). Originally published as: Norma Valle-Ferrer, *Luisa Capetillo, historia de una mujer proscrita* (Río Piedras, PR: Editorial Cultural, 1990).

[4]Ibid., 19-23.

[5]Nancy A. Hewitt, "Luisa Capetillo: Feminist of the Working Class," in Vicki L. Ruiz, et al., eds., *Latina Legacies: Identity, Biography, and Community* (Oxford: Oxford University Press, 2005), 121.

[6]Ibid., 121.

[7]Ibid., 122. Also see, Kathleen M. de Onis, "Arguing for Free Love in an Era Free of Women's Liberation: Remembering the Life of Puerto Rican Feminist and Labor Activist Luisa Capetillo," *Women & Language*, 36. 2 (Fall 2013) 92-4.

[8]Valle-Ferrer, *Luisa Capetillo*, 29, 33-34.

[9]Ibid., 33. Hewitt, "Luisa Capetillo: Feminist of the Working Class," 123.

[10]Hewitt, "Luisa Capetillo: Feminist of the Working Class," 123.

[11]Lisa Sánchez González, "Luisa Capetillo: An Anarcho-Feminist *Pionera* in the Mainland Puerto Rican Narrative/Political Tradition," in González Berry, Erlinda and Chuck Tatum. Eds. *Recovering the US Hispanic Literary Heritage, Vol. II*. Houston: Arte Público Press, 1996, 154-55.

[12]Capetillo, *Mi Opinión* (1911). Also see, *A Nation of Women: An Early Feminist Speaks Out—Mí opinión sobre las libertades, derechos y deberes de la mujer*, ed. By Félix V. Matos Rodríguez. Houston: Arte Público Press, 2004.

[13]Ibid., 39 and 52.

[14]Capetillo, *Mi Opinión* (1911), dedication page.

[15]Ibid., vii.

[16]Ibid., viii.

[17]See, Emilio Castelar, *Galería histórica de mujeres célebres* (Madrid: tipográfico de Alvarez Hermanos, 1886-1889).

[18]Capetillo, *Mi Opinión* (1911), 149-50.

[19]Ibid., 149-50.

[20]Gayle V. Fischer, *Pantaloons & Power: A Nineteenth-Century Dress Reform in the United States* (Kent, Ohio: The Kent State University Press, 2001), 83.

[21]"La 'jupe-culotte,'" *Boletín Mercantil de Puerto Rico*, Apr. 19, 1911.

[22]"De teatro," *Boletín Mercantil de Puerto Rico*, Aug. 9, 1911, 3.

[23]"Más noticias," *Boletín Mercantil de Puerto Rico*, Nov. 20, 1911.

[24]Hewitt, "Luisa Capetillo: Feminist of the Working Class," 127.

[25]See Susana Sueiro Seoane, "Una Puertorriqueña transnacional: Luisa Capetillo, Anarquista y Espiritista (1879-1922) in Aparecida de Figueiredo Fiuza, Adriana and Gabriela de Lima Grecco, *Escrituras de autoria feminina e identidades ibero-americanas* (Rio de Janeiro: UA Ediciones, 2020), 254-6.

[26]Luisa Capetillo, "Mi Primera Impresión," *Cultura Obrera*, May 18, 1912. (Capetillo's essay is dated May 15, 1912).

[27]"Pro-'Brazo y Cerebro,' *Cultura Proletaria*, May 18, 1912.

[28]Ibid.

[29]See, "For the Revolution in Spain: An Appeal for Solidarity," *Mother Earth*, 4, no. 11 (January 1910), 358-59.

[30]"It Did Not Work," *The Topeka State Journal*, June 28, 1912.

[31]Ibid. Also see, "Porto Rico Gown Created Sensation," *The Scranton Truth*, June 29, 1912.

[32]"It Did Not Work," *The Topeka State Journal*, June 28, 1912.

[33]*The Day Book* (Chicago, IL), June 29, 1912.

[34]"No Volunteers for Trousers," *The Kansas City Times*, July 1, 1912.

[35]Luisa Capetillo, "Femeninas—en pro de la mujer," *Brazos y Cerebro*, Oct. 22, 1912. Although Capetillo's essays about free love that are examined in this chapter do not appear in other edited collections, a particularly good source is: Julio Ramos, ed., *Amor y anarquía: Los escritos de Luisa Capetillo* (Río Piedras: Ediciones Huracán, Inc., 1992 and the 2nd ed. (Educación Emergente, 2021).

[36]Ibid.

[37]See, a series of short plays in: Luisa Capetillo and Lara Walker, *Absolute Equality: An Early Feminist Perspective: Influencias de la ideas modernas* (Houston: Arte Público Press, 209), pp. 129-52. Also see, Jorell Meléndez-Badillo, ed., *Páginas libres: Breve antología del pensamiento anarquista en Puerto Rico (1900-1919)*, (San Juan: Editora Educatión Emergente, 2021), 79-95.

[38]Capetillo, "Femeninas," *Brazos y Cerebro*, Oct. 22, 1912.

[39]Ibid.

[40]"La dictadura postal en los Estados Unidos," *Fuerza Consciente*, Mar. 15, 1912. Also see, Jaime Vidal, "'Brazo y Cerebro' Interceptado," *Regeneración*, Jan. 11, 1913.

[41]"Wanted—Straight Paper," *Regeneración*, March 1, 1913.

[42]"Fuerza Consciente," *Fuerza Consciente*, March 15, 1913.

[43]Capetillo, "Por la libertad femenina," *Fuerza Consciente*, Aug. 9, 1913.

[44]Ibid.

[45]Ibid.

[46]"Autoridades que dictan a las mujeres cómo deben vestir," *Fuerza Consciente*, Aug. 9, 1913.

[47]Luisa Capetillo, *Mi Opinión: Disertación sobre las libertades de la mujer*

[2nd edition] (Ybor City, FL: Imprenta de Joaquín Mascuñana, 1913).

[48]Jaime Vidal, "Dos palabras," in Luisa Capetillo, *Mi Opinión: Disertación sobre las libertades de la mujer* (Ybor City, FL: Imprenta de Joaquín Mascuñana, 1913), 85-6.

[49]"Jaime Vidal," *Regeneración*, Oct. 4, 1913.

[50]Luisa Capetillo, "Femeninas por la justicia," *Fuerza Consciente*, Nov. 15, 1913.

[51]Ibid.

[52]Ibid.

[53]"Will Preach Doctrine of Free Love in Cuba," *The Tampa Tribune*, Dec. 22, 1913.

[54]Capetillo, "Educación femenina," *Fuerza* Consciente, Feb. 28, 1914.

[55]Ibid.

[56]Valle-Ferrer, *Luisa Capetillo*, 51-2.

Loud, Hidden Voices of the Revolution: Reynalda González Parra, Organized Labor and *Feminismo Transfronterizo*

[1]Reynalda González Parra, "¡Al Abordaje!" *Germinal* (Tampico, Tamaulipas) June 14, 1917, Archivo de Librado Rivera y Hermanos Rojos, hereafter cited as ALR-HR.

[2]I thank the 'Race in History Writing Group' at Texas A&M University sponsored by the Melbern G. Glasscock Center Humanities Research, for its support and comments throughout the drafting and writing of this essay. Special thanks to April Hatfield for her assistance in crafting my argument. In some sources, Reynalda appears as Reinalda González Parra. For the consistency purposes, I use Reynalda throughout the essay. Thanks to Anna Ribera Carbó's work on women's participation and leadership in the COM Mexico City, we have some crucial data on González Parra's activism, "Mujeres Sindicalistas: Las Trabajadoras de la Casa del Obrero Mundial (1912-1916). Una Aproximación a las fuentes para su estudio," Online essay vi file:///C:/Users/soniah/Downloads/DialnetMujeres Sindicalistas LasTrabajadoras DeLaCasaDelObre-1256568.pdf [accessed October 1, 2019]. I offer a fuller discussion of Reynalda González Parra and other key anarcho-feminists in *For a Just and Better World: Engendering Anarchism in the Mexican Borderlands, 1900-1938.* University of Illinois Press, 2021.

[3]Leif Adelson, "Historia social de los obreros industriales de Tampico, 1906-1919," PhD Dissertation, El Colegio de México, 1982; Carlos

González Salas, *Acercamiento a la Historia del Movimiento Obrero en Tampico: 1887-1983.* Cd. Victoria: Autónoma de Tamaulipas, IIH, 1987; Barry Carr, *El movimiento obrero y la política en México, 1910-1929.* México City: Sep-Setentas, 1976.

[4]Hernández, *For a Just and Better World,* 8-10.

[5]Pilar Melero, *Mythological Constructs of Mexican Femininity,* 1st edition. Palgrave, 2015; Emma Perez, *The Decolonial Imaginary: Writing Chicanas into History.* Indiana University Press, 1999.

[6]Gabriela González, *Redeeming La Raza: Transborder Modernity, Race, Respectability, and Rights.* Oxford, 2018, 52.

[7]Clara Lomas, "Transborder Discourse: The Articulation of Gender in the Borderlands in the Early Twentieth Century," *Frontiers: A Journal of Women Studies,* 2003, Vol. 24, No. 2/3, Gender on the Borderlands (2003), 51-52; Pérez; González, *Redeeming La Raza.*

[8]"México, Chihuahua, Registro Civil, 1861-1997," database with images, FamilySearch, familysearch.org/ark:/61903/3 :1:33S7-95HX-SY9?cc=1922462&wc=MKCT-C6J%3A1021829501%2C1021882701: (12 March 2018), Casas Grandes, Nacimientos 1867-1889, image 147 of 425; Archivo General del Registro Civil, Chihuahua City Central Archives, Mexico; her death certificate remains elusive and the historical record stops short of González Parra's activities after 1920.

[9]Bray, Mark and Robert H. Haworth, *Anarchist Education and the Modern School: A Francisco Ferrer Reader.* PM Press, 2018.

[10]Ribera Carbó, Anna. *La Casa del Obrero Mundial: Anarcosindicalismo y revolución en México.* México: INAH, 2010.

[11]Porter, *Working Women,* 15-20; Carbó, *Mujeres Sindicalistas,* 168.

[12]Huitrón, 291.

[13]Huitrón, 291-95; Ribera Carbó, *La Casa del Obrero Mundial.*

[14]Ribera Carbó, Anna. *La Casa del Obrero Mundial: Anarcosindicalismo y revolución en México.* México: INAH, 2010.

[15]Bray and Hawarth; see also Hart for the Mexican context; the literature on anarchism is extensive. Foundational studies include but are not limited to, Peter Kropotkin, *Anarchism: A Collection of Revolutionary Writings* (1927). New York: Dover, 2002; Emma Goldman, *Anarchism and Other Essays* (1917). New York: Dover, 1969; Alexander Berkman, *What Is Anarchism?* (1929) (Oakland: AK Press, 2003); Max Nettlau, *A Short History of Anarchism* (Freedom Press, 1996); Paul Avrich, *The Russian Anarchists* (1967). AK Press, 2005) and *Anarchist Voices: An Oral History of Anarchism in America.* AK Press, 2005, among his other publications.

[16]Reynalda González Parra, "A La Mujer," *Germinal, Periódico Libertario* (Tampico), Julio 2, 1917, ALR-HR.

[17]Presidente Municipal from Ricardo Treviño, Secretario General, COM Tampico, May 26, 1917, Fondo: Presidencia, caja 1917, #1, Archivo Histórico de Tampico, hereafter cited as AHT; Barry Carr, "The Casa del Obrero Mundial, Constitutionalism and the Pact of February 1915," in Elsa Cecilia Frost, et.al (eds), *El trabajo y los trabajadores en la historia de México* (México, Tucson: El Colegio de México, University of Arizona, 1979, 605.

[18]Hart, *Anarchism and the Mexican-Working Class*; Alcayaga Sasso, Aurora Mónica, "Librado Rivera y Los Hermanos Rojos en el Movimiento Social y Cultural Anarquista en Villa Cecilia y Tampico, Tamaulipas, 1915-1932," Tesis Doctoral, Universidad Iberoamericana, 2006, 50; "Como pensaba Ferrer: A las Sociedades de Resistencia," *Luz* (Mexico City), April 3, 1918.

[19]Bertha Ulloa, *Historia de la Revolución Mexicana, periodo 1914-1917: La Constitución de 1917*. México: Colegio de México, 1983; "El control del movimiento obrero como una necesidad del Estado de México (1917-1936)," 785-813.

[20]Hart, 157-158.

[21]For all ten points see "Bases del Congreso Obrero reunido en Tampico," in *¡Luz!: Semanario Libertario, doctrinario y de protesta, escrito por trabajadores en defensa de la mujer y de los trabajadores mismos* Etapa II, November 28, 1917, ALR-HR; These points are also paraphrased in Alcayaga Sasso, 125.

[22]Reynalda González Parra, "A la Mujer," *Germinal, Periódico Libertario* (Tampico), Julio 2, 1917, AHLR-HR.

[23]Ibid.

[24]See the references to the *Centro* in *Sagitario*; Alcayaga Sasso, 50, 60, 123-125; Kevin Aguilar, "The IWW in Tampico," 127-128. While Alcayaga Sasso uses "Centro de Estudios Sociales Feministas" Aguilar uses "Centro Femenil de Estudios Sociales"; Verónica Oikión Solano, *Cuca García (1889-1973): Por las causas de las mujeres y la revolución.* México: Colegio de Michoacán; Colegio de San Luis, 2018, 170; Either shortly before co-founding the COM or soon thereafter, González Parra became active with and/or founded the *Centro Feminista*.

[25]Leobardo Castro, "La infancia en la casa del obrero mundial," *Ariete: Revista Sociológica*, Etapa 1, Octubre 24, 1915, núm. 2, pg. 5, AHLR-HR; for contrast see, Jacinto Huitrón, "Amor sin cadenas," *Revolución Social*, Orizaba, 1 de julio de 1915, Etapa II, Núm. 9., as quoted in Carbó, "Mujeres Sindicalistas."

[26]Hart, 153-155.

[27]Reinalda González Parras, "¡Al Abordaje!" *Germinal*, (Tampico), June 14, 1917, AHLR-HR.

[28]Susan K. Besse writes about what she terms a modernization of gender inequality for the Brazilian case that can be identified for the Mexican case as well, *Restructuring Patriarchy: The Modernization of Gender Inequality in Brazil, 1914-1940* (University of North Carolina Press, 2018).

[29]Hernández, For a Just and Better World, 8-10.

[30]Based on the list of contributors appearing in donor columns, the writings of González Parra reached various corners of the globe; in solidarity, organizations from abroad reprinted features from the anarchist press and González Parra's COM as well as other anarchist collectives did the same.

[31]"Administración: Entradas de Germinal," *Germinal*, July 2, 1917, AHEM. It is possible that Reynalda's donation may have been on behalf of the *Centro de Estudios Feministas*.

[32]"Acta de Formación del 'Grupo Racionalista' de San Antonio, Tex." *Regeneración*, October 9, 1915, Hispanic American Historical Newspapers database, hereafter cited as HAHN.

[33]It is important to note that there was diversity among anarcho-syndicalists and not all promoted an atheist view nor rejected God (although most did reject the hierarchical structure of the Catholic Church).

[34]Hart, *Anarchism and the Mexican-Working Class*; see also Kirwin Shaffer, "Freedom Teaching: Anarchism and Education in Early Republican Cuba, 1898-1925," *The Americas*, 60. 2 (October 2003): 151-183.

Josefina de la Grana's Letters to the Editor: A Window into her Activism in Tampa, Florida

[1]I have identified 313 contributions by Josefina de la Grana to the correspondence sections of the *Tampa Daily Times* and the *Tampa Morning Tribune* between 1927 and 1946—301 letters to the editor and twelve poems.

[2]In Tampa, the term "Latin" encompassed members of several immigrant groups—Cubans, Spaniards, and Italians—and their descendants.

[3]*Título del Registro de Nacimientos, Camargo, Tamaulipas, 1888*. Archivo General del Registro del Estado, Tamaulipas, Mexico. The couple had three more children: Miguel (1889), Rene (1894), and Sara (1896). Sara died in infancy. Documents related to the Díaz-Cannere family are available in Ancestry.com and FamilySearch.com

[4]She shared the prize with another female contestant. The essay was published in the bulletin of L'Athénée Louisianais, a francophone cultural institution founded in New Orleans in 1876 and connected to the Alliance Française.

[5]Two Spanish (Centro Español and Centro Asturiano), two Cuban (El Círculo Cubano and La Unión Martí-Maceo – the latter for Afro-Cubans), and one Italian (L'Unione Italiana).

[6]In the 1930s de la Grana worked as secretary of the Tampa Branch of the Socialist Party of Florida and special organizer of the Cigar Makers' International Union. Other sources (Baxley et al. 264) claim that she was a language teacher in Hillsborough County public schools. The 1940 census is the only census that shows an occupation for her: "Interpreter. Private Practice."

[7]On how these divisions shaped women's activism in Tampa see the classic study by Nancy A. Hewitt (2001).

[8]Not all letter writers are easily identifiable. Some used initials or pseudonyms ("A citizen," "Old Timer"). Things had not changed significantly twenty years later. In June of 1946, the month where de la Grana's last letter appeared in the *Tampa Morning Tribune*, the paper published a total of 157 pieces, twenty nine of them (eighteen percent) by authors identified as women.

[9]According to the writer this could have increased the number of votes for de la Grana from the official 138 to "upward of 500" (against 6,197 votes for the Democratic candidate). The state secretary of the socialist party made a similar argument in his report to national headquarters (Edson).

[10]After two trials, none of the defendants were punished (Ingalls, 185-199).

[11]For the role of women and children in the activities of the Tampa Committee and the importance of this discourse of "militant motherhood" in the 1930s see Varela-Lago (*Conquerors* 251-261). On Latina labor activism in Tampa during these years, see also McNamara. McNamara focuses primarily on the activities of union organizer Luisa Moreno.

AKA Frances: Francisca Flores and the Radical Roots of Chicana Feminism in California

[1]FBI document LA HR: BK Memorandum for Mr. L. M. C. Smith Chief, Special Defense Unit in Flores *FBI File 1128474-000* (8 December, 1941).

[2]This article would not have been possible without the aid and support of Dr. Maria E. Cotera (University of Texas at Austin) who not only saw value in my research but took time from her schedule to review and edit the article. A special thank you to Erin M. Blomstrand and Alex Pirehpour-Andrews for editing the article.

[3]Two different sources indicate two different dates as to her birthdate and birthplace. One source has her birth date as December 1913 in San Diego while the FBI report, which had obtained a birth certificate, has her birth date as November 3, 1913. According to the FBI's copy of Flores' certificate of birth, no. 7804, they note that Flores' given birth name was "Francisco" Flores, which could have been a typo. See FBI document LA 100-23069 in Flores *FBI File 1128474-000* (April 1, 1952) 1-3. Her place of birth is also questionable. The FBI file and Elizabeth Escobedo noted that Flores was born "in a Los Angeles barrio." See Elizabeth Escobedo, "Flores, Francisca" in *Notable American Women: Completing the Twentieth Century* ed. Susan Ware and Stacy Braukman, Harvard University Press, 2004, 214.

[4]Gilbert Gonzalez has argued that the U.S.'s first imperialistic opportunity rested with "Our-Next-Door-Neighbor" (Mexico) policy. Through economic conquest, the United States laid the seed of dependency into the twentieth century, which caused waves of Mexican migration into the US. See Gilbert Gonzalez, *Culture of Empire: American Writers, Mexico & Mexican Immigration, 1890-1930*. University of Texas Press, 2004.

[5]FBI verification indicated that she "spent seven years in the sanitarium." See FBI document LA 100-23069 (Feb. 21, 1956), 12.

[6]This sentiment was shared by Flores who indicated that men did not take women seriously and only "wanted them to make tortillas." William Flores, "Francisca Flores Eulogy," 1.

[7]The author does not specify which repatriation waves; however, Corona arrived in Los Angeles in 1936 therefore, more than likely, he was addressing the Roosevelt repatriation wave.

[8]At the Tenney Committee Hearing on February 19, 1942, Flores stated that she joined the CPUSA in 1939. FBI files differ on the year she joined the party. Later files indicate that she had been affiliated with the CPUSA as early as 1935, while others indicate a later date. See FBI document File "no. 100-1207," (June 27, 1942) 5; FBI document File "no. LA 100-23069," (N.D.) 1.

[9]FBI document File no. 100-1207, (October 18, 1940), 2.

[10]FBI document file no. LAG: JEC 100-1207, (May 19, 1941), 4-5.

[11]FBI document file no. 100-1207, (June 27, 1942), 4.

[12]FBI document file no. ND-86, (December 8, 1941), 1.

[13]FBI document file no. 100-17204-25, (May 28, 1943), 2.

[14]*El Congreso* addressed issues such as police repression, racial

discrimination, increased educational opportunities, better jobs, barrio improvement, and lower housing rents. See Zaragosa Vargas, *Labor Rights are Civil Rights: Mexican American Workers in the Twentieth-Century America*. Princeton University Press, 2005, 179-192.

[15]FBI document file no. 100-1207, (June 27, 1942), 3.

[16]See FBI document file no. SD 100-1207, (February 21, 1945), 1-3; FBI document file no. 100-1207, (May 24, 1945), 1. There is no clear indication as to what Francisca Flores' position was in UCAPAWA; however, through multiple FBI sources, we find that Flores was dismissed from her position in the CIO "because she was not a bookkeeper."

[17]FBI document file no. LA 100-23069, (April 21, 1952), 28; FBI document file no. 100-23069, (June 20, 1955), 2.

[18]FBI document file no. SD #100-1207, (November 4, 1943), 5.

[19]FBI document file no. LSD 100-1207, (April 22, 1944), 5.

[20]FBI document file no. LA 100-23069, (Feb. 21, 1956), 13.

[21]FBI document file no. 100-17204-25, (June 27, 1942), 5.

[22]FBI document file no. LA 100-23069, (April 10, 1945), 2.

[23]FBI document file no. 100-1207, (Feb. 21, 1945), 1.

[24]FBI document file no. SD 100-1207, (Feb. 22, 1945), 3.

[25]FBI document file no. LA 100-23069, (April 21, 1952), 4.

[26]FBI document file no. LA 100-23069, (April 21, 1952), 24.

[27]FBI document file no. LA 100-23069, (September 2, 1949), 4-5.

[28]FBI document file no. LA 100-23069, (April 21, 1952), 11.

[29]FBI document file no. LA 100-17204-83, (April 21, 1952).

[30]FBI document file no. LA 100-17204-83, (N.D.).

[31]FBI document file no. LA 100-23069, (January 29, 1952), 1; FBI document file no. LA 100-23069, (April 13, 1953), 1.

[32]The FBI records seemed to frantically search for Flores' whereabouts, but she could have been using an alias. FBI document file no. LA 100-23069, (May 28, 1953), 1-2.

[33]FBI document file no. LA 100-23069, (June 3, 1953), 1.

[34]The FBI letters provided very limited information. Initially, the first letter collected was said to have insufficient information to determine who wrote it. There were not enough letter characters to compare with previous letters that the FBI had on file. FBI document file no. LA 100-23069, (October 19, 1953) 1-3; FBI document file no.100-17204-85, (April 21, 1952).

[35]FBI document file no. 100-17204, (February 5, 1954), 2.

[36]FBI document file no. 100-17204-2-23, (April 21, 1952), 1.

[37]By early 1954, Flores was characterized as "Key Figure status." Her status was stamped as "Detcom." FBI document file no. 100-17204 2-23, (April 21, 1952); FBI document file no. LA 100-23069, (June 20, 1955), 3.

[38]Records indicate that there were three levels in the CPUSA regarding membership status. The no. 1 was for regular membership. The no. 1 ½ was utilized for members who participated in the underground but had daily operational contact; and the no. 2 was for those who were in the CPUSA Underground. FBI document file no. 100-23069, (December 30, 1954), 3; FBI document file no. 100-23069, (August 10, 1955), 1.

[39]FBI document file no. 100-23069, (August 10, 1955), 1.

[40]FBI document file no. 100-23069, (September 14, 1956), 3.

[41]FBI document file no. 100-23069, (April 19, 1957), 19.

[42]FBI document file no. LA 100-23069, (November 12, 1957), 19.

[43]FBI document file no. LA 100-23069, (November 12, 1957), 20.

[44]Although Flores focused on Mexican American History, courses at the California Labor School addressed multiple ethnic and gender issues such as "Negro Liberation," "The Negro People in the Struggle for Freedom," "The Jewish People in the Struggle for Democracy," "Women in a Changing World," and "Problems of the Mexican-American People." See *California Labor School, Los Angeles Division* (Winter 1949-50), Box 3, Folder 29, 93-04-12 Senate-Rules, California Un-American Activities Committee Records Files, California State Archives, Office of the Secretary, Sacramento.

[45]FBI document file no. LA 100-23069 Flores FBI File 1128474-000, (April 21, 1952), 27.

[46]FBI document file no. LA 100-23069, (November 4, 1956) ,10.

[47]FBI document file no. 100-23069, (April 19, 1957), 9.

[48]FBI document file no. LA 100-23069, (February 27, 1956), 3.

[49]FBI document file no. LA 100-23069, (February 27, 1956), 2.

[50]FBI document file no. LA 100-23069, (November 12, 1957), 20.

[51]FBI document file no. LA 100-23069, (November 12, 1957), 24.

[52]FBI document file no. LA 100-23069, (June 6, 1958), 10-11.

[53]Jerry Harris does an excellent job explaining the ideological rifts at the convention. He also argues that the 16th National Convention played a much more significant role in the exodus of CPUSA members than

HUAC persecution. See Jerry Harris, "The Center Cannot Hold: The Struggle for Reform in the Communist Party, 1957–58." *Science & Society,* 74. 4 (2010): 461–488.

[54]FBI document file no. LA 100-23069, (April 19, 1957), 10.

[55]FBI document file no. LA 100-23069, (July 8, 1958), 5.

[56]FBI document file no. LA 100-23069, (July 24, 1962), 3.

[57]FBI document file no. LA 100-23069, (July 8, 1959), 3.

[58]Flores and Dobbs had established a relationship throughout the 1950s due to their involvement in the Party. It is noted in one FBI record that Dobbs visited Flores at her home to discuss CPUSA issues. FBI document file no. LA 100-23069, (July 6, 1961), 2.

[59]FBI document file no. LA 100-23069, (July 6, 1961), 4.

[60] FBI document file no. LA 100-23069, (July 8, 1960), D.

Mujeres y mártires: Cristero Diaspora Literature

[1]It was not until 1966 when Alicia Olivera de Bonfil published *La guerra cristera: Aspectos del conflicto religioso de 1926 a 1929* that the first comprehensive study of the Cristero War appeared. This pioneering work was followed in 1973 by Jean Meyer's *La cristiada*, an exhaustive three-volume history that is still regarded as foundational to all subsequent studies of the conflict.

[2]I here use Literature of the Cristero War as opposed to Cristero Literature to encompass literature that deals with the conflict from a variety of perspectives, from propagandistic defenses of the Cristero cause to scathing critiques. See Agustín Vaca and Ángel Arias Urrutia for a discussion of these terminological choices (Vaca 1998, 71; Arias Urrutia 2002, 92).

[3]Recent book-length studies include Guy Thiébaut's 1997 *La contre-révolution mexicaine à travers sa littérature* followed by Ángel Arias Urrutia's 2002 *Cruzados de novela: las novelas de la Guerra cristera* and Álvaro Ruiz Abreu's 2003 *La cristera, una literatura negada*. A notable early exception is Manuel Pedro González's 1951 *Trayectoria de la novela en México*.

[4]Many Cristero articles appeared in the early-twentieth century US Spanish-language press, which published numerous accounts of battles and martyrs as well as editorials condemning the Mexican government. Ignacio Lozano's *La prensa* and *La opinión* are prominent examples of papers that regularly included pro-Cristero content, providing a forum for

prominent Cristero exiles to register their disdain for Calles and his government and garner transnational support for their cause (Kanellos 2000, 26; Young 2015, 65).

[5]See Meyer and Vaca for historical examples on which this literature is based. Some of the most well-known examples of this literature include *Pensativa* by Jesús Goytortúa Santos and *Los recuerdos del porvenir* by Elena Garro. For analyses of these texts, see Naranja Tamayo and León Vega.

[6]Jorge Gram was the pseudonym of Cristero canon David G. Ramírez.

[7]For a close reading of these texts, see Vaca, Chapters 3-5.

[8]See "Rubén Darío, Latino Poet" and "At the Crossroads of Circulation and Translation: Rethinking US Latino/a Modernism."

[9]The archival traces of María Guadalupe Muro are minimal and to my knowledge do not extend beyond De la Torre's *Álbum*. At this time, I have not located any other published works by her.

[10]*Revista Católica* was a Jesuit newspaper and printing house that began in New Mexico in the 1870s and relocated to El Paso, Texas in the 1910s. Once the Cristero War began, the paper became a staunch supporter of the cause. As Young explains, "At the onset of the Cristero War, the paper took an active position against the Calles government, publishing editorials criticizing the Calles regime and opining that Catholic Mexicans had the duty to rise up in arms against the government. By 1927 (if not earlier), the newspaper had been banned from circulation in Mexico" (65).

[11]See, for example, Anna Brickhouse's discussion of other narratives of martyrdom that foreground torture in *The Unsettlement of America*, especially Chapter 2.

[12]See Brickhouse Chapter 2 for a discussion of miracles in relation to narratives of martyrdom.

[13]In 2000, 25 Cristeros were officially declared martyrs by the Catholic Church, followed by a smaller group in 2006 (Young 2015, 177).

Mujeres vascas en Estados Unidos, 1850-1950: La formación de una comunidad

[1]William A. Douglass and Jon Bilbao. *Amerikanuak. Basques in the New World,* Reno: University of Nevada Press, 1975, p. 424. El autor ha traducido las citas.

[2]Anna M. Aguirre y Koldo San Sebastián. *Newyorktarrak*, Vitoria-Gasteiz: Servicio Central de Publicaciones del Gobierno Vasco, 2018, pp. 99-100.

[3]Así ocurre en los demás estados del oeste con presencia vasca: Washington, Oregon, California, Montana, Utah, Arizona, Wyoming. Colorado y New Mexico.

[4]Bilbao, Jon. "Vascos en el Oeste", Conferencia, Bilbao, 1959.

[5]Bilbao, Jon. "Vascos en el Oeste", Conferencia, Bilbao, 1959.

[6]Sydney Stahl Weinberg, Donna Gabaccia, Hasia R. Diner and Maxine Schwartz Sel. "The Treatment of Women in Immigration History: A Call for Change [with Comments and Response]", *Journal of American Ethnic History,* 11.4 (Summer, 1992), pp. 25-69.

[7]Sydney Stahl Weinberg, Donna Gabaccia, Hasia R. Diner and Maxine Schwartz Sel, "The Treatment of Women in Immigration History: A Call for Change [with Comments and Response]", *Journal of American Ethnic History,* 11. 4 (Summer, 1992), pp. 25-69.

[8]Gloria Totoricagüena. "Interconnected Disconnectedness: How Diaspora Basque Women Maintain Ethnic Identity", en Linda White & Cameron Watson, eds*), Amatxi, Amuma, Amona: Writings in Honor of Basque Women,* Reno: Center for Basques Studies, Nevada 2003, p. 101.

[9]Teresa del Valle. "Introducción", en William A. Douglass. *Cultura vasca y su diáspora. Ensayos teóricos y descriptivo*s, Donostia: Baroja, 1991, p.15.

[10]Marie Pierre Arrizabalaga. "Las mujeres pirenaicas y la emigración en el siglo XIX", en Julio Hernández Borge, Domingo L. González Lopo. *Mujer y emigración: una perspectiva plural.* Santiago: Universidad de Santiago de Compostela, 2008, pp. 107-131.

[11]Asun Garitano. *Far Westeko Euskal Herria.* Iruña- Pamiela: 2009, pp. 194-218.

[12]Joan Errea, *My Mama Marie.* Reno: Center for Basque Studies, 2013.

[13]Monique Urza. "Catherine Etchart: a Montana Love Story" en Richard W. Etulain (ed), *Basques in the Pacific Northwest.* Pocatello: Idaho State UP, 1991, pp. 40-50.

[14]Jeronima Echeverria, "The Basque hotelera: Implications for a broader study", en W.A. Douglass, C. Urza, L. White, J. Zulaika (eds). *The Basque Diaspora.* Reno: Basque Studies Program, 1999, pp. 239-248.

[15]Christy Ann Webber (dr) *Janet C. Inda. Basque Sheepherder's Daughter,* Reno: Oral History Program. U of Nevada-Reno, 1982.

[16]Mary Alustiza. *The Basque Table,* Stockton: Azitsula, 1996; M Ancho-Davies. *Chorizos in an Iron Skillet,* Reno: U of Nevada P, 2001; Ann Rogers. *A Basque history cookbook,* New York: Charles Scribner's sons, 1996, 1968.

[17]William A. Douglass. *Death in Murelaga*, U of Washington P, 1969, p. 7.

[18]Rodney Gallop. *Los vascos*, Madrid: Ediciones Castilla, 1948, p. 55.

[19]W. A. Douglass. *Death in* . . . p. 105.

[20]Pierre Lhande. *En torno al hogar vasco*, Donostia: Auñamendi, 1975, pp. 23-66.

[21]Rodney Gallop, Opus cit, 55.

[22]Amaia Mugika Goñi, "Euskal ezteiak", *en Deia*, Bilbao: 23 diciembre 2014.

[23]Marie-Pierre Arrizabalaga. *A Statistical Study of Basque Immigrants into California, Nevada, Idaho and Wyoming between 1900 and 1910*. Reno: University of Nevada, 1986, p. 20.

[24]Leonard Kasdan. "Family Structure, Migration and the Entrepreneur", *Comparative Studies in Society and History,* Vol.7, 1965, p. 350.

[25]En el Archivo Municipal de Lekeitio, existe abundante documentación sobre la solicitud de permisos para emigrar "a California" por parte de mujeres jóvenes. Referencias para Idaho, Nevada y Oregon aparecen, asimismo, en Iban Bilbao & Chantal de Eguiluz, "Matrimonios vascos en Idaho y Nevada (1862-1941)", en *Diáspora Vasca: 4*. Vitoria-Gasteiz: 1983, p. 22.

[26]A través de la obra del escritor vasco americano Robert Laxalt se puede comprender mejor la mentalidad y la tierra de aquellos vascos que emigraron a Estados Unidos. Ver, por ejemplo, *In A Hundred Graves. A Basque Portrait*, Reno: University of Nevada Press, 1972; and *The Land of my Fathers. A Son's Return to the Basque Country,* Reno: University of Nevada Press, 2000.

[27]William A. Douglass. *Echalar and Murelaga. Opportunity and Rural Exodus in two Spanish Basque Villages*, London. Hurst & Company, 1975, p. 120.

[28]Monique Selim. "Algunos aspectos sobre la migración vasca femenina a Paris", en F. Xavier Medina (comp.). *Los otros vascos. Las migraciones vascas en el s. XX*. Madrid: Fundamentos, 1997.

[29]Oral Histories, J. Chertudi, 1975, Boise Basque Museum and Cultural Center.

[30]Claude Mehats. *Organisation et aspects de l'emigration des Basques de France en Amérique, 1832-1976*, Vitoria-Gasteiz: Servicio Central de Publicaciones del Gobierno Vasco, 1995.

[31]Douglas y Bilbao, *Opus cit.*

[32]María Eugenia Cruset. "Migración y exilio: el papel de las mujeres", *Revista Trasversos*, Rio de Janeiro, (2017), p. 128.

[33]Henry de Charnisay. *Emigration Basco-Bearnaise en Amèrique*, Biarritz: J& D, 1996, p. vv.

[34]Robert Laxalt, *Swett Promised Land*, New York: Harper & Brothers, 1957.

[35]Nea Colton, *The Rivers are Frozen*, New York: Coward-Mc Cann, 1942.

[36]Ver Jeronima Echeverria. "The Basque 'hotelera': Implications for a Broader Study", en William A. Douglass, Carmelo Urza, Linda White & Joseba Zulaika (eds.), *The Basque Diaspora*, Reno: Basque Studies Program, 1999, pp. 238-248.

[37]El *arreo* es la ropa que la novia lleva al matrimonio, que había sido confeccionada por ella o sus familiares y amigas, y lo diferenciaban de la dote que es el conjunto de dinero y bienes aportados por la novia o su familia. Las muchachas empezaban desde muy jóvenes a preparar su *arreo*. Con lo ahorrado, podía comprar telas, algún encaje, botones, etc.

[38]En el caso de las vascas de Francia no existía este tipo de contratos, como señala Terexa Lekunberri: "Emazte horrek ez du sekulan ezkontza kontraturik egin bere senarrarekin. Aldiz ezkondu eta 20 urteren buruan, joan ziren notariora, "elgarren premu" (donation entre époux) aktoa izenpetzeko, zernahi gerta ere bati, bestea babestua izan zadin."

[39]*Idaho Daily Stateman*, 24 marzo 1901.

[40]Mi padre siempre presumía de que su madre había sido bautizada en una catedral.

[41]Jerónima Echevarria. *Home Away from Home. A History of Basque Boarding Houses*, Reno-Nevada: University of Nevada Press, 1999.

[42]Ibídem, p. 227

[43]Mary Grace Paquette. *Basques to Bakersfield*, Bakersfield: Kern County Historical Society, 1982, p. 5.

[44]Eva Hunt Dockery, Opus cit.

[45]Eva Hunt Dockery, Opus cit.

[46]Joan Errea, Opus cit, pp. 55-56.

[47]AUTOR, TITULO. *Idaho Statesman,* 24 nov. 1908.

[48]J. Echeverria, Opus cit, pp. 227.

[49]John B. Edlefsen. *A sociological study of the Basques of Southwest Idaho*. Washington: State College of Washington: 1948, p. 47.

[50]John B. Edlefsen, opus cit, p. 79.

[51]Carla María Plagiarulo. *Basques in Stockton. A Study of Assimilation*, Stockton: 1948, p. 32.

[52] Sylvia Yanagisako. *Transforming the Past: Tradition and Kinship Among Japanese Americans*. Stanford: Stanford University Press, 1985.

[53] Teresa Fernández Martorell. "Circunstancias de las migraciones: noticias vascas", en F. Xavier Medina, Opus cit, p. 13.

[54] Adrien Gachiteguy. *Les Basques dan l'Ouest Americain*, Bordeaux: 1955. Ezkila, p.139.

[55] William A. Douglass and Jon Bilbao, Opus cit, pp. 355-356.

[56] *The New York Times*, 21 marzo 1911.

[57] Oral Histories: Mikel Chertudi, Eugenia Acordagoitia, 4 abril 2002, Boise Basque Museum and Cultural Center.

[58] *Weekly Elko Independent,* Sept. 4, 1903.

[59] *San José Evening News*, Tuesday, 2 mayo 1911.

[60] *Idaho Statesman*, 1917.

[61] Koldo SanSebastian "Con las manos vacías". www.euskonews. eus/zbk/674/con-las-manos-vacias/ar-0674015001C/

"We Were Always Chicanos," or "We Did it Our Way:" Situated Citizenship in the Equality State

[1] I wish to extend my sincere gratitude to Annie Mejorado Vigil and Susana Vigil, as well as the entire Riverton, Wyoming Manito community for sharing their stories and struggles with the Following the Manito Trail team. The generosity and care they show their communities and Chicanx peoples more generally are rooted in an ethos of love and is a reminder of the ways in which we must be attentive to the threads of the past that teach us and guide us in the work that we do today and in the future. Thank you for your eternal commitment to, as Susana noted, *la causa*.

[2] This archive includes Annie Vigil Mejorado and Susana Vigil's personal archives as well as the archives of the Following the Manito Trail project. The FMT project archives related to Wyoming are housed at the American Heritage Center at the University of Wyoming in Laramie. Other portions of the FMT archive will be housed at the Center for Southwest Research at the University of New Mexico and the Chicana/o Research Collection at Arizona State University. The archives are intentionally separate to allow regional communities to access them. After consultation with Vigil Mejorado and Vigil, they are addressed by their first name in the essay.

[3] For more on Following the Manito Trail, see Fonseca (2017), Herrera (2017), Lovata (2017), Martínez (2019), Romero (2020), and Martinez and Fonseca (2021).

[4]A set of approximately forty interviews were conducted in various cities and towns in Wyoming by the Following the Manito Trail team in 2015 and 2016. Each interview varied in length from a few minutes (for video documentary purposes) to one or two hours (for oral history documentation). Oral history interviews (individual and group) were semi-structured based on a set of questions prepared in advance by the FMT team and approved by the University of Wyoming Institutional Review Board. Interviews took place at private residences or in public spaces including city libraries, public parks, and church halls. The oral history documentation process informed some of the questions central to the FMT project, including why families migrated to Wyoming, the material and social conditions of their new locales, and how they maintained their sense of *querencia*, or love of home, through outward migration. The interviews conducted for this project will be archived at the University of Wyoming American Heritage Center.

[5]See Cobos (2003).

[6]See Rios Bustamante (2001) and Western (2011).